Palace Ware Across the Neo-Assyrian Imperial Landscape

Culture and History of the Ancient Near East

VOLUME 78

The titles published in this series are listed at *brill.com/chan*

Palace Ware Across the Neo-Assyrian Imperial Landscape

Social Value and Semiotic Meaning

By

Alice M. W. Hunt

BRILL

LEIDEN | BOSTON

Library of Congress Cataloging-in-Publication Data

Hunt, Alice M. W.
Palace ware across the Neo-Assyrian imperial landscape : social value and semiotic meaning / by Alice M. W. Hunt.
pages cm. — (Culture and history of the ancient Near East, ISSN 1566-2055 ; volume 78)
Includes bibliographical references.
ISBN 978-90-04-30411-6 (hardback : acid-free paper) — ISBN 978-90-04-30412-3 (e-book)
1. Pottery, Assyro-Babylonian. 2. Pottery, Ancient—Iraq. 3. Pottery—Social aspects—Assyria—History. 4. Imperialism—Social aspects—Assyria—History. 5. Value—Social aspects—Assyria—History. 6. Semiotics—Social aspects—Assyria—History. 7. Assyria—Social life and customs. 8. Assyria—Antiquities 9. Iraq—Antiquities I. Title.

NK3820.H86 2015
738.093509'01—dc23

2015024960

This publication has been typeset in the multilingual 'Brill' typeface. With over 5,100 characters covering Latin, IPA, Greek, and Cyrillic, this typeface is especially suitable for use in the humanities.
For more information, please see www.brill.com/brill-typeface.

ISSN 1566-2055
ISBN 978-90-04-30411-6 (hardback)
ISBN 978-90-04-30412-3 (e-book)

This book is printed on acid-free paper.

ana iailu ištu libbī

Contents

Acknowledgements

Scientific inquiry and academic research cannot exist in a vacuum. This project took shape over years, over shared pints, cups of coffee and bottles of wine. I am grateful for each and every conversation, new perspective and question I could not answer; all of which challenged me and encouraged me. Although you are too numerous to name, you are not forgotten.

This manuscript is based on my doctoral research and I am especially grateful to my supervisors. Thilo Rehren—thank you for believing in me, supporting me to take risks, and accepting nothing less than excellence. Ian Freestone—thank you for your encouragement and for helping me refine my analytical abilities. Rachael Sparks—thank you for keeping me grounded in the archaeology, suffering through the science, and providing a shoulder when needed.

In its present manifestation, this manuscript owes much to the advice and mentorship of Karen Radner (UCL), Eleanor Robson (Cambridge), Jeff Speakman (UGA), and Katelyn Chin and the series editors. Your comments and critiques have made this a stronger work and me a better researcher.

It is my pleasure to recognize the individuals and institutions whose generosity made this project possible. Robert Speller and Ben Price (UCL) for allowing me access to and training in X-ray radiography and Johannes Sterba (Technische Universität Wien) for conducing the INAA for this study. Caroline Cartwright (The British Museum) and Yuval Goren (Tel Aviv University) for their expertise and advice during my petrographic work. John Curtis and the Trustees of the British Museum, Ralf-Bernard Wartke (Vorderasiatiches Museum), Melinda Zeder (Smithsonian Institution), the Israel Antiquities Authority, Jean-Baptiste Humbert and the École biblique et archéologique française de Jérusalem, Hartmut Kühne and Janoscha Kreppner (Freie Universität Berlin), Muzahim Mahmoud Hussein (Iraqi Department of Antiquities), Ayelet Gilboa (University of Haifa), Sy Gitin (AIAR), and David Stronach, Peter Lumsden and Eleanor Wilkinson (UC Berkeley excavation team) for allowing me access to materials and for answering endless questions.

For permission to use photographs and other graphic art media under copyright I gratefully acknowledge the following presses, museum and individuals: The British Museum, The British School of Archaeology in Iraq, Harrassowitz Verlag, Saad Jassim, Hartmut Kühne, and Walter de Gruyter.

Funding for this project was generously awarded by: The State Department Bureau of Education and Cultural Affairs, The Albright Institute of Archaeological Research, Smithsonian Institution, and the Gay Clifford Award for Outstanding Women.

List of Figures

List of Tables

List of Maps

Glossary

base	the section of the vessel opposite the rim upon which the vessel rests
base angle	measurement of the amount of turn as the base merges with the vessel body
body	the section of the vessel below the neck and above the base, the 'bowl' or hollow
body depth	height to maximum diameter / maximum diameter
BSE	backscattered electrons
collar	a vertical extention of the rim which joins it to the vessel body
EDS	energy dispersive spectrometry
form	the shape and size of a vessel
height	measurement of the total vertical space occupied by the vessel, inclusive of base, body, neck and rim/lip
height to maximum diameter	the vertical distance from the vessel base to the maximum diameter
HHV	higher heating value, the amount of heat released by a specified quantity of fuel one it is combusted and the remnants have returned to 25°C
INAA	instrumental neutron activation analysis
lip	the very edge or tip of the vessel opening
maximum diameter	the widest diameter measurement of the vessel body, usually at the vessel shoulder
minimum diameter	the most restricted diameter measurement of the vessel body, usually at the intersection of the body and neck
neck	the section of the vessel which off-sets the lip and rim from the vessel body
neck angle	measurement of the amount of turn as the neck merges with the rim
PCA	principal component analysis
PPL	plane polarized light
rim	the section of the vessel wall just below the lip
rim diameter	the diameter of the vessel lip
SEI	secondary electron image
SEM	scanning electron microscope

shoulder	the location on the vessel body where the profile changes from vertical to horizontal
shoulder angle	measurement of the amount of turn as the vessel changes from horizontal to verticle orientation
XPL	crossed polarized light

CHAPTER 1

The Palace Ware Problem

Public and academic interest in the Neo-Assyrian empire was excited during the late 19th century by the excavation of the great Assyrian cities of Aššur (Andrae 1909), Nineveh (Layard 1849), Nimrud (Layard 1852) and Dur-Šarrukin (Botta 1849), and, after the cuneiform languages were deciphered in the 1850s, the translation of the monumental inscriptions contained therein. The end of the 19th century was a period of economic, territorial and scientific growth, particularly for Great Britain and Germany, and it is against this background of Victorian imperial expansion and scientific inquiry that the material culture of the Neo-Assyrian empire was first evaluated and interpreted.

Expeditions to the great Assyrian cities, known from Biblical texts, focused on the palaces, temples and administrative buildings on the upper tells, resulting in the excavation of a large quantity and variety of luxury goods, including precious metal and stone, ivory and glass, and little information about everyday Assyrian life. Assyrian reliefs and remains were proudly displayed in museums and available for wider consumption in periodicals, such as the Illustrated London News.

In 1927, Petrie uncovered a cache of thin-walled, drabware during excavation in Palestine which reminded him of metal vessels from Assyria he had seen in the British Museum. Petrie believed the presence of these ceramics at Tel Jemmeh resulted from the occupation and administration of the city by the Neo-Assyrians during the 8th–7th centuries BCE (Petrie 1928).

Pottery was not considered worthy of great attention by most 19th and early 20th century archaeologists, so it is significant that the delicate ceramics observed by Petrie in Palestine were also commented upon at Assyrian sites by Layard (1849), Botta (1849) and Andrae (1909). However, examination of these vessels as a corpus was not undertaken until Mallowan's excavation of Nimrud (ancient Kalḫu) in the 1950s (Mallowan 1950; 1966). Rawson (1954) published general descriptions of the vessels, which he termed 'palace ware' because they were recovered from the North-west palace at Nimrud, and comments about their manufacture. These observations, modified slightly and commented upon by Oates (*née* Lines) (1954; 1959), have stood as the definitional description of Palace Ware for the last 60 years.

Simply stated, the Palace Ware problem is that the absence of clear, quantitative definitional criteria for Palace Ware often leads to its misidentification and, subsequent misinterpretation, particularly since the social and symbolic

 | DOI 10.1163/9789004304123_002

function and meaning of these vessels has not been established. In addition, archaeologists use Palace Ware as an 'index artefact' of Neo-Assyrian imperial occupation and administration when this connection has yet to be concretely established (*e.g.* Parker 2001). The Palace Ware problem is compounded by limitations inherent in the material itself and the materials available for study and analysis, most of which were excavated 60–100 years ago and for which limited archaeological information is available.

The present work addresses the Palace Ware problem by: providing quantitative formal and fabric definitional characteristics for Palace Ware classification; assessing the social function and semiotic meaning of Palace Ware in the Assyrian core and evaluating how they change across the Neo-Assyrian imperial landscape; establishing chemical and mineralogical characterisation of Palace Ware raw materials and fabrics; and determining the transport mechanism for Palace Ware throughout the Neo-Assyrian empire.

What We Know

Delicate, thin-walled pottery was recognised by early excavators of Neo-Assyrian capital cities as a distinct cultural phenomenon (*e.g.* Layard 1849). Although these vessels were neither systematically recorded nor published in detail, it is reasonable that excavators were referring to what is now called Palace Ware. The term 'Palace Ware' was first used by Rawson in 1954 to refer to all the ceramics from the North-west palace at Nimrud. The term was intended as a descriptive reference to their excavation context and was not a comment on their status or social function. While working on the ceramic assemblage at Fort Shalmaneser, Oates (1959) restricted the term 'Palace Ware' to refer only to the "egg-shell" thin vessels; correctly identifying the thicker forms as standard Neo-Assyrian tableware.

In addition to providing a name for these vessels, Rawson published technical observations about them which have since been used as definitional criteria (1954, 168–170):

- delicate eggshell thin walls
- fine-grained, highly levigated fabric
- wheel thrown and pinched rather than cut from the hump
- thrown to its current thinness
- dimpled to facilitate handling while wet from the wheel
- high fired in an oxidizing kiln
- made of clay with a low iron content
- highly specialized and difficult to manufacture

Rawson's technical notes about Palace Ware and its manufacture are based on macroscopic observation and, while quite groundbreaking for the time, are incomplete and subjective by today's standards. Perhaps the most obvious problem with the use of Rawson's observations as definitional criteria is that the two most outstanding characteristics of Palace Ware 'fine-grained' and 'thin-walled' are ambiguous due to the relative nature of the terms 'fine' and 'thin'. This relativity leads to the misidentification of Palace Ware, impacting our ability to determine the boundaries of its cultural geography and potentially obscuring the complex social and political relationships within the Neo-Assyrian imperial landscape.

At the same time Palace Ware was being described as a ware-group by Rawson and Oates, archaeologists began to associate it with cultural constructs, particularly Neo-Assyrian power and prestige (*e.g.* Mallowan 1966), reinforcing Petrie's earlier belief that the presence of Palace Ware outside the Assyrian core was indicative of Neo-Assyrian imperial occupation or administration. These associations were based on archaeological context, location of Palace Ware in palaces, administrative buildings, temples, and elite homes, and the similarity of form between Palace Ware and metal vessels recovered from similar contexts.

Discussions about skeuomorphism are discussions about materiality and value and, thus, begin to address important questions about Palace Ware social and symbolic value and meaning. Typically vessels in the less expensive or lower prestige material are believed to be skeuomorphs of forms manufactured in the more expensive and prestigious materials: expense and prestige being themselves emic cultural constructs which are often elusive for archaeologists. Ceramic is generally not considered an expensive or prestigious material in the Near and Middle East, which suggests that, in the case of Palace Ware, the ceramic forms are a cheaper, less prestigious, although not necessarily derivative, version of metal vessels. The question of which came first the metal or the ceramic vessels cannot be answered using the archaeological data currently available: the relative stratigraphic dating of vessels in these two materials is not fine-grained enough to narrow their initial occurrence by less than half a century.

The unbalanced nature of excavations at Neo-Assyrian capital cities makes it difficult to support the elite status of Palace Ware using archaeological context. Likewise, the perception of Palace Ware as the less expensive and less prestigious alternative or imitation of metal luxury goods is in conflict with Palace Ware's association with the Neo-Assyrian ruling elite, power and privilege. The correlation of Palace Ware distribution and Neo-Assyrian imperial expansion however, seems to support a dynamic relationship among empire, expansion, and the consumption of Palace Ware (map 1.1).

Palace Ware is a relatively short-lived phenomenon: first appearing in the Neo-Assyrian core during the late 9th century and disappearing after the fall of the empire to Babylon in 608 BCE. Although Palace Ware forms are, in and of themselves, not unique or even distinctly Neo-Assyrian, the combination of form and fabrication, the extreme 'fineness' of the paste and 'thinness' of the walls, is a distinctly Neo-Assyrian material expression. Therefore, what has been established archaeologically is that Palace Ware is a Neo-Assyrian phenomenon and its consumption throughout the greater Assyrian landscape appears to be related to Neo-Assyrian imperial expansion.

Previous Studies

Several descriptive studies of the shape and style of published Palace Ware vessels from within and without the Assyrian core have been conducted (*e.g.* Gatti 1986; Hausleiter 1999; Anastasio 2010). While none of these studies offer new insight or discussion of previous interpretations of Palace Ware, they provide a valuable summary of available data. Ohtsu's study of Palace Ware (1991), on the other hand, uses morphometric attributes, specifically neck length, to evaluate regional and temporal changes in Palace Ware manufacture within the Assyrian core. Unfortunately, Ohtsu used published drawings from the 1950s which are often not to scale rather than observations and measurements taken from the actual artefacts rendering his conclusion that long neck lengths are an indicator of southern Assyrian manufacture suspect.

Outside the Assyrian core, Palace Ware is often interpreted as an imported luxury ware (*e.g.* Gatti 1986; Hausleiter 1996) or a locally manufactured elite ware (*e.g.* van Beek 1973; Gilboa 1996) for consumption by the Assyrian ruling class. To date, three studies of Palace Ware provenance have been published. Freestone and Hughes (1989) conducted geochemical and petrographic analyses of Neo-Assyrian ceramics, including Palace Ware vessels, from Qasrij Cliff and Khirbet Qasrij (Iraq). They concluded that it was not possible to discern Palace Ware provenance from these sites due to the fine-grained nature of Palace Ware fabrics and the chemical and mineralogical similarity of sediments deposited along the Tigris, the likely raw material source for Palace Ware manufacture (Freestone and Hughes 1989). In a similar study of Neo-Assyrian ceramics from Khirbet Khatuniyeh (Iraq), Hughes, Freestone and Humphrey (1997) were unable to determine Palace Ware provenance petrographically due to the lack of diagnostic mineral inclusions.

The third provenance study of Palace Ware was conducted on Assyrian-style ceramics from Tel el-Hesi (Israel) by Engstrom (2004). Engstrom found that

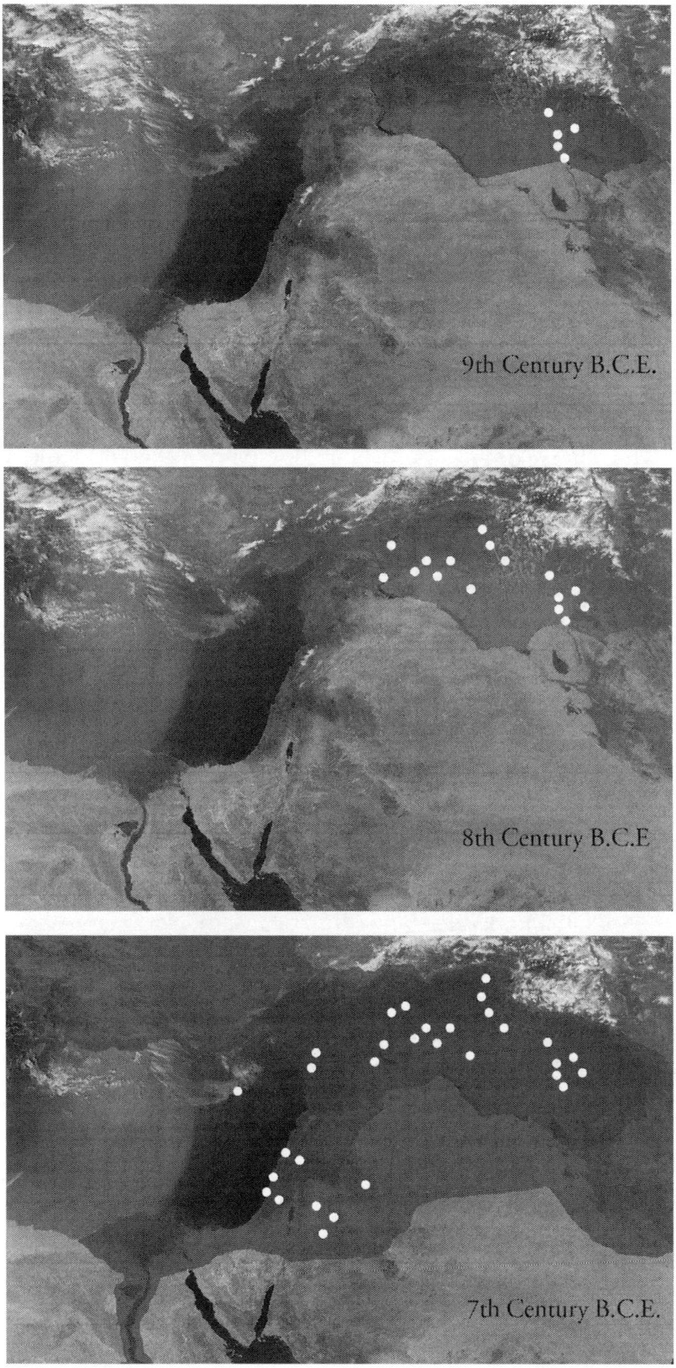

MAP 1.1 *Palace Ware finds by century. black = annexed provinces; grey = buffer zones & vassal states. (Modified from Google Earth Landsat Image.)*

the Palace Ware from el-Hesi was petrologically similar to the local sediment descriptions published by Melson and van Beek (1992) and concluded, therefore, that Palace Ware was locally manufactured at el-Hesi. Although Engstrom describes the el-Hesi Palace Ware as fine-grained and levigated, the published thin-section micrographs reveal that these vessels, while significantly finer than typical local fabrics, are made from a significantly coarser paste than their Mesopotamian counterparts. This demonstrated difference in interpretation of 'fine-grained' by excavators and analysts stems from the lack of unambiguous diagnostic criteria.

These studies raise an important methodological problem with Palace Ware analysis: our ability to determine geochemical and mineralogical provenance or, more accurately, fabric groups is limited by the 'fineness' of Palace Ware fabrics and the relative homogeneity of potential raw material sources in the Assyrian core.

Where We Go From Here

Palace Ware has the potential to contribute to our understanding of Neo-Assyrian imperial organisation and administration of the provincial system, the dynamic relationship between province and empire, and the perception of Assyria, the empire, and its administrators by populations outside the Assyrian core. In order to participate meaningfully in these larger dialogues about power and perception, we must first address three fundamental questions: what is Palace Ware?; what mechanism conveyed it across the Neo-Assyrian imperial landscape?; and what was the social function, value, and semiotic meaning of Palace Ware?

What is Palace Ware?

Any serious analysis of Palace Ware must begin by establishing an objective and unambiguous definition of Palace Ware. In order to accomplish this goal, we employ quantitative methods to: a) assess attributes that differentiate Palace Ware within the greater Neo-Assyrian ceramic assemblage; b) evaluate which attributes and attribute patterns are intentional and consistently reproduced; and c) using the attributes identified by these analyses, essential formal and fabric characteristics are used to establish quantitative definitional criteria for Palace Ware classification.

Methodologically, we approach the question 'what is Palace Ware' by examining the physical attributes and manufacture technology of Palace Ware vessels from the Neo-Assyrian core. Our selection of vessels from the imperial capital cities of Nimrud, Nineveh and Aššur is predicated on the belief that whatever cultural and social meaning and value these vessels possess—whatever 'Assyrian-ness' or 'Palace Ware-ness' they embody—will be purest and best preserved in vessels from their primary culture area. Vessels in the Palace Ware assemblage from the Neo-Assyrian core, hereafter Central Polity, were given the field classification 'Palace Ware' or identified as such by curators and researchers using the information published by Rawson and Oates (1954; 1955). Neo-Assyrian finewares and tablewares from Nimrud, Nineveh and Aššur with similar shape and style were analysed to confirm the broad typological boundaries of Palace Ware identified by Rawson and Oates.

The physical attributes of Palace Ware include: style and shape, which we evaluate using ceramic typology; formal characteristics, such as shape and size, which we quantify using morphometric analysis; and fabric characteristics, which we establish using petrographic and electron microscopy. A typology is a tool used to group and compare objects based on similar characteristics or attributes of shape and style. A seemingly infinite number of attributes can be measured on any given artefact. Pfalzner (1995) argues, therefore, that typologies should be intentionally constructed; built to answer a specific set of question within the limitations of the data set. The premise of this study is that Palace Ware is a real and meaningful category bounded by distinct formal attributes. Therefore, our typological analysis is constructed to reveal attribute patterns and describe the formal boundaries of Palace Ware.

Selection of attributes in typological analysis is theoretically determined and question driven. Arnold (1985) argues that attributes themselves are culturally meaningless and only become culturally and socially significant in relationship to each other. He further believes that this alleviates observer bias because the attribute patterns themselves describe emic categories. Adams and Adams (1991) argue that the reality of typology always falls short of its theoretical ideal and, as such, is a tool for the archaeologist and not a method of discerning ancient values, aesthetics, or emic categories. We believe ceramic typologies fall somewhere between these two positions. Ceramic typologies are able to reveal patterns and relationships among attributes which are culturally meaningful to the people who made and used them; for example neck length and rim diameter distinguishing jars of similar shape and size used to hold cereals and liquids. At the same time, we believe that typologies are essentially descriptive tools built by and for archaeologists and, therefore, necessarily use etic terminology and observations in their construction. In order to approach the typological analysis of Palace Ware with as few biases as possible, we employ the culturally neutral terminology of the form-based paradigm advocated by Hendrix *et al.* (1996). Attributes selected for typological and morphometric analyses are presented in table 1.1.

TABLE 1.1 *Definition of morphometric and typological Palace Ware attributes*

Attribute	Definition
lip	the very edge or tip of the vessel opening
rim	the section of the vessel wall just below the lip
neck	the section of the vessel which off-sets the lip and rim from the vessel body
collar	a vertical extention of the rim which joins it to the vessel body
shoulder	the location on the vessel body where the profile changes from vertical to horizontal
body	the section of the vessel below the neck and above the base, the 'bowl' or hollow
base	the section of the vessel opposite the rim upon which the vessel rests
maximum diameter	the widest diameter measurement of the vessel body, usually at the vessel shoulder
minimum diameter	the most restricted diameter measurement of the vessel body, usually at the intersection of the body and neck
rim diameter	the diameter of the vessel lip
height	measurement of the total vertical space occupied by the vessel, inclusive of base, body, neck and rim/lip
height to maximum diameter	the vertical distance from the vessel base to the maximum diameter
body depth	height to maximum diameter / maximum diameter
shoulder angle	measurement of the amount of turn as the vessel changes from horizontal to verticle orientation
neck angle	measurement of the amount of turn as the neck merges with the rim
base angle	measurement of the amount of turn as the base merges with the vessel body

Morphometric analysis is the quantitative description of form using measurements of length, width, angle and volume. Palace Ware occurs in two basic shapes which can be broken down anatomically as illustrated in figure 1.1. Each anatomical unit or attribute is a basic structural descriptor which can be quantified as a continuous variable of length, width and angle. We use vessel capacity as a measure of size and calculate Palace Ware capacity as the sum of a series of frustums (truncated circular conic sections) beginning at the base of the vessel and terminating between the shoulder and neck (figure 1.2a). Frustums were selected instead of the more traditional cylinders (*cf.* Senior and Birnie 1995) because they more closely emulate the shape of Palace Ware vessel bodies making them a more accurate measure of capacity (figure 1.2b).

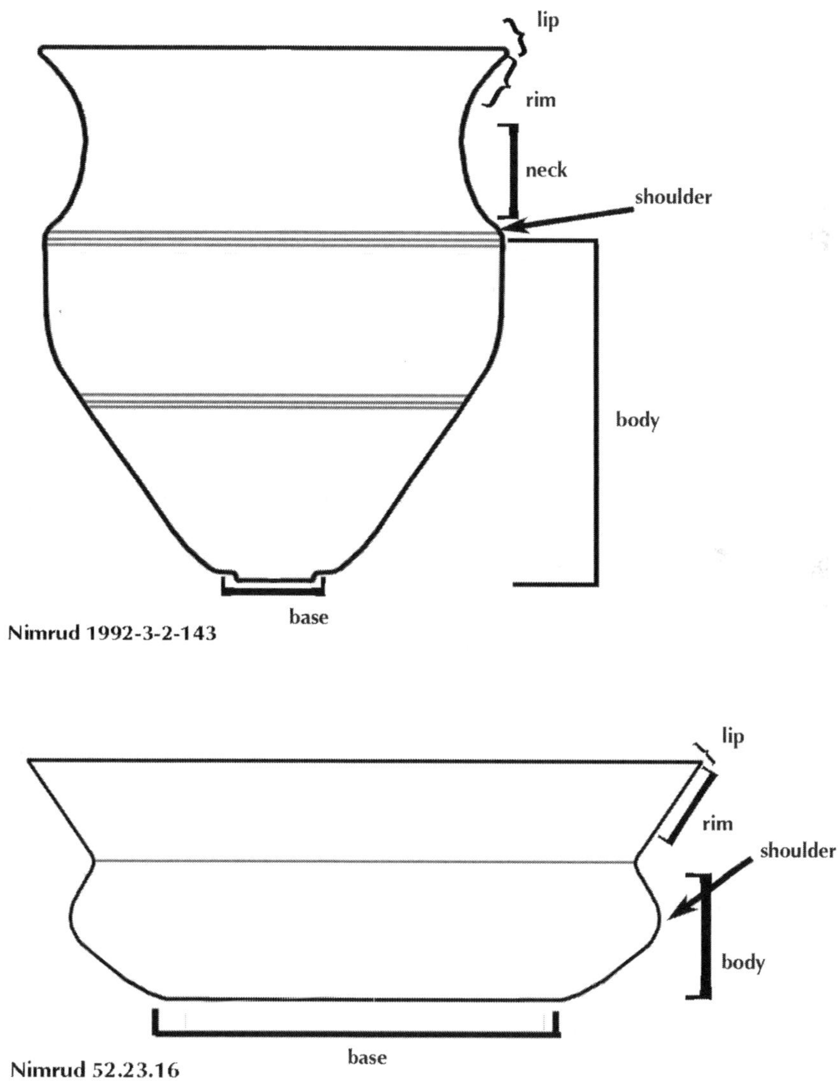

FIGURE 1.1 *Anatomical drawing of the two basic Palace Ware shapes.*

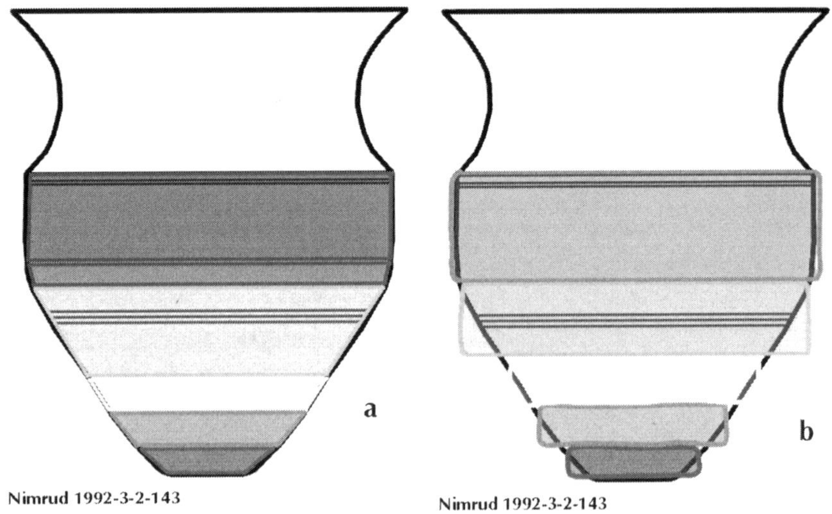

FIGURE 1.2 *Illustration of capacity measurement. (a) optimised capacity measurement as frustums (b) traditional capacity measurement as cylinders.*

The subjectivity of typologies (see the Ford/Spaulding debate in American Antiquity 1953–1954) is also a problem in morphometric studies because in both analyses the patterns observed are dependent upon the attributes selected for analysis. We ameliorate this subjectivity by employing statistical methods, specifically multi-response permutation procedures (MRPP), to identify and interpret the clustering behaviour of attributes. Patterns in the morphometric data are identified using bivariate plots of attribute pairs graphed on a Cartesian coordinate plane where the x and y axes represent a single attribute or measured continuous variable. Inherent patterns, patterns arising from natural correlation between attributes such as body length and vessel height, display visually as a linear correlation or with horizontal asymptotic behaviour (figure 1.3a). Artificial patterns, those which reflect intentional human behaviour, are identified graphically as non-linear or curvilinear clusters (figure 1.3b).

Once we identify a significant or artificial pattern in the data, it is important to assess whether the clustering behaviour could arise from random sampling or results from the intentionality of the potter. MRPP compares the observed intragroup average distances on a Cartesian coordinate system with the average distances arising from all other possible permutations of the data within the limitations of the null hypothesis. It is easier to disprove similarity than difference among populations due to inherent variability within a group, therefore the null hypothesis for MRPP is that the two observed groups are the same. If the observed clusters are different, then the average intragroup distance will

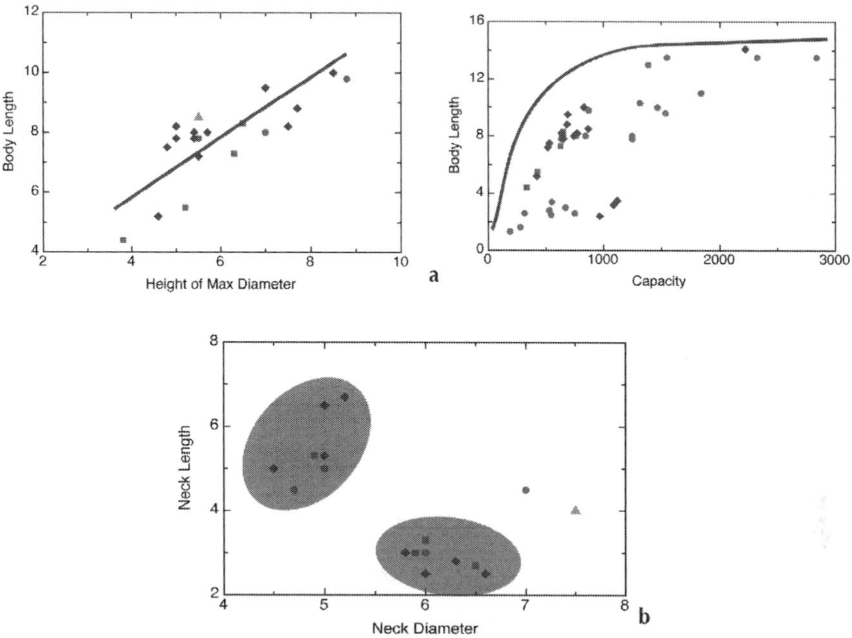

FIGURE 1.3 *Bivariate plots of attribute correlation patterns.*

be less than the average distance between all other arbitrarily assigned groups taken from the population (for a detailed description see Mielke *et al.* 1976; Berry *et al.* 1983; Mielke and Berry 2001). MRPP also calculates the strength of the clustering behaviour; defined as the difference between the average intergroup distance and the average intragroup distance (*cf.* van Sickle 1997). One of the advantages of MRPP for morphometric analysis is that it does not require assumptions about the data which cannot be met by archaeological test populations (multivariate normality, homogeneity of variance, *etc.*). MRPP also corrects for difference in group or population size because it weights the observed distances by relative group size before averaging them to generate delta (Berry *et al.* 1980).

Understanding Palace Ware manufacture technology, behaviours related to raw material acquisition and processing, vessel formation and shaping, decoration, and firing, enables us to more accurately describe the definitional formal and fabric characteristics of Palace Ware. For example, are the raw materials used to manufacture Palace Ware naturally fine-grained or does the fineness of the fabric reflect human design? Palace Ware manufacture technology also provides us with a baseline/framework for assessing the transport mechanism of these vessels.

Several scientific analytical methods are necessary to determine manufacture technology: petrographic and electron microscopy; x-ray radiography; and experimental methods, such as particle size analysis and firing of potential raw materials. Petrography, an analytical technique used in geology, is the systematic description and interpretation of the mineralogy and texture of rocks, both in hand specimen and using polarizing microscopy of thin-sections (Allaby and Allaby 2003). Ceramic petrography, by extension, is the systematic description and interpretation of the mineralogy and texture of ceramic fabrics using polarizing light microscopy of ceramic thin-sections. Our petrographic analyses were conducted using a Leica DMRX compound polarized light microscope equipt with a digital camera. Minerals were identified using the diagnostic characteristics presented in Rock Forming Minerals (Deer, Howie and Zussman 1997–2011) and the Handbook of Mineralogy (online version, Anthony *et al.* 2004–2011). Thin-section descriptions were formulated using the methodology and terminology advocated by Whitbread (1995).

The fine-grained nature of Palace Ware fabrics necessitates the use of scanning electron microscopy (SEM), in addition to optical microscopy, for the identification of mineral inclusions and analysis of ceramic fabrics. SEMs use the electrons emitted when a material is excited by a focused high energy electron beam scanning across its surface in a raster pattern to generate high magnification images. A number of atomic interactions occur when a material is stimulated by a high energy electron beam but the three most relevant for electron microscopy are secondary and backscattered electrons and x-rays.

Secondary electrons are low energy electrons emitted when a high energy electron 'bumps' an electron out of an outer atomic orbital. Images generated using secondary electrons (SEI) are useful for examining the topography of materials. Backscattered electrons, higher in energy than secondary electrons, are emitted when the high energy electron beam interacts with the atomic nuclei in the sample material. Images generated using backscattered electrons (BSE) are useful for evaluating the elemental composition of a material because the energy of the emitted backscattered electrons is related to the atomic number of the nucleus from which it derives. X-rays are also emitted at characteristic energies related to the atomic number of the element stimulated. The intensity or number of characteristic x-rays emitted is directly proportional to the concentration of the excited element in the material. These characteristic x-rays can be collected, quantified, and analysed by energy dispersive spectrometry (EDS) on an SEM equipt with an energy dispersive detector.

In this study, SEM-SEI images were taken on a Hitachi S3400N to evaluate fabric vitrification and estimate firing temperature. SEM-BSE images and EDS-SEM analyses of mineral phases were collected using a JEOL 8600 Superprobe equipt with an Oxford Instruments silicon drift detector (SDD). All samples were prepared as polished blocks using Beuhler EpoThin epoxy resin and polished according to the standard sample preparation protocol for ceramic material to 0.25 μm.

X-ray radiography, hereafter referred to as radiography, is based on the physics of x-ray attenuation. Attenuation, transmission loss, is the reduction in signal intensity with respect to distance travelled through a substance. Different materials attenuate differently, transmitting x-rays at different rates, depending upon their density and chemical composition. One of the challenges in ceramic radiography is the high attenuation of silica and silicate materials. Most minerals have a high silica content, from the clay minerals in the ceramic matrix to the fragments of rock-forming minerals included therein, therefore both the matrix and the inclusions attenuate with similar intensity making phase differentiation difficult. Air, trapped in voids created during raw material processing, vessel formation or the thermal expansion and retraction of minerals during firing, has a significantly lower attenuation than silicate materials. The differential attenuation of air and the ceramic body facilitates identification of manufacturing behaviours, particularly when and where voids are elongate or large (Middleton 1997; Berg 2008). The radiographs in this study were collected using a tungsten x-ray source (x-tek 160kV gun), a Varian Pax Scan 4030 detector and Varian Viva software (revision k3, build 45) at 400 μA, 40–45 kV and 20 frames per image.

Sometimes the evaluation of artefacts is not enough to answer questions about their manufacture and function. In these cases it is often necessary, through experimental research, to create a reference data set for the interpretation of archaeological observations. The fine-grained fabric of Palace Ware is one of its most recognisable features and was interpreted by Rawson (1954) as the result of levigation. In order to evaluate this hypothesis, we needed to determine which processes, natural and artificial, could be responsible for Palace Ware's fine fabric. Therefore, we conducted particle size analysis and levigation and sedimentation experiments on potential raw materials to both characterise the raw material sources themselves and to evaluate potential raw material processing technologies.

Particle size analysis, also called grain size distribution analysis, describes a material based on the relative amount, measured in our analysis as mass, of particles present according to their size. Our analysis used a combination of sieve and sedimentation techniques. Potential ceramic raw materials were mixed and divided using a sample divider box and the coarse fraction ($\geq \Phi$ 4) was separated from the fine fraction using standard geological sieves (nos. 5–230) and each particle size weighed. The fine fraction ($< \Phi$ 4) was

TABLE 1.2 *Sedimentation rate according to Stoke's Law*

Particle Size (Φ)	Time Elapsed
3.8	30 seconds
4.1	45 seconds
4.3	1 minute
4.8	2 minutes
5.5	5 minutes
6.3	15 minutes
6.8	30 minutes
7.3	60 minutes
7.8	2 hours
8.3	4 hours
8.8	8 hours
9.7	24 hours

thoroughly mixed and suspended in dH2O. Particles suspended in a column of water separate according to Stoke's Law which, over simplified, calculates the terminal velocity of a particle falling in fluid as a function of the mass density (mass per unit volume) or mass and size of the particle. Terminal velocity or sedimentation is longer the finer (smaller) the particle. The density of particles in the column was measured and recorded at timed intervals (table 1.2) using a hydrometer (series 020388). This data was processed and analysed as particle size histograms and log normal distributions commonly referred to as cumulative coarser curves.

Strictly speaking, levigation is the process of refining a material by grinding it, suspending the resulting powder in liquid, and allowing the suspension to flow through a series of tanks thereby removing the coarsest and heaviest particles. Sedimentation, the process described above, allows an unprocessed material suspended in liquid to settle naturally according to its terminal velocity. Although archaeologists often conflate these two processes and use the term 'levigation' to refer to any refinement of a material by water, we treat them as two separate manufacture behaviours. In order to assess whether Palace Ware fabrics resulted from levigation or sedimentation, we homogenised and separated potential raw materials using a sample divider box. Half of the material was wet milled to 50 μm (the upper limit for Palace Ware inclusions).

The resulting paste was suspended in dH2O and passed through a series of tanks. The suspended material in the last tank was collected and used to make sediment smear slides which were analysed for particle size and morphology and mineral type using petrographic microscopy. For comparative purposes, the sedimentation experiment described above for particle size analysis was repeated using the second half of the material, and 1 mL aliquots were removed from the suspension at 30 seconds, 1, 2, 3, 5, 15, 30, 45 and 60 minutes. These aliquots were used to make sediment smear slides which were analysed for particle size, morphology, and mineral type.

The firing temperature of Palace Ware informs not only our understanding of Palace Ware manufacture but also provides insight into its cost of production and, by extension, social value. Since sampling regulations for the Palace Ware in the study precluded refiring experiments or analysis of fabric texture on a fresh break, we created a reference group of ceramic textures for pore and vitrification analysis as polished blocks using experimentally fired briquettes of potential raw material sources.

Potential raw materials were homogenised and separated using a sample divider box and the coarse fraction of half of each potential material source was removed by sieving. Both the refined and coarse material was mixed with dH2O to create a paste and formed into briquettes 2 cm long, 1 cm wide, and 1 cm thick. A set of briquettes, refined and natural from each potential raw material source, was placed into a Morgan Salamander Super Graphite crucible and insulated with sterile quartz sand. The crucible was loaded into a cold Lenton 2316 furnace and heated at 5°C/min to temperature (600–1200°C, at 100°C intervals), and allowed to soak for 30 minutes before cooling naturally overnight.

Fired briquettes were prepared as polished blocks using Buehler EpoThin epoxy resin and polished according to the standard sample preparation protocol for ceramic material to 0.25 µm. SEM-SEI images taken on a Hitachi S3400N, were analysed for texture, pore and vitrification according to the procedures outlined by Tite *et al.* (1982) and Maniatis and Tite (1981).

How was Palace Ware Transported Across the Imperial Landscape?

The movement of artefacts across a cultural landscape is typically the result of trade, the migration or relocation of people, and/or the diffusion of an idea, social practice or value system across social boundaries. Each of these transport mechanisms leaves tangible evidence in the archaeological record enabling us to reconstruct the behaviour or suite of behaviours responsible for the movement of cultural materials.

Movement of Objects

Trade or transport of archaeological ceramics can be identified by the bulk chemical composition and mineralogy of their fabrics, particularly when combined with formal analysis (morphometric and typological). If Palace Ware was a traded or transported commodity, we would expect vessels inside and outside the Assyrian heartland to have the same formal and fabric characteristics and the same chemical and mineralogical profile. Mineralogical characterisation of Palace Ware fabrics was conducted using petrographic analysis, and instrumental neutron activation analysis was used to determine their bulk chemical composition. When possible, petrographic analysis of potential raw material sources was conducted for comparative purposes.

Instrumental neutron activation analysis (INAA) is a quantitative technique used to determine the bulk chemical composition of a material by measuring the concentration of elemental isotopes. Simply stated, in INAA a powdered material is bombarded with free neutrons (subatomic particles contained in the atomic nucleus). In response, atoms in the material incorporate these free neutrons into their nuclei altering the proton/neutron ratio of the atom and forming a different elemental isotope. Some of these newly created isotopes (artificial isotopes) are radioactive (radioisotopes) with unstable nuclei which spontaneously degrade or decay emitting ionising radiation (α, β and γ particles) in order to return to a stable configuration. The decay trajectory and energies of these particles are characteristic of the original elemental isotope and measurements of their relative intensities enable us to quantify the major (> 1 wt%), minor (0.1–1 wt%) and trace (< 0.1 wt%) elemental composition of the material.

The detection limits for INAA are determined by the atomic structure of the measured elements, the neutron flux of the reactor, and the elapsed time after which the γ-particles are measured. Typical values are in the range of 0.1 to 1*106 ng g^{-1}. The reactor used for this study is a TRIGA Mark-II, housed at the Atominstitut, Technische Universität Wien in Austria, which runs at a flux density of 1013 cm^{-3} s^{-1}. INAA analyses were conducted by Dipl. Ing. Dr. J. Sterba.

Characterisation of the mineralogy and bulk chemical composition of archaeological ceramics provides geological and, by extension, geographic information. As a result, chemical and mineralogical analyses of archaeological ceramics are often referred to as 'provenance studies'. The theoretical and methodological issues associated with ceramic 'provenance studies' in general and the term 'provenance' in particular are discussed in detail elsewhere. (*e.g.* Hunt 2012; Rice and Saffer 1982; Bishop *et al.* 1982). For clarity, we use the term 'fabric group' to refer to ceramic vessels with similar bulk chemistry and mineralogy.

Movement of People and Potters

The migration or relocation of people and populations are often detected archaeologically by the introduction of material culture and/or technology to a geographic region. Displaced and relocated populations bring their ideologies, values, and social practices with them to their new environment. These values and social practices are often intensified and exaggerated in the new location as a reaction to its foreignness and as a means of solidifying and confirming social and cultural identity (Sinopoli 2001; Alcock and Morrison 2001). Therefore, if the consumers of Palace Ware outside the Assyrian core were displaced Assyrians from the Central Polity, we would expect the social function, value and semiotic meaning of Palace Ware to remain the same.

Social value and symbolic meaning can be observed in the archaeological record as characteristics or attributes of an artefact which are unnecessary for its practical function or technological success and yet are intentionally and consistently reproduced. The identification and interpretation of the attributes related to social and semiotic value, meaning and function are discussed in the next section.

Potters are technologically conservative; adopting new techniques, technologies and innovations in response to external pressure and economic stress (Matson 1989; Foster 1965). Although potters may adapt to a new environment by adjusting their raw material sourcing and processing behaviours out of necessity, their basic production sequence will remain unchanged (Hendrickson 1989). Therefore, if Palace Ware vessels outside the Central Polity were manufactured by potters from or trained in the Assyrian heartland, we would expect them to be manufactured using the same chaîne opératoire (formation, shaping and decoration technology) and firing temperature and conditions as Palace Ware vessels manufactured in the Central Polity. We would also expect a high degree of morphometric conformity among Palace Ware assemblages within and outside the Central Polity. We would not, however, expect the same bulk chemical and mineralogical profiles for Palace Ware fabrics from populations from within and outside the Assyrian heartland.

Morphometric 'norms' and variation are determined and quantified as the mode and standard deviation of measurements for a given attribute. According to Blackman *et al.* (1993), the acceptable variation for a particular form or shape of vessel produced in two different ceramic workshops is twice the standard deviation of those same vessels manufactured in a single workshop or production centre. Therefore, vessels manufactured outside the heartland by Assyrian potters should have the same 'norm' and fall within the expected range of variation (two standard deviations) for Palace Ware produced in Central Polity workshops.

Movement of Ideas

Transmission of Palace Ware across the imperial landscape as a concept requires us to view artefacts as the material expression of ideas, values, and behaviours rather than simply as objects. Producers and consumers of material culture relate to the physical, material world, consciously or unconsciously, through culturally and socially constructed *urformen*, signifiers or signs—conceptual units which contain the ideal form and material of an object as well as its function (practical and social), value and meaning. Shared *urformen* are the building blocks of language and culture which facilitate inter- and intra-group communication (Eco 1976). These signs can be regionally or culturally specific, for example 'tea cup' brings different ur-forms to mind in China and England, or widely disseminated 'international' or 'intercultural' concepts such as 'wine glass'. Artisans and craftsmen, such as Riedel, may play with the 'wine glass' ur-form by removing its stem and base in their "O" series, however they play within a limited range of accepted variation, changing only one or two attributes of the ur-form at a time so that the consumer is able to identify or recognise the vessel as 'wine glass'. Similarly, when we encounter a foreign or unfamiliar object or concept, we make sense of it by relating it to and comparing it with our repertoire of *urformen* or signs—modifying the form and function of these ideals to fit the material reality we experience.

When an artefact is transmitted across cultural boundaries as an idea or social practice it is translated from the ur-form of its culture of origin into a modified ur-form from the receiving culture's repertoire. During this translation, aspects of the artefact which are culturally or socially significant to the receiving culture are often emphasised or exaggerated. Ur-forms can be identified archaeologically as morphometric and typological patterns or 'norms'. If the diffusion of Palace Ware across the Neo-Assyrian imperial landscape resulted from the dissemination of Palace Ware as a concept, we would expect to see a shift in the morphometric 'norms' or ur-form of Palace Ware vessels outside the Central Polity and/or an emphasis on different attributes related to social value, meaning and semiotic function.

A more detailed discussion of *urformen* and *urphänomen* can be found in Goethe's *Theory of Colour* (1810; republished in 1970) and his letters to Hegel (trans. Butler and Seiler 1984) and the application of semantics and semiotics to material culture is described in Eco's *A Theory of Semiotics* (1976) and *Umberto Eco: Philosophy, Semiotics and the Work of Fiction* (Caesar 1999).

What was the Social Value and Semiotic Meaning of Palace Ware?

Human behaviour is culturally conditioned. Patterns in human behaviour and its material expression as artefact reflect the values and symbols or *urformen* of that culture. Attributes and behaviours intentionally and consistently reproduced which are not required for the practical function or technological success of an artefact reflect its semiotic and social value and meaning, particularly when those attributes or behaviours are expensive or difficult to execute in terms of time, resources or skill. We can detect these socially and symbolically significant attributes in the archaeological record as artificial patterns in the morphometric analysis of artefacts which are unrelated to manufacture and function. In the Palace Ware assemblage from the Central Polity, five attributes related to social value and semiotic meaning were identified: capacity; colour; wall thinness; fabric fineness; and decoration. Continuity and change in the social function, value and semiotic meaning of Palace Ware across the imperial landscape, therefore, is revealed by changes in the patterning of these five attributes and/or the advent of additional attributes of social and symbolic significance. Additional insight into the social value and symbolic significance of Palace Ware is discerned through comparative analysis of Palace Ware consumption patterns across the imperial landscape.

CHAPTER 2

Power and Prestige: The Neo-Assyrian Imperial Landscape

Assyria first became a geographical and cultural entity in the 23rd century BCE, and continued to continuously occupy that territory, or some piece of it, until 605 BCE. Understandably, the borders and boundaries of Assyria expanded and contracted during those 1600 years. We concentrate here on the Neo-Assyrian empire or Late Assyrian period (911–605 BCE), particularly the 8th and 7th centuries, touching on the Middle Assyrian period (1400–1050 BCE) only where necessary for conceptual continuity. Although the terms 'Neo-Assyrian' and 'Late Assyrian' are often used interchangeably, we use 'Neo-Assyrian' to refer to the political-cultural complex of the Neo-Assyrian empire and 'Late Assyrian' to refer to the period of time.

From its inception, Assyrian power and identity was concentrated in the 'Assyrian triangle', cornered by the cities Aššur, Nineveh, and Arba-ilu, along and to the east of the Tigris river (map 2.1a). This area was the religious, political, and cultural centre of the empire. Scholars generally recognise the triangle to sit within a roughly heart-shaped area which extends beyond the banks of the Tigris to the west (map 2.1b). This larger region was never out of Assyrian control and cultural continuity can be demonstrated archaeologically across the '1200 BCE event' which caused the collapse of neighbouring empires (Kuhrt 1995; Caubet 1992). Radner (2006) refers to the 11 administrative provinces which comprise this heartshaped region as 'central Assyria' and in this study we refer to it as the Neo-Assyrian Central Polity.

The physical entity of Assyria is described in the literature as the 'heartland', 'Assyria proper', and *māt Aššur* (land of Assur). Each of these terms incorporates complex political, ideological, and territorial relationships and it is illustrative of the complexity of Assyrian geography to tease apart the connotations of each term. Assyrian heartland can refer to the territory defined above as the Central Polity, but is often used to describe a larger region of Upper Mesopotamia which extends from the Ǧazīra or Syrian steppe in the west to the Zagros mountains in the east (*e.g.* Kühne 1995) (map 2.1c). This second usage reflects that during times of strength during both Middle and Late Assyrian periods, this territory was not only under Assyrian control but demonstrated continuity in material culture and ideology with the Central Polity.

 | DOI 10.1163/9789004304123_003

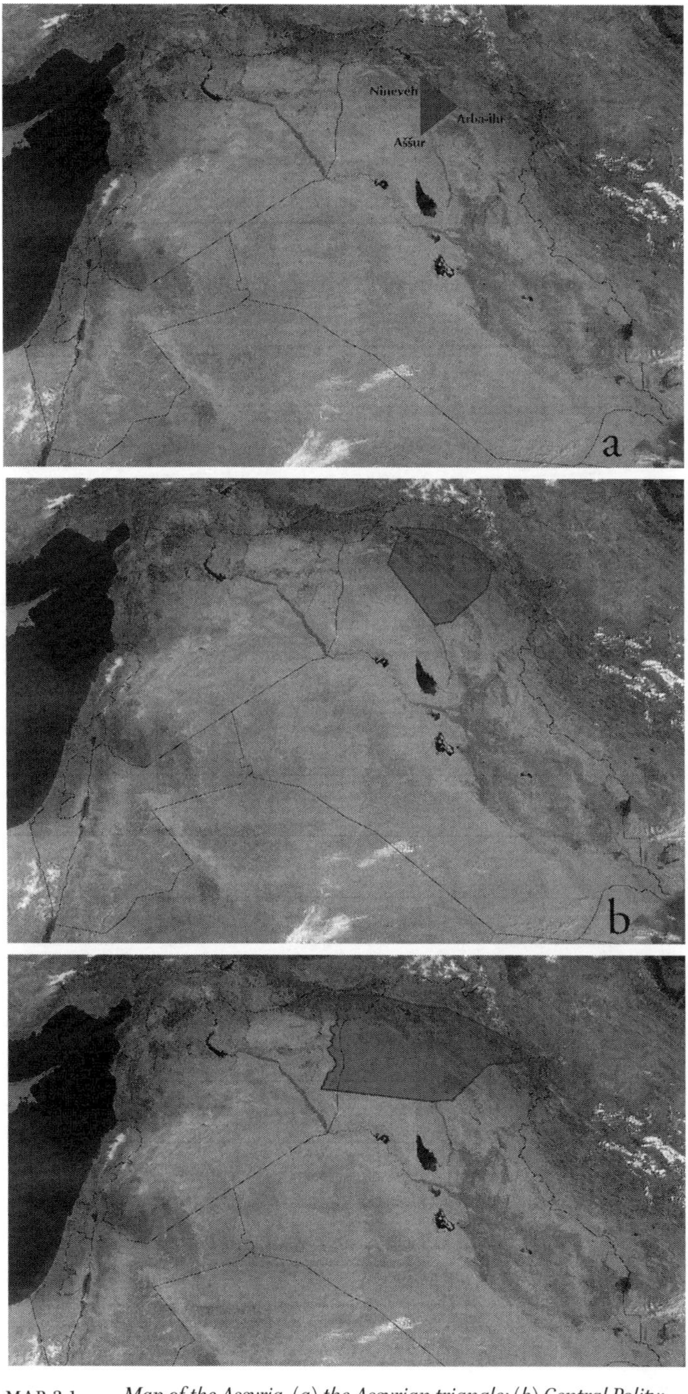

MAP 2.1 *Map of the Assyria. (a) the Assyrian triangle; (b) Central Polity; (c) Assyria Proper. (Modified from Google Earth Landsat Image.)*

Māt Aššur, first used in the Middle Assyrian period, reflects emic Assyrian geographic ideology in which all land and people incorporated into the imperial administrative system of *ḫalṣū* (provinces) were understood to be Assyrian, part of the 'land of Assur' (Postgate 1992). This ideology is discussed in detail below, however it is important to note here that from an Assyrian perspective, territories were either *māt Aššur* or not. The political realities and nuances of vassal states and buffer zones, while acknowledged in the cuneiform literature as both necessary and extant during the Late Assyrian period, are nonetheless considered 'not Assyria' despite their economic and administrative ties to the Assyrian heartland.

Assyria proper, like *māt Aššur*, typically refers to all territory organised into the Assyrian provincial system. Therefore, like 'land of Aššur', it is a fluid area defined by the changing boundaries and foreign policies of its kings. Postgate (1995) demarcates the 'home provinces' as those incorporated into *māt Aššur* before the reign of Tiglath-pileser III (744–727 BCE), an area roughly equivalent to the broader definition of heartland and our Central Polity. As a result, Assyria proper is sometimes equated with these 'home provinces'. We prefer the more general definition of Assyria proper, and employ it rather than *māt Aššur* when referring to the physical, geographic entity of Assyria for the following reasons: (a) *māt Aššur* is an ideological concept and does not reflect the complex geopolitical reality of the Neo-Assyrian empire; and (b) the term 'Assyria proper' itself implies that a region can be improperly Assyrian (*i.e.* a vassal state), providing a more accurate geographical picture of the empire by including both 'proper' and 'improper' territories.

Imperial Ideology

Simplified, Assyrian cosmogony and cosmology describe a dualist world divided between the divine and profane. Humans were created to serve the gods, to feed, clothe, and care for them, and to worship and adore them. The divine realm is governed by a trinity of great gods and a pantheon of lesser deities. The hierarchy in the divine realm is complicated by interdeity relationships and, as a result, the chief deity changed and evolved over time (Greenwood 2010; Hunt 2010; Strawn et al 2006; Porter 1997; also *cf.* Parpola 2000). The human realm is governed by the king, who, while not divine himself, is chosen by the gods, and serves as Aššur's representative on earth (*i.a.* Grayson 1999; Parpola 1999; Michalowski 1990). Much of the Assyrian royal and imperial ideology is shaped by the king's relationship with Aššur and Aššur's relationship with the land (*i.a.* Holloway 2002; Livingstone 1997), illustrated in SAA 3 11 lines 15–18:

^{d}aš-šur LUGAL ^{d}aš-šur-ma LUGAL ^{m}aš-šur–DU3–[A x] xx [xxx] ^{d}aš-šur bi-nu-ut ŠU.2-šu$_2$	Aššur is king-indeed Aššur is king! Assurbanipal is the [scion] of Aššur the creation of his hands.
DINGER-MEŠ GAL-MEŠ lu-kin$_2$-nu BALA-šu$_2$ li-ṣu-ru[ša ^{m}aš-šur]-DU3 A MAN KUR–aš-šur ZI-MEŠ-šu$_2$	May the great gods make firm his reign, may they protect the life [of Assurba]nipal, king of Assyria!
GIŠ.PA i-šir-tu a-na ru-up-pu-uš KUR u UN-[MEŠ-šu$_2$] lid-di-nu-niš-šu$_2$	May they give him a straight scepter to extend the land and his peoples!
BALA-šu$_2$ li-te-diš GIŠ.GU.ZA LUGAL-ti-šu$_2$ a-na da-ra-a-ti lu-kin$_2$-nu	May his reign be renewed, and may they consolidate his royal throne for ever!

Aššur was the land (*i.a.* Postgate 1992; Lambert 1983). Aššur was also, to a certain extent, the flora, fauna, and people who dwelt on the land. The term *Aššūrāyu*, 'Assyrian', literally translates "of Aššur" and the Assyrians were not simply those who worshipped Aššur, but those who were literally 'of Aššur', *i.e.* lived on/in "the land of Aššur" (*māt Aššur*) (Parpola 2004; Oded 1979). This suggests that ideologically there was no distinction among the 'people of Aššur' whether they lived in the Assyrian Central Polity or a distant province. All people residing in *māt Aššur* were 'people of Aššur'. When a new territory was added to Assyria proper the king declared: *itti nišē māt Aššūr amnušunūti* "and I called/considered them Assyrians" (*e.g.* Nimrud Prism, Keilinschriftliche Bibliothek ii). An alternative reading of this phrase suggested by Parpola (2004) reads: "I counted them as citizens of Assyria".

It was a divine mandate that the Assyrian king would increase the power and might of Aššur (Kuhrt 1998). The king demonstrated the supremacy of Aššur over the entire world in several ways: first, by incorporating territory into *māt Aššur* (*ibid.*); and, second, by increasing the diversity of peoples, flora, fauna, and natural resources over which Aššur was sovereign (Thomason

2005). These two strategies were not mutually exclusive. When foreign lands were annexed into the empire, the diversity of *māt Aššur* increased because the annexed territories included foreign customs, languages, deities, material culture, and local flora and fauna. This diversity reflected the power and domain of Aššur over all things (Holloway 2002). Therefore, the so-called 'Assyrianization' of the Near and Middle East was not an imperial mandate but rather the consequence of contact or a conscious choice on the part of the local or native populations in the Annexed Provinces and Unincorporated Territories (Parpola 2004).

An ideological tension existed with regard to *māt Aššur*. On the one hand, land was either *māt Aššur* or 'other'. Nuances of political relationship, such as allies, were simplified by the phrase "I called them Assyrians" (*e.g.* SAA 10 118; Tadmor 1999, Ann. 9.1.4; for discussion see Parpola 2004, note 38). Being "called Assyrian" incorporated those territories ideologically into *māt Aššur* (Parpola 2004). The Assyrian king was obligated to go on annual campaigns and increase the glory and power of Aššur through the acquisition of land, through conquest, annexation, or treaty (*e.g.* SAA 3 3; SAA 3 11).

On the other hand, all land was, in actuality, *māt Aššur*. Aššur was the supreme deity and sovereign over all things, therefore, it was not possible for something to exist over which he did not have dominion (*cf.* the Assyrian version of the Enūma Eliš and Assyrian *akitu* festival). Rather than conquering new lands, the king was returning land to Aššur (*e.g.* Holloway 2002). It is unclear whether the people living on that land were considered lapsed Assyrians, unenlightened Assyrians, or squatters on *māt Aššur*. That they were considered 'other' in addition to being Assyrian is another tension in the imperial ideology illustrated in the reliefs where the diversity of peoples over whom Aššur ruled is indicated by their styles of dress and grooming, for example the Black Obelisk of Shalmaneser (see also SAA 2 6 for the title "foreign citizen" and discussion in Parpola 2004). Given the importance of unified diversity for Neo-Assyrian imperial ideology, the Assyrians would not have imposed their culture on annexed provinces, vassal states, or buffer zones (Parpola 2004; Liverani 1979). According to Sinopoli (2001), all empires require a tension to exist between conformity and diversity in order to function, and the ideological construct of *māt Aššur* combines and explains the necessity of both.

The second imperial strategy to increase and demonstrate the diversity of Aššur's dominion was imperial collecting. Not unlike the practice in Victorian Britain (Pratt 2008; Crosby 2004), the Assyrians collected specimens of exotic flora and fauna, transported them to the Assyrian core, and raised them in royal and public botanical gardens and menagerie (Thomason 2005). These collections were confirmation of the supremacy of Aššur which the Assyrian state displayed for the gods, foreign dignitaries, and the people (Foster 1998; Stronach 1990).

Although the ideology of *māt Aššur* provided the overall shape of Assyrian foreign policy, the strategies employed evolved over the 300 years of the Neo-Assyrian empire. We know the most about the policies of the later kings, from Tiglath-pileser III to Assurbanipal, because their archives have been excavated and are being translated and published as part of an ongoing effort by the State Archives of Assyria Project (SAA) and individual Assyriologists around the world. The present study is particularly concerned with the 8th and 7th centuries BCE, to which the majority of translated texts relate.

Radner (2011) effectively employs cold war terminology to describe the different foreign policies of the Late Assyrian kings: aggressive acquisition under Tiglath-pileser III and Shalmaneser V earns them the title 'hawks'; while the gentler policies of buffer zones and alliances earn Sargon II, Sennacherib, and Esarhaddon the title 'doves'. Neo-Assyrian hawks and doves have the same end game, to increase the power and diversity of *māt Aššur*, however the *modus operandi* of the hawks was "weakness must be exploited", while "military engagement must be avoided if at all possible" was the strategy employed by the doves (Radner 2011).

The underlying assumption which governs the foreign policy of both the Neo-Assyrian 'hawks' and 'doves' is that it is to the advantage of the foreign elite to align and ally themselves with the Assyrian empire (Lanfranchi 1997). For the hawks, this need or dependence upon Assyrian economic and political stability was a weakness which could be exploited and justified, not simply by the mandate of Aššur, but by coming to the aid of an ally through military intervention and, ultimately, annexation (Radner 2011). For the doves, once a foreign elite recognised the supremacy of Aššur and the Assyrian empire it was to their advantage to be loyal and, therefore, it was more cost effective for the Assyrian empire to establish them as vassal states or buffer zones, which did not require Assyrian governors, administration, or military action (Radner 2011; Otzen 1979). This is not to say that if and when treaties were broken or vassal states disloyal the doves did not take military action, simply that it was not necessary under the doves for all weaker territories to be annexed and become part of Assyria proper (Radner 2011).

One of the consequences of these ideological tensions and ambiguities for archaeologists and Assyriologists is that traditional core-periphery models of empire, based on World Systems Theory (Wallerstein 1974, 1980, 1989), are inadequate to explain the subtlety and diversity of interregional interactions and relationships encompassed within the Neo-Assyrian imperial system. Critiques of World Systems Theory have been elegantly and extensively published elsewhere, Stein (2002) for example, and include its monolithic and homogenising nature (Thomas 1994), overemphasis on the importance of the core in interregional interaction (Schrieber 2005), simplification and gloss of the unique cultural contribution of the periphery (Stein 1998), and reduction of complex human behaviour into dualist or binary interaction (Meskell 1998; van Dommelen 1998). One of the most problematic extensions of interregional interaction models based on World Systems Theory is the equation of colonial or imperial material culture with colonial or imperial identity. Such conflation of geographic political boundaries, materiality and identity exaggerates the prominence of the 'core' in terms of influence and inflates the importance of 'peripheral' territories.

Neo-Assyrian imperial ideology is more subtle and complex than traditional World Systems Theory core-periphery interactions. Increasingly, there has been movement away from global interpretive models and toward context driven narratives which focus on the "recursive relationship between social structure and the strategic actions of individuals or small groups" within a particular imperial or colonial system (Stein 2005, 7). We use a context driven narrative in this study in order to elucidate (a) the social, cultural and political relationships between Palace Ware consumers and the Neo-Assyrian empire and (b) the social value, function and semiotic significance of these vessels for their consumers. As such, we abandon core-periphery terminology. Administrative provinces which were always culturally, politically and territorially Assyrian are referred to as the Central Provinces (map 2.2). All other administrative provinces are referred to as Annexed Provinces. The term annexed was selected because it implies being included into a more powerful, but not necessarily bigger, entity without implying inferiority which perfectly describes the context of many of these territories. Improperly Assyrian territories, vassal states, buffer zones, etc., are referred to as Unincorporated Territories.

Much has been made of the Assyrian policy of deportation as a method of control and "annihilation of local identities" (Lanfranchi 1997, 81). However, diversity was both encouraged by and a necessary part of Neo-Assyrian imperial ideology. While it would be foolish to deny the efficacy of controlling people by removing them from their homeland (see discussion of deportation as a form of Assyrian imperial control in Oded 1979 and Oded 1970), deportation also appears to have had an economic motive: deported populations were used to bolster the work forces in the Annexed Provinces and convert these

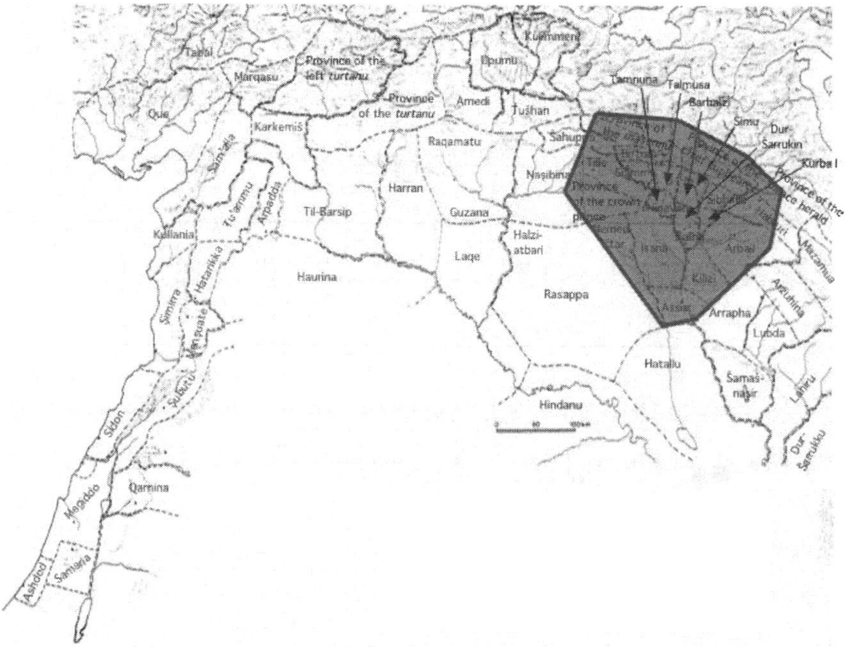

MAP 2.2 *Provincial map of the Neo-Assyrian empire. Highlighted region approximates the Central Polity. (After Radner 2006, karte 2, 3, 4.)*

territories into productive farm land (Oded 1995). Often the ruling class were the only portion of a population deported from the Annexed Provinces and Unincorporated Territories where they were incorporated into the Assyrian court and could witness first-hand the power and importance of the empire, reinforcing the necessity and advantage of their alliance with Assyria (Parpola 2004). There is no evidence, textual or archaeological, for the intentional annihilation of local identities and/or material culture and practice by the Neo-Assyrian imperial administration.

Imperial Geography

At the beginning of the Late Assyrian period (911 BCE), Assyria proper occupied only the heartshaped region we refer to as the Central Polity (figure 2.3a). By the end of the 9th century, Assyria had extended north into Syria, Turkey, and Anatolia, as a result of the foreign policies of Adad-nirari II, Assurnasirpal II, Shalmaneser III, and Šamši-adad V, encompassing the region

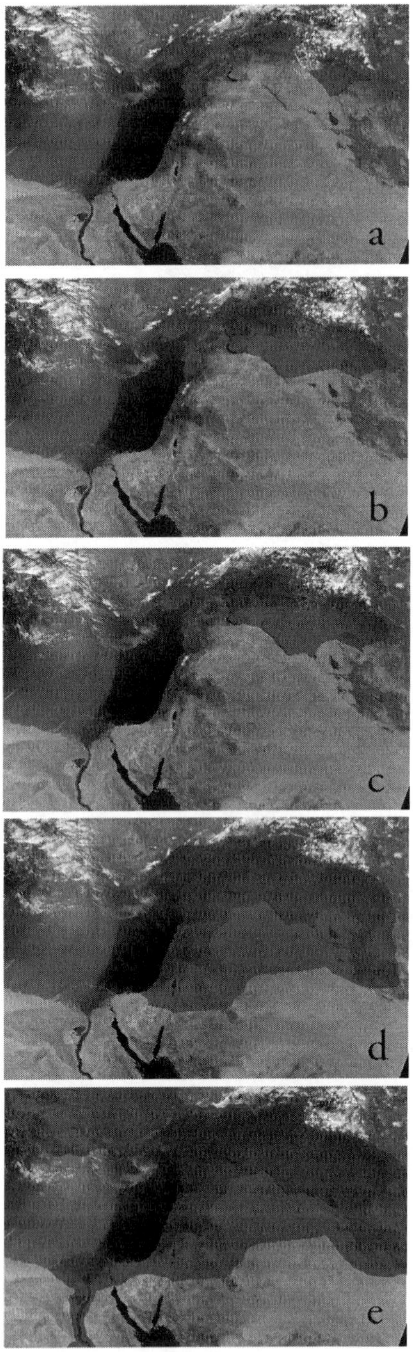

MAP 2.3 *Neo-Assyrian imperial expansion. (a) 10th century* BCE*; (b) 9th century* BCE*; (c) 8th century* BCE*; (d) Tiglath-Pileser* III *& Shalmaneser* V*; (e) 7th century* BCE *black = Assyrian provinces; grey = vassal states & buffer zones. (Modified from Google Earth Landsat Image.)*

commonly referred to as the heartland (Postgate 1992; Postgate 1995; Hawkins 1995; Radner 2006) (figure 2.3b). During the 8th century, there was moderate expansion under Adad-nirari III, followed by a period of stagnation until 744 BCE (Kuhrt 1995; Radner 2006) (figure 2.3c). Foreign policy at the end of the 8th century, under Tiglath-Pileser III and Shalmaneser V, was aggressive and in their combined 22 regnal years the Neo-Assyrian empire doubled its territorial holdings and sphere of influence (Otzen 1979; Na'aman 1995; Hawkins 1995; Kuhrt 1995; Radner 2006; Radner 2011) (figure 2.3d). Territorial expansion slowed in the 7th century under Sargon II, Sennacherib, Esarhaddon, and Assurbanipal, with only 5 new provinces added to *māt Aššur* (Kuhrt 1995; Radner 2006; Radner 2011) (figure 2.3e). However, Assyrian vassal states and buffer zones increased in size and number during this period; reflecting the change in foreign policy (Lanfranchi 2000; Parpola 2003; Radner 2006; Radner 2010; Radner 2011) (figure 2.3e).

Organisation & Administration

The administration of the Neo-Assyrian empire is the subject of several important works, such as Matilla 2000, Postgate 2007 and Ponchia 2012. Despite its extensive study, the nature of the power structure and relationships within the imperial system remain ambiguous. Postgate (2007, 358) believes that, unlike the bureaucratic Middle Assyrian administration, Neo-Assyrian administration was relational and contextual, dependent upon "institutional loyalty and personal interaction". This non-bureaucratic approach to government means that the administrative hierarchy is all but invisible archaeologically and textually, no matter how well developed and effective; and there can be no doubt that the Neo-Assyrian administrative system was well developed and highly functional given its ability to establish and maintain control over such a large and diverse empire.

Assyria was organised into administrative provinces; as Postgate (1992) famously remarked "If you are in Assyria, you are in a province; outside Assyria, not". At the height of its power, the Neo-Assyrian empire was composed of approximately 60 provinces occupying more than 540,543 square miles or 140,000,000 hectares. Administration of each province was the responsibility of a provincial governor (*bēl pāḫiti*) appointed by the king. Newly crowned kings often replaced provincial governors with loyal members of their own entourage to ensure loyalty and prevent mutiny or insurrection (Grayson 1999). Tiglath-pileser III even divided up large, powerful provinces into smaller ones upon ascending the throne in order to neutralise potential insurrection (Radner 2010a; Postgate 1979). The crown prince (*mār šarri*) and highest state officials were often awarded the provincial governorship of strategic or sensitive provinces (*e.g.* next to buffer zones or the imperial capital) requiring fierce loyalty and military responsibility (Mattila 2000).

Provincial governors reported directly to the king, probably in person, and were endowed with the authority to act autonomously (Postgate 2007). Once a year, provincial governors were obligated to have a formal audience with the king (*e.g.* SAA XVII 52, 130; SAA XVIII 68) at which time they renewed their loyalty oaths (*adê*) as part of a royal banquet (*e.g.* SAA II 3, 4, 6, 8; see also discussion in Parpola 1987a). The responsibilities of the provincial governors were diverse and included civic, state and military obligations. We can deduce from the existing letters between provincial governors and the king that their duties included: calculating, collecting, and paying taxes to the king (*e.g.* SAA I 220; SAA II 206; SAA XVI 96); calculating and regulating *ilku* service (*e.g.* SAA I 99); regulating trade and monitoring prices (*e.g.* SAA I 179; SAA V 143; CEDAR); monitoring agricultural productivity and conditions (*e.g.* SAA I 36, 83, 92, 176; SAA V 21, 26, 97, 127); reporting on foreign affairs and providing military intelligence (*e.g.* SAA I 1, 29; SAA V 2; SAA XV 113); providing labour and materials for, and overseeing public works (*e.g.* SAA I 26, 99, 124; SAA XI 15, 19, 21); providing fodder and food for the standing army (*e.g.* SAA V 126, 250); hosting foreign dignitaries (*e.g.* SAA V 52, 194); maintaining *ḫūl šarri* (royal roads) and *bīt mardītus* (road stations) (SAA I 177; SAA X 361; see also discussion in Kessler 1997); keeping the peace (*e.g.* SAA I 173, 174; SAA V 149); and acting as a representative of the king (Radner 2008).

Although the governance and administration of each province was ultimately the responsibility of its provincial governor, he was aided by several tiers of support staff (figure 2.1), including a deputy governor (*šaniu*), major-domo (*rab bēti*), city overseer (*ša muḫḫi āli*) and village inspector (*rab ālāni*) (Postgate 2007). The major-domo was responsible for the administration of the three branches of the provinical army, the king's men (*ṣab šarri*), the reserves (*ša kutalli*) and the corvee (*dullu ša šarri*), and its civilian support staff (*ibid.*). The responsibilities of the city overseer and village inspector are less clear, although presumably they involved the administration of the cities and villages within the province.

Every city was organised into neighbourhoods governed by 'councils of men' (van der Mieroop 1999; Evans 1950; Jacobsen 1943). Each city and village also had a mayor (*ḫazannu*), appointed by the king, who oversaw the government and administration of these neighbourhood councils and the city/village at large and reported to the province's city overseer or village inspector

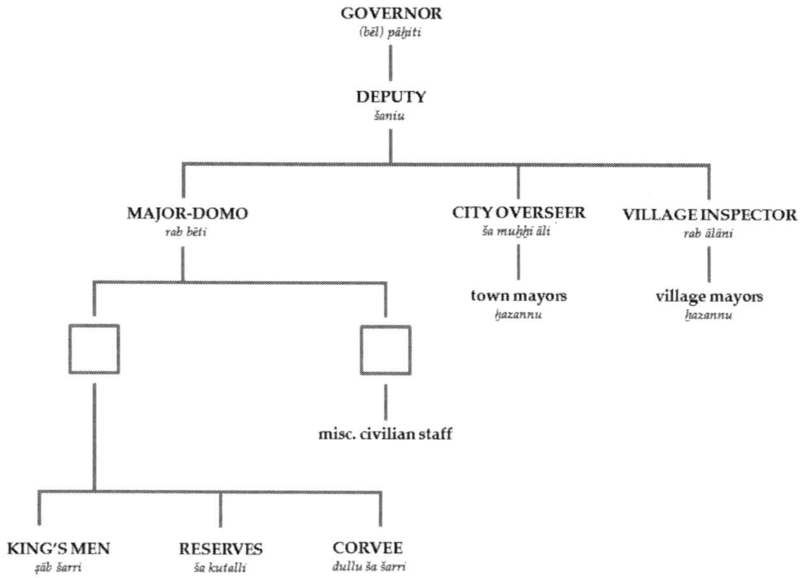

FIGURE 2.1 *Neo-Assyrian provincial government. Box indicates internal structure or hierarchy. (After Postgate 2007.)*

(Postgate 2007). Beyond this, the details of urban and provincial government and administration are vague. In part, this is because the Neo-Assyrian ethos of administration was non-bureaucratic and, in part, because every citizen had the right to appeal directly to the king in matters of civic, state or military governance, obscuring further an already "invisible" administrative hierarchy (*ibid.*).

At the State level, provincial government was one of five departments which reported directly to the king (figure 2.2) (Postgate 2007). Military government and administration was the responsibility of the *kiṣir šarrūti* or "royal cohort" and was divided between two departments the *rab ša rēši* and the *qurrubtu*. The *rab ša rēši* or "chief eunuch" oversaw the *ša ēkalli* or "palace guard" (Bonatz *et al.* 2008) and, according to Postgate (2007), his administrative responsibilities and troops were located in the imperial review palaces. *Qurrubtu* has been translated as "body guard" but Postgate argues is better understood as "aide-de-camp" since the texts make clear that the *qurrubtu* was a trusted confidant and advisor (2007: 341). The responsibilities of the *qurrubtu* and his troops were located in the royal palaces and included a branch of "personal" or "body" guards, the *ša šēpē* (Postgate 2007) (for a detailed description of the duties of the *qurrubtu* see Klauber 1910).

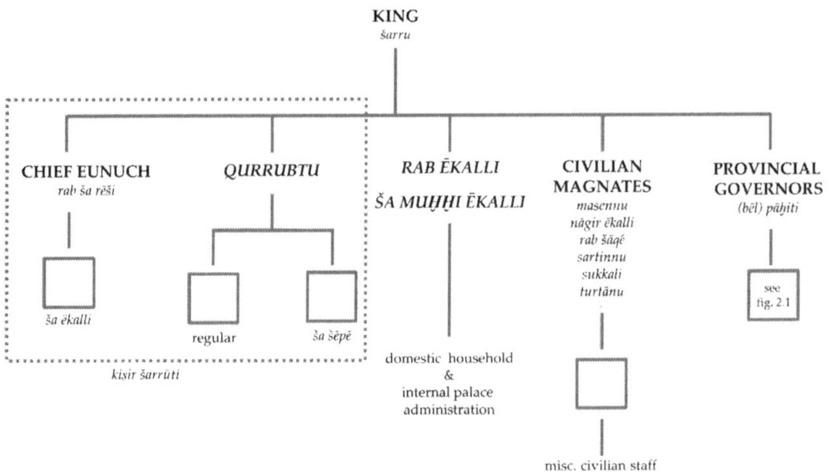

FIGURE 2.2 *Neo-Assyrian imperial government. Box indicates internal structure or hierarchy. (After Postgate 2007.)*

Administration of the royal palaces themselves and/or the royal household was overseen by a department headed by the *rāb ēkalli* or "palace manager" and the *ša muḫḫi ēkalli* or "officer in charge of the palace" (Postgate 2007), often translated "major-domo" (*c.f.* Matilla 2000). Between them, these two officials oversaw the domestic household and internal palace administration (Postgate 2007). The remaining civilian administrative functions were overseen by a department composed of a collection of officials, referred to as the civilian magnates by Postgate (2007) and the king's magnates by Matilla (2000). Officials within this department included, but were not necessarily limited to, the *masennu* or "chief treasurer", the *nāgir ēkalli* or "palace herald", the *rab šaqê* or "chief cup bearer", the *sartinnu* or "chief justice", the *sukkali* or "chief vizier" and the *turtānu* (Matilla 2000). Although Matilla (2000) and others have attempted to sketch the administrative responsibilities of these positions (*e.g.* Deller 1971; Grayson 1993), much about their respective administrative functions remains unclear and unknowable.

Each of the four State departments located in the imperial capital city would have had its own internal structure or "invisible hierarchy" and a building or apartment from which to conduct their affairs (Postgate 2007). However, in the provinces all of these functions—residence, ceremony, administration, storage, etc.—would have been contained in a single structure, the provincial governor's palace (*ibid.*).

Another administrative system operating in Neo-Assyrian cities and provinces was the guild system (*kārum*) for craftsmen, such as carpenters, metalworkers and potters, and professionals, such as bakers, eunuchs and merchants (Deller 1999; van der Mieroop 1999; see also Kraus 1982 and Weisberg 1967) (*c.f.* Ponchia 2012 for use of *qinnu* as 'guild'). Like other Neo-Assyrian administrative bodies, the structure and function of the guild system is largely "invisible" (Postgate 2007). From extant texts we can surmise that craftsmen practiced their art in identified and communal locations and/or workshops (see for example È.LÚ.UŠ.BAR.MEŠ "weaving establishment" in BCM 1 and *bīt* [LÚ]*ašlāki* "house of the bleacher" in Maqlû 2) and were organised into associations or guilds by craft (Oppenheim 1964). Each guild appears to have had an internal structure with one or more officials whose duties included distributing funds and keeping accounts (*c.f.* Cambyses 129) and negotiating and intervening with the civic and state administration on behalf of guild members (Ponchia 2012; Weisberg 1967). For example, a guild administrator writes to the king complaining that four cooks had been drafted illegally into *ilku* service; the provincial governor explains to the king, in response to his enquiry into the matter, that only one of the men was drafted illegally and that he has since been returned to service and a replacement found (Weisberg 1967).

The independence of these guilds from state, provincial and civic administration is widely debated and in Oppenheim's words "independence—in the sense of the independence of medieval guilds—is unlikely for economic reasons, such as the difficulty of procurement of raw materials and the absence of a free market economy" (1964:80). There is evidence, however, that guilds were not an extension of the state but functioned as independent negotiating bodies. For example, groups of craftsmen were issued charters or contracts, on the king's authority, with the administration of palaces and temples (*e.g.* YBC 3499) (Weisberg 1967). It is not clear whether these groups of craftsmen represented different guilds of carpenters, for example, chapters within the city/province/state guild of carpenters, or were simply the men from the guild of carpenters chosen for that particular job. Whichever the case, these contracts follow the standard formula for dialogue documents and, as such, were between independent parties acting of their own free will (*ibid.*). In fact, the existence of contracts between guilds of craftsmen and the state/civic administration suggests implicitly that these men were independent of state or civic government control.

Raw material procurement was the responsibility of the organisation or individual hiring the guild/craftsmen, although there does appear to be some level of state control/regulation of raw material resources (*e.g.* SAA 1 18, 27 and 19 153). In text YBC 3457, the contract between the administrators of the Temple of Eanna and a baker guild states "in case you do not make (the flour) fine, the seven and one-half minas (worth) of barley..... (which are) at your disposal give back" (Weisberg 1967, 76).

Craftsmen were issued with "work permits" or "union cards" (šaṭarānu ša dullu) which enabled them to collect raw materials and/or wages and allowed them access to the worksite (Weisberg 1967). In text YBC 4115, for example, Bēlšunu, son of Rimmanu (?) is ordered to bring his work document to the temple administrators:

> ša-ṭa-r[a]-ni-šú šá dul-lu li-na$_7$-šam-ma a-na
> ^{Id}AG.LUGAL.URÙ LÚ.SAG.LUGAL
> u LÚ.EN.MEŠ pi-qi-ni-ti ina È.AN.NA
> ú-kal-lam ^{I}ÌR.^{d}AG A-šú šá ^{Id}30 [KÁM]

Taken together, and in the absence of a market economy, the charters and work permits suggest that Neo-Assyrian craftsmen, while themselves independent freemen, were contracted to practice their craft at or supply their craft to a specific place for a specific period of time, such as baking bread for a temple. Neo-Assyrian potters, as craftsmen organised into guilds, would likewise have been hired by state, civic and religious institutions to supply the vessels required for that specific organisation, office, or temple.

Symbols of Power

Authority and power were made tangible in the Neo-Assyrian empire through the use of seals (*unqu*). These imperial seals were stamp seals, rather than the cylinder seals typically used for personal identification, probably because stamp seals were more practical for sealing a variety of objects, such as jars, boxes, cuneiform tablets, etc. (Radner 2008; Herbordt 1992; Postgate 1973). Another reason for the use of stamp seals for state administrative seals was to differentiate between their private and official function and, by extension, private and official actions of the seal bearer. Watanabe (1999) has argued, on the basis of SAA 15 224, that the royal seal used by the king was a signet ring. All of the official seals recovered archaeologically, however, have been stamp seals (*e.g.* Klengel-Brandt 1994) which, together with SAA 15 224 and 5 234, has been used to suggest that the administrative seal of the king, his seal of office, was made of gold or other precious metal which was subsequently reused (Radner 2008; Herbordt 1992; Collon 1987; 1996), possibly to make the succeeding king's seal.

In addition to the royal seal of the 'office' of the king, crown prince and queen (Nadali 2009–2010), several tiers of administrative seal are also in evidence including seals of office for high ranking officials and the use of more generalised administrative seals. Of the latter, the seal, sealing and/or seal impression most frequently recovered archaeologically is that depicting the king slaying a lion, which functioned as a state seal of the imperial administration and was used by high officials directly under the king, such as the civilian magnates (*i.e.* Radner 2008; Winter 2000; Herbordt 1992). The use of this state or imperial seal identified these officials to others as working in or for the Neo-Assyrian central administration but also functioned recursively to remind these officials that they were part of the larger apparatus of state government (Nadali 2009–2010).

Provincial governors, as part of the central administration of the Neo-Assyrian empire, were issued state seals (Radner 2008; Ponchia 2007) in addition to seals of office (Radner 2008; Postgate 1973). Although no provincial governor's seals have been recovered archaeologically, extant seal impressions of the seal of the governor of Nimrud suggest that these stamps bore the inscription "governor of X" (*e.g.* CTN 2 132, 133, 170, 171, 172, 173; Watanabe 1993; Herbordt 1992; 1994).

In his discussion of the iconography of the Neo-Assyrian state seal, Nadali describes the production of Assyrian images as being intentionally synthesised as iconic signs and symbols and linked to analytic narrative (2009–2010).

> The seal ... image can be considered as the result of a symbolic principal, where the king-and-lion combat implies the strong link of both the seal itself as object and the officials as people who used the state seal, with the kingship in general, and with the palace administration, specifically. (Nadali 2009–2010, 222)

We will discuss a similar function of Palace Ware as a symbol of imperial power in chapter 6.

The most dramatic symbol of power in the Neo-Assyrian empire was the 'conspicuous consumption' of resources by the king and imperial administration. Thorstein Veblen coined the term 'conspicuous consumption' in 1899 to describe the practice of acquiring goods and/or services for the specific purpose of publicly manifesting social power and prestige, real or imagined, rather than for the intrinsic value of those goods and services. According to this definition, Assyrian imperial ideology actually required the conspicuous consumption of resources as a tangible expression of the wealth and power of Aššur and, by extension, the power and prestige of the king. The practice of imperial collecting and display in public gardens and menagerie is an excellent example of ideologically sanctioned and/or compulsory conspicuous consumption.

The Neo-Assyrian practice of conspicuous consumption extended beyond the annexation of territory and imperial collecting. Royal and imperial building projects, which included temples, palaces and twice the entire imperial capital and administrative complex, were one of the most excessive displays of Neo-Assyrian wealth and power; conspicuously consuming both human and raw material resources simply because it could (Liverani 2003). Other practices of conspicuous consumption included feasting, banqueting and the exchange of gifts (Parker 2011) and personal adornment and furnishings (Thomason 2010). These latter practices, while participated in by individuals within the imperial administration and in the absence of a true market economy served not only as symbols of power and wealth but also prestige and royal favour since access to commodities, such as fine cloth and exotic foodstuffs, was controlled and rationed by the imperial administration and at the discretion of the king.

Prestige & Favour

Archaeologically, favour and prestige are difficult to detect because they are relational constructs which may or may not have a material manifestation. Favour, for example, is a partiality for or approval of someone by another person, the actor. The Neo-Assyrian king, for example, might favour an individual and tangibly express that favour by appointing him to an office or awarding him land. Prestige, on the other hand, refers to a reputation or the esteem in which someone, something or a situation is held and is awarded by the audience to the object or actor. For example, white bread was once considered prestigious and a symbol of wealth because it was expensive and made from milled flour processed to remove the bran and germ from the wheat kernel. The people who ate white bread may or may not have been aware that it was prestigious, but for those who ate brown bread made from hand ground flour from the entire wheatberry, often containing chunks and bits, the prestige of white bread was apparent.

Favour and prestige were fluid in the Neo-Assyrian imperial world; ebbing and flowing with both the changing tides of royal regime and expansion of the imperial geography. One manifestation of royal favour was appointment to provincial governorship. Provinces in the Neo-Assyrian Central Polity were ancient in origin, wealthy, and wielded considerable political power and influence (Radner 2010). In fact, many of these provincial governorships were reserved for high ranking court officials and magnates, such as the 'province of the crown prince' on the western border of the Central Polity and the 'provinces of the *masennu, rab šāqê,* and *nāgir ēkalli*' located on the border between Assyria and Urartu to the north (map 2.2). The strategic location of these provinces required the absolute loyalty of its governor and appointment to one of these governorships was a mark of high royal favour and trust. As a result, governorship of these provinces was highly prestigious, despite the fact that they were relatively small and possessed few natural resources.

As the Neo-Assyrian empire expanded, governorship of Annexed provinces along the Mediterranean coast and inland trade routes acquired great prestige (Radner 2010). These provinces controlled access to both commodities and international trade and often possessed valuable raw material resources, such as tin, copper, lumber and precious stones. The wealth of these provinces and their critical role in maintaining imperial communication networks, trade routes and military access roads across the imperial landscape increased the prestige of their governor and the favour shown by the king in appointing them.

As mentioned above, eating and drinking were also associated with prestige and favour, particularly the quality, variety and amount of food and drink a person was served or had access to (Brunke 2011). Wine, particularly grape wine, was a prestige or luxury good used by the Neo-Assyrian imperial administration to show favour. During the 8th and 7th centuries BCE, grape wine may have become more accessible to the upper and middle classes, composed of imperial officials and merchants/mid-level military leaders respectively, but was by no means common (Fales 1994). However, in the absence of a market economy, grape wine was an expensive and rationed commodity under the control of the imperial administration (Kinner Wilson 1972). The Nimrud Wine Lists offer a glimpse of how this prestige good and symbol of favour and, possibly, power was distributed and controlled by the Neo-Assyrian imperial administration. It is possibly, even probable, that the prestige of grape wine was inversely proportional to a person's access to it: the crown prince, for example, may not have considered grape wine particularly special however to a servant or freeman who received no wine ration at all, its prestige would have been great.

CHAPTER 3

Palace Ware from the Central Provinces: Nimrud, Nineveh and Aššur

In order to assess changes in Palace Ware meaning and function across the Neo-Assyrian imperial landscape, we must first have a clear understanding of the characteristics which constitute Palace Ware and describe its social significance and semiotic value. This chapter presents the results of the scientific analysis of Palace Ware from Nimrud, Nineveh, and Aššur and provides: quantitative formal and fabric characteristics for Palace Ware classification; chaîne opératoire for its manufacture; chemical and mineralogical profile for Palace Ware fabrics; and consumption patterns.

The Palace Ware assemblage from the Central Polity comes from the Neo-Assyrian collections at the British Museum and Vorderasiatisches Museum. Forty three Palace Ware vessels from Nimrud, Nineveh and Aššur were available for non-destructive analysis and an additional 24 sherds from Nimrud and Nineveh were available for invasive scientific study. While many of the vessels in the Central Polity assemblage were relatively complete (≥ 60% complete), not all attribute measurements were possible for every vessel. This means that the number of cases for each attribute analysis may vary, sometimes significantly, from the total number of vessels in the study population.

Morphometric Analysis

Archaeological ceramics are generally classified in the field and placed into 'ware' groups according to their formal and macroscopic fabric characteristics. Field classification of Palace Ware is highly subjective owing to their ambiguous definitional criteria. An additional complication with the field classification of Palace Ware is that Palace Ware forms are not unique either to the Palace Ware corpus or the Late Assyrian period. Their shapes can be traced to at latest the early Middle Assyrian period (1400–1050 BCE) and often occur in Neo-Assyrian ceramic assemblages in coarse or common ware fabrics (Gatti 1986; Anastasio 2010). The exception is Palace Ware form A plates, which appear to be uniquely Neo-Assyrian (*cf.* Howes Smith 1986 and Gjerstad 1946 for discussion about the origin of this form).

 | DOI 10.1163/9789004304123_004

Ceramic 'wares' are defined by their form (shape and size) and fabric, independent of raw material provenance (Rice 1976). In this study, we use morphometric analysis to quantitatively determine the formal characteristics of Palace Ware which can be used for field classification and to build a typology of forms.

Initial Classification

Traditionally, initial shape classification is based on the ratio of vessel height to maximum diameter in order to establish orientation of the form (Rice 1982; Sinopoli 1991). A biplot of Palace Ware height against maximum diameter identified both orientations in the assemblage (figure 3.1): horizontally oriented forms (maximum diameter ≥ height) and vertically oriented forms (maximum diameter < height).

The second basic classification of vessel shape is the openness of a form or the relationship between the maximum diameter or width of the vessel and its mouth or opening (Rice 1982). Restricted or closed forms are vessels for which the mouth is < 50% of the maximum diameter and unrestricted or open forms are vessels for which the mouth is ≥ 50% of the maximum diameter (Hendrix *et al.* 1996). According to our initial classification, all vessels in the Palace Ware assemblage are unrestricted forms.

Multiple trends are apparent in the Palace Ware population, indicating that several shapes and/or sizes are incorporated into the general classifications unrestricted-vertical and unrestricted-horizontal. Comparison of neck length and capacity refines the Palace Ware corpus into three basic forms

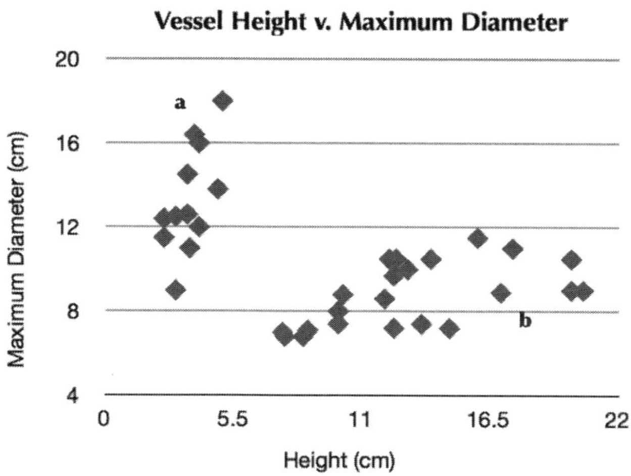

FIGURE 3.1 *Analysis of vessel orientation revealing both vertically oriented (a) and horizontally oriented (b) Palace Ware forms.*

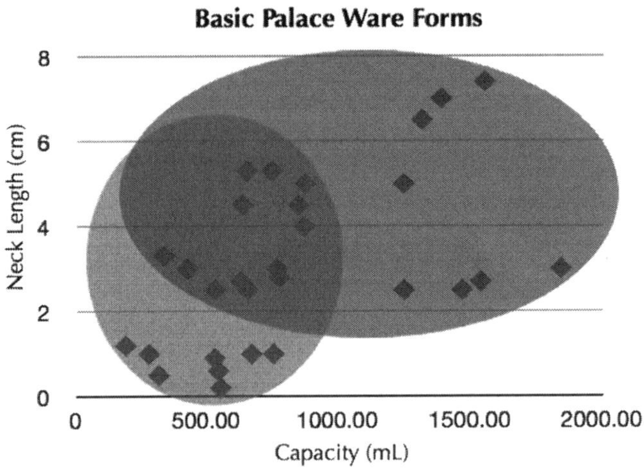

FIGURE 3.2 *Biplot of neck length vs. capacity revealing three Palace Ware formal clusters.*

(figure 3.2). The vessel capacity discontinuity at 1000 cm^3 describes two size clusters in the assemblage: vessels whose capacity is between 200–900 cm^3 and those whose capacity is between 1250–1850 cm^3. A second discontinuity in neck length divides the assemblage into two shape clusters: vessels with neck lengths ≤ 1.5 cm and vessels with neck lengths ≥ 2.5 cm.

The three basic Palace Ware forms can be described as: form A, unrestricted-horizontal vessels with capacity measurements ≤ 800 cm^3 and neck length ≤ 1.5 cm; form B, unrestricted-verical vessels with capacity measurements between 300–900 cm^3 and neck lengths between 2.5–5.5 cm; and form C, unrestricted-vertical vessels with capacity measurements ≥ 1250 cm^3 and neck lengths between 2.5–7.0 cm. Multi-responsive permutation procedure (MRPP) analysis indicates that these clusters reflect intentional formal differences in the assemblage and that each form originates from a distinct, statistically significant, population ($\delta_{obs} = 0.9$; $\delta_{exp} = 1.6$; p-value = $9.7^{*}10^{-11}$).

The "eggshell thin" walls of Palace Ware vessels are one of their most noteworthy and diagnostic characteristics (Oates 1959). A histogram of Palace Ware wall thickness reveals that, regardless of vessel shape and size, Palace Ware is 0.15–0.35 cm thick with a distinct mode at 0.20 (figure 3.3). Subtle shifts in the central tendency of wall thickness (mean, median, and mode) were observed among the three forms (figure 3.4). The central tendencies of each form were analysed using a MRPP simulated t-test to assess whether these shifts reflect statistically significant differences among the forms. Form B (mean = 0.24 cm, median = 0.23 cm, mode = 0.20 cm) and form C

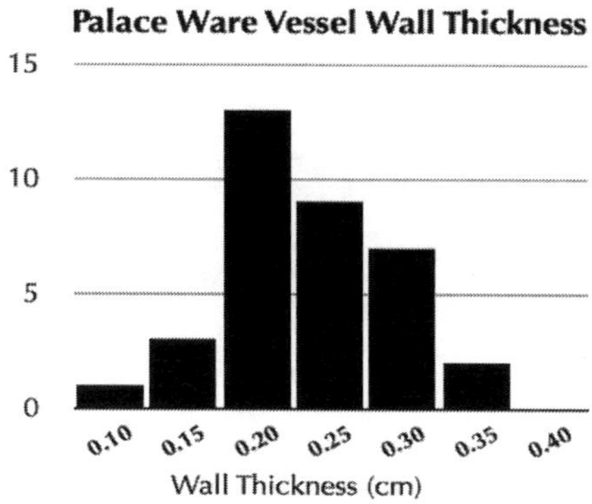

FIGURE 3.3 *Histogram of Palace Ware wall thickness revealing the extreme thinness of the vessel walls.*

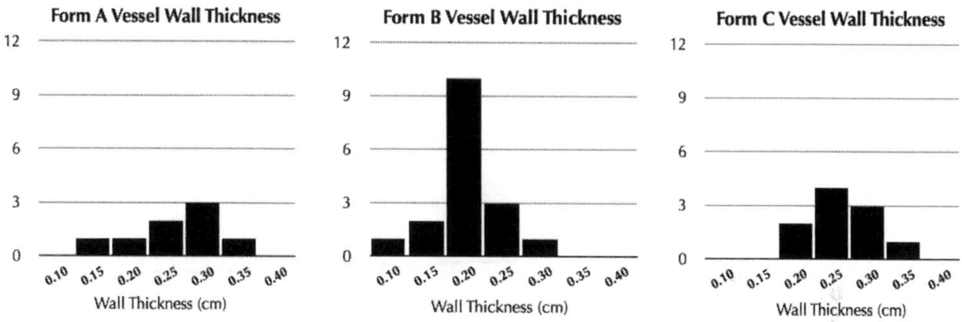

FIGURE 3.4 *Histograms of Palace Ware wall thickness by form.*

(mean = 0.28 cm, median = 0.28 cm, mode = 0.25 cm) are statistically similar (p-value = 0.47) and come from the same population of origin despite the observed difference in central tendency. The central tendency of form A (mean = 0.30 cm, median = 0.30 cm, mode = 0.30 cm) is slightly thicker than forms B and C, however forms A, B and C all come from the same population of origin (p-value = 0.26) and the observed difference in thickness is not statistically significant.

Characterisation of Forms

Form A

The 8 form A vessels are unrestricted-horizontal in shape, 2.5–4.0 cm in height, 9–14 cm at their widest, with necks 0.2–1.2 cm long, walls 0.30 cm thick, and hold between 200–800 cm^3. The depth of the vessel body is generally < 20%

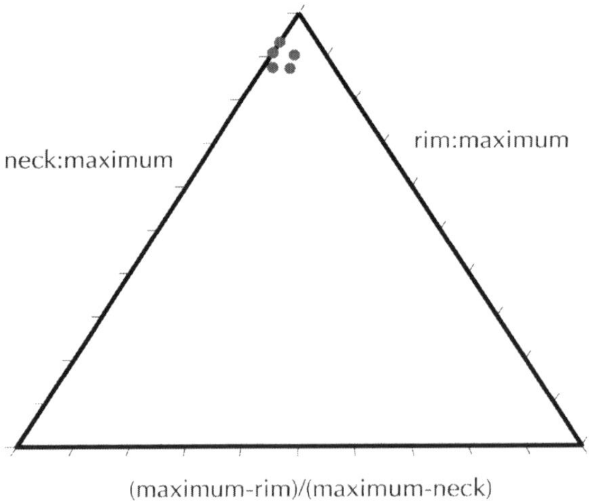

FIGURE 3.5 *Sneed & Folk ternary diagram of Palace Ware form A maximum, rim & neck diameters.*

however, two vessels were slightly deeper with depth measurements of 22 and 23%.

Maximum diameter, rim diameter, and neck diameter, plotted on a Sneed and Folk ternary diagram illustrate the regularity of the form (figure 3.5). Sixty percent (3/5) of form A vessels have a X:X:X-1 relationship among these variables while the other 40% exhibits a X:X-1:X-2 relationship, indicating two potential shape variants.

The ratio of vessel height to neck length is 4:1 for 60% of the form A population (3/5) and 3:1 for the other 40%. MRPP requires at least 6 cases for analysis and there were only 5 vessels in the form A assemblage for which all three of these measurements were available, therefore the statistical significance of this observation could not be verified. However, these two groups do not correlate with the two potential variants delineated by the relationship among maximum, rim, and neck diameters.

Given the small population of form A vessels in the assemblage from the Central Polity and our failure to find overlapping attribute patterns therein, we were unable to refine the form A population into sub-forms.

Form B

Form B is the largest population in the Palace Ware assemblage. These 24 vessels are unrestricted-vertical in shape, 7.6–14.8 cm in height, 4.0–9.7 cm at their maximum diameter, with necks 2.5–5.5 cm long, walls 0.15–0.30 cm thick, and

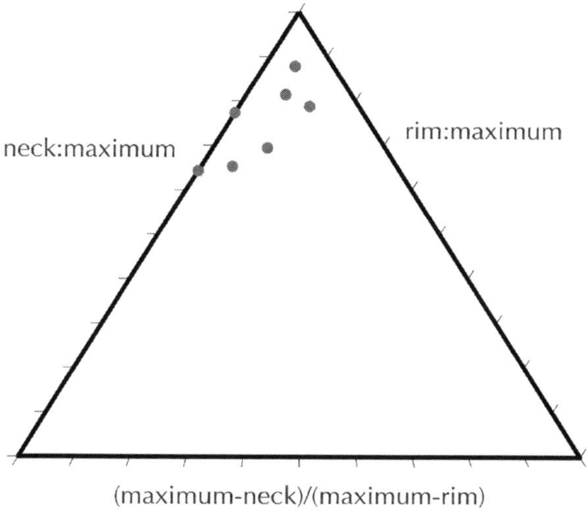

FIGURE 3.6 *Sneed & Folk ternary diagram of Palace Ware form B maximum, rim & neck diameters.*

hold between 300–900 cm^3. The depth of form B vessels clusters as follows: 60–70% deep for 43% of the population (9/21); 80–100% for 38% of the population; and >100% for 19% of the population. These clusters suggest 3 potential shape variants of form B.

Form B vessels are relatively homogeneous, illustrated by the relationship among maximum, rim, and neck diameter (figure 3.6). Three trends are observed among these variables: 40% of the vessels (4/10) exhibit a X:X:X-1 relationship among them; another 40% exhibit a X:X:X-2 relationship; and 20% exhibit a X:X-1:X-2 relationship among the three diameter measurements. This tripartite division supports the possibility of three potential formal variants in the population suggested by analysis of vessel depth. However, the difference among the diameter variables is ≤ 1 cm, which is very subtle and may result from the natural variability inherent in a single form manufactured by multiple potters.

Blackman *et al.* (1993) explore standardisation in ceramic manufacture by comparing the standard deviation in morphometric attributes for vessels from a single workshop with those from other workshops. They conclude that one can reasonably argue for standardised production if vessels from the two workshops vary by ≤ 2 σ of the variance of a single workshop (Blackman *et al.* 1993). The average standard deviation for the maximum, rim, and neck diameters of form B vessels from Nineveh, Nimrud and Aššur is 0.40, 1.1 and 1.6 cm

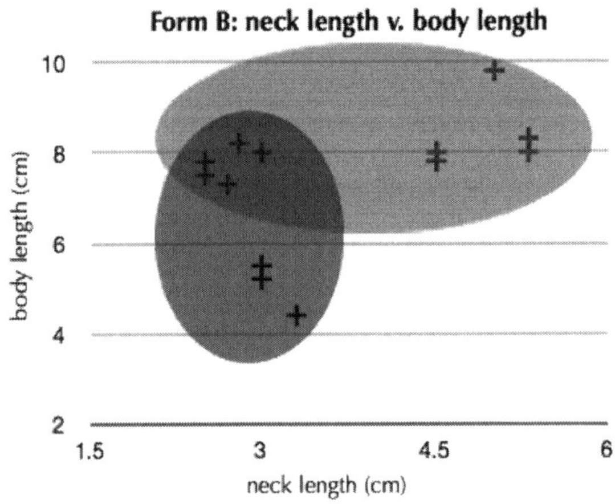

FIGURE 3.7 *Biplot of Palace Ware form B neck length against body length revealing three sub-form clusters.*

respectively and the mean standard deviation of the entire form B population for these variables is 1.3 or approximately 1 cm. Therefore, variation in vessels ≤ 2 cm is considered the result of multiple potters producing standard forms in different workshops. The 3 clusters observed in the maximum, rim and neck diameter data are explained, therefore, as the natural variation arising from the manufacture of a single, standardised form by multiple workshops.

The curvature of form B vessels is also highly uniform. The base angle is typically between 25–62° (mean = 43°, median = 41°, and mode = 49°), shoulder angle is 120–153° (mean = 137°, median = 138° and mode = 145°), and the neck angle is 69–90° (mean = 81°, median = 83° and mode = 84°). Indicating that Palace Ware form B jars were executed with a high degree of precision in multiple workshops by multiple potters throughout the Central Polity.

A biplot of vessel B neck length against body length reveals three clusters, despite the relative homogeneity of the variables themselves (neck length: mean = 4.1, median = 3.9, mode = 3.0; body length: mean = 7.8, median = 9.0, mode = 8.0) (figure 3.7). Two body length clusters, 4–6 cm and 7–10 cm, were statically verified as originating from different populations using MRPP (δ_{obs} = 1.1; δ_{exp} = 1.6; p-value = 0.0013). An MRPP simulated t-test of vessel capacity for these two body length clusters indicates that they come from statistically different populations of origin (p-value = 0.00005). Form B vessels with body lengths 4–6 cm have capacities between 334–425 cm^3 and vessels with body lengths 7–10 cm have capacities between 517–872 cm^3. This means that the observed difference in body length is related to vessel size and

describes two variants of form B: form B1, body length 4–6 cm, capacity 300–450 cm^3, and a neck length of 3 cm; and a larger variant whose body length is 7–10 cm and capacity 500–900 cm^3.

The larger form B vessels are discontinuous according to neck length: one group has necks 4.5–5.5 cm in length while the other has shorter necks 2.5–3.0 cm in length. MRPP analysis of these clusters confirms that they originate from different and statistically significant populations (δ_{obs} = 1.0; δ_{exp} = 1.6; p-value = 0.0017) and represent two additional variants of form B: form B2, neck length 2.5–3.0 cm, capacity 500–900 cm^3, and body length 7.3–8.0 cm; and form B3, neck length 4.5–5.3 cm, capacity 500–900 cm^3, and body length 7.8–9.8 cm.

Form C

The 11 form C vessels are unrestricted-vertical in shape, 10.0–20.5 cm high, with maximum diameters between 8.8–11.5 cm, necks 2.5–7.2 cm long, walls 0.20–0.30 cm thick, and capacities between 1200–3000 cm^3. Form C vessels are > 100% deep (105–202%), with one outlier at 82%.

A Sneed and Folk ternary diagram comparing maximum, rim, and neck diameter indicates the same homogeneity of shape as previously detected for forms A and B (figure 3.8), and divides into 4 relatively even groups according to the relationship among these measurements: 30% (3/10) exhibit a X:X-1:X-2 relationship; 30% a X:X-2:X-3 relationship; 20% exhibit a X:X-1:X-3 relationship;

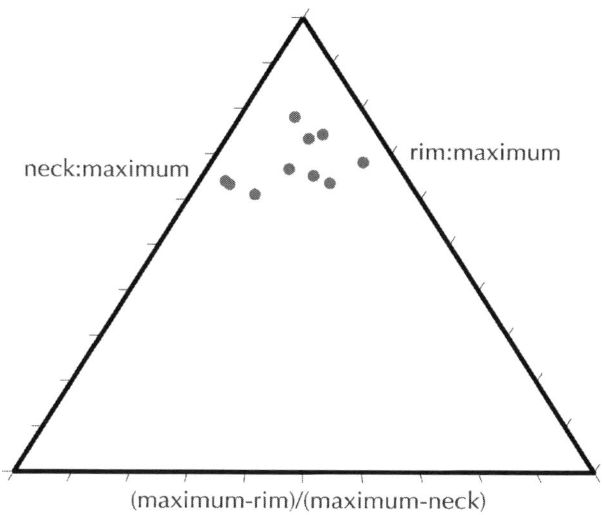

FIGURE 3.8 *Sneed & Folk ternary diagram of Palace Ware form C maximum, rim & neck diameters.*

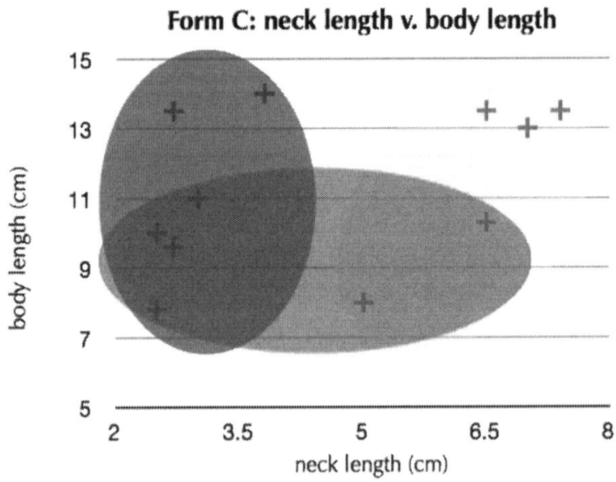

FIGURE 3.9 *Biplot of Palace Ware form C neck length against body length revealing four sub-form clusters.*

and 20% exhibit a X:X:X-3 relationship among the diameter variables. The average standard deviation for the maximum, rim, and neck diameters of form C vessels is 1.1 or approximately 1 cm. Therefore, the deviation among these variables in the form C population of ≤ 2 cm can be explained as the natural variation arising from the manufacture of a single, standardised form in multiple workshops.

The homogeneity of form C extends to the curvature of the vessel: base angle is typically 18–40° (mean = 30°, median = 28°, mode = 40°) with two outliers at 16° and 63°; shoulder angle is between 96–152° (mean = 132°, median = 136°, mode = 142°); and neck angles between 67–87° (mean = 80°, median = 82°, mode = 82°). A biplot of form C neck length against body length reveals 4 clusters: 2 body length clusters (8–11 cm and 13–14 cm); and 2 neck length clusters (2.5–3.8 cm and 5.0–7.4 cm) (figure 3.9).

MRPP simulated t-tests of vessel capacity and body length and body length and depth indicate that the two body length clusters come from statistically significant different populations of origin in terms of vessel size (p-value = 0.009) which are unrelated to vessel depth (p-value = 0.63). Therefore, the form C population contains 2 size variants: body length 8–11 cm, capacity 1250–1800 cm^3; and body length 13–14 cm, capacity 1500–3000 cm^3. Each of these size variants further divides into two shape variants: neck length 2.5–3.8 cm and 5–7.4 cm. An MRPP simulated t-test confirms that these two neck length clusters describe different and statistically significant form C shapes (p-value = 0.0013).

TABLE 3.1 *Summary of diagnostic morphometric attributes for Palace Ware form classification*

form	neck length	body length	capacity
form A	0.2–1.2 cm	2–3 cm	200–800 cm^3
form B			
form B1	3cm	4–6 cm	300–450 cm^3
form B2	2.5–3 cm	7–8 cm	500–900 cm^3
form B3	4.5–5.3 cm	7.8–9.8 cm	500–900 cm^3
form C			
form C1	2.5–3 cm	8–10 cm	1250–1840 cm^3
form C2	2.7–3 cm	13.5–14 cm	2800–3050 cm^3
form C3	5–6.5 cm	8–10 cm	1250–1300 cm^3
form C4	6.5–7.4 cm	13–13.5	1400–2300 cm^3

The 4 form C variants can be described as: C1, neck length 2.5–3.0 cm, body length 8–10 cm, capacity 1250–1840 cm^3; C2, neck length 2.7–3.0 cm, body length 13.5–14.0 cm, capacity 2800–3050 cm^3; C3, neck length 5.0–6.5 cm, body length 8–10 cm, capacity 1250–1300 cm^3; C4, neck length 6.5–7.4 cm, body length 13–13.5 cm, capacity 1400–2300 cm^3. MRPP analysis confirms that these clusters describe 4 sub-forms in the form C corpus originating from statistically significant different populations ($\delta_{obs} = 0.6$; $\delta_{exp} = 1.6$; p-value = 0.0002).

Diagnostic morphometric criteria for Palace Ware forms A, B, and C are summarised in table 3.1.

Typology

Shape names, such as 'goblet', 'bowl', and 'jug', are socio-culturally and regionally specific, subjective, and associated with culturally conditioned functions (*e.g.* Potts 1997). For example, the formal and fabric characteristics of two vessels may be identical, however, when one is labelled 'bowl' and the other 'pot' we unconsciously shift them into different functional spheres. In an effort to objectify the classification process, we adopt the form-based paradigm for ceramic typology advocated by Hendrix *et al.* (1996).

According to the form-based paradigm, all vessels can be described by three root forms: all unrestricted vessels are 'bowls'; restricted vessels with a pouring lip are 'jugs'; and all other vessels are 'jars' (Hendrix *et al.* 1996). One of the difficulties arising from applying the form-based paradigm to the Palace Ware assemblage is that the form-based paradigm does not differentiate bowls from jars based on the presence/absence of a neck element, and yet none of the bowl branch forms have necks. Palace Ware forms B and C are unrestricted vessels: even the neck diameter of these two forms, while often narrower than the rim diameter, is ≥ 50% of the maximum diameter. The neck elements of these forms are also quite substantial, accounting for 20–40% of the total vessel height. Therefore, we describe forms B and C as 'jars' rather than bowls, despite the unrestricted nature of these forms.

Vessels in the root form 'bowl' can be classified into branch forms first by size and then by shape. Bowl size is described in the form-based paradigm in terms of maximum diameter and depth (Hendrix *et al.* 1996). Form A vessels are < 20% deep and <10 cm maximum diameter which means that they are classified as very small, shallow bowls or branch form 'plates'.

Vessels in the root form 'jar' can be classified into branch forms first by size and then by the presence of other attributes, such as spouts or strainers. Jar size is described in the form-based paradigm in terms of total vessel height (Hendrix *et al.* 1996). Form B vessels are all < 15 cm high and form C vessels are between 10–20 cm high which means that they are classified as very short and very short-short jars respectively. Palace Ware vessels are devoid of functional features, such as handles, strainers, pouring lips, etc. The only branch form which describes very short to short jars without additional features is 'bottle'. Therefore, we refer to form B and C vessels as jars or bottles.

The following typology details the shape, style and decoration of Palace Ware forms A, B and C. However, it is important to remember that the chronological component of traditional ceramic typologies is not possible for Neo-Assyrian Palace Ware. Palace Ware is a relatively short lived phenomenon, approximately 150–200 years, and relative stratigraphic dating for these vessels is not sufficiently fine-grained to refine their date to less than half a century.

Form A

Form A bowls (figure 3.10) are unequal biconical with flat or disk bases. It is interesting to note that the flat bases are not particularly stable; vessels rock slightly when balanced on them. Form A rims are out-curving, horizontal and everted with a rounded lip. Three vessels, AX, AR and AW, have short incurving collars. There is no correlation between basal type and the presence/absence of a neck. Form A plates are typically undecorated but vessel AS had incised

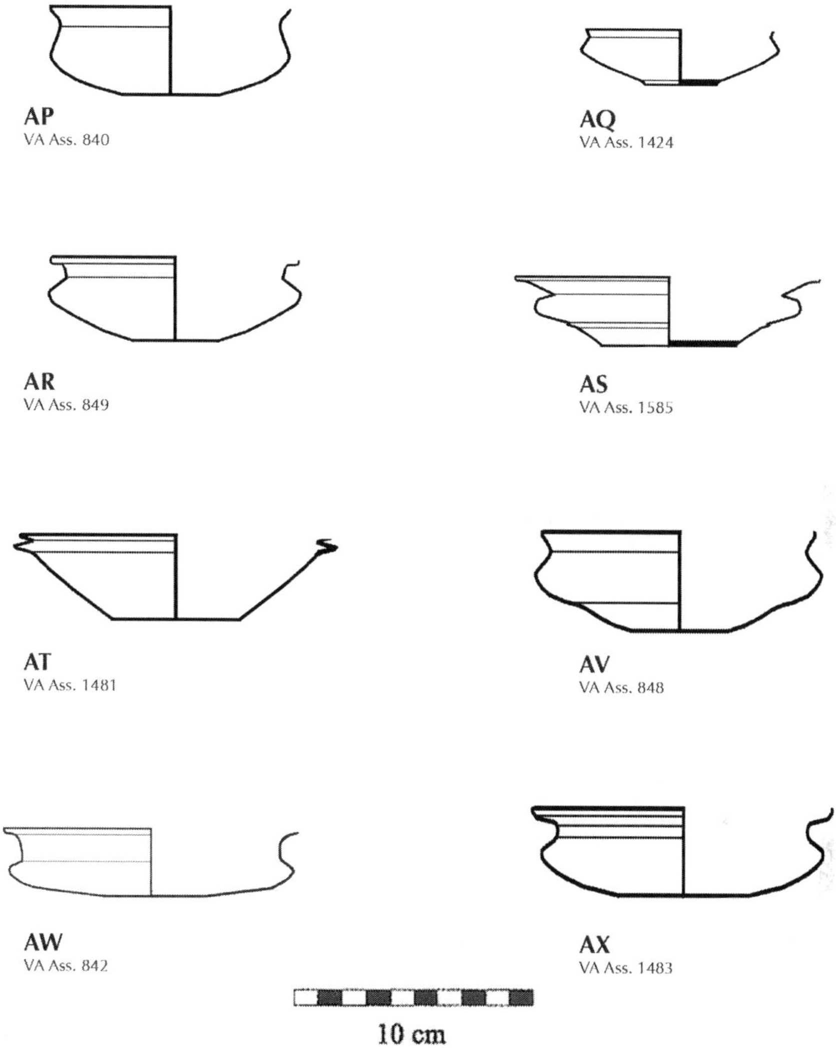

FIGURE 3.10 *Palace Ware form A bowls.*

ridges around its body similar to the pinched or stepped detail common to Assyrian bowls (figure 3.11).

Form B

Form B jars are generally unequal biconical with incurving necks, out-curving horizontal, everted rims, and thinned or rounded lips (figures 3.12–3.14). Basal elements range from flat to pointed to knob to ring, however it should be noted

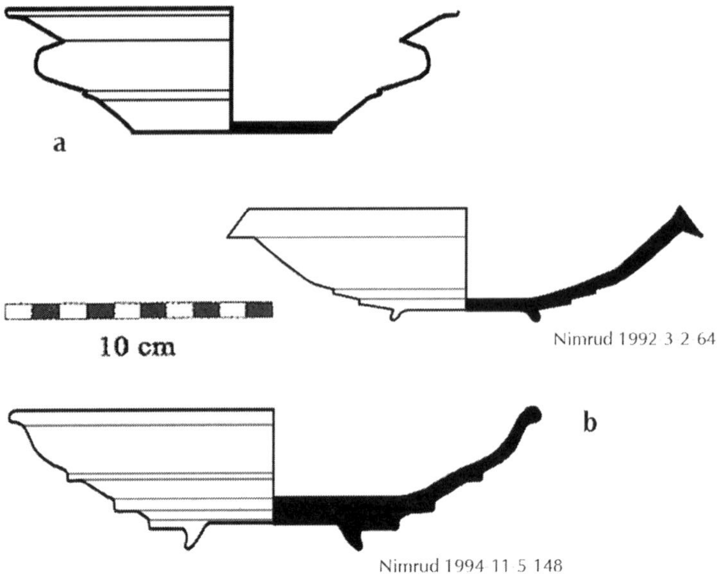

FIGURE 3.11 *Comparison of the pinched decoration on Palace Ware form A bowl* AS *(a) & the stepped decoration found of Assyrian tableware bowls.*

that, with the exception of form B1 jars, form B vessels are unable to stand on their bases. Form B jars can be undecorated but typically (83% or 10/12) are decorated with 2–3 rows of dimples, pressed depressions in the body wall. Twenty-five percent of the dimpled vessels also have incised linear decorations around the circumference of the body, often between the registers of dimples. There is no relationship between the basal element and type of body decoration.

Form B1 jars (figure 3.12) have disk bases, the only functional bases in the form B assemblage, and vessel NC has an additional 'step' between the base and vessel body creating a unique profile, similar to the stepped profile of Assyrian bowls (figure 3.15). All three form B1 jars have 2 rows of dimples between their base and shoulder, containing between 6–9 dimples each. Vessel ND has two registers of 3 incised lines running just below the shoulder and between the rows of dimples. Despite the more elaborate body decoration of vessel ND, it has a plain neck while vessels KJ and NC each have a moulded ring just below the vessel lip, which has been 'pinched' to a blunt point.

Form B2 jars (figure 3.13) have disk, pointed and flat bases, none of which are functional and able to support the vessel in an upright position. These jars are very similar in style to form B1; decorated with 2 rows of dimples

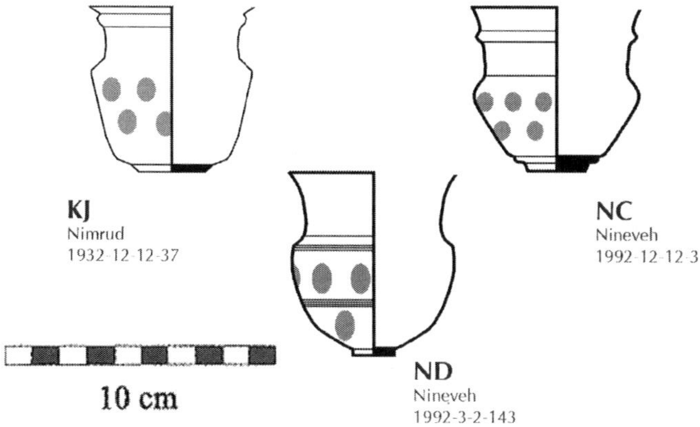

FIGURE 3.12 *Palace Ware form B1 cups.*

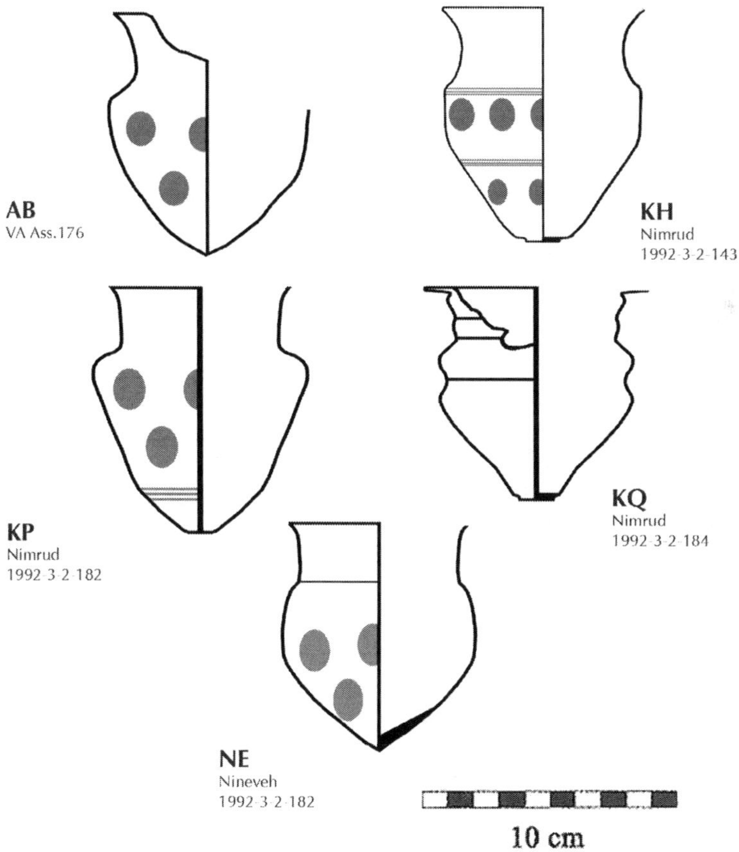

FIGURE 3.13 *Palace Ware form B2 cups.*

between the base and shoulder, each of which contains 3–9 dimples. One vessel, KH, has 2 registers of 3 incised lines running just below the shoulder and between the rows of dimples. However none of the B2 jars have moulded rings around their neck.

Vessel KQ is unique. Instead of 2 rows of dimples, the entire body is warped to produce 2 protuberances in the vessel wall and another 2 in the vessel neck (figure 3.13). The rim of KQ is t-shaped, rather than horizontal, everted—another stylistic feature unique to this vessel. Despite these stylistic differences, jar KQ is morphometrically a Palace Ware form B2 vessel.

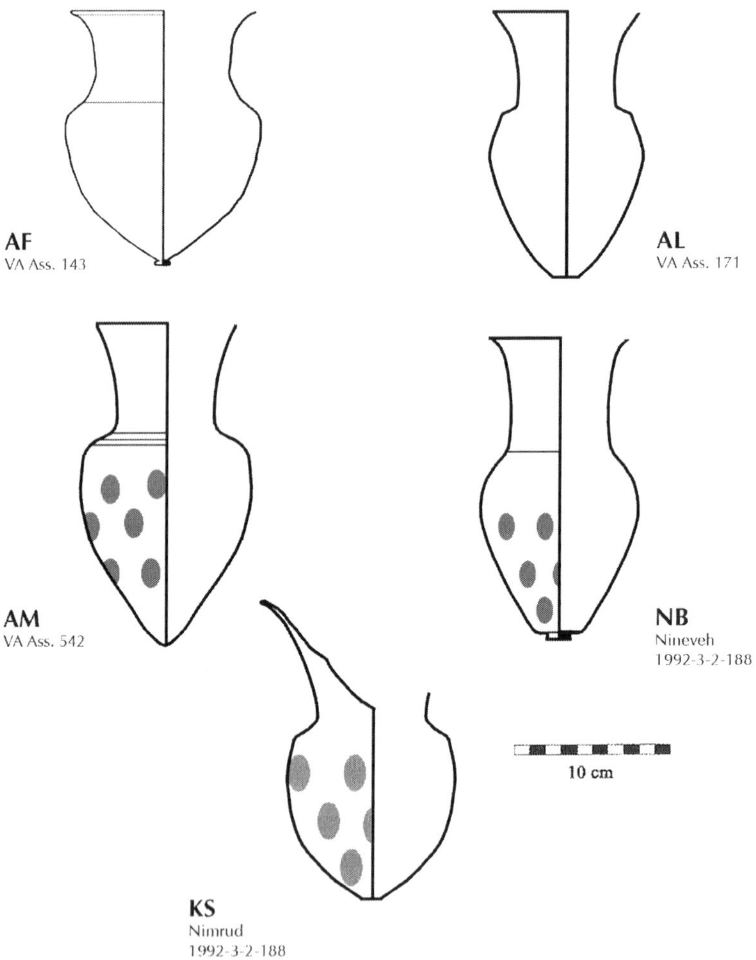

FIGURE 3.14 *Palace Ware form B3 cups.*

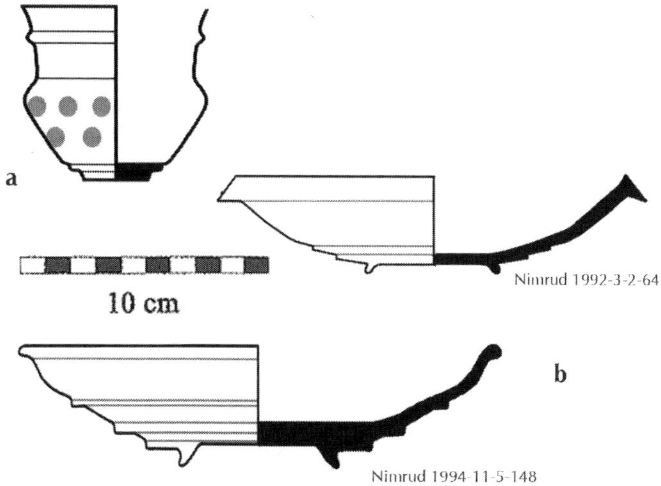

FIGURE 3.15 *Comparison of the pinched decoration on form B1 cup NC (a) and the stepped decoration found on Assyrian tableware bowls (b).*

Form B3 jars (figure 3.14) have pointed, flat, disk, and knob bases, none of which can support the vessel body in an upright position. Forty percent of the B3 population is undecorated while the other 60% is decorated with 3 registers of dimples, each containing 2–6 dimples. None of the B3 jars have incised linear decorations or moulded neck rings and there is no correlation between base type and body decoration.

Form C

Form C jars are, in general, unequal biconical with incurving neck, out-curving, horizontal everted rims with thinned or slightly thickened lips (figures 5.16–5.19). Basal elements range from flat to pointed to rounded to disk, but are primarily flat (55% or 6/11). Form C jars are very similar to form B vessels in shape, however they have significantly larger capacities. Form C jars are predominantly undecorated (55%) or have 2–3 rows of dimples each containing 4–7 dimples (45%). Two types of neck decoration are common: 1–2 moulded neck rings, pinched to a blunt point (36% or 4/11), or a thick band of incised rings around the vessel lip (18% or 2/11). There is no correlation between basal element and body decoration.

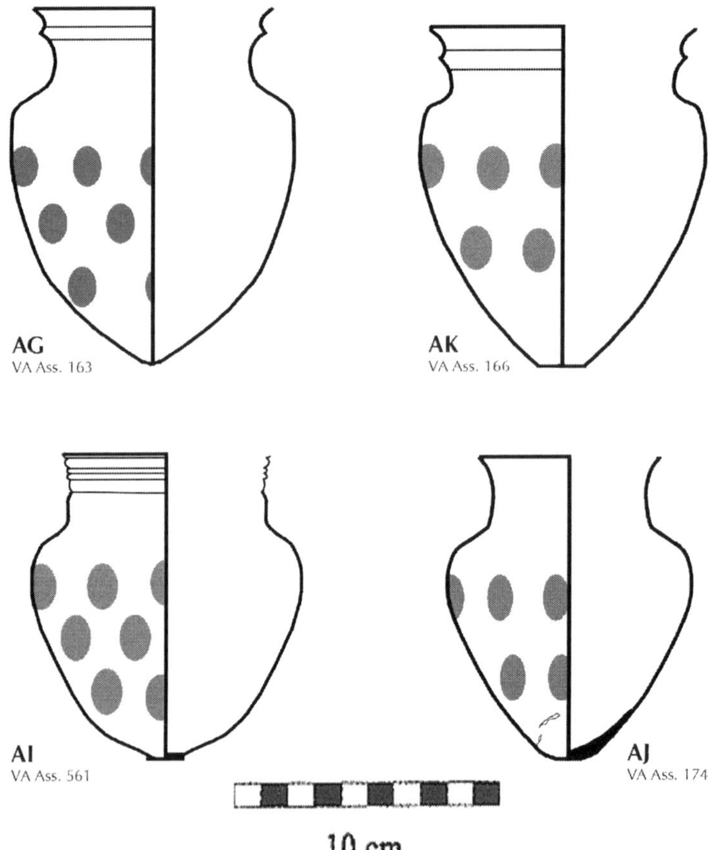

FIGURE 3.16 *Palace Ware form C1 jars.*

Form C1 jars (figure 3.16) have a variety of bases (pointed, disk, and flat) but are consistently decorated with registers of 5–8 dimples. Half of the vessels have 2 rows of dimples while the other half has 3. Form C1 jars are the most elaborately decorated vessels in the form C population; they are also the smallest. These jars may be decorated with pinched moulded rings below the lip (50%) in addition to the registers of dimples. Vessel AI is a bit of an exception with a 1.5 cm thick band of incised rings around the vessel lip.

Form C2 jars (figure 3.17) are the only Palace Ware vessels which are not unequal biconical. These two vessels are globular, ovoid-upright in shape, have rounded bases and undecorated bodies and necks. These vessels are unique in the Palace Ware assemblage in shape and style, but meet the morphometric criteria for Palace Ware and so are included in our study.

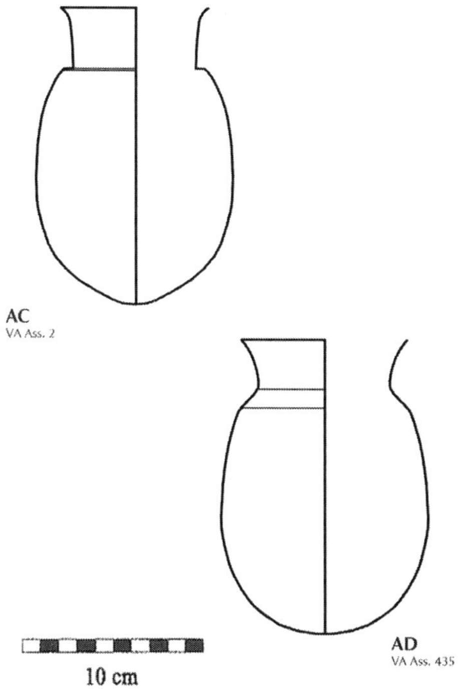

FIGURE 3.17 *Palace Ware form C2 jars.*

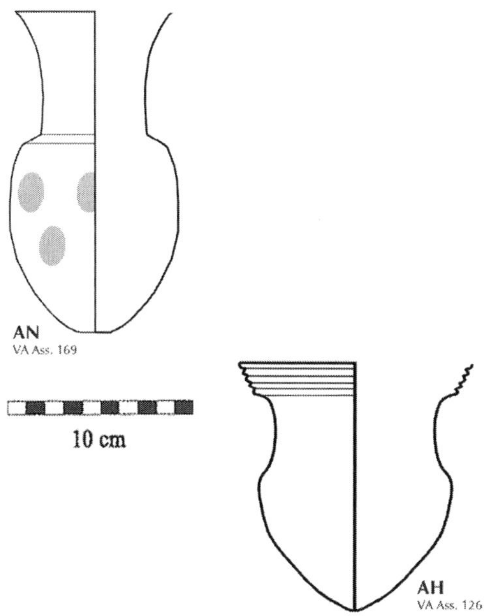

FIGURE 3.18 *Palace Ware form C3 jars.*

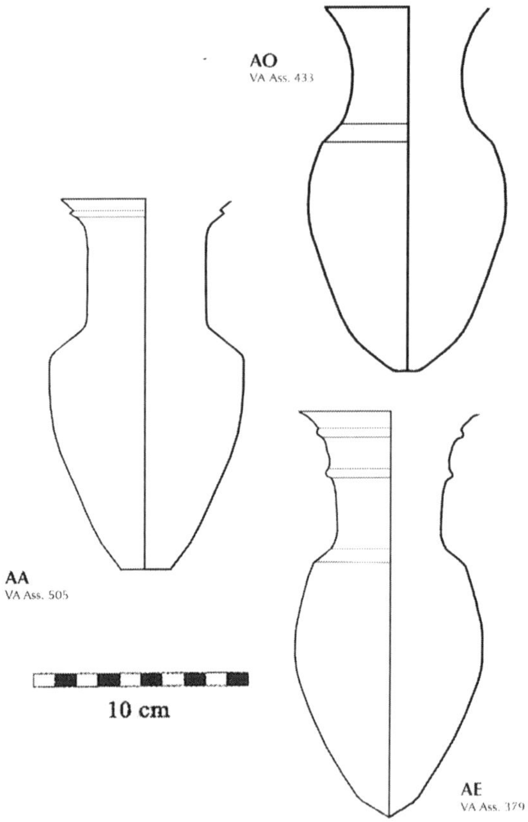

FIGURE 3.19 *Palace Ware form C4 jars.*

The two form C3 jars (figure 3.18) have flat or pointed, non-functional bases. One vessel (AH) has an undecorated body and a 1.5 cm thick band of incised lines around its lip, a traditional Mesopotamian motif, dating from at least the Ur III period (Delougaz 1952). Despite this divergence in decorative style from the rest of the Palace Ware population and since it meets the morphometric criteria for Palace Ware, jar AH is included in this study. The other vessel (AN) has a plain neck but 2 registers of dimples between its base and shoulder, each containing 4–5 dimples.

Form C4 jars (figure 3.19) have flat (2/3) and pointed (1/3) non-functional bases and undecorated bodies. However, pinched moulded neck rings are common (2/3), and vessel AE has 2 of these rings; one just below the lip and the other 3 cm below the lip.

Figure 3.20 provides a visual summary of Palace Ware typology.

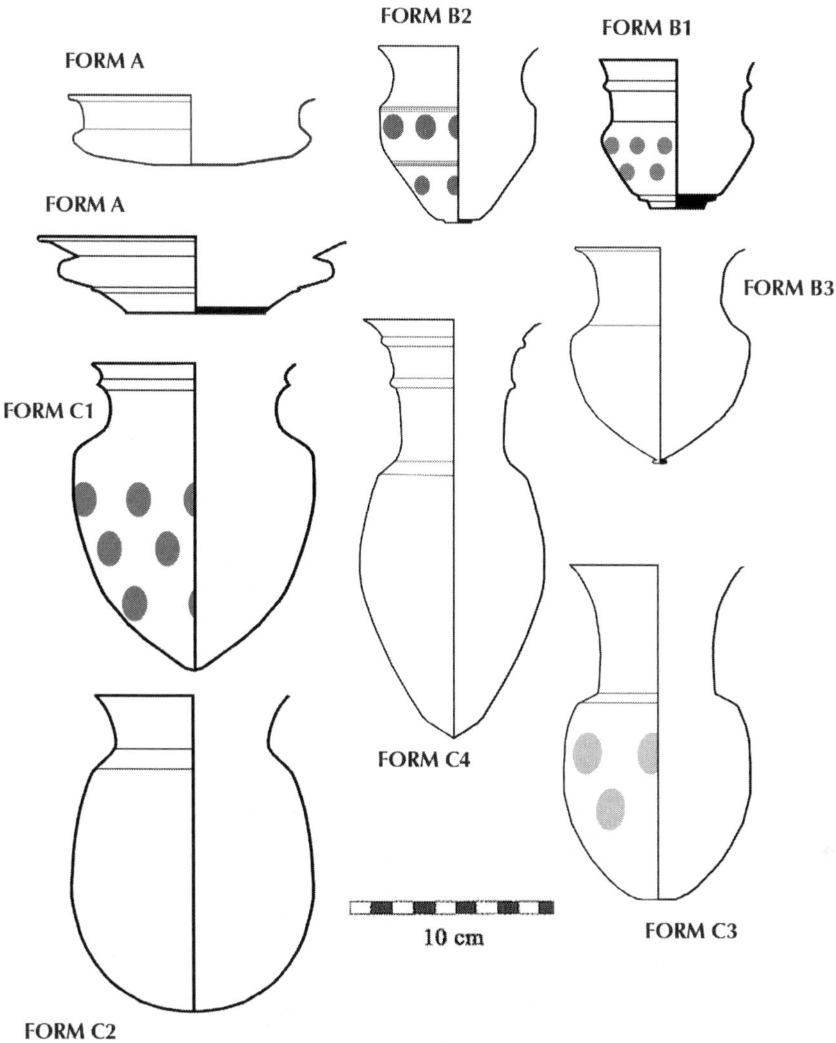

FIGURE 3.20 *Palace Ware typology—summary of forms.*

Chaîne Opératoire

Raw Materials Processing

Geological Raw Materials

Potential ceramic raw materials in the Neo-Assyrian core come from alluvial deposition in the Foothill Zone of the Unstable Shelf in northern Iraq. The location and method of harvesting this raw material (sediment) is uncertain:

extensive irrigation and water management in and around Neo-Assyrian urban centres would impact the rate and type of deposition near major settlements, such as Nimrud, Nineveh, and Aššur. Ethnographic analogy suggests that potters in the Mosul region are willing to travel to collect suitable raw material rather than use the inferior material available locally: "Clay had been brought

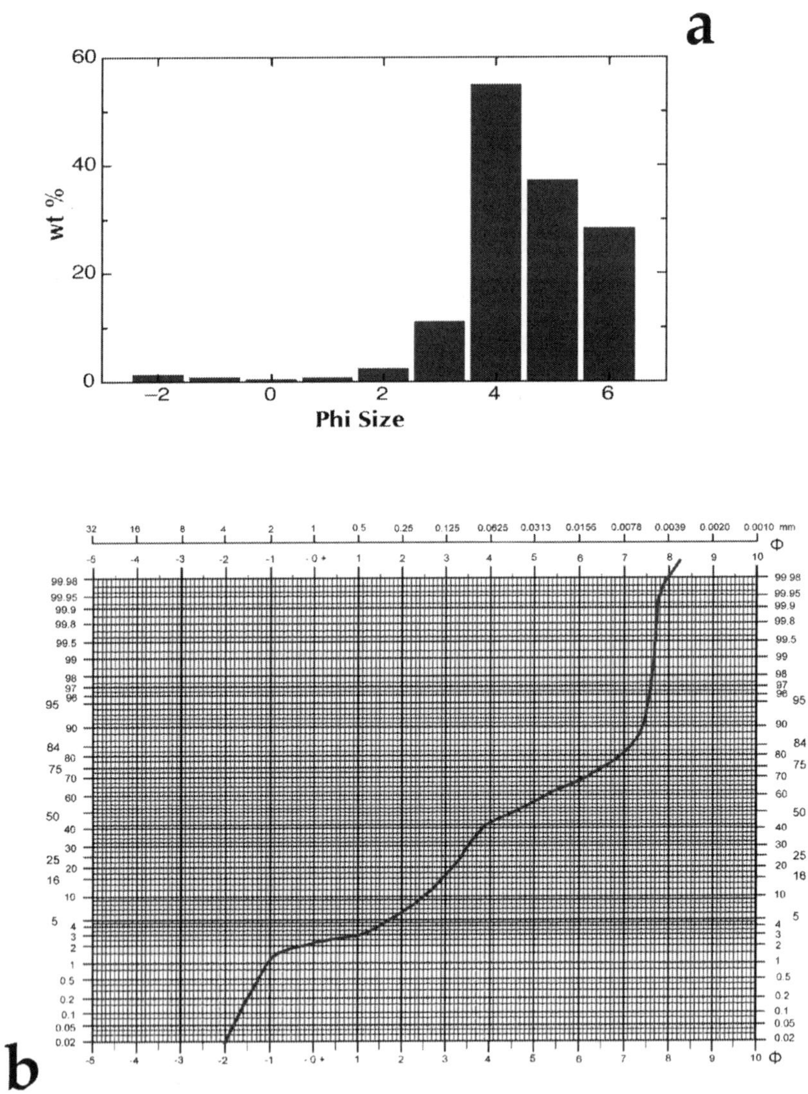

FIGURE 3.21 *Particle size analysis of sediments from the Tigris River (a) histogram (b) cumulative coarser curve.*

TABLE 3.2 *Bulk chemical composition of Palace Ware fabrics by SEM-EDS*

chemical compound	weight %
Na_2O	0.93
MgO	4.56
$A1_2O_3$	13.52
Sio_2	47.12
K_2O	1.83
CaO	20.35
Tio_2	0.76
FeO	10.98
total	100

from a place an hour and a half distant by boat" (Campbell Thompson 1923, 239). In order to fully understand where and how Assyrian potters selected their raw materials, an extensive survey and analysis of potential raw materials resources is required.

In this study, we were only able to obtain geological sediment from one location—the east bank of the Tigris at Nimrud. I am indebted to Muzahim Mahmoud Hussein of the Iraqi Department of Antiquities for collecting this sample and transporting it to London for analysis. It should be noted that conclusions drawn from the analysis of this single sediment sample are suggestive rather than determinative, and a more detailed study of raw material resources is required to confirm these observations.

The Tigris sediment is well-sorted, dark (7.5YR 5/1—grey) and smells 'rich' and 'organic', although very little (< 1%) vegetal matter was contained in it. Particle size analysis indicates that the sediment is fine-grained and composed almost entirely of very fine sand and silt (Φ size 3.8–7.3) (figure 3.21). Interestingly, the sediment contains hardly any clay (0.38 wt.% or 99.6% cumulative coarser). Bulk chemical analyses of Palace Ware from the Central Polity (table 3.2) indicated that clay minerals are present ($Al_2O_3 \sim 13$ wt.%), so it is probable that this analysis is skewed due to flocculation of the clays.

Particle morphology is consistent with alluvial deposition: grains are subrounded to well-rounded and spherical to discoidal, and loess, wind-blown

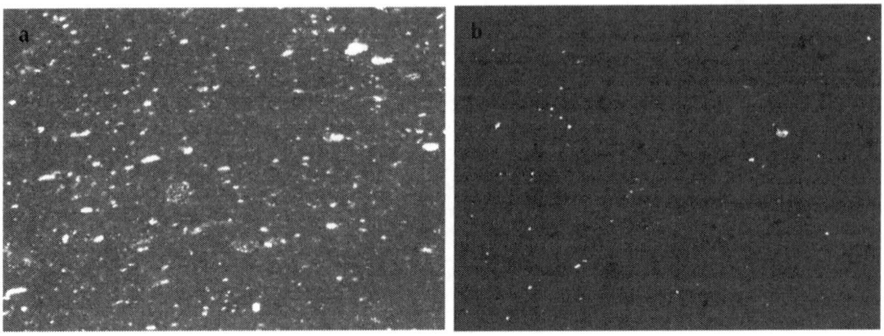

FIGURE 3.22 *Micrographs of Palace Ware fabric from Nimrud (N1-2) taken in (a) PPL and (b) XPL. (field of view = 1.7 mm)*

sediments, are composed of angular and sub-angular grains. Mineral inclusions, identified by optical microscopy of a smear slide, include in order of abundance: quartz, mica (biotite and muscovite); plagioclase; amphibole; pyroxene and zircon. Red and black opaques, probably iron and titanium-rich minerals, such as magnetite and rutile, were abundant.

The modern Tigris River, 60 km north of Mosul city, has a high flow velocity which agitates the fine particles, keeping them in suspension and enabling them to be transported down river while the low flow velocity around the dam regulator confines the coarse particles upstream (al-Ansari and Rimawi 1997). It is possible that the sorting of the modern Tigris sediment in our analysis is artificial due to the dam, however, the Tigris appears to have always been a well-sorted system with few particles above sand (al-Ansari and Rimawi 1997).

Raw Material Processing

Petrographic analyses of Palace Ware fabrics from Nimrud and Nineveh, discussed in detail below, reveal that it is an extremely fine-grained and well-sorted fabric microscopically as well as macroscopically: containing no inclusions > 0.05 mm and fewer than 2% inclusions in the ceramic matrix (figure 3.22). A ceramic matrix is typically defined as particles < 0.02 mm (approximate Φ size 5.5) (Whitbread 1995). Palace Ware fabrics have < 2% cumulative coarser particles at Φ 5.5, while the Tigris raw sediment has 63% cumulative coarser at Φ 5.5. This discrepancy between the fineness of the ceramic matrix and the fineness of the raw material indicates human intentionality—mechanical processing of the raw material, exploitation of natural processes, such as differential particle size distribution along a flood plain and/or seasonal changes in composition and particle size of alluvial load.

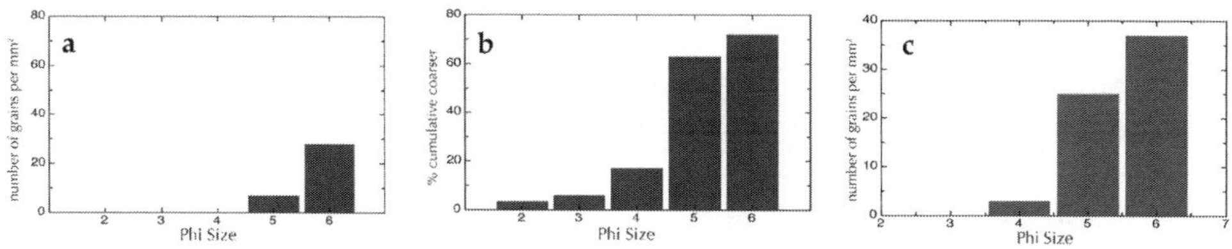

FIGURE 3.23 *Histograms of mineral inclusions in (a) Palace Ware fabrics (b) Tigris River sediments (c) non-Palace Ware Neo-Assyrian tableware.*

When matrix-size particles are removed from the particle size distribution histogram for the Tigris sediment and compared with a histogram of the inclusion size distribution for Palace Ware, the same pattern is observed in both (figure 3.23a-b): a unimodal distribution with an increase in particles at Φ 5 (4.1–5.0) and a clear mode at Φ 6 (5.1–6.0). A histogram of inclusion size distribution in non-Palace Ware Neo-Assyrian ceramic fabrics from Nimrud echoes the unimodal pattern observed in both the Tigris sediment and Palace Ware fabric (figure 3.23c). However, Palace Ware has the narrowest particle size distribution with a sharp truncation in grain size at 0.05 mm (approximate Φ size 4.3–4.2). Geological processes and seasonal changes are unlikely to create such a clean discontinuity in particle size distribution. Therefore, this truncation indicates that, while all three materials are fine-grained, Palace Ware fabrics result from artificial raw material processing and standard Neo-Assyrian ceramic fabrics do not.

Inclusions in Palace Ware fabrics are well-sorted to very well-sorted, subrounded to well-rounded and spherical to discoidal. If the raw material were crushed or ground, the necessary first step for levigation, particles would be less spherical and more angular. Palace Ware particle morphology, however, suggests that the sediments were refined using sedimentation: the process whereby a material is suspended in water and allowed to separate naturally by gravity in accordance with Stoke's Law.

Basins containing sediment and fragments of clay tablets excavated in scribal and administrative contexts at Tell ed-Dēr, dating to the Old Babylonian period (20th–16th century BCE) (Veldhuis 1996), and Nippur, dating to the Ur III period (2112–2004 BCE) (Zettler 1992), have been put forward as evidence of tablet 'recycling' and settling tanks for refining raw materials for tablet production (Taylor 2011). An unpublished report from Tell ed-Dēr describes the results of "levigation (*sic.*)" experiments using broken tablets and states that soaking in these basins created fabrics with inclusions < 0.01 mm (*ibid.*). Although our sedimentation experiment did not produce fabrics as fine as

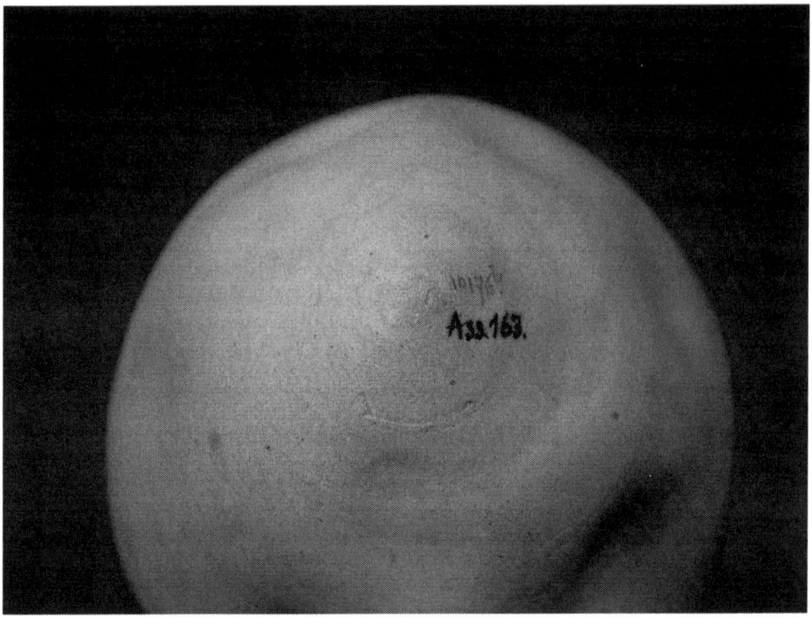

FIGURE 3.24 *Photograph of diagnostic spiral on the external basal surface of a Palace Ware jar from Aššur (VA Ass. 167).*

those at Tell ed-Dēr, our results confirm that the sharp truncation in Palace Ware inclusion size at 0.05 mm can be reproduced after 1–1 1/2 minutes of sedimentation, and that all inclusions larger than 0.02 mm are removed from the sample after 1 hour. Allowing the sample to 'settle' for an additional period of time (2, 4 and 8 hours) does not significantly change the fineness of the fabric.

Based on the fineness of the fabric and particle morphology, raw material processing for Palace Ware manufacture probably involved combining the raw sediment with water, agitating it thoroughly and, after 1–2 minutes, pouring off the suspended fine-fraction into a container to evaporate. Given the temperature and evaporation rate in Iraq, the entire refining process, from raw sediment to a workable paste, could take as little as an hour or two.

Ledgers from an Ur III (2112–2004 BCE) ceramic workshop at Umma record the amount of 'work' or production time required to manufacture vessels with different capacities (Potts 1997). Waetzoldt (1970–1971) believes that these calculations take into consideration all the labour involved, from harvesting the raw material to throwing. According to these records a 500 mL vessel 'cost' 1/4 of a day's labour or 3 hours (Potts 1997). Ur III pottery, made from a coarse paste which included organic and sand temper (Moorey 1994), would have had a shorter drying time than the dense Palace Ware fabrics. Ur III vessels were also hand formed; a relatively slow process compared to throwing on the wheel. It is probable that the increased drying and shorter formation time of Palace Ware vessels balance each other so that 4–5 form B vessels per day is a reasonable estimate of production costs and labour.

Formation

Formation

Macroscopic examination of Palace Ware vessels reveals spiral rhythmic grooves on the interior surface of the base associated with vessel manufacture by rotative kinetic energy or being thrown on a potter's wheel (Rye 1981). Spiral or 'shell' patterning on the external surface of some bases is also indicative of wheel-thrown vessels and results when vessels are cut from the wheel while it is rotating rapidly (figure 3.24) (Rye 1981). Typically, wheel-thrown vessels exhibit rilling, undulating ridges and rhythmic striations on their internal and

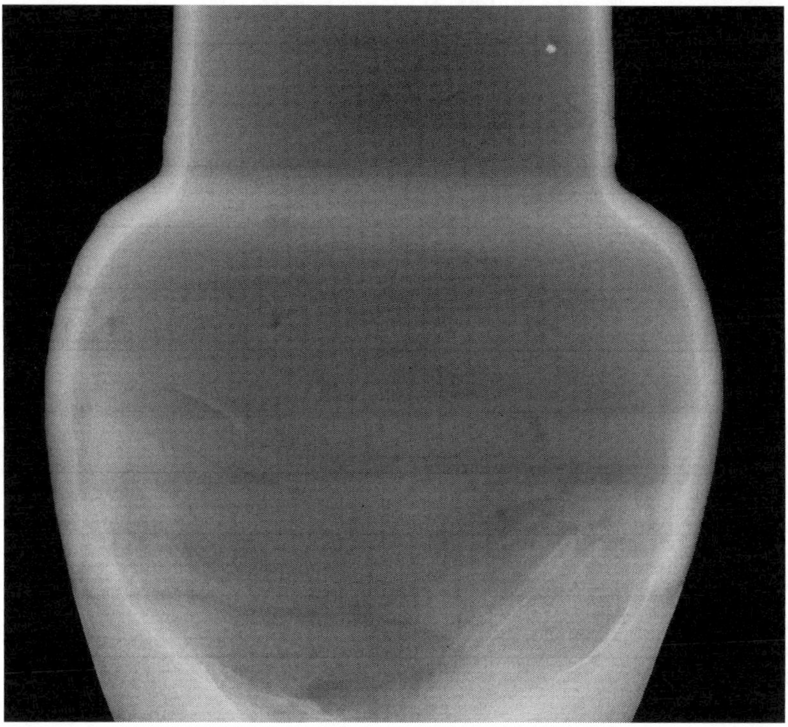

FIGURE 3.25 *Radiograph of a Palace Ware form B cup from Nimrud (UCL Institute of Archaeology ND 1312d) illustrating the diagonal orientation of elongate voids.*

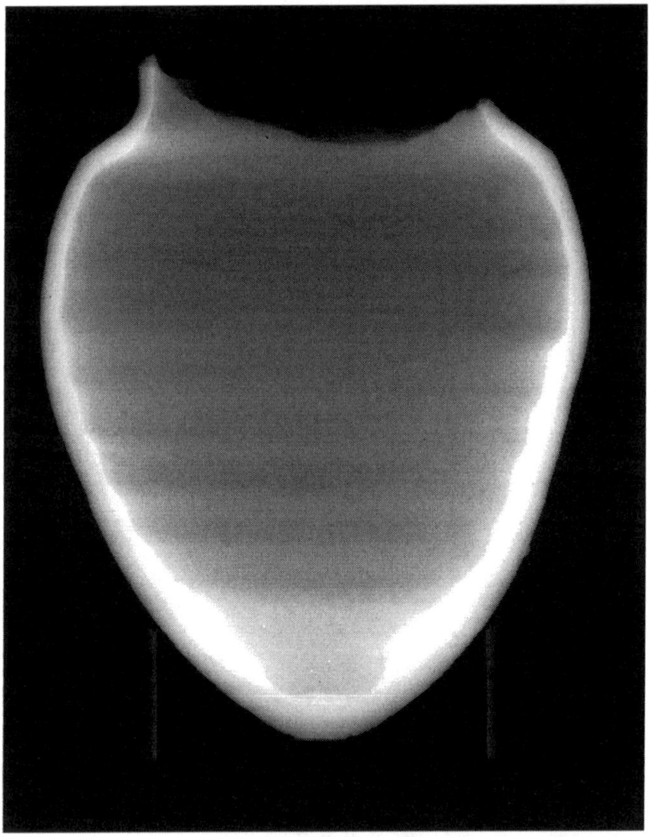

FIGURE 3.26 *Radiograph of a Palace Ware form B cup from Nimrud (UCL Institute of Archaeology ND 1312d) illustrating the subtle variation in wall thickness indicative of wheel-thrown pottery.*

external surfaces (Rye 1981; Rice 1987), however, these indicators are largely absent in the Palace Ware assemblage.

Radiographs of wheel-thrown vessels typically reveal a diagonal preferential orientation of elongate particles normal to the vessel surface (Berg 2008). The matrix-rich or dense Palace Ware fabric is devoid of elongate particles precluding detection of this diagnostic alignment. However, when rare voids are present in the ceramic body they are diagonally oriented (figure 3.25). Radiographs of form B2 jars also reveal subtle variation in wall thickness from base to rim, undetectable using callipers (figure 3.26): a feature created when the paste is drawn upward or lifted while the wheel is in motion (Middleton 1995). Spiral patterning on the base, preferred diagonal orientation of voids, and evidence of lifting all suggest that Palace Ware was formed by throwing on a potter's wheel. Archaeological evidence of the potter's wheel in Mesopotamia is scarce, however it is generally accepted, based on the pottery itself, that the potter's wheel was widely used by the second half of the 3rd millennium BCE (Courty and Roux 1995). Woolley (1956) believed he found remnants of a ceramic potter's wheel (0.075 m thick and 0.75 m in diameter) at Ur, dating to ~2900–2350 BCE. He reports that the wheel is: "heavy enough to spin of its own momentum; the central pivot-hole was covered in bitumen (or perhaps the bitumen was for attaching a peg which itself would revolve in a socket in the lower board) and

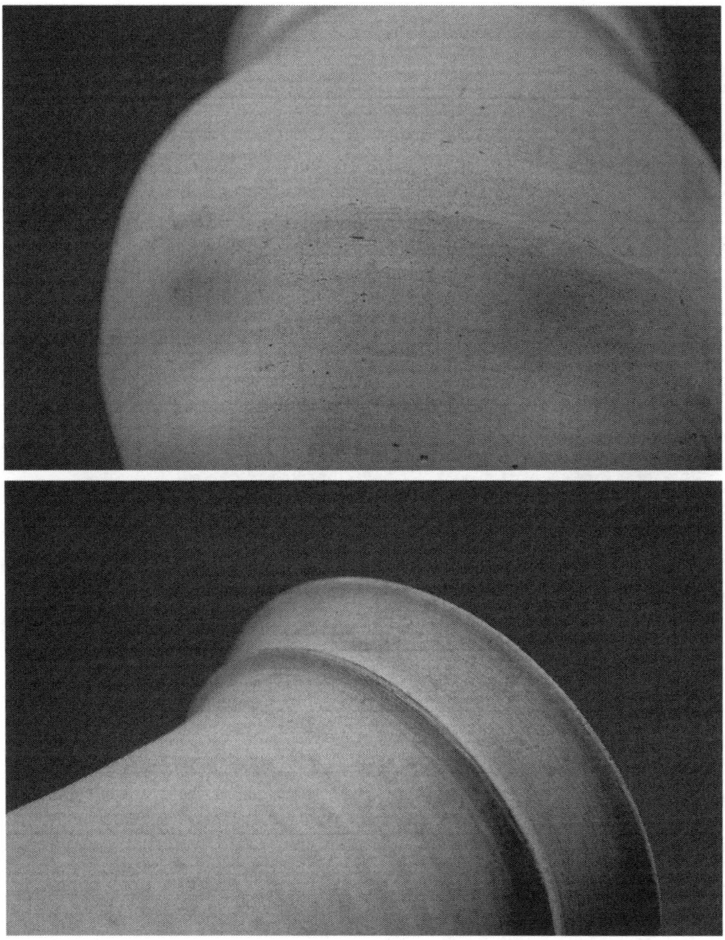

FIGURE 3.27 *Photographs of the rhythmic striations on the external surface of a Palace Ware vessel from Aššur (VA Ass. 171).*

at one point near the edge on the upper surface there were small holes into which could be put the stick-handles that served to turn the wheel" (1956, 28). A similar wheel was excavated at Abu Salabikh, also dating to the Early Dynastic period (2900–2350 BCE) (Postgate 1990) and it is likely that these ceramic potter's wheels were the 'norm' during this period (Moorey 1994).

No potter's wheels have been preserved from the Late Assyrian period, which Moorey (1994) believes indicates a technological transition from ceramic to organic or wooden wheels. However, the lack of excavated potter's wheels could also be a reflection of the small number of identified potter's workshops excavated which date to the Late Assyrian period. Regardless of what Neo-Assyrian potters' wheels were constructed from, the long history of wheel thrown pottery in Mesopotamia indicates that our observations of Palace Ware manufacture are consistent with available technology.

Shaping

The absence of rilling and the smooth, uniform surface of Palace Ware walls suggests that vessels were shaped after they were thrown (figure 3.27). Modern potters often throw a rough-out or approximation of a vessel which is reshaped or 'cut down to size'. Cutting a vessel down to size involves scraping the vessel surface, internally and externally, with a rib while the wheel is in motion to remove excess clay—thinning the vessel walls and refining the shape and size of the form. This technology is called 'turning'. During the leather-hard stage, turning produces patches of shiny, compressed clay on the vessel surface, simi-

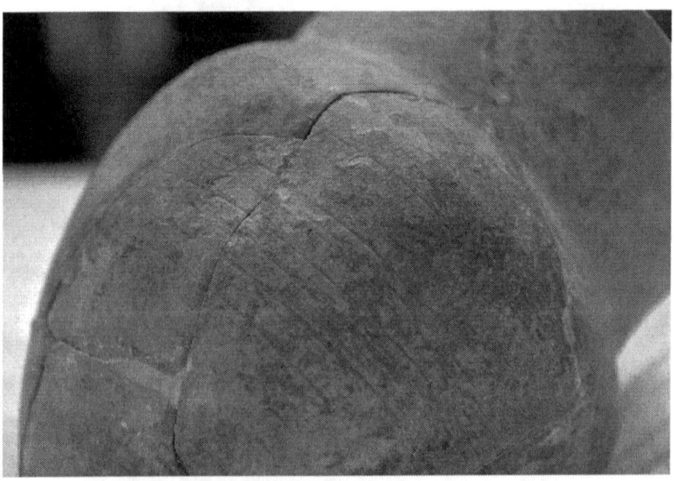

FIGURE 3.28 *Photograph of the 'greasy' texture of a Palace Ware vessel from Nimrud (1992-3-2-182).*

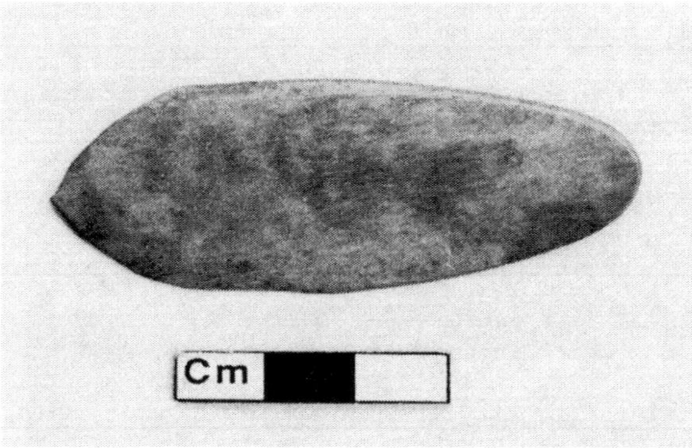

FIGURE 3.29 *Bone tool, possibly a potter's rib, excavated from a Neo-Assyrian ceramic workshop at Nineveh.* PHOTOGRAPH COURTESY OF S. LUMSDEN.

lar to the effect produced by burnishing (Berg 2008). Most Palace Ware vessels have a waxy or greasy texture and a dull sheen on their exterior surface, either uniformly or in patches, indicating turning while the vessel was leather-hard (figure 3.28).

Franken and Kalsbeck (1984, 82) identified a shaping stage for wheel thrown ceramics in the Old Babylonian period (2000–1600 BCE) at Tell ed-Dēr: "the lower part of jars and bowls was often thinned down by scraping away the surplus clay after a period of drying. Since the presence of a large quantity of organic material made turning rather difficult, this was done with a knife while the pot was supported with one hand." Knife trimming during the leather-hard stage leaves sharp-edged marks and, depending upon the force applied, the ceramic body may have a slight sheen as a result of compression (Berg 2008). Knife trimming also creates distinctive faceted texture on the vessel surface (Rye 1981).

Palace Ware vessels do not have either sharp-edged marks or a faceted surface indicative of knife trimming and, since they are not tempered with organics, it is probable they were shaped by turning on the wheel. A bone 'tool' similar in size and shape to a modern potter's rib, was recovered from the Neo-Assyrian pottery workshop at Nineveh, excavated by UC Berkeley (figure 3.29) (Lumsden 2009). It is possible that this tool was used to shape Palace Ware rough outs by turning.

Several of the form B vessels (30%), have a rough texture on the internal surface of the base (figure 3.30). Turning creates a smooth, even surface, both internally and externally (Rye 1981), suggesting that this rough texture is an intentional addition. Old Babylonian potters used clay liberally tempered with

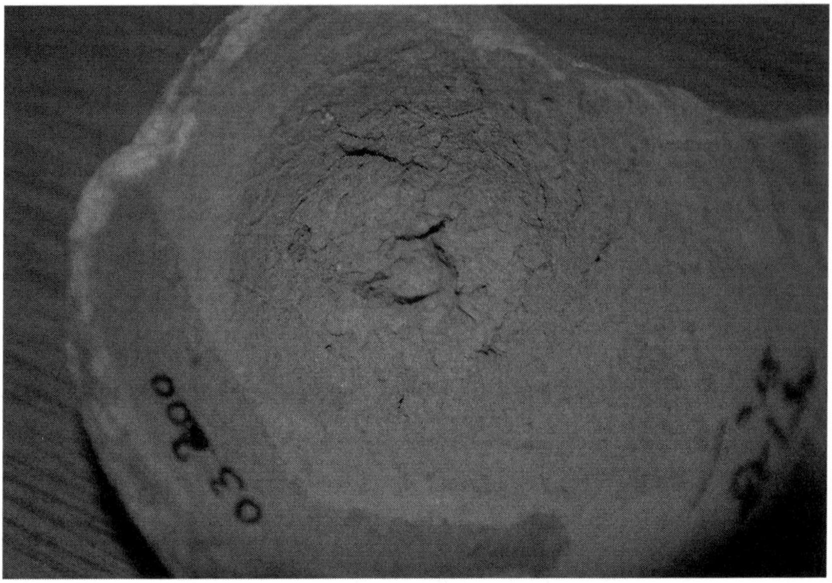

FIGURE 3.30 *Plugs of coarse, heavily organic tempered clay in the base of Palace Ware vessels to prevent failure during drying (vessel from Nineveh* NV *1–9).*

organics to prevent drying and firing cracks in the bases of vessels (Moorey 1994). We believe the rough texture on the internal surface of Palace Ware vessels indicates a similar use of heavily organic tempered 'plugs' to regulate vessel drying and prevent basal cracking during the drying and firing processes.

Decoration

Surface Treatment

The absence of rilling, smooth surface, and dull sheen of Palace Ware vessel walls were previously explained by the application of a slip (Oates 1959). Slips are often easily identified macroscopically or using a hand lens, particularly when they are a different colour than the ceramic body (Rice 1987). Palace Ware sherds are, generally, a consistent colour from surface to core, indicating that if a slip is present it is the same colour as the paste. However, macroscopic and microscopic analysis did not reveal evidence of a slip on Palace Ware fabrics.

Optical microscopy does however reveal an irregular 'layer' or crusting with a clear to merging boundary on the body of some vessels (figure 3.31). This layer is irregular both in terms of its thickness and coverage, often occurring in patches. Slips and glazes are ordinarily applied to create an even texture

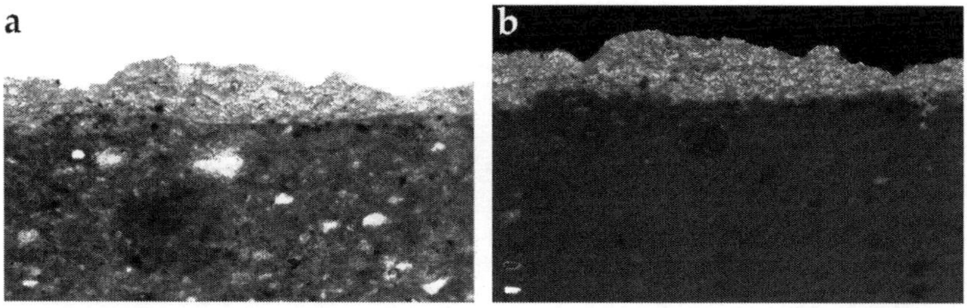

FIGURE 3.31 *Micrographs of mineral encrustation on the external surface of a Palace Ware cup from Nineveh (NV 1–2) in (a) PPL and (b) XPL. (field of view = 0.54 mm)*

and colour to the vessel exterior, therefore, this irregular layer is unlikely to be a slip or a glaze. Possible explanations for this layer include a pseudo-slip, an artefact of vessel shaping, or secondary mineralisation during deposition. Pseudo-slips are generated during shaping: when force of scraping compresses the paste and distributes it in a thin layer across the vessel surface. The variation in the application of force and multiple, overlapping scraping events could explain the patchy nature of the layer. If the layer is the result of shaping, we would expect it to be chemically and mineralogically identical to the ceramic body and, perhaps, exhibit preferential orientation of inclusions perpendicular to the vessel height. However, pseudo-slips, like applied slips, are typically opaque in plane polarised (PPL) and crossed polarised light (XPL). The layer on the surface of Palace Ware fabrics is colourless in PPL and exhibits high fourth order birefringence in XPL, consistent with post-depositional secondary calcite mineralisation.

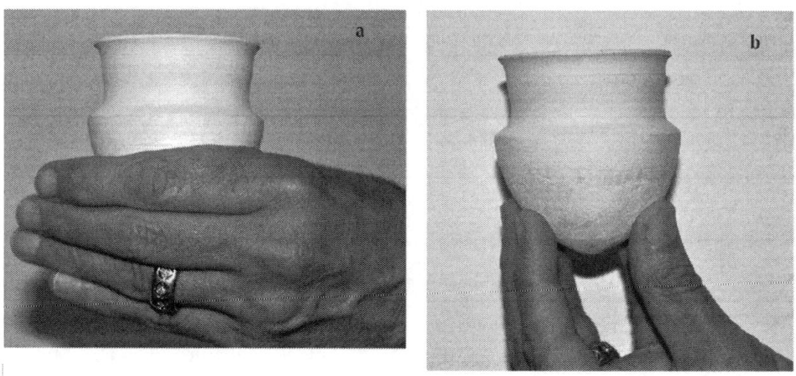

FIGURE 3.32 *Two orientations for gripping Palace Ware form B cups (a) around the body and (b) by the base. (Note: vessel in figure is a modern reconstruction.)*

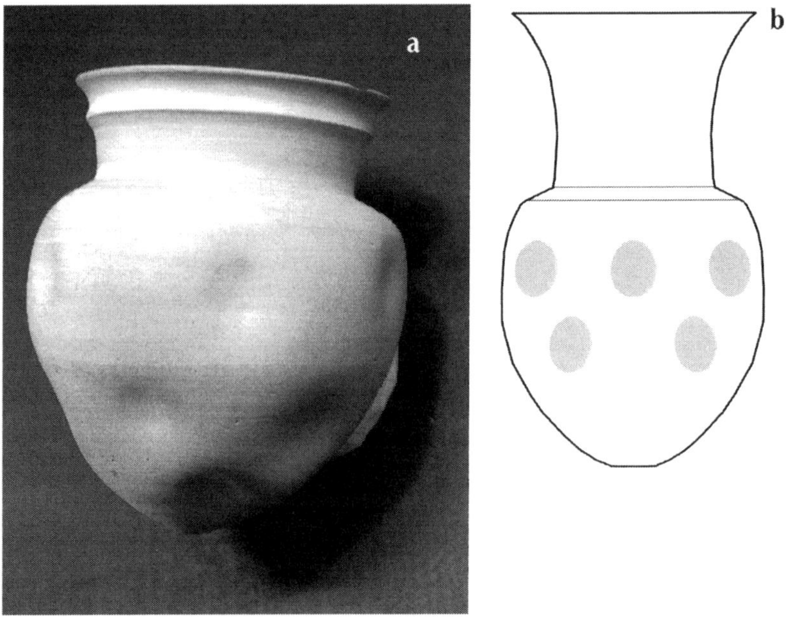

FIGURE 3.33 *Orientation of dimples on Palace Ware form B and C vessels. (a) photograph of form C vessel* AG *from Aššur and (b) drawing of form B vessel* KH *from Nimrud.*

Dimpling

Dimples are the most frequent and identifiable decorative element on Palace Ware vessels, present on 65% of the combined form B and C population. No other Neo-Assyrian or Middle Assyrian ceramic ware is decorated with dimples, making them unique to the Palace Ware corpus. Rawson (1954) suggests that the dimples are finger holds or grips to make vessels easier to grasp and use. There are two possible configurations for gripping a Palace Ware form B cup: around the vessel body, hand parallel to the vessel base (figure 3.32a) or using the fingertips to grip the tapering end of the body above the base (figure 3.32b).

Palace Ware dimples are oval and oriented with their long axis perpendicular to the base (figure 3.33). If Palace Ware dimples are designed to facilitate gripping the body, we would expect the dimples to be oriented with the long axis parallel to the base so that the long axis of the fingers would fit into the long axis of the dimple. The irregular, warped vessel body created by the dimples probably provided sufficient traction for a firm grip on the vessel body, however, if dimpling was designed to create finger holds for gripping the vessel body we would expect them to be oriented parallel to the base.

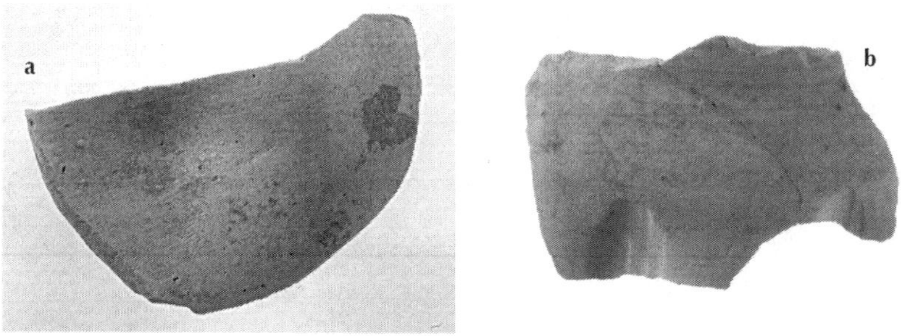

FIGURE 3.34 *Possible 'tool' marks on the obverse of Palace Ware dimples: (a) 'fingerprint' and (b) tool mark.*

The average adult hand measures between 17–20 cm from wrist to the tip of the index finger and creates a pinched 'claw' 4–7 cm from the hollow of the hand to the fingertips. The distance between the vessel base and the first register of dimples on form B jars is 1.0–3.5 cm from the base (mean = 2.0 cm; median = 2.0 cm; mode = 2.0 cm) which is within range for a comfortable grip of Palace Ware vessels by the base for hands between 17–20 cm. The orientation of the dimples supports the idea that vessels were gripped in this manner: the long axis of the finger pad aligns with the long axis of the depression. It is possible, therefore that dimples developed to facilitate gripping Palace Ware vessels by their tapering lower body. A second or third register of dimples may be decorative or designed to accommodate different hand sizes. This functional explanation of Palace Ware dimples does not, however, explain why 16% of the form B assemblage and 54% of the form C assemblage are undimpled. The relatively large number of undimpled vessels indicates that, while dimples may have served a practical purpose, this was a secondary development and dimples were not considered essential for the function of Palace Ware by their primary producers or consumers.

The dimples themselves were pressed into the clay during the leather-hard stage of drying, indicated by the dendritic cracking on the reverse surface of some dimples. The obverse of the dimple is typically smooth and without toolmarks. A small collection of sherds from Nineveh have ridged impressions, similar to fingerprints, on the obverse of the dimple depression (figure 3.34a) and one vessel has what appears to be the impression left by a small, smooth, rounded tool (figure 3.34b).

It is generally assumed that the dimples were made by impressing the clay body with a fingertip (Rawson 1954), an assumption consistent with their general size and shape. Why then does such a small percentage of the form B population have 'fingerprints' inside their dimples? It is probable that during

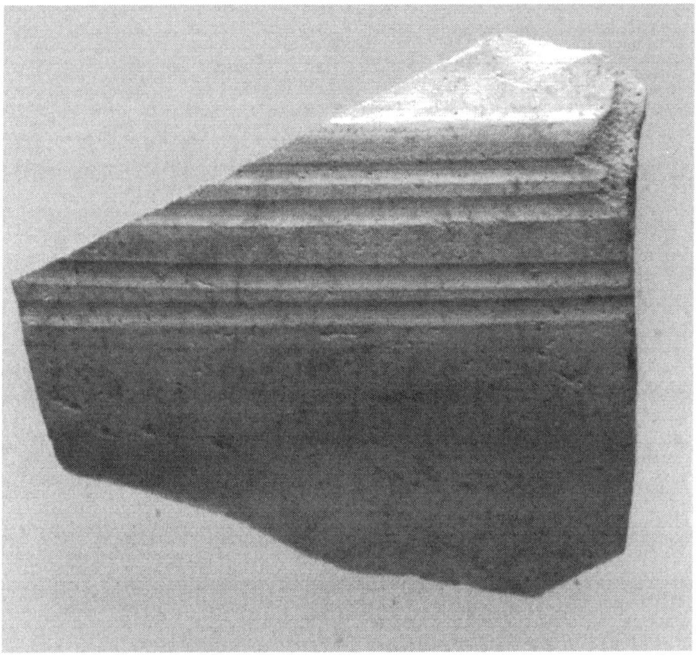

FIGURE 3.35 *Photograph of incised decoration on a Palace Ware sherd from Nineveh* (NV 1–12).

the leather-hard stage, the green strength of the vessel is weak enough to allow deformation of the vessel wall but strong enough to resist forming an impression of the finger pad. The sherds whose dimples contain possible fingerprints may have been 'dimpled' at a different stage of drying.

Incisions

The registers of incised lines around the circumference of the vessel body are evenly spaced and uniform in depth, indicating that they were made using a multi-pronged tool which was pressed against the vessel while it was rotating (figure 3.35) (Rye 1989). The valley of the incision is rounded suggesting that the tips of the tool were round and the even margins of the incision wall indicate that the vessel was leather-hard when the incisions were cut. Although simple, these registers of incised lines are elegantly executed, probably requiring significant skill and/or experience.

Firing

Firing temperature of archaeological ceramics can be estimated in several ways: experimental refiring to evaluate and compare the colour, texture and vitrification of sherds at different temperatures (*e.g.* Daszkiewicz *et al.* 2006); identification of temperature altered mineral inclusions, such as hornblende which alters from green to brown at 800°C (Deer, Howie and Zussman 1997); and quantification of voids and fabric vitrification (*e.g.* Wolf 2002; Tite *et al.* 1982). We were unable to acquire sufficient sample to conduct refiring experiments and the limited mineralogy of Palace Ware fabrics precluded minerals diagnostic of firing temperature. However, we were able to estimate firing temperature by quantifying the voids and fabric vitrification.

The bulk chemical composition of Palace Ware ceramic matrix, determined using EDS-SEM, is presented in table 3.2 and can be approximated as a clay mineral, after Önal 2006, as: $Na_{(0\cdot01)}$ $K_{(0\cdot04)}$ $Ca_{(0\cdot27)}$ $(Al_{(1)}Ti_{(0\cdot05)}$ $Fe^{3+}{}_{(0\cdot46)}$ $Fe^{2+}{}_{(0\cdot113)}$ $Mg_{(0\cdot45)})(Si_{(3\cdot63)}$ $Al_{(0\cdot27)})$ O_{10} $(OH)_2$ $^{*}nH_2O$—chemically similar to a calcium montmorillonite. Montmorillonite, a member of the smectite group, is the most abundant clay mineral in Iraq (al-Bassam and Hak 2006). Our Tigris sediment sample contained only a 0.4 wt. % clay fraction ($\Phi \geq 8.0$) and while it is possible, even probable, that the clay minerals in the Tigris sediment sample flocculated and were measured in the silt fraction, we should be cautious about describing the Palace Ware matrix as composed of montmorillonite clay (*cf.* Jacobs 1992).

The liquidus of a substance with the same bulk chemical composition as the Palace Ware matrix, CaO (30 wt.%) Al_2O_3 (19 wt.%) SiO_2 (51 wt.%), is 1265°C. When we take the magnesium content into consideration, CaO + MgO (35 wt%) Al_2O_3 (17 wt.%) SiO_2 (48 wt.%), the first liquid phase appears at a significantly higher temperature, 1307°C. These liquidus, solidus and eutectic temperatures describe the thermal behaviour of discrete mineral phases (*e.g.* Rase and Roy 1955) and are presented here as informational values only. The actual temperatures at which vitrification first appears in the Palace Ware ceramic matrix will be lower, since it is both a more complicated chemical system and a less dense structure. However, it is important to understand that materials with a high calcium content are refractory and maintain their structure at relatively high temperatures.

Calcareous ceramics are defined as containing >5 wt.% CaO (Maniatis and Tite 1981). As we have seen, Palace Ware fabrics have ~15 wt.% CaO classifying them as calcareous. Fabric colour is a common, but problematic, indicator of firing temperature for calcareous ceramics (Nicholson and Patterson 1989; Mirti and Davit 2004). Post-depositional processes, secondary mineralisation, soil composition, and humidity can all alter the colour of archaeological ceramics. With this caution in mind, the decomposition of calcium carbonate ($CaCO_3$) and its reaction and interaction within a ceramic matrix can be correlated with fabric colour. At temperatures above 750°C, calcium carbonate decomposes

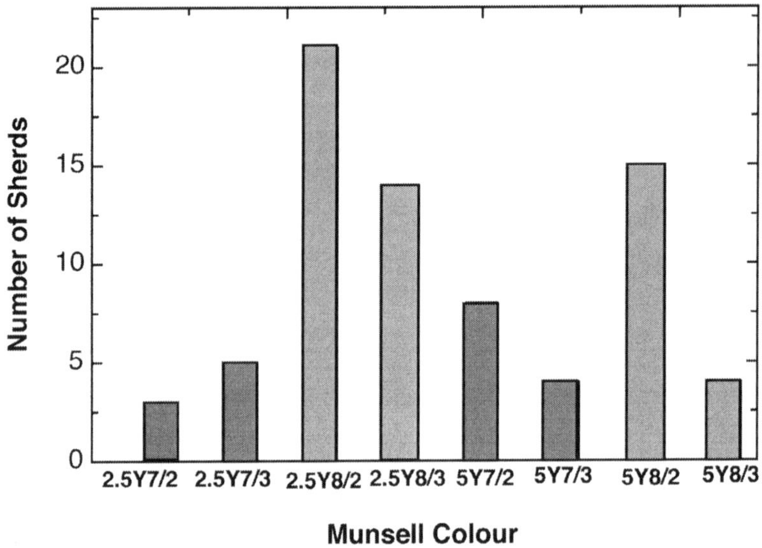

FIGURE 3.36 *Bar chart of Palace Ware fabric colours in the Central Polity.*

to form calcium oxide (CaO) or lime. At temperatures above 1000°C this lime reacts with the ceramic matrix precipitating or crystallising white calcium silicates and/or pale yellow calcium ferrosilicates which produce a cream or buff ceramic body (Molera *et al.* 1998; Shoval 2003; Nakai 2005). Calcareous ceramic bodies turn greenish or olive when they are highly vitrified, usually at temperatures of 1100°C and above (Matson 1971). Palace Ware fabrics occur in a limited range of colours—from pale yellow (2.5Y 8/2) to pale olive (5Y 6/3) (figure 3.36). This colour range suggests that Palace Ware was fired to at least 1000°C and not more than 1100°C.

Firing temperature and soak time estimation of calcareous ceramics based on vitrification and fabric texture is complicated by the relatively stable structural behaviour of these fabrics between 850–1050°C (Maniatis and Tite 1981). However, calcareous fabrics fired over 1050°C vitrify rapidly and exhibit coarse rather than fine bloating pores (Maniatis and Tite 1981). Secondary electron images of Palace Ware fabrics reveal the honey-comb texture indicative of fine bloating pores (figure 3.37a). However, they also exhibit merging mineral phase boundaries (figure 3.37b) and coarse bloating pores (figure 3.37c), albeit more rarely. In our reference collection of Tigris sediment briquettes fired to 600–1200°C, merging boundaries of mineral phases and coarse bloating pores begin to appear at 1100°C (figure 3.38). Therefore, we estimate that Palace Ware was fired between 1050–1100°C. These results are consistent with our firing temperature estimate based on fabric colour.

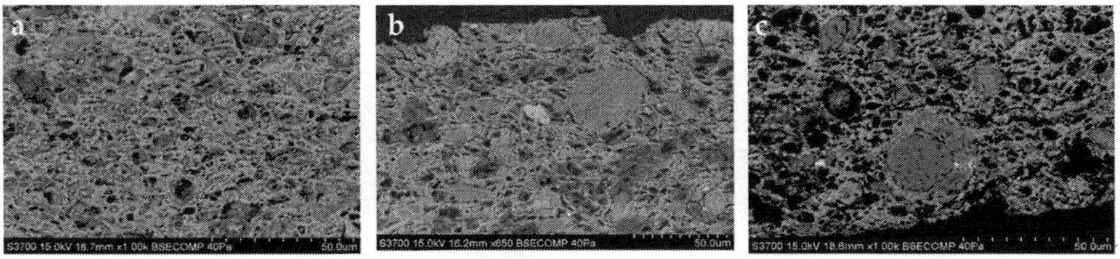

FIGURE 3.37 *SEM-BSE images of Palace Ware fabrics illustrating (a) fine bloating pores (b) merging phase boundaries and (c) gross bloating pores.*

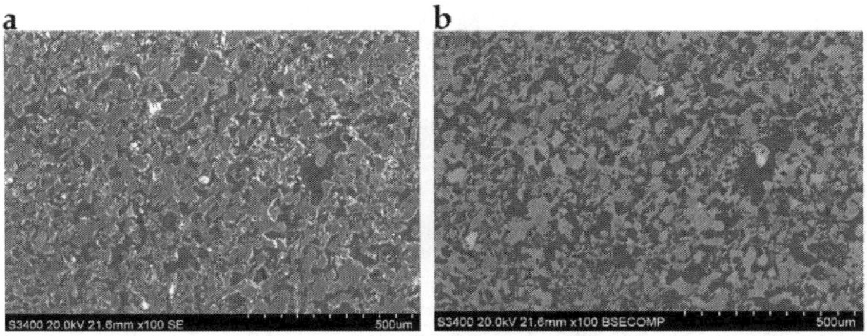

FIGURE 3.38 *SEM images of an experimental briquette of Tigris River sediment fired to 1100°C (a) SEI and (b) BSEI.*

The earliest recorded kiln in Mesopotamia, from Yarim Tepe I, dates to the 6th millennium BCE, and indicates that pyrotechnology was well developed at this early date. The kiln contains a well defined subterranean fire box, and internal architecture separating the fire box from the vaulted heating chamber (Oates and Oates 1976). Reconstruction of a kiln at Qasrij Cliff, dating to the Late Assyrian period, appears to use the same basic architecture and technology, with a subterranean fire box, perforated floor separating the two chambers, and a vaulted heating chamber (Curtis 1989).

Intact heating chambers for Neo-Assyrian kilns have not been recovered archaeologically and it is possible, therefore, that the vault of Neo-Assyrian kilns was semi-permanent or temporary and only 'capped' before firing (Moorey 1994). Van As and Jacobs (1985) recreated an experimental, two-chamber updraft kiln of this kind, with a temporary vaulted roof, and found that it was highly efficient—reaching temperatures ± 900°C after 3 hours using palm leaves as fuel, and demonstrating that a permanent roof was not required to reach high temperatures. Rehder (2000) has calculated that a small kiln with a fire box 3–5 m^2 can generate temperatures of 1200°C or more. Neo-Assyrian

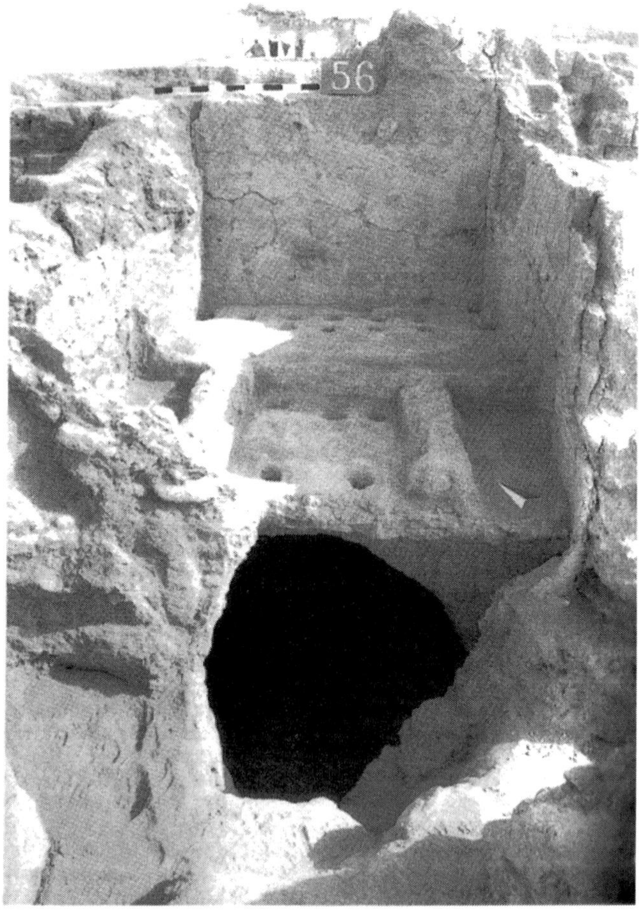

FIGURE 3.39 *Photograph of the Neo-Assyrian kiln at Aššur. Originally published in Rijad 2002.*

pottery in general is estimated to have been fired to between 850–1050°C (Tite and Maniatis 1975), which is within the heating range of As and Jacobs' experimental kiln. We estimate that Palace Ware was fired to between 1050–1100°C, which is within the theoretical temperature range for a kiln of this size and construction.

Our investigation of the social value of Palace Ware, requires an understanding of its production cost in terms of consumables, such as fuel, as well as time and labour. Fuel consumption, heating efficiency, and maximum temperature can be calculated from the measurements of the kiln structure (Rehder 2000). To date, only a few kilns dating to the Late Assyrian period have been excavated in the Central Polity: an unpublished kiln was excavated by the UC Berkeley team in the lower town at Nineveh in 1988–1989, and a possible ceramic kiln was excavated at Aššur (Rijad 2002). Unfortunately, analysis and publication of the Nineveh kiln is not scheduled and publication of the Aššur kiln is cursory—little more than a mention and photograph. However, working from photographs and unpublished excavation reports we can estimate the size of these two structures.

The Nineveh kiln has a long, narrow, oval fire box, approximately 2 m wide by 5 m long or 7.85 m^2. Despite its unorthodox shape, the installation is considered a kiln because it is associated with wasters, some of which are Palace Ware, and potter's tools (Lumsden 2009). The Aššur kiln has a rectangular fire box and elaborate internal architecture with a flat, multi-chambered perforated floor separating the fire box from the heating chamber (figure 3.39). The heating chamber is almost square, measuring approximately 1.7 m wide and 2 m long (3.4 m^2). We are unable to estimate the area of the fire box from the published photograph of the Aššur kiln, however Neo-Assyrian kilns have the same architecture and approximate size as Middle Assyrian updraft kilns, for example Tell Sabi Abyad (Akkermans and Duistermaat 2001). The ratio of floor area of the fire box to the floor area of the heating chamber for the Tell Sabi Abyad kiln is approximately 5:2. If we use the same ratio for the Neo-Assyrian kilns we can estimate the fire box floor area of the Aššur kiln to be 8.5 m^2. Conversely, we can reconstruct the heating chamber floor area of the Nineveh kiln to 3.14 m^2. These calculations indicate that despite the difference in shape, the kilns from Aššur and Nineveh are similar in size.

Fuel consumption and heating efficiency of the two kilns was probably different, however, due to their shape. Without a detailed analysis and full publication of these kilns, we are unable to determine whether the difference in shape had technological advantages or was a reflection of the preference or cultural origin of the potter's guilds at these two locations.

There is no evidence of kiln furniture being used for unglazed ceramics in Mesopotamia (Moorey 1994). Given the high level of vitrification observed in the Palace Ware ceramic bodies, firing stacked vessels in the heating chamber appears to be extremely risky; vessels could potentially fuse together. We know that the Neo-Assyrians were highly skilled pyrotechnicians from the chemical and technical texts (*e.g.* Oppenheim 1970). Therefore, it is reasonable that Neo-Assyrian potters could have fired multiple tiers of Palace Ware without kiln furniture or a prohibitive risk of failure. For the purpose of this exercise, we will assume Neo-Assyrian potters were able to fire two tiers of form B vessels in a single load.

TABLE 3.3 *Higher heating values* (HHV) *of common biomass fuels (compiled from Rehder 2000 & Winterhalter* et al. *1974*)

fuel type	HHV in MJ/kg
grape pomace	21.8
walnut shells	19.5
olive pits	19.4
oakwood	18.7
dung	18–17
straw	13.5

If the heating chamber of a kiln is 3.2 m² (the average of the heating chambers from Nineveh and Aššur) and the average maximum diameter for form B vessels is 7.4 cm, occupying approximately 43 cm², then 744 vessels would fit in the first tier. The second tier would need to be placed in the interstitial space created by the first tier and could hold 405 vessels loaded either base or rim facing down. Together these two tiers bring the size of a full kiln load to 1,149 form B vessels. The average form B vessel weighs 57 g, making our hypothetical load approximately 65.49 kg of ceramic material.

If we accept 0.84 kJ per kg per °C as the heat content of clay (Rehder 2000), then to reach a firing temperature of 1100°C, 1 kg of Palace Ware requires 0.84*1100 = 924 kJ of heat. The thermal efficiency of ancient ceramic kilns was between 1–2% (Rehder 2000), meaning that the average Neo-Assyrian kiln required 924/0.015 = 61,600 kJ or 61.6 MJ of energy from the fuel to achieve a firing temperature of 1100°C. As a point of comparison, non-Palace Ware Neo-Assyrian pottery, estimated by Tite and Maniatis (1975) to be fired between 850–1050°C, requires only 30.6–58.8 MJ of energy from the fuel.

No textual reference to the technological aspects of ceramic manufacture have been found to date. Without analyses of ash from the fire box of an actual kiln it is impossible to know what type of biomass fuel was used in Neo-Assyrian ceramic manufacture. Expensive fuels, such as charcoal and wood, however were probably reserved for the manufacture of glass, glazed ceramics and metals (*e.g.* Oppenheim 1970). Biomass fuels for ceramic manufacture would likely have been agricultural and industrial waste, such as chaff and dung. Table 3.3 presents the higher heating values (HHV) of some available biomass fuels in the Neo-Assyrian core.

According to Rehder (2000), 1 kg of ceramic material requires between 1–3 kg of biomass fuel to reach and maintain the target firing temperature, meaning that our hypothetical load would require somewhere between 65.50–196.50 kg of fuel. For the purpose of this exercise, we use dung as our biomass fuel. To calculate the amount (kg) of dung required to heat 1 kg of Palace Ware to 1100°C we divide the energy required from the fuel by the higher heating value of the fuel (61.6 MJ/17–18 MJ/kg). Heating and maintaining 1 kg of Palace Ware at 1100°C requires 3.6–3.4 kg of dung. Therefore, our sample load of 1,149 form B vessels (65.49 kg of ceramic material) would consume between 253.78–222.68 kg of dung: approximately 30% more fuel than Rehder's estimate for a standard ceramic load and between 10–50% more fuel than a non-Palace Ware ceramic load of similar weight. There are no records explicitly indicating the monetary value of biomass fuels in the Neo-Assyrian heartland, but it is evident from this exercise that their drying, storage, and consumption could have been a considerable expense even if the actual kiln load was smaller than our hypothetical load.

Mesopotamian craftsmen in all periods were organised into guilds or workshops. Texts from Ur III Umma indicate that ceramic workshops consisted of 2–10 potters and a supervisor, and were typically attached to or affiliated with establishments such as breweries (*é-bappir*) or state kitchens (*é-muhaldim*) (Potts 1997). Detailed accounts of the productivity of these workshops were kept with raw material 'debts', materials and labour loaned from the state, balanced against manufactured ceramics (Waetzoldt 1970–1971). Potts has suggested that the "60 talents (1800 kg) of reeds ... noted in the debt section of [text] MW124" was fuel for the kiln. Another Ur III account of consumables for a state feast for Inanna at Garšana lists "20 bundles of reeds: soup has been cooked with them" (Brunke 2011)—suggesting that reeds might have been the biomass fuel standard in Mesopotamia. Whatever biomass fuel was used for ceramic manufacture, these texts suggest that biomass fuel management and distribution was a function of the state.

Chemical and Mineralogical Characterisation

In order to evaluate the transport mechanism for Palace Ware across the Neo-Assyrian imperial landscape, particularly the movement of the vessels themselves, we must establish mineralogical and chemical fabrics group(s) for Palace Ware from the Central Polity.

Regional Geology of Assyria

Assyria, located in northern Iraq, is dominated geologically by the anticlinal Zagros and Anti-Taurus mountains to the north and north-east, and the Tigris and Euphrates river systems. These geographical features shape the political and economic boundaries of the empire in the Late Assyrian period. The present study is concerned with ceramic production, therefore the scope of this discussion is limited to the alluvial systems, the sediments they transport, and the potential source rocks from which they derive.

Both the Tigris and the Euphrates originate in the Anti-Taurus mountains near Lake Van. The Euphrates then flows southward through the semi-arid Syrian desert with no permanent tributaries once it crosses into Iraq. The river is 2700 km in length, 1213 km of which are in Iraq, and has a catchment of 7,650,000 km^2 (Krásný *et al.* 2006). The average flow rate of the Euphrates is 1100 m^3/s, however during its spring spate in May, this can increase to 50,000 m^3/s (*ibid.*). The Tigris, on the other hand, is fed by four tributaries inside Iraqi borders: the Upper and Lower Zab; the Adhaim, and the Diyala. Although the Tigris is significantly shorter than the Euphrates, flowing only 1718 km (1418 km of which are in Iraq) with a catchment of 375,000 km^2, it has a significantly greater capacity and an average flow rate of 4000 m^3/s, reaching 80,000 m^3/s during its spate in March and April (*ibid.*).

The Pleistocene terraces of the Tigris and Euphrates generally occur as narrow belts, no more than 2 km on either side of the river, however preferential expansion can occur on the eastern bank of the Tigris south of Mosul, which reaches 10 km in width (Aqrawi *et al.* 2006). Four main terraces are associated with the Tigris and Euphrates, and the coarseness of the Quaternary sediments (up to cobble size) deposited on the Tigris terraces and along the flood plain indicate a high carrying capacity of the river during this time (*ibid.*; Philip 1968). Quaternary and recent flood plain and suspended sediments from the Tigris and Euphrates consist of loam, composed primarily of clayey silts and silty clays (Aqrawi *et al.* 2006; Berry *et al.* 1970; Philip 1968). It is possible to differentiate sediments from the Tigris and Euphrates based on heavy mineral analysis and chemical composition (*cf.* Ali Jawad 1984; Minarikova 1979). However, by the time the Euphrates enters Iraq it has lost 45% of its load, and the Tigris deposits 52% of its load north of Bagdad (Philip 1968).

Rainfall in Iraq varies from 50 mm/year in the south-west to 1200 mm/year in the north-east, and typically falls in bursts between October and May (Krásný *et al.* 2006). During the rainy season, precipitation can exceed 40 mm in 24 hours, facilitating the drainage of wadis into the Euphrates (*ibid.*). In the Zagros foothills, rainfall averages 300–700 mm/year, and can exceed 700 mm/year in the mountains (*ibid.*). It is, therefore, not surprising that the Assyrian heartland is located in the foothills of the Zagros mountains where conditions

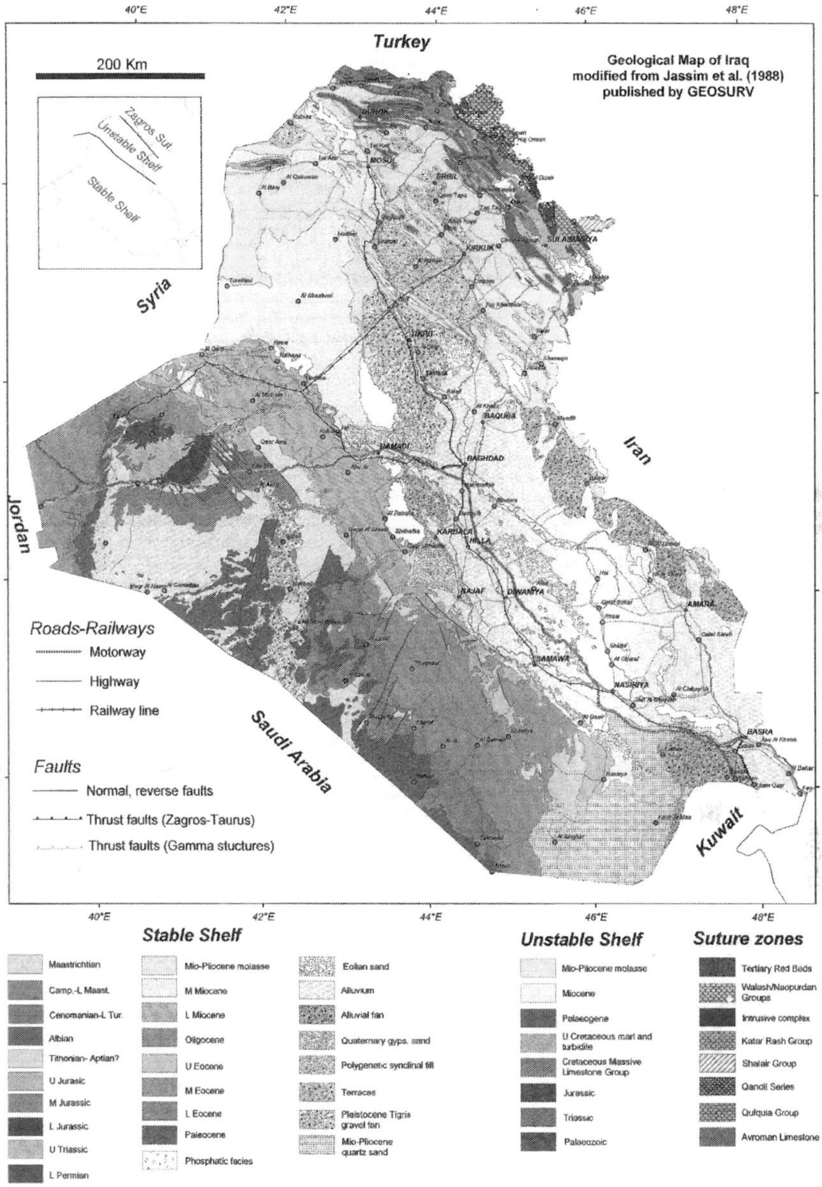

MAP 3.1 *Geological map of Iraq.*
JASSIM 2006, FIGURE 1–2.

are optimal for irrigation and aquifer agriculture of cereals (al-Amiri 1983). Although both rivers are significant ideologically, the Tigris, Upper and Lower Zab rivers flow through the Assyrian heartland and are, therefore, the most likely source for ceramic raw material for this region.

Annual evaporation is between 2500–3000 mm, of which 400–500 mm occur in July and August (Krásný *et al.* 2006). However, aeolian deposits are limited to three belts in southern Iraq, outside of the Assyrian heartland (Aqrawi *et al.* 2006). It is unlikely, therefore, that aeolian sediments are a source of ceramic raw material for the Central Polity.

The morphology, structural and surface geology of Iraq is complex, comprising three distinct tectonic units: the Stable Shelf, which is bounded to the north by the anticlinal Makhul-Hemrin-Peshti-Kuh range; the Unstable Shelf, extending from the Makhul-Hemrin-Pesht-i-Kuh range, or foothills, to the Zagros and Taurus Suture belts; and the Zagros Suture zone (map 3.1). The Assyrian core spans two of them, occupying the northern edge of the Ruthba-Jezira and Salman Stable Shelf subzones, and the Foothill and High Folded Zone Unstable Shelf subzones. The postulated Precambrian basement composition for this area includes granites, amphibolites, gabbros, diorites, and ophiolites (Jassim 2006). The Tigris cuts into bedrock on its western bank as it flows through the Assyrian core, and detrital minerals from the exposed basement contribute to the composition of Tigris sediment deposits (Aqrawi *et al.* 2006). However, detrital minerals and sediments from the Unstable Shelf and Suture Zones are transported by the Tigris and Zab tributaries, and comprise the majority of the alluvial load.

As the Tigris flows from its source in the Anti-Taurus through the Zagros it passes through the Northern Thrust (Ora) and High Folded subzones of the Unstable Shelf. Both subzones were uplifted during the Cretaceous and are characterised by steep anticline structures (Jassim and Buday 2006a; Jassim and Buday 2006b; Buday and Jassim 1987). The Northern Thrust Zone can be considered allochthonous, probably originally part of the Anti-Taurus in Turkey (Jassim and Buday 2006b; Buday and Jassim 1987). Major rock types in these zones include: amphibole, gabbro, diorite, limestone, dolomitic limestone, breccia, acid volcanics, and volcanic ash (Buday and Jassim 1987). The Northern Thrust Zone also contains igneous outcrops rich in barite, celestine, and pyrite (al-Bassam and Hak 2006).

The Upper and Lower Zab rivers flow out of the Zagros in the east, potentially transporting regionally diagnostic metamorphic and volcanic detrital minerals from the Zagros Suture. The Upper Zab is formed by two tributaries originating in the Balambo-Tanjero Zone of the Unstable Shelf and the Shalair Zone of the Zagros Suture. The Balambo-Tanjero Zone is composed of fluvial and marine clastics dating to the Maastrichtian and later, and is characterised by imbricated structures which override local anticlines (Jassim and Buday 2006a; Jassim and Buday 2006b; Buday and Jassim 1987). The Shalair Zone is charac-

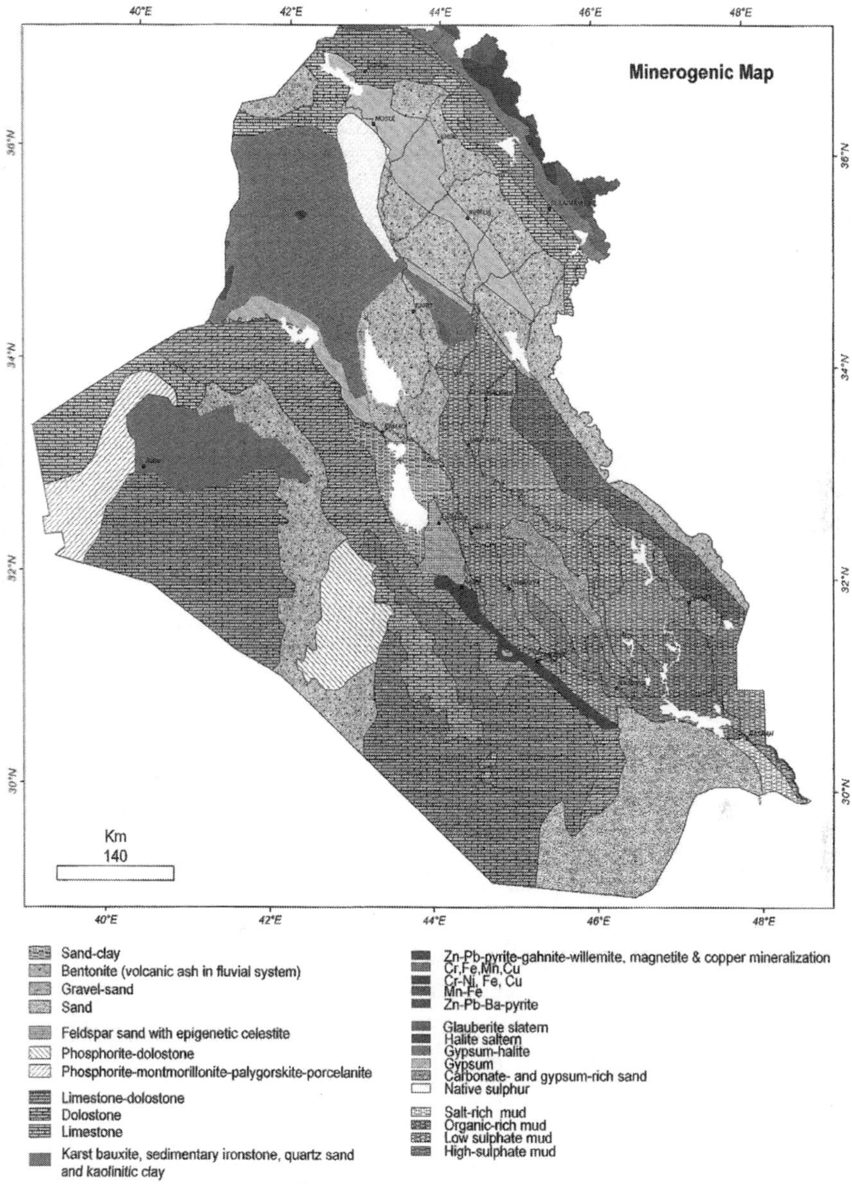

MAP 3.2 *Industrial minerals map of Iraq.*
AL-BASSAM & HAK 2006, FIGURE 20–1.

terised by Paleozoic metamorphic sequences overlain by Jurassic-Cretaceous low-grade meta-sediments and meta-volcanics, and Upper Cretaceous arc volcanics (Jassim and Buday 2006a; Jassim and Buday 2006b; Jassim *et al.* 2006; Buday and Jassim 1987). These tributaries form the Upper Zab in the High Folded Zone (described above), which then flows through the long anticlines and broad Miocene-Quaternary molasse containing synclines of the Foothill Zone where it meets the Tigris (Jassim and Buday 2006a; Jassim and Buday 2006b). Major rock types along the Upper Zab include: alkali olivine basalt, alumina rich basalt, tholeiitic dolerite, basaltic andesite, andesite, rhyolite, calc-shist and green schist, limestone, and amphibolite (Buday and Jassim 1987).

The Lower Zab originates in the High Folded Zone inside the drainage basin of the Penjween-Walash subzone of the Zagros Suture. The Penjween-Walash Zone is composed of Cretaceous ophiolites, metamorphic and sedimentary rocks, and Eocene arc and fore-arc units (Jassim and Buday 2006a; Jassim and Buday 2006b; Jassim *et al.* 2006; Buday and Jassim 1987). The Lower Zab flows out of one of the Penjween-Walash drainage basins, through the High Folded Zone, and joins the Tigris south of Aššur in the Foothills Zone. Major rock types associated with the course of the Lower Zab include: metabasalt, green schist, olivine tholeite, basaltic tuff, greywacke, dunite, peridotite, pyroxenite, basic and ultrabasic banded gabbro and coarse gabbro, and serpentinite (Buday and Jassim 1987).

Both kaolinitic and montmorillonitic clays are found in the Assyrian core associated with fluvial deposition: kaolinites from the western mountains and montmorillonites from the Foothills and High Folded Zones (al-Bassam and Hak 2006). Montmorillonite *sensu stricto* and palygorskite are the most abundant clay minerals in Iraq, generally associated with Upper Cretaceous and Tertiary formation in the Unstable Shelf (al-Bassam and Hak 2006). However, kaolinite *sensu stricto* is associated with older deposits in the Zagros, and illite *sensu stricto* can be found in alluvial deposits in the Foothills and High Folded Zones (Sal-Bassam and Hak 2006). The Upper and Lower Zab rivers flow through bentonite *sensu stricto* deposits in the Foothill Zone before they meet the Tigris (al-Bassam and Hak 2006) (map 3.2).

Typical detrital light minerals suspended in or deposited by the Tigris during its course through the Assyrian core include: quartz, cryptocrystalline silica (radiolarian chert), carbonates, mica (biotite, muscovite, chlorite), and plagioclase feldspar (intermediate to basic) (Philip 1968). Heavy detrital minerals include: iron ores (magnetite, ilmenite, hematite), epidote (primarily pistachite, but also zoisite, and clinozoisite), amphiboles (primarily hornblende, also actinolite), pyroxene (primarily augite, also diopside, enstatite, and hypersthene), garnet, rutile, zircon, apatite, olivine, tourmaline, sphene, and spinel (al-Juboury *et al.* 1999; Philip 1968).

Mineralogical Profile

As mentioned above, Palace Ware fabrics are extremely fine-grained (< 2% inclusions; inclusions < 0.05 mm) and well-sorted to very well-sorted (figure 3.22). The inclusions themselves are sub-rounded to well-rounded and spherical to discoidal—consistent with alluvial sediment from the Tigris which has been processed by sedimentation. The mineralogy of Palace Ware fabrics from the Central Polity is consistent with the igneous and volcanic geology of the Northern Thrust and High Folded Zones in northern Iraq. Analysis of 24 thin-sections from the Central Polity reveals that Palace Ware fabrics are homogeneous and can be described as follows (a table of thin section descriptions is provided in appendix A):

> The matrix is olive to pale yellow-brown and opaque in PPL; optically inactive in XPL. Devoid of foraminifers. Rare (0.5–1%) planar voids (up to 0.5 mm) with frequent secondary calcite formation in the interstitial space. Opaques (2%) of haematite, rutile, magnetite, sphene and spinel, between a few microns and almost 20 µm. The inclusions ($f{:}c_{0\cdot062}$mm = 98:2) contain very well-sorted, sub-rounded to well-rounded, fine sand particles of quartz and plagioclase (rare) and amphibole and mica (very rare) up to 0.05 mm. Heavy minerals (monazite-xenotime, baryte-celestite, zircon, epidote, apatite) (very rare) up to 0.03 mm could be identified.

Palace Ware fabrics from Nimrud and Nineveh are almost indistinguishable. However, fabrics from Nimrud have a subtle difference in mineralogy and those from Nineveh have a slightly greater number of inclusions. Nimrud Palace Ware fabrics contain more plagioclase inclusions that Nineveh fabrics and they also contain apatite, a mineral not found in any of the Nineveh samples. Nineveh fabrics, on the other hand, are slightly more inclusion rich: fine:coarse (0.062mm) fraction = 98:2 rather than 99:1.

It is possible that these differences reflect the exploitation of different and local raw material resource at Nimrud and Nineveh. Nineveh sits 30 km north of Nimrud along the Tigris and the river and its deposits likely contain a greater number of inclusions at Nineveh than they do by the time they reach Nimrud. This geographic difference would explain differences in mineralogy if Nineveh fabrics contained mineral inclusions not found at Nimrud or in greater abundance at Nineveh. The opposite it true. The introduction of a new mineral type at Nimrud suggests the exploitation of a new raw material source or a mixture of sources for local Palace Ware manufacture at Nimrud. The Upper Zab contributes alkali basaltic material to the Tigris just south of

Nimrud which could explain the mineralogical differences between Nimrud and Nineveh fabrics, particularly if local potters were using sediments from the Upper Zab and/or mixing Upper Zab and Tigris sediments for Palace Ware manufacture.

These subtle differences in Palace Ware fabrics from Nimrud and Nineveh are too minor to differentiate them petrographically as different geological fabric groups (1–5 inclusions differ per thin-section), particularly since we believe that the raw materials were prepared by sedimentation—a process that alters both the number and type of mineral inclusions in a ceramic fabric. However, these results suggest that petrographic differentiation of ceramics from Nimrud and Nineveh might be possible for coarser fabrics and that Palace Ware manufacture was undertaken locally, by different workshops exploiting local resources and not the result of a single centralised production. The potential regional differences between Nimrud and Nineveh Palace Ware fabrics are highlighted below:

Nimrud

The matrix is olive to pale yellow-brown and opaque in PPL; optically inactive in XPL. Devoid of foraminifers. Rare (0.5–1%) *planar voids (up to 0.5 mm)* with frequent secondary calcite formation in the interstitial space. Opaques (2%) of haematite, rutile, magnetite, sphene and spinel, between a few microns and almost 20 µm. The inclusions (*f:c*$_{0\cdot062}$*mm = 99:1*) contain very well-sorted, sub-rounded to well-rounded, fine sand particles of quartz and *plagioclase*, amphibole and *apatite (rare)* and mica (very rare) up to 0.05 mm. Heavy minerals (zircon, monazite-xenotime, baryte-celestite, epidote) (very rare) up to 0.03 mm could be identified.

Nineveh

The matrix is olive to pale yellow-brown and opaque in PPL; optically inactive in XPL. Devoid of foraminifers. Rare (0.5–1%) *planar voids (up to 0.3 mm) with common (~15%) secondary calcite formation in the interstitial space.* Opaques (2%) of haematite, rutile, magnetite, sphene and spinel, between a few microns and almost 20 µm. The inclusions (*f:c*$_{0\cdot062}$*mm = 98:2*) contain very well-sorted, sub-rounded to well-rounded, fine sand particles of quartz (rare) *plagioclase*, amphibole and mica (very rare) up to 0.05 mm. Heavy minerals (baryte-celestite, monazite-xenotime, zircon, epidote) (very rare) up to 0.03 mm could be identified.

Chemical Profile

The geochemical profiles for Palace Ware fabrics from Nimrud and Nineveh, using INAA, are illustrated in figure 3.40 (a table of the data is provided in appendix B). Fabrics from Nimrud and Nineveh are very similar and cluster together in biplots of elemental ratios, such as Th:Hf against Eu:Ta (figure 3.41). However, more sophisticated statistical analysis using principal components analysis (PCA) reveals subtle geochemical differences between Palace Ware from Nimrud and Nineveh and two chemical sub-groups within the Nimrud Palace Ware population (figure 3.42).

Although the sample size is too small for these groups to be statistically defensible, Nimrud sub-group 1 has slightly higher chromium (Cr) and lower hafnium (Hf) concentrations than the Nineveh fabrics and both of these compositional groups have higher Cr and Hf concentrations than Nimrud sub-group 2. Clearly, multiple raw material resources are being exploited at Nimrud. These results suggest not only local manufacture of Palace Ware forms using local raw material resources, but that local Palace Ware production was not necessarily centralised/specialised to a single workshop within a single city. The samples from Nimrud available for INAA were undiagnostic body sherds with little or no contextual or typological information. We are therefore unable to evaluate the nature of these two geochemical sub-groups/ workshops at Nimrud. We know that guilds of potters in Assyria were often associated with institutions and organisations. Do these subgroups indicate a

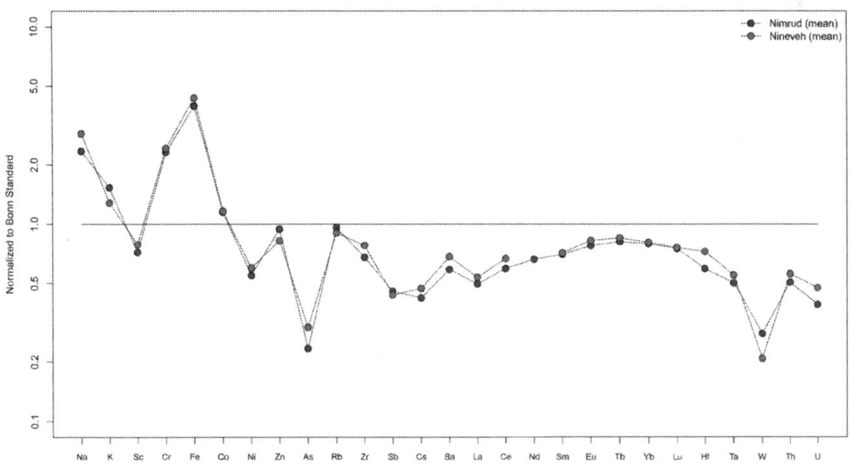

FIGURE 3.40 *Combined INAA chemical profile for Palace Ware from Nimrud & Nineveh.* GRAPH COURTESY OF J. STERBA.

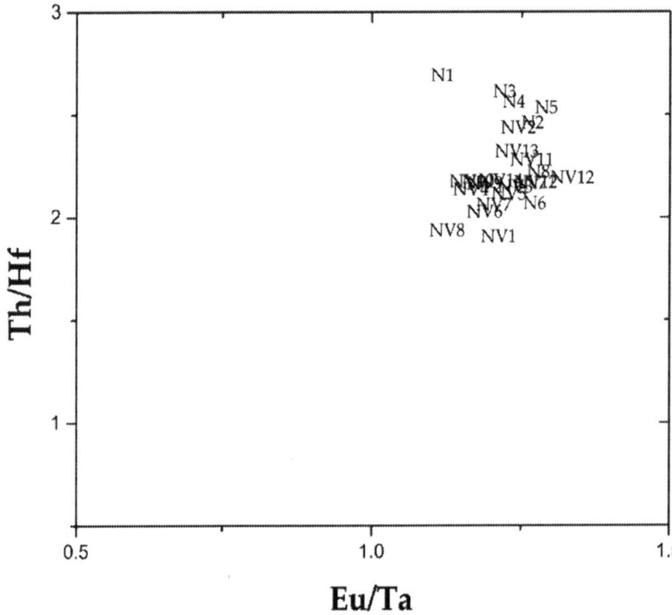

FIGURE 3.41 *Biplot of elemental ratios Eu:Ta vs Th:Hf illustrating the chemical compositional similarity between Palace Ware fabrics from Nimrud (N) and Nineveh (NV).*

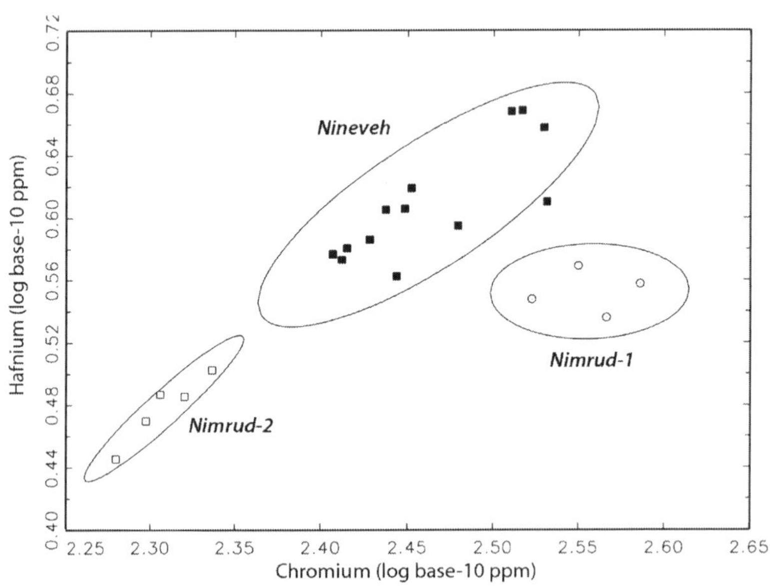

FIGURE 3.42 *Principal component analysis revealing three chemical compositional groups: Nineveh, Nimrud-1 & Nimrud-2.*
FIGURE COURTESY OF J. SPEAKMAN.

guild which supplied Palace Ware to the palace and another which supplied Palace Ware to the temples? Alternatively, did one workshop specialise in form A Palace Ware bowls while the other manufactured form B and C cups and jars? These are important questions that can only be answered by a more comprehensive archaeological, geochemical and petrographic analysis of Palace Ware from Nimrud and throughout the Central Polity.

Palace Ware Function

Determining the practical function and/or social function of archaeological ceramics is complicated, particularly when organic residue and phytolith analyses to determine vessel contents are not possible. In this section, we isolate and evaluate the practical function of Palace Ware, without the aid of residue or phytolith analysis, by focusing on performance characteristics, such as size, permeability and shape.

Palace Ware vessels do not have obvious indicators of practical function, such as pouring lips, spouts, strainers or handles. All three Palace Ware forms are unrestricted vessels with outward flaring rims—a feature not indicative of or conducive with fastening a lid or closure. The moderate to high vitrification of their ceramic bodies would render Palace Ware vessels impermeable. However, their relatively small capacities and thin, delicate walls limits their usefulness as transport or storage vessels for bulk liquids or grains.

Four form B and one form C vessel in the study assemblage from the Central Polity were crusted with a black resinous substance (figure 3.43a) suggesting that they may have been used to transport expensive substances, such as refined oils, resins or perfumes. Three of these vessels are also stained with blackish drips, as if dark fluid from inside the vessel dripped onto the external surface during or after being poured (figure 3.43b). Freestone and Hughes (1989) suggest that a Palace Ware-style vessel imported from the Central Polity to Khirbet Qasrij, dating to the Late Assyrian period, was lined with bitumen to 'waterproof' the vessel for the transport of liquids. However, the vitrified ceramic body of Palace Ware vessels would render any additional 'waterproofing' unnecessary. In addition, the resinous substance is 'caked', generally in the vessel base, rather than coated on the inside of Palace Ware vessel walls, suggesting that the resinous substance was mixed with or was itself the intended content of the vessel.

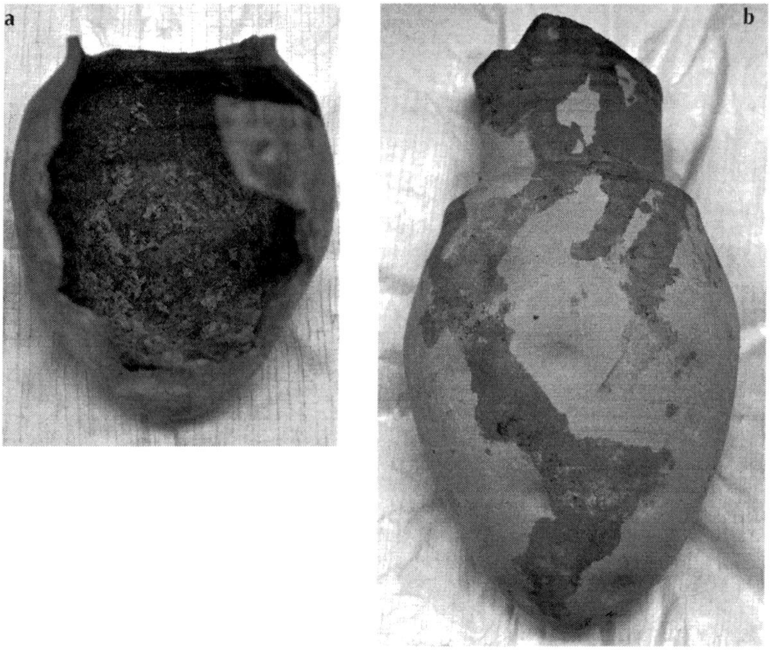

FIGURE 3.43 *Photographs of resinous encrustation on Palace Ware interior surfaces (a) and dripped down their external faces (b).*

The function and form of Mesopotamian ceramics are, generally, related to their contents (Potts 1997). Compare, for example, the archaic logogram and Sumerogram for 'beer' (*kaš*) and 'cereal ration' (*ninda*) and the associated ceramic forms (figure 3.44). The archaic logograms for the Akkadian words 'oil' (*šamnu*) and 'resin' (*erēšu*), like the logogram for 'beer', depict vessels with pointed. According to Waetzoldt (1970–1971), the Sumerian word ^{dug}*šagan* 'oil jar' refers to a biconical vessel with a pointed base, similar in shape to Palace Ware form B and C jars. The similarity in overall shape and resinous residue found in some Palace Ware jars suggests that they may have stored oils, resins or perfumes. However, a third liquid, wine, is also associated with biconical vessels with pointed bases.

'Wine' (*geštin*) first appears in the cuneiform literature in the 3rd millennium, and so 'wine' does not have an archaic logogram (Powell 1996). The Sumerogram for 'wine' (figure 3.45), from which the Akkadian word *karānu* is rendered, is a curious sharp-pointed, inverted chevron with a small rectangle above it: a stylised biconical vessel with a pointed base? The Akkadian *karānu* can be translated 'wine', 'grape' or 'grapevine', suggesting that the biconical,

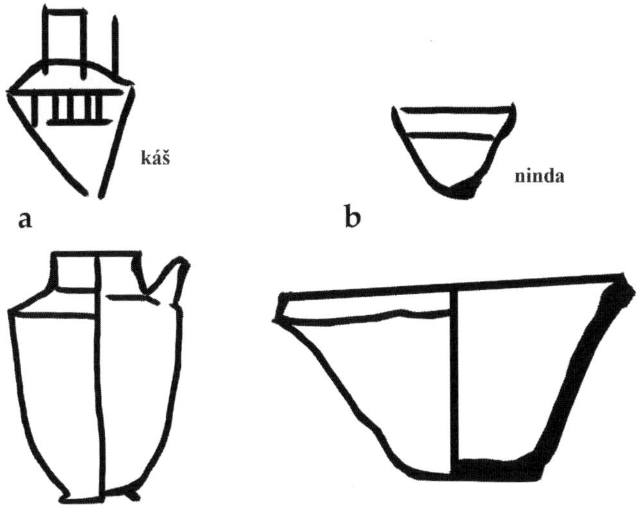

FIGURE 3.44 *Archaic cuneiform logograms & Sumerograms for (a) beer and (b) cereal ration with their associated ceramic forms.*
REDRAWN FROM NISSEN, DAMEROW & ENGLUND 1990; PONGRATZ-LEISTEN 1988; LABAT 1976; DELOUGAZ 1952.

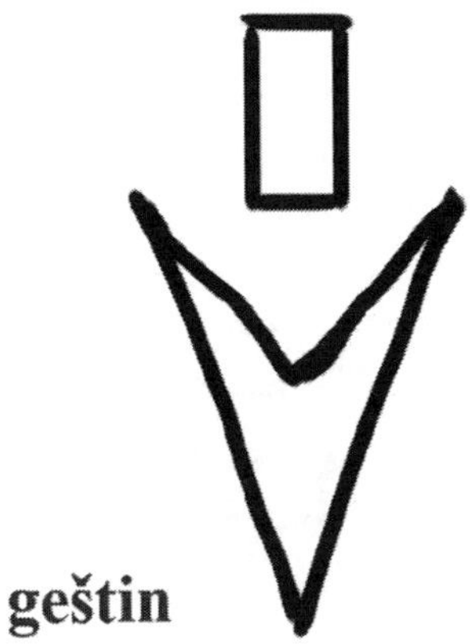

FIGURE 3.45
Sumerogram for wine.
REDRAWN FROM LABAT 1976.

pointed vessel depicted in the Sumerogram was used for grape rather than barley or date wine. If Palace Ware vessels were used to hold wine, the resinous residue caked inside several form B and C jars may have been added as a preservative to slow down the oxidation process and help retard grape wine from turning to vinegar.

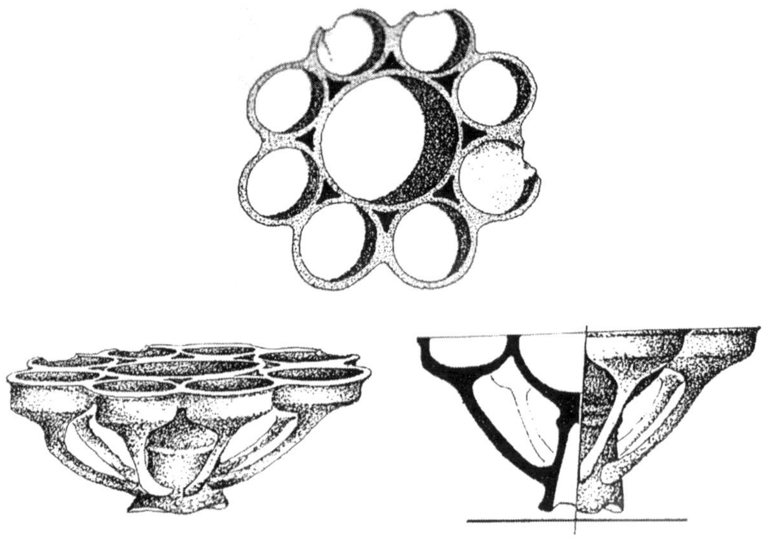

FIGURE 3.46 *Ceramic stand from the Queens' tomb at Nimrud.* REPRINTED WITH PERMISSION OF THE BRITISH INSTITUTE FOR THE STUDY OF IRAQ FROM HUSSEIN 2008, FIGURE 12.

A Late Assyrian palace relief from Nineveh illustrates a biconical jar, similar in shape to a Palace Ware form C jar, supported by a ring stand (figure 6.2) A ceramic ring stand was excavated at Nimrud (Hussein 2008) which appears to support one large vessel and eight smaller vessels (figure 3.46). Calculating the size of the stand from the published drawing, the large central support has a diameter of 12 cm and a jar depth of 4.6 cm, and the eight smaller supports have diameters of 5 cm and jar depths of 2.6 cm. Form B vessels have an average maximum diameter of 7.4 cm which tapers downward to a point. The body diameter of form B vessels is approximately 5 cm between 2–3 cm above the base, which means form B vessels could fit into the eight small supports. The average maximum diameter of form C vessels is 10 cm—too small to fit into the large central support, even at its maximum diameter. Form C jars may instead have been supported by the individual ring stands depicted in the cylinder seals, a compound stand with a smaller central support or had another function altogether. However, given the similarity in shape between form B and C vessels it is probable that they served related practical functions.

A relief from Nineveh depicts Assurbanipal feasting or at least drinking with his queen-consort Aššur-šarrat (figure 6.2). The queen is holding a vessel with a similar shape to a form A Palace Ware bowl. It is possible, therefore, that form

A vessels were also used to consume a beverage. However, there is very little additional archaeological or iconographic evidence for the practical function Palace Ware form A bowls.

Palace Ware forms A and B, and probably form C, appear to have functioned as drinking vessels which suggests that they held beer or wine rather than oil. This practical function is consistent with their shape, size, and impermeability. Forms B and C were probably used for the consumption of grape wine, however the beverage consumed out of form A vessels is less clear. Without gas chromatography-mass spectrometry (GC-MS) analysis to evaluate the contents of Palace Ware vessels, we cannot further define their practical function. However, given the general practical function of form B jars as drinking vessels and their relatively small size, we believe they were held in the hand and can be classified as cups.

Palace Ware Consumption

One of the ways we can evaluate changes in the social function, value and symbolic meaning of Palace Ware across the Neo-Assyrian imperial landscape is by investigating changes in its consumption patterns, both in terms of where Palace Ware was consumed and the relative consumption of forms. One of the challenges with a comparative analysis of Palace Ware consumption is the disparity in contextual information available for these vessels in the Central Polity, the Annexed Provinces and the Unincorporated Territories. Information about Palace Ware consumption in the Central Polity is biased. Until excavation of the lower tels and residential contexts are as extensively excavated as the upper tels and public or official contexts, we need to be careful about how we use contextual information. What we can say for certain is that Palace Ware was consumed simultaneously at Nimrud, Nineveh and Aššur.

Palace Ware from Nimrud was excavated in primary public and official contexts, such as reception rooms in the North-west palace, Governor's palace and the Nabu temple, and private contexts, such as houses, burials and the residential quarters of the North-west palace. No contextual information is available for the Palace Ware vessels from Nineveh, however Palace Ware from Aššur was also excavated in public or official contexts, such as the Anu and Adad temple, but primarily was recovered from secondary private contexts, specifically burials. The Neo-Assyrian residences at Aššur also yielded several Palace Ware vessels, however, to date, these have not been published and were unavailable for study (*cf.* Rijad 2002).

In terms of Palace Ware consumption by form, form B jars predominate the assemblages from Nimrud and Nineveh, representing 74% and 100% of the total population respectively. At Nimrud, form B vessels are found in both public and private contexts, including burials, but the majority of the population (79%) comes from primary public/official contexts. Form A bowls are also present at Nimrud, generally in primary public or official contexts, although two bowls were recovered from a private residence of a court official on the upper tel. A possible explanation for the low consumption of form A vessels at Nimrud and Nineveh is that metal form A vessels were more commonly used in the Central Polity than ceramic form A bowls (see discussion in chapter 6).

Form A vessels are more prevalent at Aššur, where they constitute 32% of the Palace Ware population, and come from burial contexts. In fact, 80% of the Palace Ware population from Aššur comes from private burials dating to the Late Assyrian period, which may explain why such a variety of forms was recovered at this site. All of the form C jars in this study were excavated at Aššur and, like the form B jars from this site, come primarily from secondary burial contexts with only a single form C vessel and 4 form B vessels recovered from the Anu and Adad temple (Andrae 1909). Table 3.4 summarises Palace Ware consumption patterns in the Neo-Assyrian Central Polity.

TABLE 3.4 *Palace Ware consumption patterns in the Neo-Assyrian Central Polity*

	Primary Context		**Secondary Context**	
	Public (temple, palace, etc.)	**Private (residence, etc.)**	**Public (midden, fill, etc.)**	**Private (burial, etc.)**
Nimrud				
Form A	3	2		
Form B	11	1		2
Form C				
Aššur				
Form A				8
Form B	4			2
Form C	1			10

Definitional Criteria for Palace Ware Classification

To summarise, Palace Ware vessels are wheel-thrown and subsequently thinned with a rib by turning to approximately 0.2 cm thick, have a homogeneous fabric, and are made from local alluvial sediment which has been refined by sedimentation to its current fineness and sorting of particles ≤ 0.05 mm and < 2% total inclusions. Vessels are fired to approximately 1050–1100°C, producing a moderate to highly vitrified ceramic body which is olive (5Y 6/3) to buff (2.5Y 8/2) in colour. The high firing temperature and requisite fuel consumption and careful manufacture of these vessels suggests that Palace Ware was expensive to produce and, therefore, probably had a different social value than common or tablewares. Palace Ware vessels are unrestricted typically with unequal biconical bodies; the exception being form C2 vessels which have globular bodies.

Formal and fabric characteristics for Palace Ware classification in the field and laboratory based on morphometric, typological and fabric analysis of Palace Ware from the Neo-Assyrian core are as follows:

Field Classification

Form A

unequal, biconical, unrestricted horizontal bodies
outcurving, horizontal everted rim with rounded lip
incurving neck possible
rounded or flat base
possible incised lines or ridged decoration
vessel walls 0.15–0.35 cm (mode 0.30 cm)
2.5–4.0 cm in height
maximum diameter 9–14 cm
average capacity 500 mL
colour 2.5Y7/2–2.5Y8/3 and 5Y7/2–5Y8/3

Form B

unequal, biconical, unrestricted vertical bodies
outcurving, horizontal everted rim with thinned or rounded lip
incurving neck 2.5–5.5 cm in length
pointed base most frequent but may also be rounded, knob, ring or disc
possible decorative motifs include registers of dimples, incised lines and/or moulded rings
vessel walls 0.15–0.30 cm (mode 0.20 cm)

7.6–14.8 cm in height
maximum diameter 4.0–9.7 cm
average capacity for form B1 400 mL and 700 mL for forms B2 and B3
colour 2.5Y7/2–2.5Y8/3 and 5Y7/2–5Y8/3

Form C

unequal, biconical, unrestricted vertical bodies, form C2 jars have globular bodies
outcurving, horizontal everted rim with thinned or slightly thickened lip
incurving neck 2.5–7.2 cm in length
flat base most frequent but may also be rounded, knob, ring or disc
possible decorative motifs include registers of dimples, incised lines and/or moulded rings
vessel walls 0.20–0.35 cm (mode 0.25 cm)
10.0–20.5 cm in height
maximum diameter 8.8–11.5 cm
average capacity 1.5 L and 3 L
colour 2.5Y7/2–2.5Y8/3 and 5Y7/2–5Y8/3

Laboratory Classification

fine grained fabric, mineral inclusions ≤ 0.05 mm and < 2% total inclusions
very well sorted inclusions, sub-rounded to well-rounded and spherical to discoidal
igneous and volcanic mineralogy, primarily metal oxides (haematite, rutile, magnetite, sphene, spinel), heavy detrital minerals (monazite-xenotime, baryte-celestite, zircon, epidote, apatite), and common silicates (quartz, amphibole, plagioclase and mica)
calcareous fabric, approximately 10–15% CaO
moderate vitrification with merging mineral phases and fine bloating pores common and less common coarse bloating pores

CHAPTER 4

Palace Ware from the Annexed Provinces: Dur-Katlimmu & Guzana

As discussed in chapter 2, core-periphery models of empire, while convenient, are not consistent with Neo-Assyrian imperial ideology, nor do they reflect the complexity of the political relationships established and maintained during the Late Assyrian period. Arguably, the etic nature of the models is not sufficient cause, in and of itself, to abandon them, however the terminology is problematic. 'Peripheral' implies marginality. As we have seen, the non-central provinces in the Neo-Assyrian empire are both powerful and important political and economic entities, therefore, we avoid even an unconscious association with subordination. Annexed, the term adopted in this study, is perhaps a more accurate description of these non-central provinces because not all provinces were ceded to the empire through treaty. The implication imbedded in the term 'annexed' is one of inclusion into a more powerful, but not necessarily larger, entity rather than inferiority; a more accurate reflection of Neo-Assyrian foreign relationships.

When selecting a site or sites from among the Annexed Provinces it is important that the site be: (a) positively and indisputably identified as occupied during the Late Assyrian period; (b) that the site be excavated rather than simply surveyed; and (c) that the material culture from the site be available for analysis. Although many excavated sites are within the identified Neo-Assyrian Annexed Provinces, most are in modern Turkey, Syria, Lebanon, and Iran, which makes it difficult to find sites which meet all of the above criteria. Dur-Katlimmu, modern Tall Šēḫ Ḥamad, and Guzana, modern Tell Halaf, were selected to represent the Annexed Provinces because they both met the selection criteria and served as Neo-Assyrian provincial capitals.

Palace Ware from a coastal province would have been an ideal addition to this study. Unfortunately, Palace Ware from the capital city of the Neo-Assyrian province Magiddû (Meggiddo), excavated in the early 20th century, has been lost and, therefore, unavailable for study. We hoped the recent excavations at Ashdod-North, in the Neo-Assyrian province of Asdudu, conducted by the Israel Antiquities Authority, would yield Palace Ware. However, when we examined the ceramic assemblage, no Assyrian-style vessels were present. One possible piece of Palace Ware from the Ashdod province was excavated at Ekron

 | DOI 10.1163/9789004304123_005

(Gitin 1997, figure 12). However, this vessel was misplaced and unavailable for analysis. Published Assyrian-style ceramics from Dor have been interpreted as Palace Ware (*e.g.* Gilboa 1996), which is interesting since Dor was never annexed into the Neo-Assyrian administrative structure (Radner 2006; however confer Na'aman 2009). Our examination of the Assyrian-style vessels at Dor did not reveal Palace Ware in the assemblage and the Assyrian-style vessels were not available for detailed and/or destructive analysis.

The Palace Ware populations from Dur-Katlimmu and Guzana, were identified as Palace Ware in the field according to Oates' definition (1959). Palace Ware from Dur-Katlimmu comes from the monumental structure referred to as the Red House rather than from the Neo-Assyrian residences, and was previously published by Kreppner (2006) as 'ware B'. Since the majority of these vessels are housed in Syria, in a number of cases we were required to work from the published drawings, which are detailed and to-scale, photographs and measurements taken by Kreppner. This means that while our information about the Dur-Katlimmu assemblage is relatively complete, we do not have all measurements from every vessel and, as a result, the number of cases for each attribute analysis may vary from the total number of vessels in the Palace Ware assemblage.

Palace Ware from Guzana, housed in the Vorderasiatisches Museum, is composed primarily of complete vessels. It was not possible to take samples for petrographic and chemical analysis and so, our study of the Palace Ware from Guzana does not include fabric characterisation or a discussion of raw material provenance. Since fabric fineness is one of the key definitional criteria for classifying vessels as Palace Ware, we were unable to conclusively identify these vessels are Palace Ware. However, we were able to conduct a complete morphometric and typological analysis to assess whether their form, shape and style are consistent with Palace Ware from the Central Polity. Several of the vessels are incomplete, and so the number of cases in a given attribute analysis may vary.

Dur-Katlimmu

Dur-Katlimmu was located in the Rasapa (Nergal-eresh) province of the Neo-Assyrian empire until the reign of Tiglath-pileser III in the late 8th century when, to redistribute power in an attempt to stabilise the southern empire, Rasapa was divided and Dur-Katlimmu became part of the Laqe province (map 4.1) (Radner 2002). The city itself served as a provincial capital during the

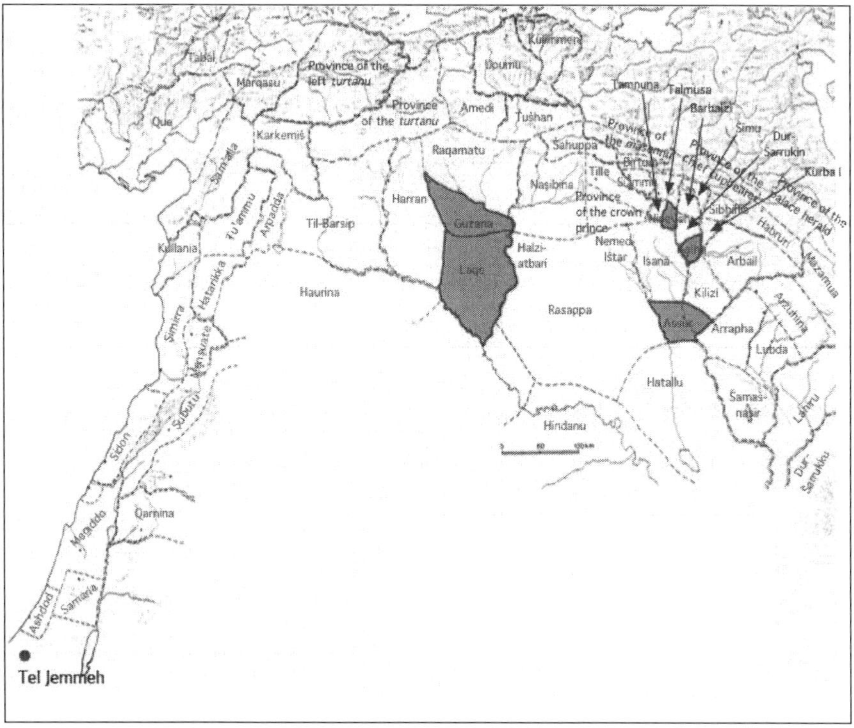

MAP 4.1 *Map of the Neo-Assyrian provincial system. Provinces included in this study are highlighted.*
AFTER RADNER 2006, KARTE 2, 3, 4.

Middle Assyrian period, housing a regional governor and cuneiform archive, and, during the Late Assyrian period, the role of Dur-Katlimmu was probably that of an administrative, if not provincial, capital (Kühne and Luther 1998). Cuneiform evidence also suggests that during the Late Assyrian period Dur-Katlimmu also functioned as a garrison for elite imperial chariot troops, their equipment, and horses (Kühne 2010).

Dur-Katlimmu was 'discovered' in 1879 when local workman engaged in a construction project near the site unearthed fragments of an Adad-nirari III stele (Kühne 1996). The site was subsequently excavated by Rassam, however, the results of this work are unpublished. Systematic large scale excavation of the site did not begin until 1975, under the direction of Wolfgang Röllig from the Eberhard Karls Universität Tübingen (*ibid.*). In 1978, direction of the excavation passed to Hartmut Kühne of the Freie Universität Berlin, under whose leadership it remains today. Excavation of Dur-Katlimmu is ongoing and, therefore, information about the site is continually growing, changing and being reinterpreted in light of new data.

The site itself is located in Syria on the left bank of the Ḥābūr river, a tributary of the Euphrates, about 230 km west of Aššur. Two wadis, Sa'ib Óamad and Garibe, supply additional water to the city and supported its thriving agriculture through an extensive canal system (Pucci 2010). During the Late Assyrian period, the city expanded to include 60 hectares of intramural and 50 hectare of suburban settlement housing more than 7,000 people within and without the 4 km city wall (Kühne 2008).

The 3 hectare citadel is located in the south surrounded by a fortified wall, 25 m above the river basin. The citadel at Dur-Katlimmu has not been extensively published, and therefore little is known about its occupation during the Late Assyrian period. However, during the Middle Assyrian period the citadel housed administrative palaces and archives, including the palace of Aššur-iddin, Royal Vizier (Kühne 1996), and it is reasonable to assume similar public and monumental buildings were in use during the Late Assyrian period.

Most of our information about the Neo-Assyrian settlement of Dur-Katlimmu comes from the excavations of Lower Town II and the 'Assyrian Residences'. Although the Assyrian Residences have not yet been published, the adjacent Red House has been extensively studied (Kreppner 2006) and the cuneiform archives, including the library of Šulmu-šarri, have been published (Radner 2002).

Palace Ware analysed in the current study is courtesy of Kühne and comes from the Red House assemblage, previously published by Kreppner (2008; 2006). The excavators believe that the ceramics from the Red House were made and used by a local 'squatter' population after the fall of Assyria (the Neo-Assyrian empire) in 615 BCE rather than by the building's occupants during the Late Assyrian period. They argue cultural continuity between the two populations (*e.g.* Kreppner 2008), and regardless of whether the pottery at the Red House was manufactured and consumed by the local population during the Neo-Assyrian period or by the same population as squatters after the fall of the empire, the pottery at the Red House reflects the values of the local, Neo-Assyrian inhabitants of Dur-Katlimmu.

Twelve vessels were available for destructive and non-destructive analysis and an additional 15 vessels were available as morphometric drawings, since the political climate in Syria prevented our travel to Dur-Katlimmu to examine them in person.

Typology

In our analysis of Palace Ware from the Central Polity, we began with the quantitative morphometric analysis of vessels in order to identify patterns related

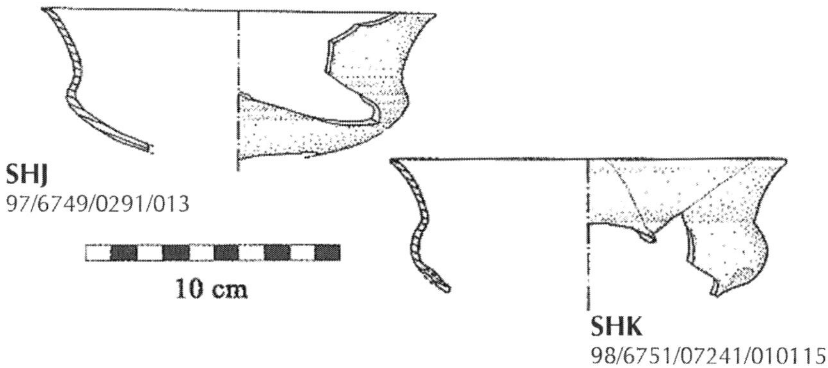

FIGURE 4.1 *Palace Ware form A bowls from Dur-Katlimmu.*
REPRINTED WITH PERMISSION FROM KREPPNER 2006, TAFEL 96.

to vessel form before assessing their typological characteristics. In our analysis of Palace Ware from the Annexed Provinces and Unincorporated Territories, we begin by separating the assemblages into preliminary groups based on typological criteria before confirming their type/form classification through morphometric analysis. We reverse this process outside of the Assyrian heartland intentionally because typological analysis is relatively quick and easy to do in the field, making it a logical first step for Palace Ware analysis. Since we intend these definitional criteria and classifications to be applied to other Palace Ware assemblages in the future, we designed our analysis to reflect the reality of field classification before laboratory analysis.

Form A

Only 2 vessels in the Palace Ware assemblage from the Annexed Provinces met the typological criteria for form A bowls (figure 4.1). Both vessels are unequal biconical, with incurving necks, out-curving, horizontal, everted rims and thinned lips, consistent with form A bowls from the Central Polity (figure 3.10). The basal elements of both vessels are missing; however their undecorated bodies are also consistent with Palace Ware form A bowls.

Both of these bowls are from Dur-Katlimmu, precluding regional stylistic analysis. However, comparative stylistic analysis between form A bowls from the Central Polity and Dur-Katlimmu reveals a consistent aesthetic or style for form A bowls from these two areas of the empire. Form A bowls without necks were not part of the Palace Ware assemblage from the Annexed Provinces, which may reflect: (a) the local preference at Dur-Katlimmu; (b) the sample size of form A vessels from the Annexed Provinces; or (c) that form A bowls with necks were more socially or symbolically significant in the Annexed Provinces than form A bowls without necks. A larger sample of form A vessels from a greater portion of the Annexed Provinces is necessary to evaluate these possibilities.

Form B

Eight vessels from Dur-Katlimmu (≥ 70% extant) are typologically consistent with Palace Ware form B cups with unequal biconical bodies, incurving necks, out-curving, horizontal, everted rims and thinned or rounded lips (figures 4.2–4.3). Like their Central Polity counterparts, form B cups from the Annexed Provinces have non-functional basal elements which range from pointed and rounded, to disk and knob, to a rather elaborate stepped design. Thirtyeight percent (3/8) of the form B population from Dur-Katlimmu is undecorated, compared to the 17% (2/12) undecorated form B vessels in the Central Polity; the remaining vessels in the form B population from Dur-Katlimmu are decorated with the dimples typical of form B and C vessels in the Assyrian heartland.

In the Palace Ware assemblage in the Central Polity, forms B1 and B2 are primarily differentiated typologically by the functional basal element of B1 cups (figures 3.12 and 3.13). Since none of the form B cups from the Annexed Provinces can stand on their bases, we are only able to differentiate forms B2 and B3 typologically.

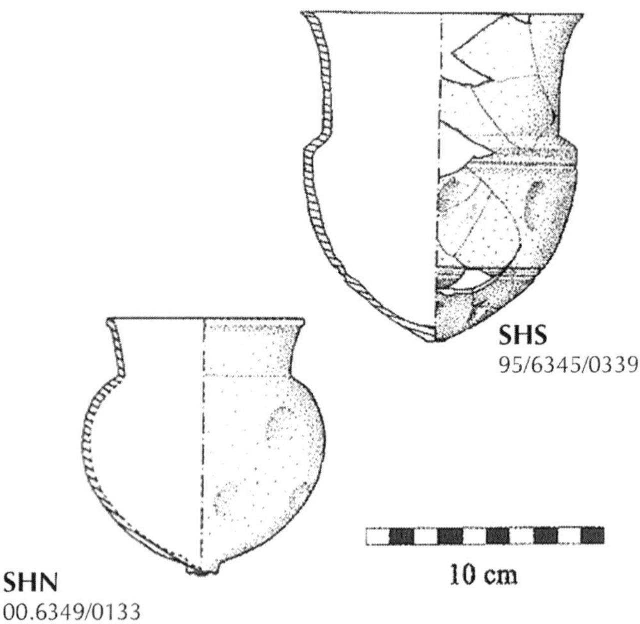

FIGURE 4.2 *Palace Ware form B2 cups from Dur-Katlimmu.*
REPRINTED WITH PERMISSION FROM KREPPNER 2006, TAFEL 97.

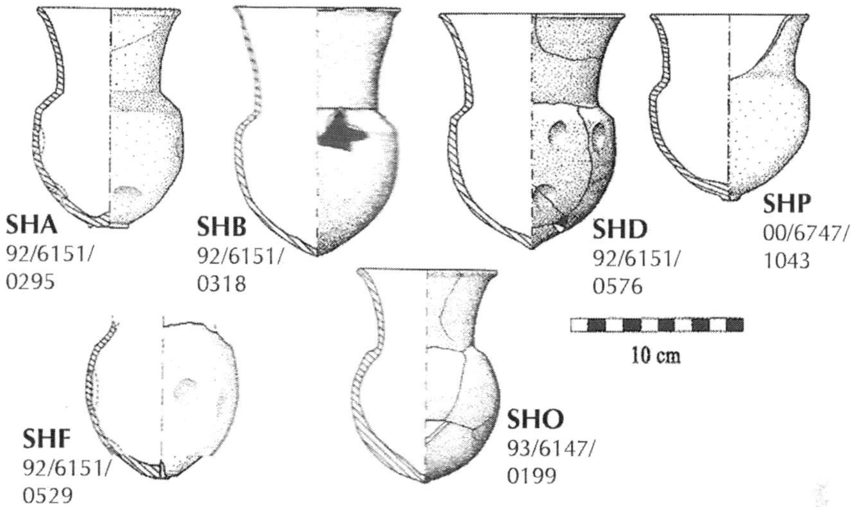

FIGURE 4.3 *Palace Ware form B3 cups from Dur-Katlimmu.*
REPRINTED WITH PERMISSION FROM KREPPNER 2006, TAFEL 11, 97, 98.

Two vessels from Dur-Katlimmu (SHN and SHS) are typologically consistent with Palace Ware form B2 cups from the Central Polity with dimpled bodies comprised of 2 rows of 3–9 dimples each and undecorated necks (figure 4.2). In addition to the two rows of dimples, vessel SHS also has 2 registers of 3 incised lines running just below the shoulder and between the rows of 'dimples. This decorative style is similar to vessel KH in the form B2 population from the Central Polity (figure 3.13). Like vessel KH, vessel SHS is the most elaborately decorated form B2 cup in its population.

Of the 6 form B3 cups from Dur-Katlimmu (figure 4.3), 3 are undecorated and 3 are decorated identical to the even split (50:50) between undecorated and decorated vessels found in the Central Polity B3 population (figure 3.14). The 3 decorated vessels have 2 rows of dimples, each containing 3–6 dimples, consistent with the decorated B3 cups from the Assyrian Core.

Form C

Twelve vessels in the Palace Ware assemblage from Dur-Katlimmu are typologically consistent with form C jars: primarily (67% or 8/12) unequal biconical with incurving necks, out-curving, horizontal everted rims with thinned or rounded lips (figure 4.4–4.6), similar in shape and style to Palace Ware form B cups and form C jars. Like their Central Polity counterparts, form C jars from the Annexed Provinces have non-functional basal elements, which range from pointed to stepped to disk to knob but do not include flat bases which are the most common type of basal element in the Central Polity form C population (55% or 6/11). The most common basal element in the form C population from Dur-Katlimmu is stepped (40% or 4/10), followed closely by disk bases (30%).

Form C jars in the Central Polity are fairly evenly split between undecorated and dimpled bodies, 55% and 45% respectively. At Dur-Katlimmu, the percentage of dimpled bodies to undecorated vessels is also fairly even, 58% (7/12) to 42% (5/12). Of the two types of neck decoration common to form C jars in the Central Polity, only the moulded ring decoration is present in the form C assemblage in the Annexed Provinces.

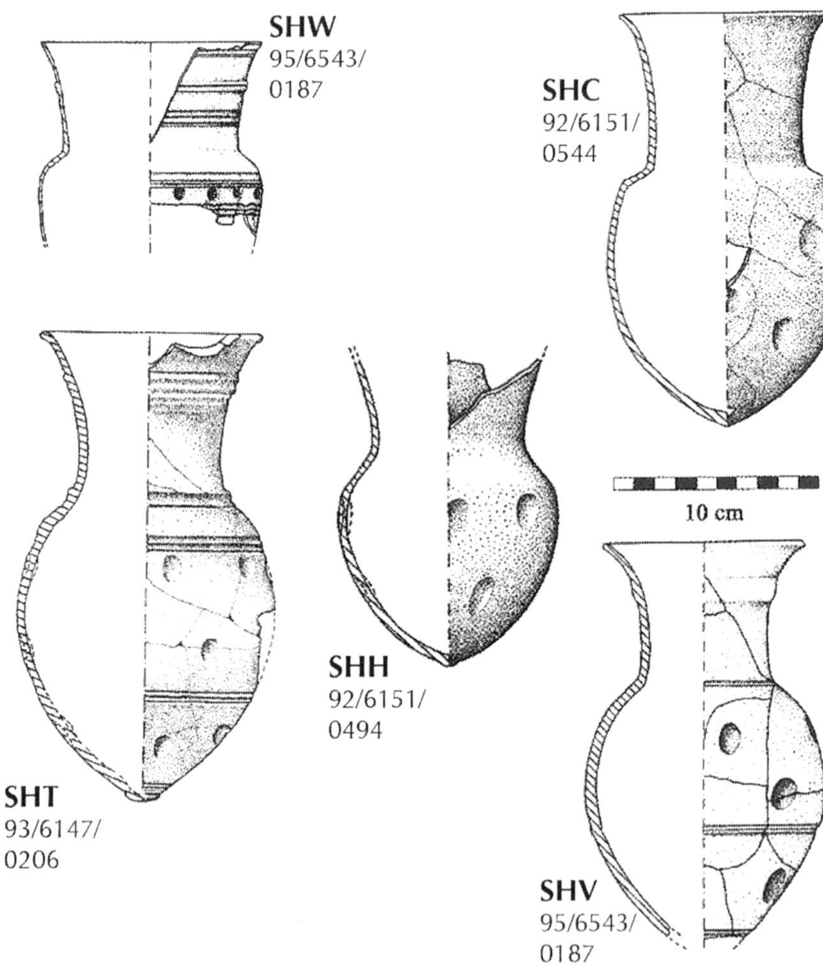

FIGURE 4.4 *Palace Ware form C1 jars from Dur-Katlimmu.*
REPRINTED WITH PERMISSION FROM KREPPNER 2006, TAFEL 11, 97, 98.

Five vessels from Dur-Katlimmu are typologically consistent with Palace Ware form C1 bowls (figure 4.4): 2 of these vessels are decorated with 3 rows of 5–8 dimples, while another 2 are decorated with 2 rows of 4–7 dimples, and 1 vessel (SHW) is too fragmentary to see more than a single row of dimples. Like their Central Polity counterparts, form C1 bowls in the Annexed Provinces are the most elaborately decorated vessels in the form C population. Of the 4 form C1 bowls with extant necks, only one (SHC) is undecorated. The other 3 vessels (SHT, SHV, and SHW) all have moulded rings decorating their necks; vessel SHV has a single moulded ring at the intersection of the neck and rim, while vessels SHT and SHW have more elaborate neck decorations consisting of 1–3 moulded rings with registers of 2–3 incised lines decorating them (figure 4.4). In addition to the neck decoration and dimples, vessels SHT, SHV and SHW also have 2–3 registers of 3 incised lines around their shoulders and between their rows of dimples. Registers of incised lines around the vessel body are not a decorative element associated with form C jars in the Central Polity where they typically manifest on form B1 and B2 cups (figures 3.12 and 3.13).

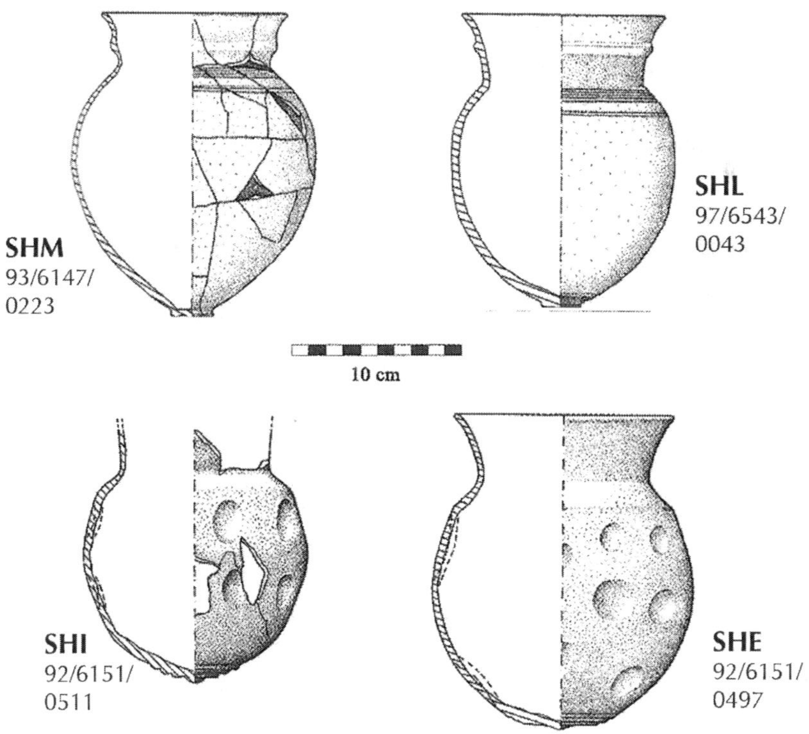

FIGURE 4.5 *Palace Ware form C2 jars from Dur-Katlimmu.*
REPRINTED WITH PERMISSION FROM KREPPNER 2006, TAFEL 11, 97.

Form C2 jars are globular, ovoid-upright in shape with rounded bases and undecorated bodies (figure 3.17). All 4 vessels from the Annexed Provinces form C assemblage that are globular, ovoid-upright in shape are from Dur-Katlimmu (figure 4.5). Unlike their Central Polity counterparts, these 4 vessels have decorated bodies and non-functional stepped or disk basal elements. Vessels SHE and SHI both have dimpled bodies with 3 and 2 rows of 4–6 dimples, respectively, and elaborate stepped bases. Vessels SHL and SHM are decorated with a thick register of 4–5 incised lines at the intersection of the neck and the body, and a smaller register of 2–3 incised lines around the vessel shoulder, and have non-functional disk bases. It is interesting that form C2 jars only occur in the form C population from Dur-Katlimmu and that 2 style variants are present within that population neither of which are consistent with the style of C2 jars from the Central Polity, although the decorative motifs are themselves undoubtedly Assyrian. These stylistic differences in the C2 population may reflect the local or regional aesthetic at Dur-Katlimmu or may indicate an intentional hyper-Assyrianisation of style.

No form C3 jars were identified in the Palace Ware assemblage from the Annexed Provinces.

Form C4 jars in the Central Polity have undecorated bodies, with non-functional pointed or rounded bases and 67% of the population (2/3) are decorated with moulded neck rings (figure 3.19). Three vessels in the form C population from Dur-Katlimmu are typologically similar to C4 jars with their undecorated bodies and moulded neck rings decorating 1 of the 2 vessels with extant necks (SHR) (figure 4.6). Vessel SHR also appears to have 2 incised lines running through its moulded neck ring, similar to those found on form C2 jars from Dur-Katlimmu. The basal elements for the form C4 vessels from Dur-Katlimmu range from stepped (SHQ) to knob (SHR) to pointed (SHY), only the latter of which is found in the Central Polity form C4 bowl population.

There are two potential regional trends in the form C population from the Dur-Katlimmu. Comparison between the form C assemblages from the Central Polity and Annexed Provinces in general reveal that form C vessels in the Annexed Provinces are more elaborately decorated than their counterparts in the Assyrian Heartland. Form C1, C2 and C4 vessels decorated with registers of incised lines are unique to Dur-Katlimmu; incised decorations are not associated with form C vessels in the Central Polity or, as we shall see, elsewhere in the Annexed Provinces. Second, the only C2 vessels in the form C assemblage from the Annexed Provinces are from Dur-Katlimmu, suggesting that the practical, social or symbolic function associated with this form was important for consumers of Palace Ware at Dur-Katlimmu but either unknown or unimportant at Guzana.

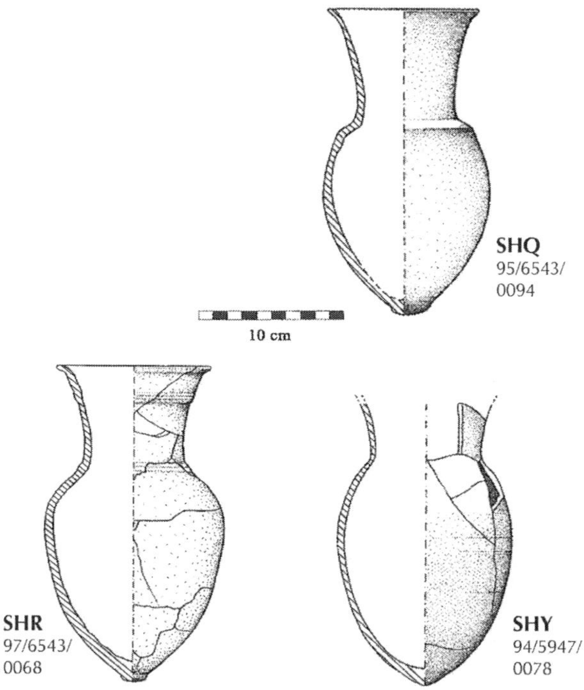

FIGURE 4.6 *Palace Ware form C4 jars from Dur-Katlimmu.* REPRINTED WITH PERMISSION FROM KREPPNER 2006, TAFEL 97, 98.

Morphometric Analysis

Form A

Like their Central Polity counterparts, form A bowls from Dur-Katlimmu are unrestricted-horizontal in shape. Despite their similarity in shape and style however, form A bowls from Dur-Katlimmu are subtly different in form from Central Polity vessels. For example, although the basal elements are missing from both vessels, SHJ, the more complete of the two (70% extant), stands 6.5 cm in height—2.5 cm higher than the tallest form A plate in the Central Polity. Vessel SHJ also has an estimated extant depth of 25%, which is deeper than the average form A plate from the Central Polity whose depth is < 20%. However, two Central Polity plates have depths of 22 and 23% and so it is possible that vessel SHJ is consistent with a deeper form A variant from the Central Polity. A larger sample of form A vessels from both the Central Polity and Annexed Provinces is necessary to confirm this hypothesis.

The maximum diameter of both form A vessels from Dur-Katlimmu is 16 cm, with neck lengths 2 cm and 2.5 cm, compared to maximum diameter measurements for form A Central Polity vessels which are 9–14 cm with neck lengths of 0.2–1.2 cm. The walls of the form A bowls from Dur-Katlimmu are 0.3 cm thick (mean = 0.28 cm; median = 0.3 cm; mode = 0.3 cm), the same as Central Polity bowls, and the estimated capacity of SHJ is 505 cm^3 which is within range of the definitional criteria for form A bowls.

The relationship among maximum, rim and neck diameter for form A bowls from Dur-Katlimmu is internally consistent (16 cm, 17.5 cm and 15 cm, respectively). However, the maximum diameter, rim diameter and neck diameter measurements for the vessels from Dur-Katlimmu are consistently larger that those in the Central Polity. For example, the rims of form A bowls from Dur-Katlimmu are 1.5 cm wider than the maximum diameter suggesting a subtle change in shape in the Annexed Provinces. Analysis of vessel curvature, however, reveals that Palace Ware form A bowls from the Annexed Provinces are consistent with one of the three trends found in the form A assemblage in the Central Polity: with neck angles 60° and 55° and shoulder angles 110° and 115° respectively.

These subtle morphometric variations in the form A population from Dur-Katlimmu do not significantly alter their shape or appearance. Therefore, since the form A bowls from Dur-Katlimmu meet the formal (shape and size) definitional criteria for Palace Ware and the definitional criteria for fabric, discussed below, we classify them as Palace Ware.

Form B

Form B cups from Dur-Katlimmu meet the basic morphometric definitional criteria for Palace Ware: they are unrestricted-vertical in shape, have walls 0.2–0.3 cm thick (mean = 0.24 cm, median = 0.2 cm, mode = 0.2 cm) and hold between 418–792 cm^3. Analysis of vessel curvature and the relationship among maximum, rim and neck diameters confirm the uniformity of shape between form B cups in the Central Polity and at Dur-Katlimmu. Vessels from Dur-Katlimmu have base angles between 22–38° (mean = 32°, median = 33°, no mode available), shoulder angles between 132–142° (mean = 137°, median = 139°, mode = 140°), and neck angles between 66–88° (mean = 75°, median = 76°, mode = 76°); consistent with base, shoulder and neck angles from Central Polity form B cups. Similarly, form B cups from Dur-Katlimmu cluster with Central Polity form B Palace Ware cups on a Sneed and Folk diagram of maximum, rim and neck diameter (figure 4.7). However, the relationship among these variables at Dur-Katlimmu does not exhibit the clear trends detected in the Assyrian Core; of the 7 vessels for which these measurements were available, 29% (2/7) exhibited a X:X-1:X-2 relationship among them and the remaining 5 vessels each displayed a different relationship (X:X:X-1, X:X:X-2, X:X-1:X-3,

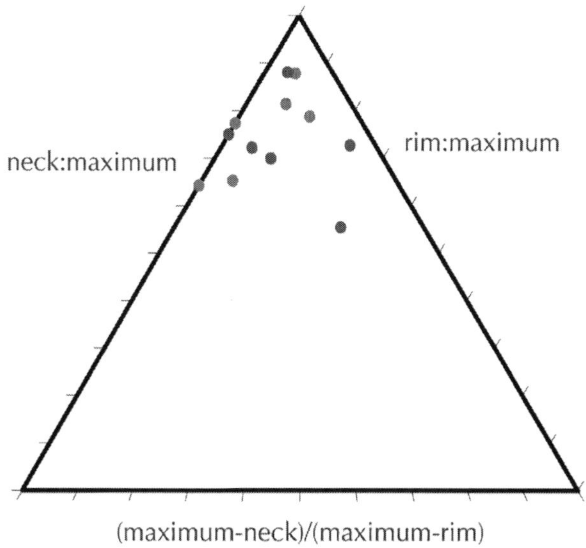

FIGURE 4.7 *Sneed & Folk ternary diagram comparing Palace Ware form B rim, neck & maximum diameters from Dur-Katlimmu (black) and the Central Polity (grey).*

X:X-2:X-3, X:X-2:X-4). As in the Central Polity, the difference between these measurements is typically ≤ 1 cm, although it can be as great as 1.5 cm in the Annexed Provinces, and therefore, can be accounted for as the natural variability inherent in the manufacture of a single form by multiple potters.

However, form B cups from Dur-Katlimmu are subtly taller (height = 10–16 cm), wider (maximum diameter = 9–13.5 cm), have longer necks (neck length = 2–6 cm) and are shallower than their Central Polity counterparts (depth = 40–60% for 38% of the population 80–100% for 62% but no vessels > 100%). While these subtle differences do not affect the overall shape or appearance of the form B vessels from Dur-Katlimmu, they make morphometric classification and confirmation of formal variants difficult. As discussed in chapter 3, we consider 1.56 cm our acceptable margin of error for morphometric classification of Palace Ware.

The three formal variants of Palace Ware form B cups are described morphometrically as follows (adapted from table 3.1):

formal variant	body length	capacity	neck length
B1	4–6 cm	300–450 cm^3	3 cm
B2	7–8 cm	500–900 cm^3	2.5–3 cm
B3	8–10 cm	500–900 cm^3	4.5–5 cm

Five vessels in the form B population from Dur-Katlimmu have capacities < 500 cm^3: SHA, SHB, SHD, SHN, SHO. However, none of them have body or neck lengths consistent with form B1 cups. These 5 vessels were classified typologically as form B2 (SHN) and form B3 (SHA, SHB, SHD, SHO) cups. Vessel SHN has a body 8 cm long and a neck 2 cm long, consistent with form B2 vessels in the Central Polity, and a capacity of 470 cm^3. The 4 form B3 vessels have body lengths between 8–10 cm, neck lengths between 5–6 cm, consistent with form B3 vessels in the Central Polity, but capacities between 455–487 cm^3, except for vessel SHO which has a capacity of 419 cm^3.

MRPP analyses of capacity against body length for the form B2 and B3 populations from the Central Polity and Annexed Provinces indicates that they are from the same statistical population of origin (B2: $\delta_{obs} = 1.57$; $\delta_{exp} = 1.54$; p-value = 0.53; B3: $\delta_{obs} = 1.15$; $\delta_{exp} = 1.56$; p-value = 0.0082). Therefore, we classify vessel SHN as a Palace Ware form B2 cup and vessels SHA, SHB, SHD, SHO as Palace Ware form B3 cups despite their smaller capacities.

In addition to vessel SHN, vessel SHS was also classified as form B2 cups based on typological criteria. SHS meets the morphometric definitional criteria for Palace Ware form B2 cups: body length 10 cm, capacity 793 cm^3, and neck length 5.5 cm.

The 2 remaining vessels classified typologically as form B3 cups, SHF and SHP, like vessels SHA, SHB, SHD and SHO, have bodies 8–10 cm long and neck lengths 5–6 cm, consistent with the morphometric definitional criteria for form B3 Palace Ware cups. The capacities of these vessels are also consistent with B3 cups from the Central Polity ranging from 624 cm^3 to 880 cm^3.

With the exception of the form B2 and B3 cups from Dur-Katlimmu with capacities < 500 cm^3, no regional morphometric trends were observed in the Palace Ware form B population.

Form C

Form C jars from Dur-Katlimmu meet several of the general definitional morphometric criteria for Palace Ware form C jars: they are unrestricted-vertical in shape, have necks 2.5–8 cm long, and walls 0.2–0.3 cm thick (mean = 0.3 cm, median = 0.3 cm, mode = 0.3 cm). The overall height of Dur-Katlimmu form C jars (16–25 cm), however, differs from those in the Central Polity by more than the acceptable 1.56 cm margin of error; of the two components of vessel height, neck length and body length, only neck length is within the acceptable range of variance. The maximum diameters of form C jars from Dur-Katlimmu (11–15.5 cm) are also significantly larger than their Central Polity counterparts; the difference between the widest form C bowl from the Central Polity and Dur-Katlimmu is close to 4 cm. Together the larger maximum diameter

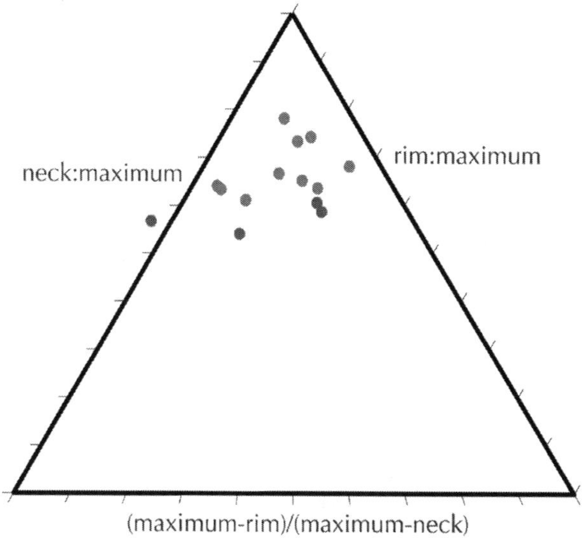

FIGURE 4.8 *Sneed & Folk ternary diagram comparing Palace Ware form C rim, neck & maximum diameters from Dur-Katlimmu (black) and the Central Polity (grey).*

and longer body length indicate a formal variant unique to Dur-Katlimmu or less precision during the manufacture of form C vessels in the Annexed Provinces, possibly related to local production by local potters. However, if this difference in vessel form were related to manufacture of Palace Ware by local potters, we would expect to see similar formal variation in the Palace Ware bowl and cup populations at Dur-Katlimmu. The fact that we do not, suggests that these alterations are intentional, possibly related to a change in their social or semiotic function at Dur-Katlimmu.

The relationship among maximum, rim and neck diameter in the form C population at Dur-Katlimmu exhibits similar behaviour to that observed in the Central Polity form C population (figure 4.8), although clear trends in the relationship among these variables were not detected. Analysis of vessel curvature confirms the uniformity of vessel shape between form C jars from Dur-Katlimmu and Central Polity: base angle 20–42° (mean = 32°, median = 31°, mode = 42°), shoulder angle 126–143° (mean = 134°, median = 134°, mode = 136°), and neck angle 70–86° (mean = 77°, median = 75°, mode = 86°). These results suggest that the variation in maximum diameter is not related to an intentional alteration in vessel shape.

Form C bowl capacities from Dur-Katlimmu are unexpected, ranging from 538–1967 cm^3 rather than the 1200–3000 cm^3 observed in the Central Polity.

There are three capacity clusters in the Dur-Katlimmu form C population: (a) 538–751 cm^3; (b) 1049–1060 cm^3; and (c) 1207–1967 cm^3. In the Palace Ware assemblage from the Central Polity vessels with capacities in the 'a' range would be classified as form B cups and no Palace Ware vessel, regardless of form, has capacity measurements approximating 1 litre, range 'b'. This suggests that either the form C vessels from Dur-Katlimmu with capacities in the 'a' or 'b' range are not Palace Ware; that the capacity specific definitional criteria observed in the Central Polity assemblage are not observed or adhered to as strictly by potters at Dur-Katlimmu; or that the consumers of Palace Ware at Dur-Katlimmu required several form C size variants not found/required in the Central Polity.

In support of the latter, form C jars from Dur-Katlimmu are the same depth as their Central Polity counterparts with depths >100%. While the subtle morphometric differences between form C Palace Ware jars from the Central Polity and Dur-Katlimmu do not affect the overall shape and appearance of the vessels, they make morphometric classification and confirmation of formal variants C1, C2, C3 and C4 difficult.

The four formal variants for Palace Ware form C jars are described morphometrically as follows (adapted from table 3.1):

formal variant	body length	capacity	neck length
C1	8–10 cm	1250–1840 cm^3	2.5–3 cm
C2	13.5–14 cm	2800–3050 cm^3	2.7–3 cm
C3	8–10 cm	1250–1840 cm^3	5–6.5 cm
C4	13–13.5 cm	1400–2300 cm	6.5–7.4 cm

The 5 vessels from Dur-Katlimmu typologically classified as form C1 bowls have body lengths between 11–17 cm, capacities between 537–1967 cm^3 and necks 5.5–8.0 cm long. Of the vessels for which capacity measurements were available, only one vessel (SHT) had a capacity within the expected range, measuring 1967 cm^3. The body and neck lengths of SHT, however, are longer than expected for form C1 jars and fall outside the 1.56 cm acceptable margin for inherent variation. The remaining form C1 jars (SHC, SHG, SHH and SHV) have capacity measurements between 538–1056 cm^3, significantly smaller than C1 jars from the Central Polity, and yet they also have body and neck lengths longer than Central Polity jars and outside the acceptable margin of variability.

The 4 vessels classified typologically as form C2 jars, SHE, SHI, SHL and SHM, have bodies 12.5–13.5 cm long and neck lengths 2.5–3 cm, consistent with the expected morphometric criteria for Palace Ware form C2 jars. However, their capacity measurements are significantly smaller than expected: 1060–1545 cm^3 rather than 2800–3050 cm^3.

A similar phenomenon of compliance and non-compliance with expected morphometric patterns is observed in the typologically form C4 population from Dur-Katlimmu. The 3 vessels in this population (SHR, SHY and SHQ) have capacities smaller than expected, 1381, 1226 and 674 cm^3 respectively, but SHR and SHY have body lengths significantly longer than expected, 16 cm each, and SHQ, the smallest vessel, has a body length within the acceptable range. The neck lengths of SHR and SHQ are both within the acceptable range for form C4 jars measuring 8 and 6.5 cm respectively: the neck of SHY is incomplete.

MRPP analysis of capacity against body length for the form C1, C2 and C4 populations from the Central Polity and Dur-Katlimmu indicate that they are from the same statistical population of origin: C1—$\delta_{obs} = 1.27$; $\delta_{exp} = 1.55$; p-value = 0.012; C2—$\delta_{obs} = 0.85$; $\delta_{exp} = 1.51$; p-value = 0.012; C4—$\delta_{obs} = 1.48$; $\delta_{exp} = 1.59$; p-value = 0.248). Therefore, we classify the C1, C2 and C4 vessels from Dur-Katlimmu as Palace Ware despite their morphometric differences.

In the Central Polity, Palace Ware is distinguished from the greater Assyrian ceramic assemblage by its thin walls (0.15–0.3 cm), fine fabric ($f{:}c_{0\cdot062mm}$ = 98:2), and restricted capacity. The form C population from Dur-Katlimmu meets the definitional criteria for Palace Ware wall thinness and, as will be discussed below, vessels from Dur-Katlimmu also meet the criteria for fabric fineness. However, the form C vessels from Dur-Katlimmu are not discontinuous in terms of capacity, nor are they restricted to the expected range of 1200–3000 cm^3. One possible explanation for this discrepancy is that the social function or factors which necessitated the restricted vessel capacities for form C jars in the Central Polity were not operational or at least not essential for the consumption of these vessels in the Annexed Provinces and/or at Dur-Katlimmu. Another possible explanation is that the discontinuity in vessel capacity observed in the Central Polity form C vessels is an artefact of sampling: the entire form C assemblage came from burial contexts in Aššur.

Chaîne Opératoire

Raw Materials Processing

Geological Raw Materials & Processing

Potential ceramic raw material at Dur-Katlimmu comes from alluvial deposition by the Ḫābūr river and/or the Wadis Sa'ib Hamad and Garība in the Lower Ḫābūr region of Syria. Unfortunately, we were unable to acquire samples from these potential raw material sources. Instead, we used the extensive geological, chemical and geomorphological analysis of the region surrounding

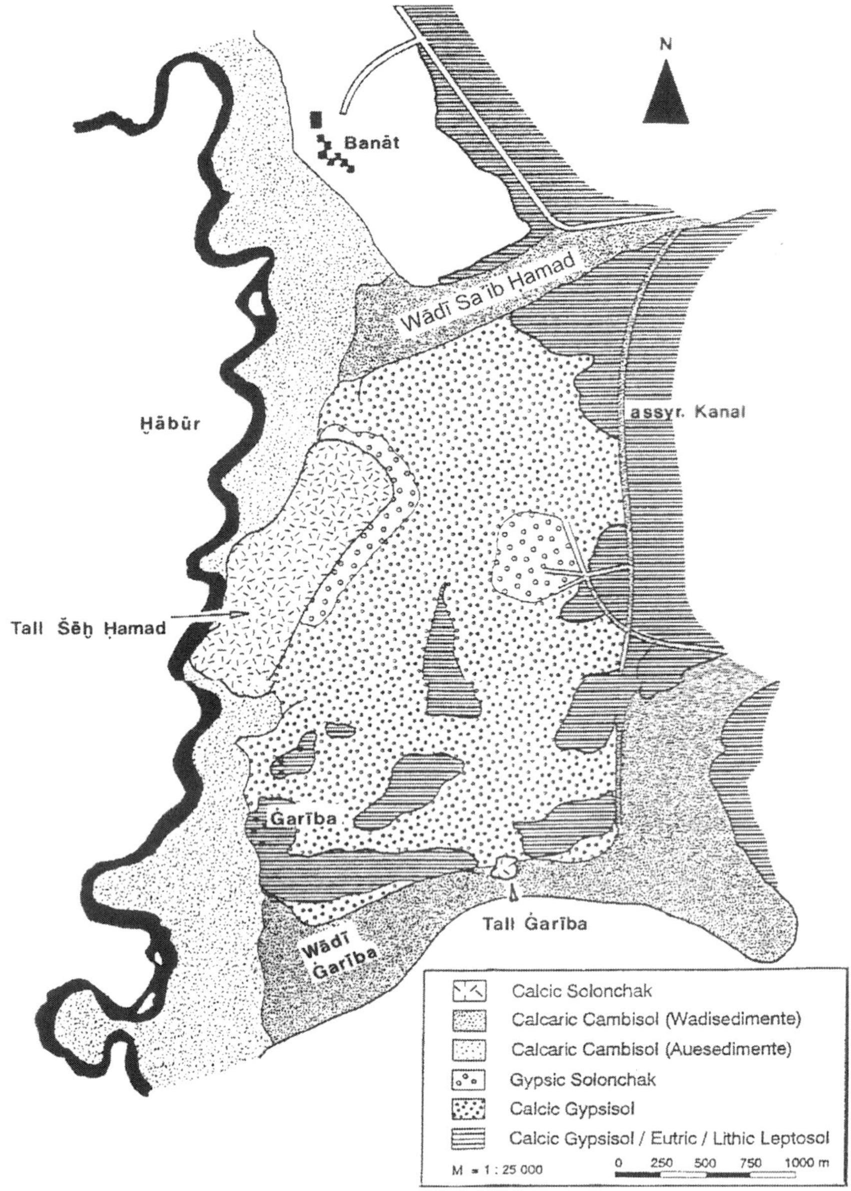

MAP 4.2 *Geological map of the region surrounding Dur-Katlimmu.*
REPRODUCED WITH PERMISSION FROM SMETTAN 2008, ABB. 02,2.

Dur-Katlimmu, published by Smettan in 2008 to establish a general raw material profile of local resources at Dur-Katlimmu.

The Lower Ḫābūr region around Dur-Katlimmu is characterised by calcareous cambisols along the banks of the Ḫābūr and in the Wadis, and calcareous and gypsic solonchak and calcarious gypsisol adjacent to the tell (map 4.2) (Smettan 2008). The Ḫābūr flows through several basalt exposures north of Dur-Katlimmu near Ard esh-Sheikh and there is a large basalt exposure directly opposite Dur-Katlimmu on the west bank of the Ḫābūr (Schneider 2006). Comparative particle size distribution analysis of the alluvial and wadi sediments indicates that the alluvial sediments are substantially finer (1–15% sand; 29–36% silt; 67–53% clay; 0% gravel and stones) than the wadi sediments (37–55% sand; 14–28% silt; 28–40% clay; 1–2% gravel and stones) (Smettan 2008). Characterisation of the clay fraction reveals that the alluvial sediment contains less palygorskite and more smectite/vermiculite and Mg-chlorite than the wadi sediments but equivalent amounts of kaolinite (Smettan 2008). Although analysis of the mineral inclusions in these sediments is not provided by Smettan, petrographic and XRD analysis of locally manufactured Middle and Late Assyrian ceramics, conducted by Schneider, indicates that the sediments likely contain (in order of abundance): calcite, plagioclase (anorthite), gypsum, quartz, pyroxene (diopside), olivine, and wollastonite (Schneider 2006).

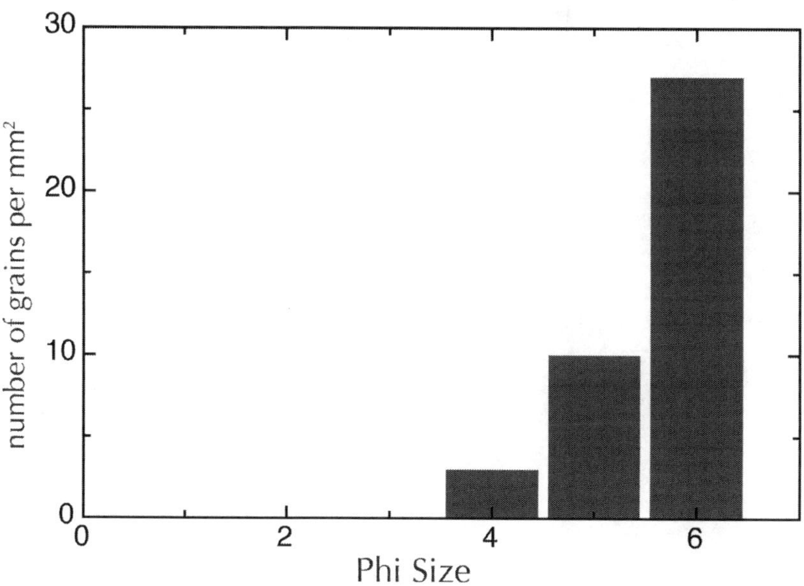

FIGURE 4.9 *Particle size histogram of inclusions in Palace Ware fabrics from Dur-Katlimmu.*

A histogram of particle size distribution for alluvial and wadi sediments and the mineral inclusions in Palace Ware from Dur-Katlimmu indicate processing of the raw material before Palace Ware manufacture (figure 4.9). The distribution of inclusions in the Palace Ware fabric exhibits a unimodal distribution with a sharp truncation at Φ 5 (4.1–5.0) and a clear peak at Φ 6, consistent with Palace Ware fabric in the Central Polity. This profile could result from the sedimentation of either the unimodal alluvial or bimodal wadi sediments local to Dur-Katlimmu.

Mineral inclusions in the Palace Ware fabric from Dur-Katlimmu are well-sorted to very well-sorted, sub-rounded to well-rounded and spherical to discoidal, consistent with alluvial sediments: mineral inclusions in aeolian and/or wadi sediments are typically more angular (subangular to subrounded) (Allaby and Allaby 2003). However, we are unable to positively identify the alluvial sediments from the Ḫābūr river as the raw material used for Palace Ware production based on particle morphology without a comparative morphological analysis of the alluvial and wadi sediments themselves.

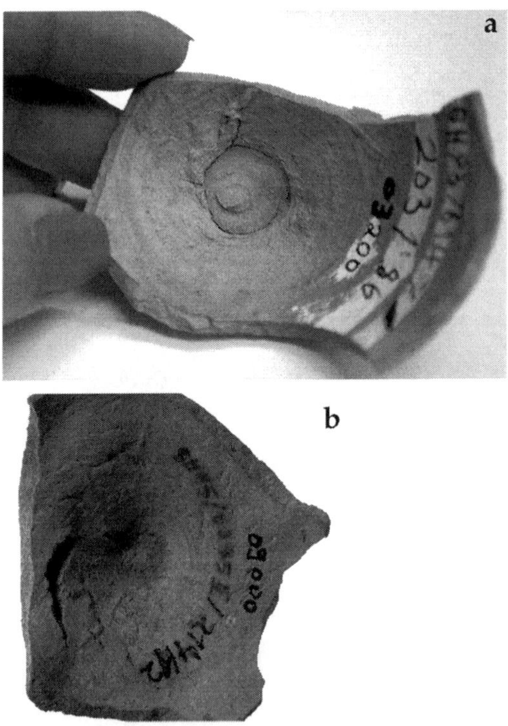

FIGURE 4.10 *Photographs of basal drying defects in the Palace Ware assemblage from Dur-Katlimmu illustrating (a) basal collapse and (b) tearing.*

Formation

Formation & Shaping

Macroscopic examination of Palace Ware from Dur-Katlimmu reveals rhythmic grooves on the interior of form B and C bases indicative of formation by wheel throwing (Rye 1981). One of the 9 basal sherds from Dur-Katlimmu we were able to examine in Berlin appears to have had an internal collapse of its basal element, which is depressed and has a drying crack along the interior circumference of the base (figure 4.10a). In addition, a base sherd from Dur-Katlimmu exhibits diagonal tears or cracks in its lower body, 1.5 cm above the base (figure 4.10b). The s-shaped drying cracks and spiral pattern of the remaining drying cracks along the planes of weakness created during wheel throwing are further evidence that Palace Ware was formed on the wheel at Dur-Katlimmu.

The absence of rilling and fine, continuous rhythmic striations on the exterior surface of some vessels indicates a secondary shaping stage on the wheel after vessel formation (Rye 1981). The interior surface of the vessels are also smooth and even, which suggests Palace Ware vessels at Dur-Katlimmu, like those in the Central Polity, were first thrown as rough-outs and subsequently cut down to size, internally and externally, by turning on a wheel. The waxy or greasy texture and dull sheen of Palace Ware vessels from Dur-Katlimmu is indicative of turning during the leather-hard drying stage (Berg 2008).

Another indication of technological continuity between the Central Polity and Dur-Katlimmu is the use of 'plugs' composed of heavily organic tempered clay in 3 of the 9 form B bases we were able to examine from Dur-Katlimmu (figure 4.11). These 'plugs' were used to prevent drying and firing cracks in the Central Polity, a technology which dates back to the Old Babylonian period (Moorey 1994). The presence of these 'plugs' in the Palace Ware assemblage from Dur-Katlimmu indicates a high degree of familiarity with Neo-Assyrian ceramic technology and/or Palace Ware chaîne opératoire at this site despite the morphometric and stylistic variations in the completed forms.

Decoration

Evidence of a slip or pseudo-slip was not detected macroscopically or using a hand lens on Palace Ware vessels from Dur-Katlimmu. However, vessels were heavily encrusted with the drusy greyish crystals (figure 4.12a) also found on Palace Ware in the Central Polity. In thin-section, these crystals form an irregular 'layer', transparent in PPL with high birefringence colours in XPL (figure 4.12b), which suggests calcium enrichment or post-depositional secondary crystallisation of calcium carbonate or calcium hydroxide, similar to that found on Central Polity Palace Ware.

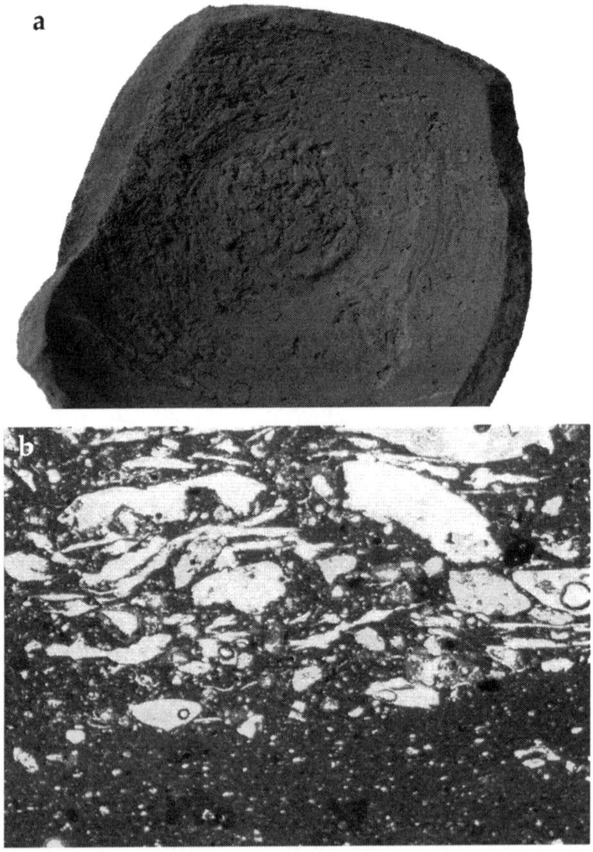

FIGURE 4.11 *Plugs of coarse, heavily organic tempered clay used in the bases of Palace Ware form B cups at Dur-Katlimmu to prevent vessel failure during drying.* (*a*) *photograph;* (*b*) *micrograph in* PPL (*field of view = 1.7 mm*)

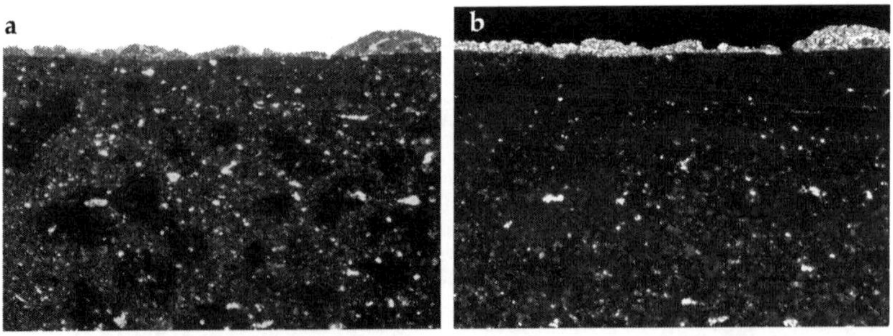

FIGURE 4.12 *Micrographs of mineral encrustation on the external surface of Palace Ware from Dur-Katlimmu in* (*a*) PPL *and* (*b*) XPL. (*field of view = 3.5 mm*)

Dimples, the most frequent and identifiable decorative element in the Palace Ware assemblage from the Central Polity, are also the most frequent decoration at Dur-Katlimmu, occurring on 59% or 13/22. In the Annexed Provinces, as in the Central Polity, Palace Ware dimples are oval and oriented with their long axis perpendicular to the base and are approximately 1 cm along their longest axis, consistent with formation by pressing a fingertip into the vessel wall while it was still pliable. Unlike Central Polity Palace Ware however, none of the dimples on Palace Ware from the Annexed Provinces have ridged 'fingerprint' impressions inside their exterior depression, suggesting secondary smoothing or wiping with a cloth after dimpling or that the dimples in the Annexed Provinces were made when the vessel was too dry to retain the impression of a finger but still pliable enough to deform under pressure.

The registers of incised lines around the vessel circumference are evenly spaced and uniform in depth suggesting that, like their Central Polity counterparts, they were made using a multi-pronged tool while the vessel was in motion or rotating on the wheel. The margins of the incisions are smooth and even, indicating that they were made when the vessel was in the leather-hard drying stage (Rye 1981) and the valley of the incisions are rounded, indicating that the tips of the tool were rounded, similar to the tool we believe was used to incise Palace Ware in the Central Polity.

The protruding or raised rings around the necks of Palace Ware forms B and C from Dur-Katlimmu were likely moulded, since there is no evidence of smoothing or deformation around the margins of the ring (Rye 1981).

TABLE 4.1 *Bulk chemical composition of Palace Ware from Dur-Katlimmu by SEM-EDS*

chemical compound	weight %
Na_2O	1.18
MgO	6.37
Al_2O_3	13.91
SiO_2	48.23
K_2O	0.67
CaO	21.43
TiO_2	0.94
FeO	7.25
total	100

It is possible subsequent smoothing of the vessel's exterior surface could have obscured evidence of appliqué or carving, however, like their Central Polity counterparts, thin-section micrographs from Dur-Katlimmu Palace Ware of these rings illustrates that they are continuous with the ceramic body.

Firing

Bulk chemical composition of Palace Ware ceramics from Dur-Katlimmu, determined using SEM-EDS, is presented in table 4.1. The wt.% of CaO in these fabrics is ~15 wt.%, classifying them as calcareous (Mantiatis and Tite 1981). Given the relatively high concentration of magnesium in the Palace Ware matrix from Dur-Katlimmu (4–7 wt.%, compared to 2–3 wt.% in the Central Polity) we combined calcium and magnesium concentrations for the purpose of this analysis. On a CaO-SiO_2-Al_2O_3 ternary phase diagram, the bulk composition of Palace Ware from Dur-Katlimmu plots close to the eutectic line at 1264°C. As discussed in chapter 3, the actual temperature at which the Palace Ware ceramic matrix begins to 'melt' or vitrify is lower than 1264°C, given the complexity and density of the matrix material, but it is a useful upper boundary or guideline.

Palace Ware vessels from Dur-Katlimmu occur in a broader range of colours that those from the Central Polity—from light brown (7.5YR 6/4) to very pale brown (10YR 8/3) to pale yellow (5Y 8/2) to light grey (2.5Y 7/2) (figure 4.13). Sixtyfour percent (16/25) of the assemblage is similar in colour to the pale yellow (2.5Y 8/2) and pale olive (5Y 6/3) of Palace Ware in the Central Polity. The remaining 36% of the assemblage, which is 'redder' in colour, is mottled with patches of pale yellow and grey.

During firing, the iron contained in a ceramic body acts as a strong colouring agent up to about 1000°C: colouring the vessel fabric black under reducing conditions as the iron reduces to Fe_3O_4 and FeO; and reddish or pink under oxidising conditions as the iron oxidises to Fe_2O_3 (Matson 1971). As discussed previously, at about 900°C the colour of the ceramic body begins to be strongly influenced by the crystallisation of calcium silicates and calcium ferrosilicates which turn the vessel pale yellow or buff (Shoval 2003; Nakai 2005; Molera *et al.* 1998). Therefore, we estimate that at Dur-Katlimmu Palace Ware was fired to between 900–1000°C, the transition temperature for calcium-iron colour dominance in a calcareous fabric, and probably closer to 1000°C or for a sufficient soak time for calcium silicates and calcium ferrosilicates to dominate vessel colour.

A Late Assyrian kiln was excavated at Dur-Katlimmu adjacent to the Red House and contemporaneous with its occupation (Kreppner 2008). The kiln is

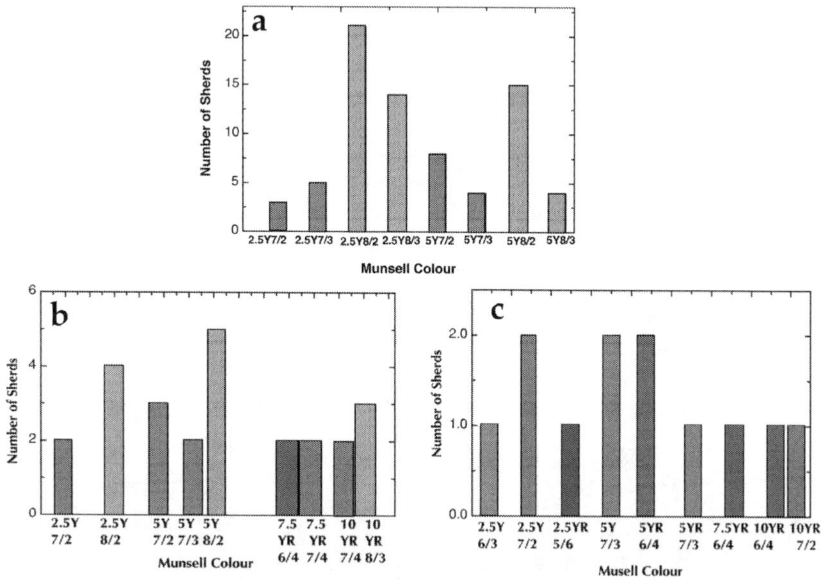

FIGURE 4.13 *Bar charts comparing Palace Ware vessel colour in (a) the Central Polity, (b) Dur-Katlimmu and (c) Guzana.*

structurally similar to the Late Assyrian kiln from Aššur: a simple two chamber updraft kiln with a rectangular firebox and heating chamber floor (figure 4.14). Although complete plans of this kiln have not yet been published, we estimate the floor of the heating chamber to be 1.3 m by 2 m or 2.6 m^2, which is almost 1 m^2 (0.8 m^2) smaller than the kiln at Aššur. The firebox of the Dur-Katlimmu kiln can be approximated at 6.5 m^2, using the 5:2 ratio of floor area to firebox area known from Middle Assyrian kilns.

We were able to analyse a 2 1/2 cm section of the kiln wall and a slag prill from the firebox using SEM-EDS. Figure 4.15 illustrates the vitrification gradient or depth of thermal penetration into the kiln wall: 1/2 cm into the wall the matrix is glassy and mineral phases are merging and indistinct, bubbles (spherical voids) form as volatiles are released; 1 1/2 cm into the firebox wall, the matrix is solidified but distinct mineral phases are easily identifiable and the void space is irregular, preserving the vughs and vesicles created during the formation of the kiln wall. Closer examination reveals the partial decomposition of calcium carbonates (calcite) at 1 1/2 cm (figure 4.16a) and the complete decomposition of calcium carbonates and formation of calcium hydroxide crystals at 1/2 cm (figure 4.16b). This indicates that the firebox wall (1/2–1 1/2 cm) experiences temperatures of at least 750°C but not more than 900°C, since the crystals

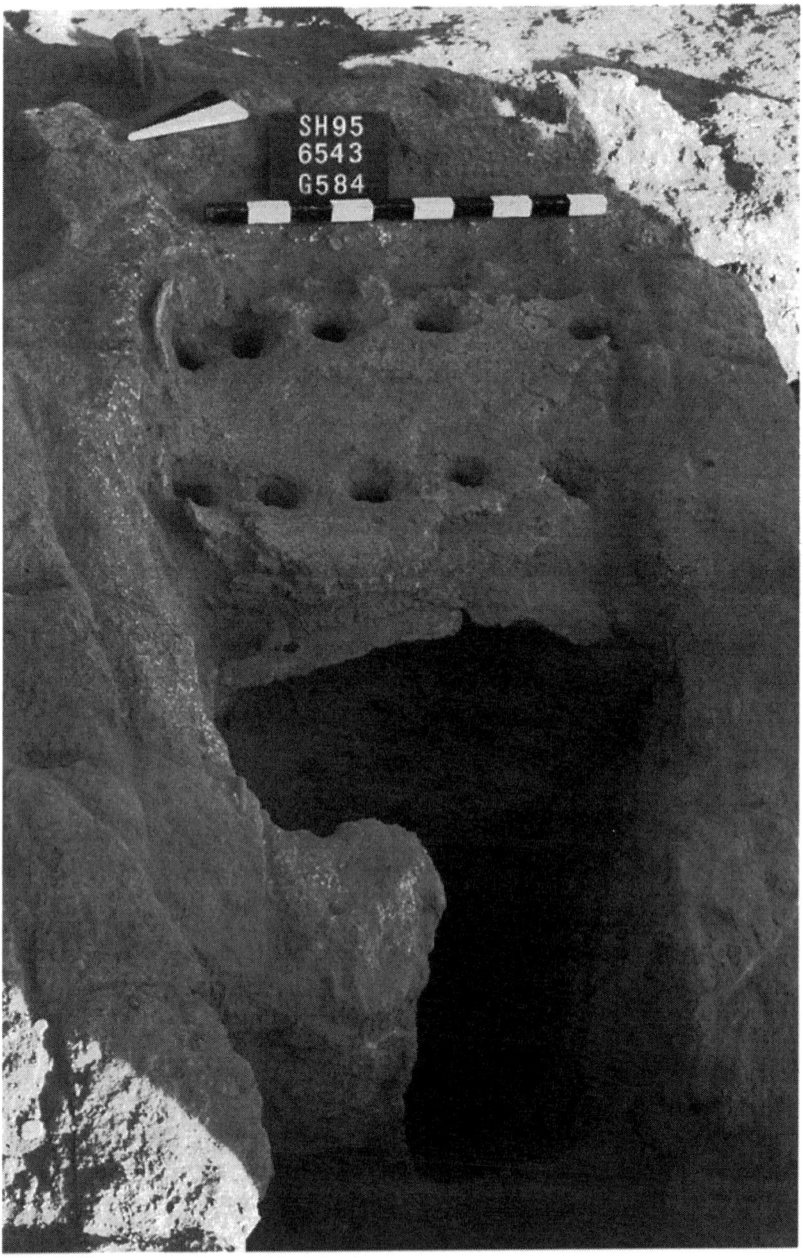

FIGURE 4.14 *Photograph of Neo-Assyrian kiln from Dur-Katlimmu.*
REPRINTED WITH PERMISSION FROM KREPPNER 2008.

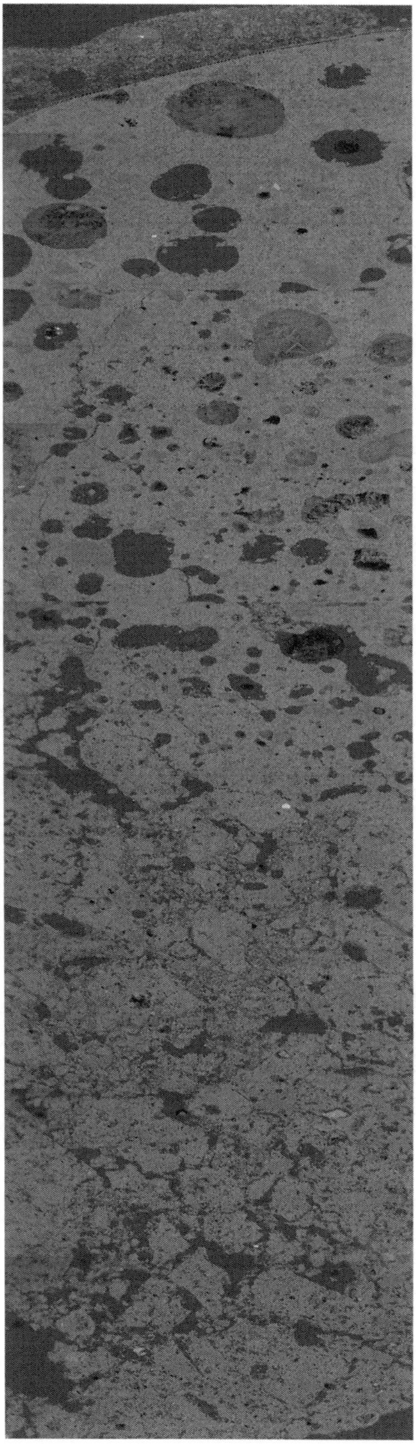

FIGURE 4.15
SEM-BSE image of the kiln wall profile from Dur-Katlimmu.

which formed from the decomposition of calcium carbonate were calcium oxide rehydrated to calcium hydroxide rather than calcium ferrosilicates or calcium silicates (Matson 1971).

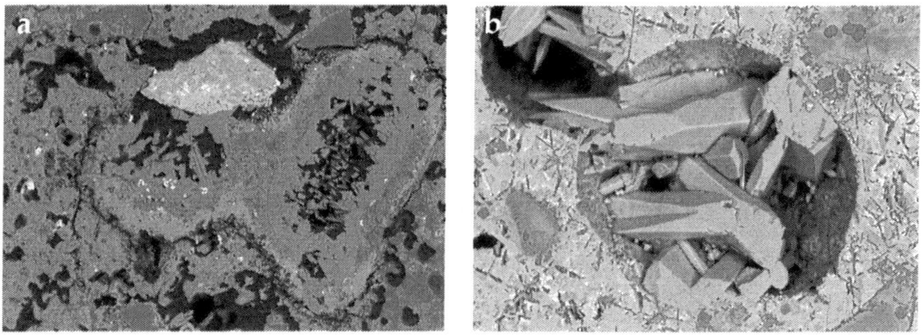

FIGURE 4.16 *SEM-BSE images of calcium carbonate mineral phases in the kiln wall from Dur-Katlimmu illustrating (a) partial decomposition of the phases and (b) formation of calcium hydroxide crystals.*

TABLE 4.2 *Bulk chemical composition of Neo-Assyrian kiln wall from Dur-Katlimmu by SEM-EDS*

chemical compound	exterior wall (wt %)	interior wall (wt%)	slag prill (wt%)
Na_2O	1.53	1.18	2.11
MgO	8.15	6.37	4.99
$A1_2O_3$	11.46	13.91	14.89
SiO_2	44.95	48.25	49.07
K_2O	1.75	1.87	2.82
CaO	25.43	21.43	19.00
Tio_2	1.06	0.94	1.68
FeO	5.67	6.05	5.43
total	100	100	100

The bulk chemical composition of the firebox wall is similar to the Palace Ware ceramic composition, indicating that specialised refractory materials were not used in its construction. An increase in wt.% of potassium is subtle but present as we move from the external wall (1 1/2 cm) to the internal wall (1/2 cm) to the slag prill (table 4.2), indicative of combustion using biomass fuels. When we plot these three compositions, taking into account the different concentrations of potassium, onto a CaO-SiO_2-Al_2O_3 ternary phase diagram we see that the temperature in the firebox needed to reach at least 1307°C for the slag prill to form. Again, these temperatures are estimates of the maximum temperature required for vitrification and do not take into consideration the complexity and density of a ceramic matrix or length of exposure to thermal radiation or 'soak' time.

We arrive, perhaps, at a more accurate temperature estimate by evaluating relict minerals included in the slag prill itself. Figure 4.17 illustrates a partially melted alkali feldspar (chemical composition provided in table 4.3). A phase diagram of the albite-orthoclase solid solution system indicates that an alkali feldspar 73% Or has a solidus or 'melting' point at 1100°C and is completely liquid (liquidus) over 1200°C. This estimate is consistent with the firing temperature estimate for Palace Ware from Dur-Katlimmu between 900–1000°C.

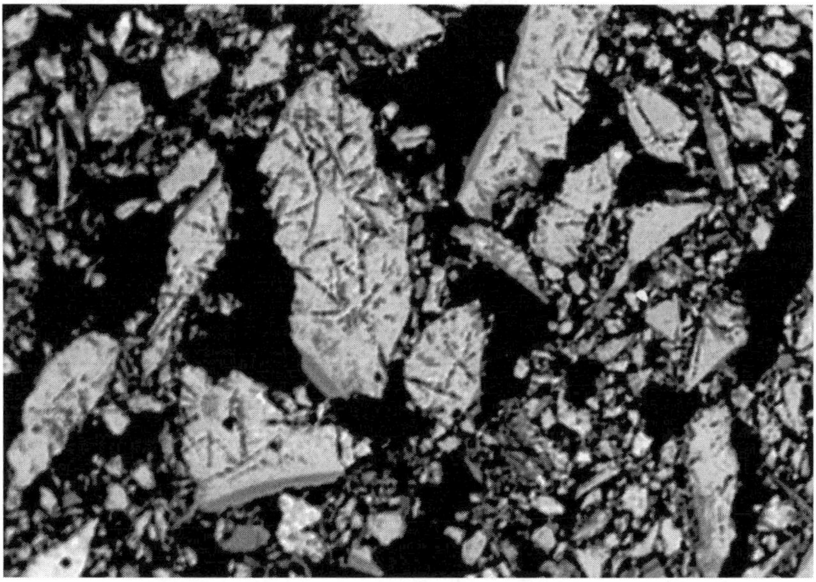

FIGURE 4.17 *SEM-BSE image of a decomposing alkali feldspar in the kiln wall from Dur-Katlimmu.*

TABLE 4.3 *Bulk chemical composition (SEM-EDS) of a decomposing feldspar in the kiln wall from Dur-Katlimmu*

chemical compound	weight %
Na_2O	3.12
MgO	1.46
$A1_2O_3$	14.24
SiO_2	69.99
K_2O	8.53
CaO	1.31
FeO	1.35
total	100

Chemical and Mineralogical Characterisation

Mineralogical Profile

As discussed in chapter 3, Palace Ware fabrics are extremely fine-grained (< 2% inclusions; inclusions < 0.05 mm) and well-sorted to very well-sorted (figure 3.22). The inclusions themselves are sub-rounded to well-rounded and spherical to discoidal—consistent with alluvial sediment from the Tigris which has been processed by sedimentation. The mineralogy of Palace Ware fabrics from the Central Polity is consistent with the igneous and volcanic geology of the Northern Thrust and High Folded Zones in northern Iraq.

Palace Ware fabric from Dur-Katlimmu, like Palace Ware fabric in the Central Polity, also is extremely fine-grained (< 3% inclusions; inclusions ≤ 0.05 mm) and well-sorted to very well-sorted (figure 4.18). The inclusions themselves are sub-rounded to well-rounded and spherical to discoidal—consistent with particle morphology in alluvial sediments. Analysis of 12 thin-sections from Dur-Katlimmu reveals that Palace Ware fabrics are homogeneous and can be described by the following petrographic description:

> The matrix is pale yellow brown to olive (rare) and opaque in PPL; optically inactive in XPL. Devoid of foraminifers. Rare (0.5–1%) planar voids (up to 0.7 mm) with frequent secondary calcite formation in the interstitial space. Opaques (2–3%) of magnetite, ilmenite and spinel between a few microns to almost 20 µm. The inclusions ($f{:}c_{0\cdot062\text{ mm}}$ = 97–96: 3–4) contain very well-sorted, sub-rounded to well-rounded, fine sand

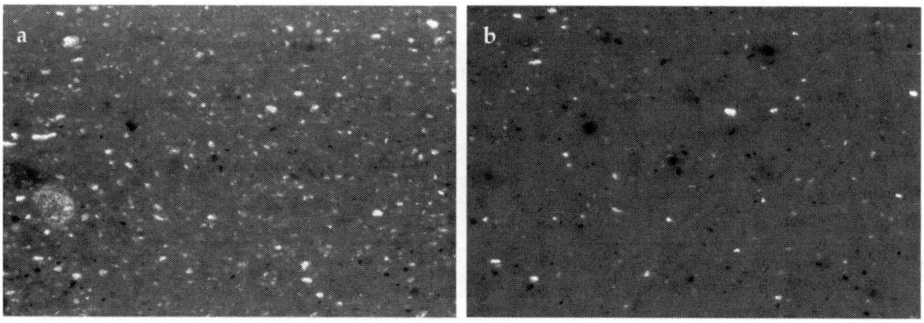

FIGURE 4.18 *Micrographs of Palace Ware fabric from Dur-Katlimmu* (SH 1–11) *in* (*a*) PPL *and* (*b*) XPL. (*field of view = 1.7 mm*)

particles of relict calcite, calcic plagioclase, quartz, pyroxene and olivine-like minerals, up to 0.06mm.

The mineralogy of Palace Ware fabrics from Dur-Katlimmu is consistent with alluvial sediments from the Ḫābūr river around Dur-Katlimmu. Palace Ware fabrics from Dur-Katlimmu are petrographically distinct from Central Polity Palace Ware fabrics in several important ways. First, the relatively low abundance of quartz grains (the most frequent mineral phase in Central Polity fabrics) and occurrence of pyroxene and olivine-like minerals suggest a mafic/basic basalt contribution to the raw material source. Although basic basalts potentially contribute to the mineral composition of alluvial sediments deposited along the Tigris, the Palace Ware fabrics from the Central Polity do not include pyroxene or olivine. This may reflect the relative proximity of the parental basalts: adjacent to Dur-Katlimmu in the case of the Ḫābūr and 100 km or more north for Nimrud and Nineveh along the Tigris.

Second, Palace Ware fabrics from Dur-Katlimmu are more likely to exhibit secondary calcite formation in void spaces that those from the Central Polity and often contain relic calcite and limestone fragments. This difference in mineralogy also reflects a distance raw material profile local to Dur-Katlimmu: the abundant calcic mineral content of these fabrics is probably contributed by the calcareous cambisols on the banks of the Ḫābūr. Together, these two mineralogical differences suggest that different raw material resources where exploited to manufacture Palace Ware at Dur-Katlimmu and in the Central Polity.

Chemical Profile

The geochemical profiles for Palace Ware from Nimrud, Nineveh and Dur-Katlimmu, using INAA, are illustrated in figure 4.19. Geochemically, Palace

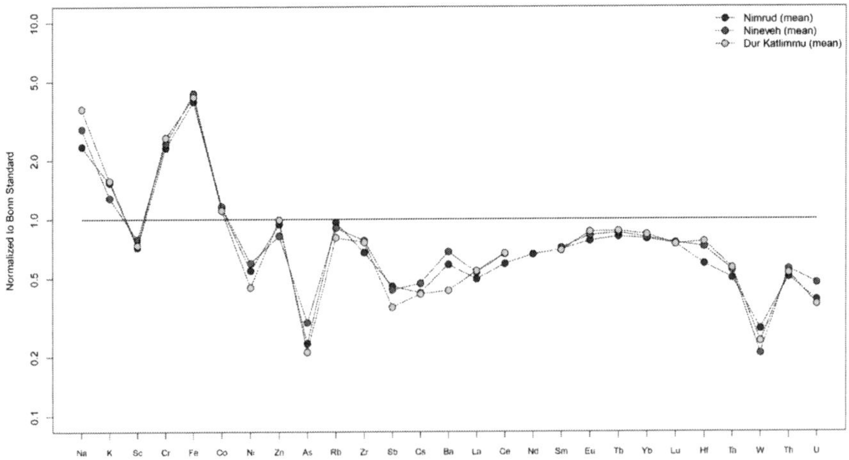

FIGURE 4.19 *Combined INAA bulk chemical profile for Palace Ware from Nimrud, Nineveh & Dur-Katlimmu.*
GRAPH COURTESY OF J. STERBA.

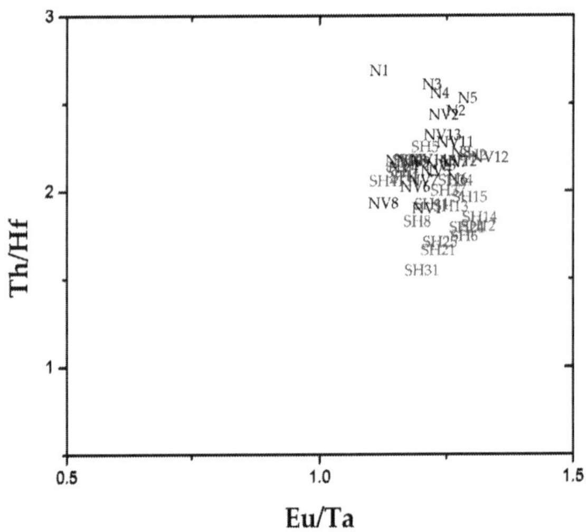

FIGURE 4.20 *Biplot of elemental ratios Eu:Ta vs. Th: Hf illustrating the chemical compositional similarity among Palace Ware from Nimrud (N), Nineveh (NV) & Dur-Katlimmu (SH).*

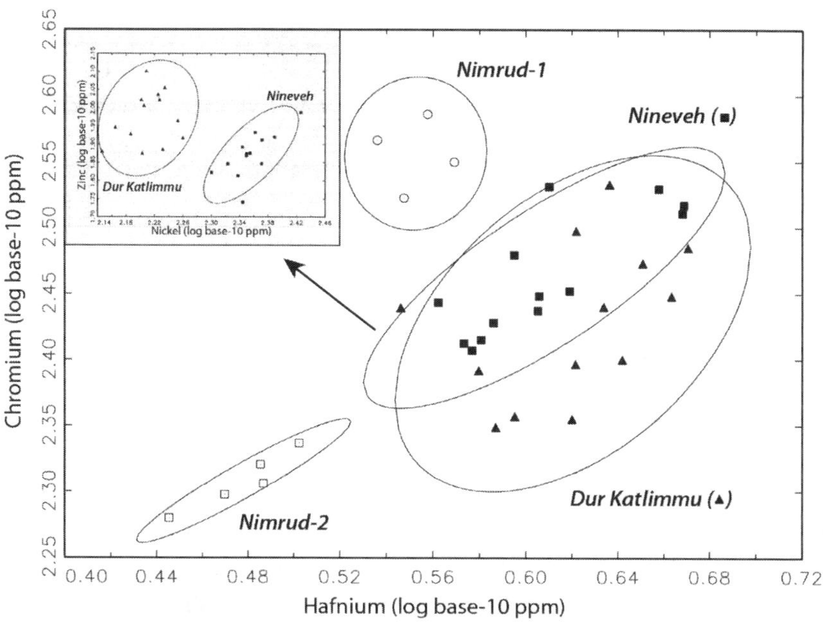

FIGURE 4.21 *Principal component analysis revealing four chemical compositional groups: Nineveh, Nimrud-1, Nimrud-2 & Dur-Katlimmu.*
FIGURE COURTESY OF J. SPEAKMAN.

Ware from Dur-Katlimmu and the Central Polity are very similar and cluster together in a biplot of Th:Hf against Eu:Ta, albeit with subtle but discernible internal structure (figure 4.20). However, principal component analysis reveals that Palace Ware from Dur-Katlimmu is manufactured from a geochemically as well as petrographically distinct raw material source (figure 4.21).

Dur-Katlimmu Palace Ware is easily distinguished from Nimrud Palace Ware by its Cr and Hf composition however, it is the differences in nickel (Ni) which confirm that Dur-Katlimmu Palace Ware was manufactured using a local raw material source. Ni is a common impurity in the lattice of certain clay minerals, particularly montmorillonites. The most abundant clay mineral in the Tigris is montmorillonite; the most abundant clay minerals in the Euphrates and Ḫābūr are chlorite and vermiculite. It is probable that the higher Ni content in Palace Ware fabrics from the Central Polity is related to their greater abundance of montmorillonite minerals.

Together the petrographic and geochemical data suggest local Palace Ware manufacture at Dur-Katlimmu exploiting local raw material resources, probably alluvial deposits along the Ḫābūr.

Palace Ware Consumption

Consumption patterns of Palace Ware at Dūr-Kaltimmu, like those in the Central Polity, are biased by currently available and excavated material and contextual information. Although lower tel residential areas of Dur-Katlimmu have been excavated, namely the Neo-Assyrian residences, at the time of writing they have not been published. Our analysis of Palace Ware consumption at Dur-Katlimmu, therefore, is restricted to the Red House.

The Red House is a monumental structure adjacent to the Neo-Assyrian residences (Kreppner 2008). Palace Ware from the Red House comes from secondary deposition, fill deposits above the primary floor levels (Kreppner 2008). The excavators believe that Palace Ware was used in the Red House and is particularly associated with room LW which functioned as a reception room (Kreppner 2008). Since the majority of the Palace Ware in the Central Polity available for analysis comes from public/monumental architecture, consumption of Palace Ware in the reception room of the Red House could indicate a contextual continuity in Palace Ware consumption between these two.

In terms of Palace Ware consumption by form at Dur-Katlimmu, form C jars are the most abundant (57%) in the Palace Ware population, followed closely by form B cups (35%). This is a change from formal consumption patterns in the Central Polity at the public/monumental contexts of Nimrud and Nineveh, where form C vessels are not consumed at all. While this may be related to the sample size of these populations, it is interesting to note that Nimrud, like Dur-Katlimmu, consumed a small percentage of form A bowls (7 and 9 % of their respective populations).

TABLE 4.4 *Palace Ware consumption patterns in the Annexed Provinces*

	Secondary Context		Unknown Context
	Public (temple, palace, etc.)	**Private (residence, etc.)**	
Dür-Katlimmu			
Form A	2		
Form B	8		
Form C	12		
Guzana			
Form A			
Form B			7
Form C			3

The formal Palace Ware consumption pattern in the Central Polity that most closely resembles that from Dur-Katlimmu is from the burials at Aššur (table 4.4). Burials are complicated contexts to understand. Grave goods are meaningful, socially, culturally and even symbolically, however these meanings are often unclear to archaeologists. Whatever their practical, social or symbolic function, form C Palace Ware jars were considered important/meaningful enough to be incorporated as grave goods. Assuming a certain degree of social and cultural continuity between Dur-Katlimmu and Aššur or the Central Polity, it is possible that whatever value made these vessels meaningful for inclusion in burial at Aššur made them meaningful to consume at Dur-Katlimmu; that their consumption and perhaps all Palace Ware consumption at Dur-Katlimmu was socially or symbolically, rather than practically, motivated.

Guzana

Guzana is located at the headwaters of the Ḫābūr river in north-eastern Syria and served as the capital of the similarly named Neo-Assyrian province. The city is referred to in the cuneiform literature by its Aramaic name, even after the Aramean city-state in which it was located, Bīt-Baḫiani, became an official province in the 8th century BCE (Dornemann 1997; Radner 2006).

The Neo-Assyrian city was laid out roughly in a rectangle with 1.9 km of fortified wall guarding the 21.6 hectare city. The 3 hectare citadel was also circumscribed by a fortified wall and accessed through the two chambered 'scorpion gate'. The citadel is situated on a mound in the northern portion of the site and consisted of monumental architecture such as the Western Palace with its columns shaped like deities, the North-East Palace and associated private residences, and vaulted tombs (Cholidis 2010).

Guzana was first excavated by M. von Oppenheim in 1899, whose four soundings at different loci revealed monumental sculptures just beneath the topsoil (Dornemann 1997). Lacking official permission, von Oppenheim carefully backfilled his trenches with the intention of launching a large scale expedition once the proper permissions were acquired (*ibid.*). He returned to Guzana in 1911 and concentrated his efforts on the citadel until 1913, when excavation was interrupted by WWI (von Oppenheim 1931). He launched two additional campaigns in 1927 and 1929 before work at Guzana ceased for 77 years (Dornemann 1997). In 2006, a joint mission of the Staatliche Museen zu Berlin, Direction Générale des Antiquités et des Musées de Damas, Eberhard Karls Universität Tübingen, and Martin-Luther-Universität Halle-Wittenberg resumed excavation.

In 1943, the Tell Halaf-Museum in Berlin was bombed during an air raid. Significant damage was sustained by the larger basalt objects; the limestone orthostats, plaster casts, and pottery were completely destroyed (Cholidis 2010). Salvage operations between 1943–1944 recovered nine truckloads of debris which the Tell Halaf-Projekt began restoring in 2001. No ceramic artefacts from von Oppenheim's excavations have survived.

Palace Ware from Guzana included in this study comes from the renewed excavations courtesy of the Vorderasiatisches Museum. Eleven vessels were available for non-destructive analysis however, contextual information for these vessels is not available at present.

Typology

Form B

Seven vessels from Guzana (≥ 70% extant) are typologically consistent with Palace Ware form B cups with unequal biconical bodies, incurving necks, out-curving, horizontal, everted rims and thinned or rounded lips (figures 4.22–4.23). Like their Central Polity counterparts and form B cups from Dur-Katlimmu, these vessels have non-functional basal elements which range from pointed and rounded, to disk and knob, to a rather elaborate stepped design. Seventyone percent (5/7) of the form B population from Guzana is undecorated, compared to the 17% (2/12) undecorated form B vessels in the Central Polity. The remaining vessels in the form B population from Guzana are decorated with the dimples typical of form B and C vessels in the Central Polity.

One vessel (HC) is typologically consistent with Palace Ware form B2 cups from the Central Polity with a dimpled body decorated with 2 rows of 3–9 dimples each and a ridge or moulded ring at the intersection of the neck and the rim (figure 4.22). Neck decoration is not a feature of form B2 vessels in the Central Polity: moulded neck rings are found only on form B1 forms. However, since the most outstanding typological feature of form B1 vessels is their functional base, a feature missing from HC, we preliminarily classify it as form B2, pending morphometric analysis.

Of the 5 form B3 cups from the Annexed Provinces (figure 4.23), 80% (4/5) are undecorated and 20% (1/5) are decorated compared to the even split (50:50) between undecorated and decorated vessels found in the Central Polity B3 population. The decorated cup from Guzana (HD) has a plain, undecorated body but a moulded ring where the neck and the rim intersect, similar to the one on vessel HC, and an elaborate stepped base—neither of which are decorative elements associated with B3 cups in the Central Polity. However,

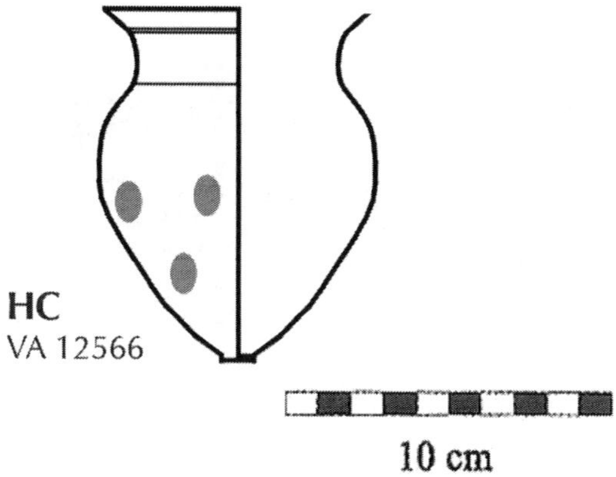

FIGURE 4.22 *Palace Ware form B2 cups from Guzana.*

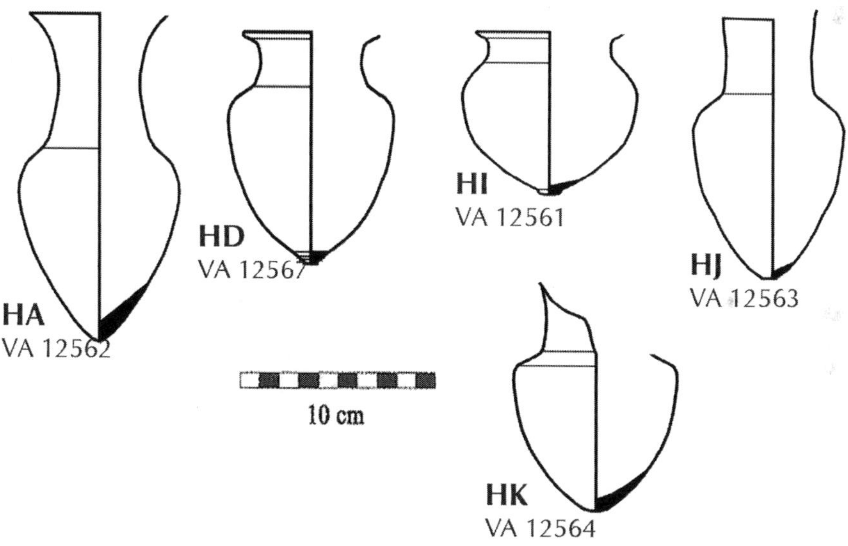

FIGURE 4.23 *Palace Ware form B3 cups from Guzana.*

the only form B cups in the Central Polity which have undecorated bodies are form B3, therefore we preliminarily classify it as a B3 cup pending morphometric analysis.

We were unable to classify vessel HF according to the typological criteria from the Central Polity (figure 4.24). Vessel HF is unequal biconical, with an incurving neck, out-curving, horizontal, everted rim with a flattened lip and rounded base. Like many form B vessels it has a body decorated with rows of

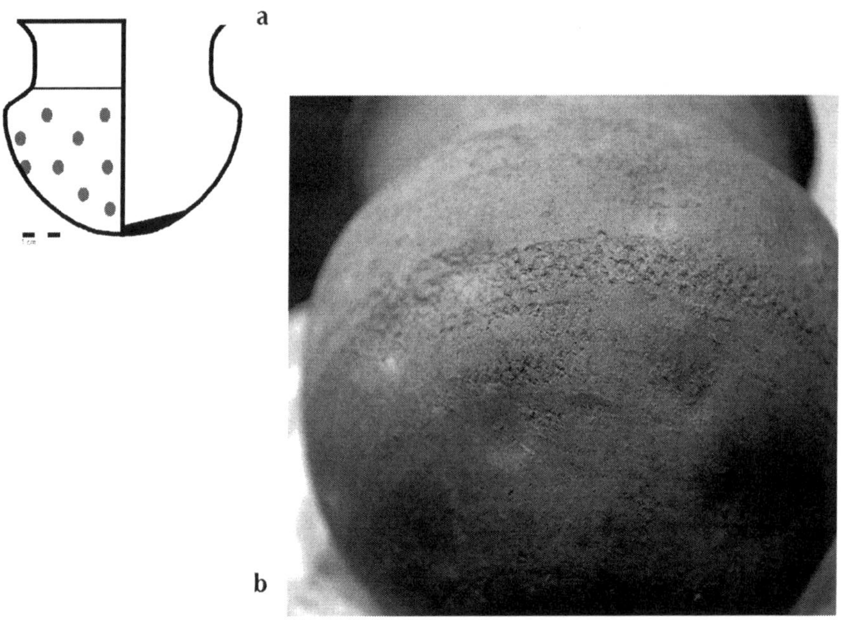

FIGURE 4.24 *Palace Ware cup* HF *from Guzana exhibiting microdimples in (a) drawing and (b) photograph.*

dimples. However, unlike form B1, B2 and B3 vessels with 2 rows of 2–9 dimples, HF has 5 rows of irregularly spaced 'micro-dimples' with 2–8 micro-dimples per row. Each micro-dimple is approximately half the size of a typical Palace Ware dimple, 0.3–0.5 cm on its longest axis as opposed to 1 cm. Micro-dimples are unique to Guzana in the Palace Ware assemblage from the Annexed Provinces and this vessel in particular at Guzana, and are unknown in the Central Polity. We classify it, tentatively, as a form B vessel because the profile created by the micro-dimpling is similar to that of form B2 vessel KQ from Nimrud.

Form C

Three vessels in the Palace Ware assemblage from Guzana are typologically consistent with form C jars: unequal biconical with incurving necks, out-curving, horizontal everted rims with thinned or rounded lips (figure 4.25–4.26). Like their counterparts from Dur-Katlimmu and the Central Polity, form C jars from Guzana have non-functional basal elements, which range from pointed to stepped to disk.

Form C jars in the Central Polity are fairly evenly split between undecorated and dimpled bodies, 55% and 45% respectively. At Guzana, the percentage of dimpled bodies outweighs the undecorated vessels 67% (2/3) to 33% (1/3). However, given the small sample size of form C vessels from Guzana it is not possible to draw any meaningful conclusion from this pattern. The 2 decorated form C jars from Guzana are typologically consistent with Palace Ware form C1 bowls (figure 4.25): HE is decorated with 3 rows of 5–8 dimples and a moulded neck ring and vessel HG has 4 rows of 4–6 dimples and stepping at the join between the vessel body and neck element (now missing). Like their Central Polity and Dur-Katlimmu counterparts, form C1 bowls at Guzana are the most elaborately decorated vessels in the form C population.

No form C2 or C3 jars were identified in the Palace Ware assemblage from Guzana.

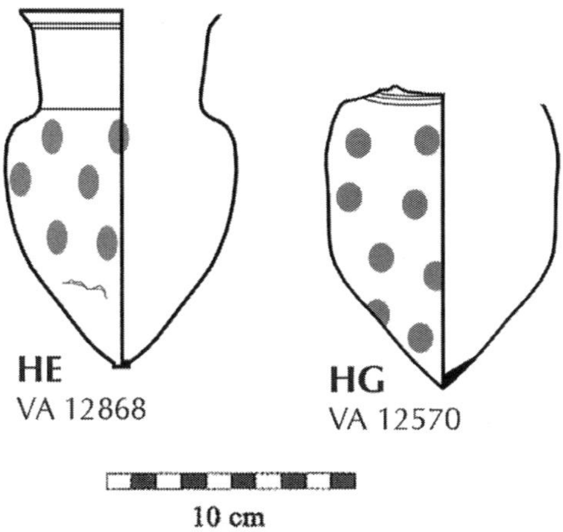

FIGURE 4.25 *Palace Ware form C1 jars from Guzana.*

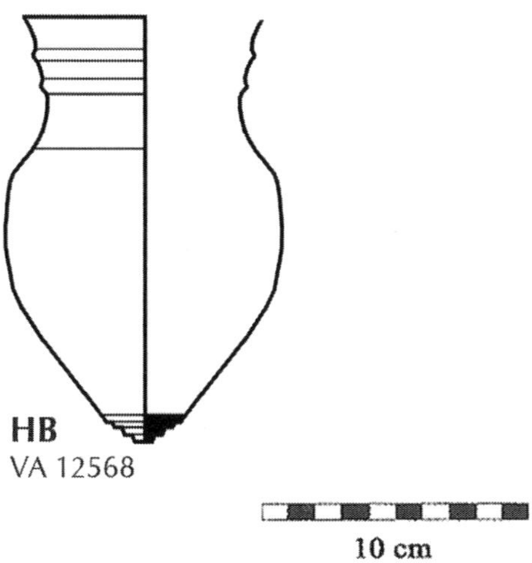

FIGURE 4.26 *Palace Ware form C4 jars from Guzana.*

Form C4 jars in the Central Polity have undecorated bodies, with non-functional pointed or rounded bases and 67% of the population (2/3) are decorated with moulded neck rings. The single vessel from Guzana (HB) typologically similar to C4 jars has an undecorated body and 2 moulded neck rings (figure 4.26). Vessel HB also has the most elaborate base in the form C population at Guzana, a non-functional, complex stepped base, unknown in the Central Polity but quite common in the Dur-Katlimmu form C population.

Morphometric Analysis

Form B

Form B cups from Guzana meet the basic morphometric definitional criteria for Palace Ware: they are unrestricted-vertical in shape, 6.5–14.5 cm in height, maximum diameter 7.1–8.5 cm wide, necks 1.8–5.5 cm long, have walls 0.15–0.3 cm thick (mean = 0.21 cm, median = 0.2 cm, mode = 0.2 cm) and hold between 327–879 cm^3. However, like the vessels from Dur-Katlimmu, they have subtly shallower bodies than their Central Polity counterparts; depth profiles of 40–60% for 43% of the population and 60–100% for the remaining 57%, but no vessels > 100% deep, a profile for 19% (4/21) of the form B population in the Central Polity.

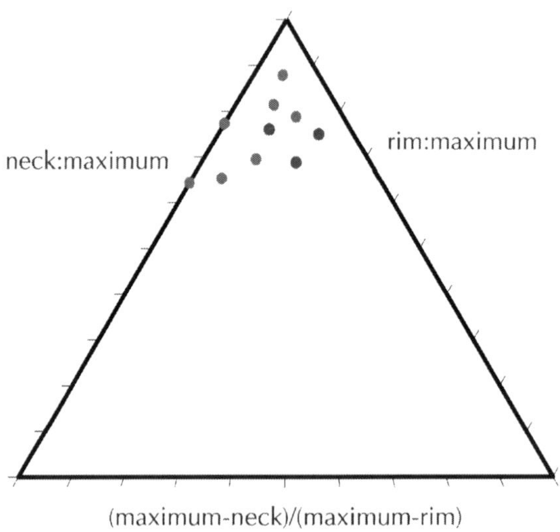

FIGURE 4.27 *Sneed & Folk ternary diagram comparing Palace Ware form B rim, neck & maximum diameters from Guzana (black) & the Central Polity (grey).*

Analysis of vessel curvature and the relationship among maximum, rim and neck diameters confirm the uniformity of shape between form B cups in the Central Polity and Annexed Provinces. Vessels from Guzana have base angles between 25–44° (mean = 33°, median = 33°, no mode available), shoulder angles between 111–146° (mean = 135°, median = 138°, no mode available), and neck angles between 73–90° (mean = 81°, median = 80°, mode = 78°); consistent with base, shoulder and neck angles from Central Polity vessels. Similarly, form B cups from Guzana cluster with Central Polity form B Palace Ware cups on a Sneed and Folk diagram of maximum, rim and neck diameter (figure 4.27). However, the relationship among these variables at Guzana does not exhibit the clear trends detected in the Assyrian Core, probably due to the small sample size. Of the 5 vessels for which these measurements were available, each displayed a different relationship among these variables (X:X:X-1, X:X:X-2, X:X-1:X-2, X:X-1:X-3, X:X-2:X-2). As in the Central Polity and Dur-Katlimmu, the difference between maximum, rim and neck diameter is typically ≤ 1 cm and can, therefore, be accounted for as the natural variability inherent in the manufacture of a single form by multiple potters.

The three formal variants of Palace Ware form B cups are described morphometrically as follows (adapted from table 3.1):

formal variant	body length	capacity	neck length
B1	4–6 cm	300–450 cm^3	3 cm
B2	7–8 cm	500–900 cm^3	2.5–3 cm
B3	8–10 cm	500–900 cm^3	4.5–5 cm

One vessel in the form B population from Guzana has a capacity < 500 cm^3. Vessel HF also has a body length and neck length consistent with form B1 cups, 4.5 cm and 2 cm respectively. Although HF meets the morphometric criteria for a form B1 cup, it is typologically anomalous with 5 rows of 'micro-dimples' rather than the expected 2 rows of full-size dimples. However, since form B1 cups are the most elaborately decorated vessels in the form B population in the Central Polity, we preliminarily classify vessel HF as a Palace Ware form B1 cup.

Vessel HC was classified as a form B2 cup based on typological criteria and meets the morphometric definitional criteria for Palace Ware form B2 cups: body length 7.4 cm, capacity 696 cm^3, and neck length 6 cm. The 5 remaining form B vessels from Guzana were classified typologically as form B3 cups (HA, HD, HJ, HK and HI). These vessels have bodies 8–10 cm long, neck lengths 3.5–6.5 cm, and capacities 624–880 cm^3, consistent with the morphometric definitional criteria for form B3 Palace Ware cups. Therefore, all 7 typologically form B vessels from Guzana are classified as Palace Ware form B cups.

Form C

Form C jars from Guzana also meet the general definitional morphometric criteria for Palace Ware form C jars: they are unrestricted-vertical in shape, are 13–15 cm in height, with maximum diameters between 9–10 cm, necks 3.5–4 cm long, walls 0.2–0.3 cm thick (mean = 0.25 cm, median = 0.25 cm, no mode available) and capacities 1207–1959 cm^3. The relationship among maximum, rim and neck diameter in Guzana exhibits similar behaviour to that observed in the Central Polity form C population (figure 4.28) and analysis of vessel curvature confirms the uniformity of vessel shape between form C jars from Guzana and the Central Polity: base angle 30–45° (mean = 35°, median = 30°, no mode available), shoulder angle 121–158° (mean = 137°, median = 133°, no mode available), and neck angle 83–84° (mean = 83.5°, median = 84°, no mode available). Form C vessels from Guzana are also the same depth as their Central Polity counterparts (>100%). In fact, the 3 form C jars from Guzana are a better morphometric fit with form C jars from the Central Polity than those from Dur-Katlimmu.

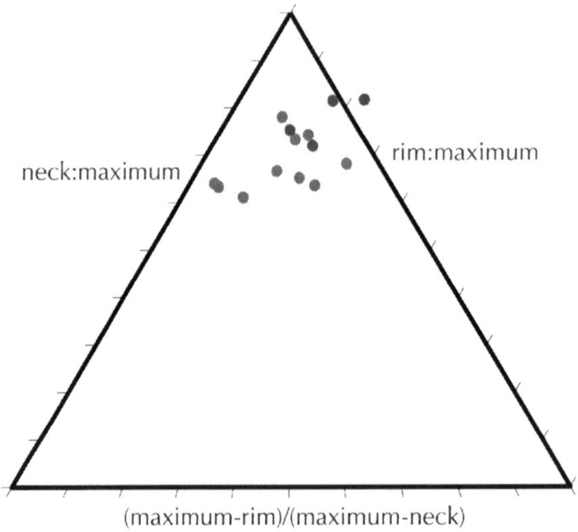

FIGURE 4.28 *Sneed & Folk ternary diagram comparing Palace Ware form C rim, neck & maximum diameters from Guzana (black) & the Central Polity (grey).*

The four formal variants for Palace Ware form C jars are described morphometrically as follows (adapted from table 3.1):

formal variant	body length	capacity	neck length
C1	8–10 cm	1250–1840 cm^3	2.5–3 cm
C2	13.5–14 cm	2800–3050 cm^3	2.7–3 cm
C3	8–10 cm	1250–1840 cm^3	5–6.5 cm
C4	13–13.5 cm	1400–2300 cm	6.5–7.4 cm

The 2 vessels from Guzana typologically classified as form C1 jars (HE and HG) have body lengths of 10 and 14.5 cm, capacities of 1207 and 1959 cm^3 and HE has a neck 3.5 cm long. Although the capacity and neck lengths are within the expected range for C1 jars, the body of HG is longer than expected for form C1 bowls and falls outside the 1.56 cm acceptable margin for inherent variation.

A similar phenomenon of compliance and non-compliance with expected morphometric patterns is observed for the typologically form C4 jar from Guzana. Vessel HB has a capacity of 1504 cm^3, the only vessel with a capacity within range for form C4 vessels, but its neck and body lengths are smaller than expected and outside the 1.56 cm acceptable margin of error, measuring 4 cm and 11 cm respectively.

Chaîne Opératoire

Raw Materials Processing

Geological Raw Materials & Processing

Potential ceramic raw material resources at Guzana include the complex alluvial system of the Ḫābūr Basin or Upper Ḫābūr, particularly deposition by the Ḫābūr river and the karstic springs around Ras al-'Ain. Unfortunately, we were unable to acquire samples from these potential raw material sources. Instead, we used an unpublished regional survey and geochemical analysis of the Upper Ḫābūr conducted by Bishop and Blackman to establish a general raw material profile of local resources at Guzana.

The available information about potential ceramic raw material in the Upper Ḫābūr is far from comprehensive. The region is characterised by sedimentary rock formations of limestone, sandstone and marls (Geological Map of Syria, Syria Arab Republic). Although Bishop and Blackman found that all sediments in the region around Guzana were calcareous, the wt.% of CaO is highly variable from wadi to wadi (2010). Petrographic analysis of locally manufactured cuneiform tablets from the Neo-Assyria city of Sikan, across the Ḫābūr river from Guzana, conducted by Goren suggest that local ceramic raw materials

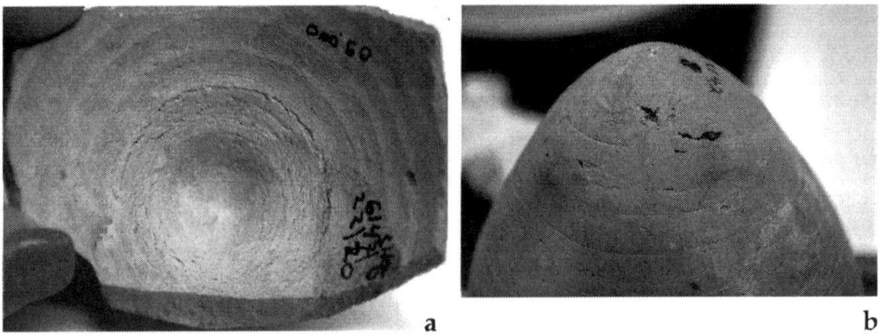

a b

FIGURE 4.29 *Photographs of basal drying defects in the Palace Ware assemblage from Guzana illustrating (a) basal collapse and (b) tearing.*

contained primarily calcite, quartz and mica and did not contain igneous rock fragments or detrital minerals (Goren *et al.* 2004).

As mentioned above, we were unable to sample Palace Ware vessels from Guzana for scientific analysis. Therefore, we are unable to characterise their fabric, precluding their positive identification as Palace Ware and limiting our ability to assess local production vs. Central Polity importation.

Formation

Formation & Shaping

Macroscopic examination of Palace Ware from Guzana reveals rhythmic grooves on the interior of form B and C bases indicative of formation by wheel throwing, similar to the patterns found on Palace Ware from the Central Polity and Dur-Katlimmu. Vessel HA from Guzana has a series of drying cracks or small tears in the fabric which occur in a spiral pattern on the interior of its base (figure 4.29a) and vessel HE exhibits diagonal tears or cracks in its lower body, 1.5 cm above the base (figure 4.29b). The spiral pattern of the drying cracks along the planes of weakness created during wheel throwing support the manufacture of Palace Ware on the wheel at Guzana.

Like Palace Ware from Dur-Katlimmu, vessels from Guzana exhibit fine, continuous rhythmic striations on the exterior surface of some vessels and are devoid of rilling suggesting a secondary shaping stage on the wheel after vessel formation (Rye 1981). The interior surface of the vessels are also smooth and even, which suggests Palace Ware vessels at Guzana, like those at Dur-Katlimmu, were first thrown as rough-outs and subsequently cut down to size, internally and externally, by turning on a wheel (figure 4.30). The waxy or greasy texture and dull sheen of Palace Ware vessels from Dur-Katlimmu and

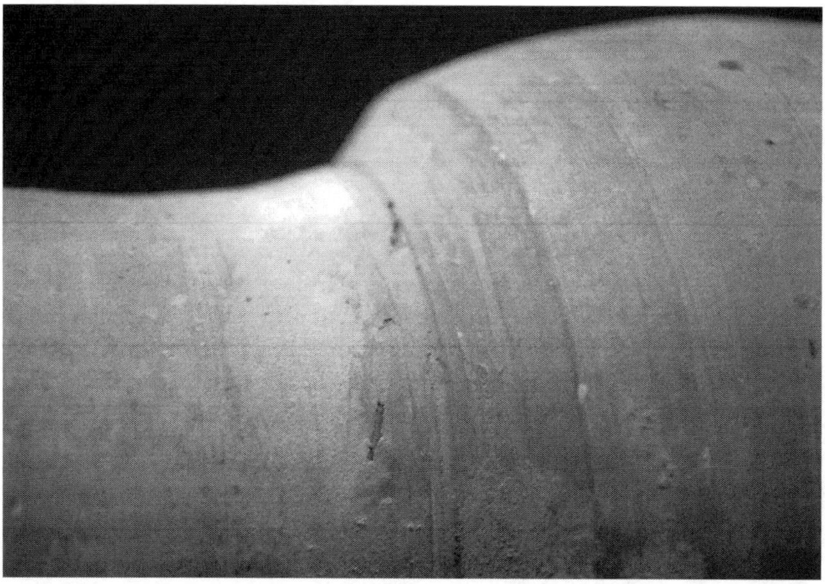

FIGURE 4.30 *Photograph of rhythmic striations indicative of wheel thrown pottery on the external surface of Palace Ware vessel* VA *12563 from Guzana.*

Guzana is indicative of turning on a fast wheel during the leather-hard drying stage (Berg 2008).

Decoration

Evidence of a slip or pseudo-slip was not detected macroscopically or using a hand lens on Palace Ware vessels from Guzana however, vessels were heavily encrusted with drusy greyish crystals also found on Palace Ware in the Central Polity suggestive of calcium enrichment or post-depositional secondary crystallisation of calcium carbonate or calcium hydroxide.

Forty percent (4/10) of the vessels from Guzana are dimpled and, like their Central Polity counterparts, the dimples are oval and oriented with their long axis perpendicular to the base. With the exception of vessel HF, dimples at Guzana are approximately 1 cm along their longest axis, consistent with formation by pressing a fingertip into the vessel wall while it was still pliable. Vessel HF is decorated with 'micro-dimples', 0.3–0.5 cm along their longest axis, which are spherical rather than ovoid and have a deep, smooth, round depression on the exterior surface of the dimple suggesting formation with a tool rather than fingertip. Tool marks are known to be associated with dimples in the Central Polity Palace Ware assemblage.

The protruding or raised rings around the necks of Palace Ware forms B and C from Guzana were likely moulded, consistent with ringed decorations from the Central Polity and Dur-Katlimmu. Although this cannot be confirmed using thin-section analysis, there is no evidence of smoothing or deformation around the margins of the ring (Rye 1981) suggesting that the rings are one with the body and not the result of appliqué.

Firing

We were unable to conduct our own bulk chemical analysis of Palace Ware from Guzana and published INAA analyses of locally manufactured pottery and raw material sources from Guzana provide only the diagnostic trace element profiles (*cf.* Davidson and McKerrell 1976; 1980). Even if major element composition of these ceramics were available, INAA is typically unreliable for calcium measurements (Hancock 1985). However, Guzana is located in a calcium-rich sedimentary environment along the Ḫābūr river. It is reasonable to assume, therefore, that like Palace Ware from Dur-Katlimmu (approximately 60 km downriver), the Palace Ware at Guzana is composed of a calcareous matrix.

Palace Ware from Guzana occurs in pale yellow (2.5Y 7/3) to light grey (10YR 7/2) to light yellow brown (10YR 6/4) to reddish brown (5YR 5/3) to pink (5YR 7/3) (figure 4.13). Only 40% of the population is similar in colour to Palace Ware from the Central Polity, while 60% (6/10) is mottled and/or reddish in colour. We estimate, therefore, that the Palace Ware assemblage at Guzana was fired between 900–1000°C, but probably closer to 900°C or for an insufficient soak time for the vessel colour to be dominated by the crystallisation of calcium silicates and calcium ferrosilicates.

Palace Ware Consumption

Without contextual information for the Guzana Palace Ware, we are limited to consumption patterns by form, and even here caution is advised because the sample is very small (n = 11). That said, form B cups are the most prevalent form at Guzana, making up 70% of the total population (table 4.4); a similar pattern to Nimrud and Nineveh Palace Ware consumption. However, like Dur-Katlimmu, form C vessels are also consumed at Guzana. This difference in Palace Ware consumption between the Central Polity and Annexed Provinces may, as mentioned above, be an artefact of sample size both in the Assyrian Heartland and Annexed Provinces, but may also reflect a change in value and/or social meaning of Palace Ware in general and form C jars in particular in the Annexed Provinces.

Palace Ware Transport Mechanism

Geochemical and petrographic analyses of Palace Ware from Dur-Katlimmu indicate that Palace Ware in the Annexed Provinces was manufactured locally rather than imported from the Central Polity leaving us with two important questions: *how* did Palace Ware spread to the Annexed Provinces?; and *why* did Palace Ware spread to the Annexed Provinces? Deferring the question of *why* until chapter 6, the dissemination of Palace Ware across the imperial landscape could be explained by either the relocation of potters from the Neo-Assyrian Central Polity to the Annexed Provinces or the transmission of Palace Ware as an idea or symbol as the result of interregional interaction.

The relocation of people and/or populations for economic purposes was not uncommon in the Late Assyrian period, and, from what we understand of the nature and structure of the Neo-Assyrian guild system, it is possible that craftsmen and artisans from guilds or chapters of guilds were contracted by provincial governor's palaces. Bakers, cooks, confectioners, potters, carpenters, metalworkers, etc. would all have been essential to the construction, maintenance and proper function of these institutions. If these craftsmen and artisans were from or trained in the Central Polity, the transport mechanism for Palace Ware across the Annexed Provinces may have been the relocation of potters as part of the household/administrative support of the provincial governor.

Palace Ware in the Central Polity has a high degree of inter and intra-site conformity in both form and fabric. For example, in the Central Polity inter-site variation (variance) for Palace Ware vessel height, maximum diameter and neck length across the three forms is 0.39, 0.45 and 0.29 respectively. We would expect Palace Ware from sites in the Annexed Provinces fall within the same range of intersite variation as that for the three Central Polity sites if it were manufactured by Central Polity or Central Polity trained potters: that is the variance between Palace Ware from Dur-Katlimmu and Aššur, for example, would approximate the variance between Aššur and Nineveh. However, as we have seen, formal Palace Ware variation in the Annexed Provinces is outside the accepted range of variability for manufacture of Palace Ware by different Central Polity workshops. Intersite variance in the Annexed Provinces for Palace Ware vessel height, maximum diameter and neck length is quite large, 0.92, 4.13 and 5.55 respectively, indicating that Palace Ware manufacture is not internally consistent across the Annexed Provinces negating the possibility of two Palace Ware traditions, one for the Central Polity and one for the Annexed Provinces.

There are several possible explanations for the formal difference between Palace Ware in the Central Polity and Annexed Provinces: Palace Ware manufacturers in the Annexed Provinces were local, non-Central Polity trained potters; Palace Ware was manufactured by Central Polity trained potters but for consumers requiring something different from their vessels than consumers in the Central Polity; or a combination of the two. The Palace Ware chaîne opératoire in the Annexed Provinces is very close to the one used to manufacture Palace Ware in the Central Polity. At Dur-Katlimmu, potters even used heavily tempered 'plugs' to facilitate basal drying in 1/3 of the form B cups. These similarities in chaîne opératoire and overall execution of Palace Ware shapes suggest that the potters responsible for Palace Ware in the Annexed Provinces had extensive knowledge of and/or familiarity with Assyrian ceramic technology in general but, perhaps, not the nuances of Palace Ware production specifically. The ambivalence of these results, the familiarity with Assyrian potting traditions and yet, significant formal variation from Central Polity vessels may indicate that Palace Ware was transported to the Annexed Provinces as a concept or symbol, modified locally to meet the needs of its consumers. As such, it is possible that the potters were from or trained in the Central Polity and fully conversant in Palace Ware production and that the consumers of Palace Ware in the Annexed Provinces were either not from the Central Polity or required something different from their Palace Ware than Central Polity consumers.

When an artefact is transmitted across cultural boundaries as a concept or symbol, it is translated from the ur-form of its culture of origin to a modified ur-form from the receiving culture's repertoire. During this cultural translation of signs, aspects of the artefact which are culturally and socially significant to the receiving culture are often emphasised or exaggerated. Ur-forms are identified in the archaeological record as morphometric and typological patterns or 'norms', particularly patterns which necessary for the manufacture or use of the object. If the diffusion of Palace Ware across and beyond the Neo-Assyrian imperial landscape resulted from the transmission of Palace Ware as a concept or sign, perhaps via foreign dignitaries or provincial governors, than we would expect to see a shift in the morphometric and typological norms of Palace Ware vessels in the Annexed Provinces and Unincorporated Territories and/or emphasis on different attributes.

As we discuss in greater detail in chapter 6, the Palace Ware ur-form in the Central Polity for forms B and C is a decorated, dimpled, thin-walled, fine-grained unequal biconical or globular, buff-green vessel with a specific capacity. These patterns suggests that the ur-form for Palace Ware cups and jars in the Central Polity was a modified version of the standard Assyrian bottle. The ur-form for Central Polity form A bowls is an undecorated, thin-walled, fine-grained unequal biconical plate with an out-curving rim which is buff-green in colour and also has a specific capacity.

In the Annexed Provinces, the Palace Ware 'norms' are also thin-walled, fine-grained, unequal biconical and globular cups and jars and unequal biconical bowls. However, Palace Ware vessels in the Annexed Provinces do not occur in the restricted range of colours and capacities found in the Central Polity assemblage. In addition, Palace Ware from the Annexed Provinces is more extensively and elaborately decorated than their Central Polity counterparts, particularly at Dur-Katlimmu, with typical Assyrian decorative elements and motifs, some of which are not associated with Palace Ware in the Central Polity, and the neck/rim elements of form A and B vessels are elongated. These patterns suggest that the sign translated to create a Palace Ware ur-form in the Annexed Provinces for forms B and C was related to the typical Assyrian bottle or storage jar ur-form, a common cultural concept or sign shared with the Central Polity, and preserved many of the modified features of the Central Polity Palace Ware ur-form, such as wall-thickness and fabric-fineness. However, the Palace Ware ur-form in the Annexed Provinces was translated into a regionally meaningful sign by modifying and exaggerating Palace Ware attributes, such as decoration, and ignoring others, such as capacity and colour. Similarities and differences between Palace Ware ur-forms in the Central Polity and Annexed Provinces indicate a high degree of semantic relationship between the two signs. However the emphasis on the 'Assyrian-ness' of Palace Ware in the Annexed Provinces over other attributes, such as colour and capacity, distinguish this characteristic as possessing increased social significance in this region.

We conclude, therefore, that Palace Ware in the Annexed Provinces was not transported or traded from the Central Polity but locally manufactured. While it is possible, even likely, that the potters were from or trained in the Central Polity, Palace Ware does not appear to have been transmitted by the manufactures as part of a standard 'Assyrian' ceramic repertoire. Rather, Palace Ware was produced in the Annexed Provinces to serve a specific social or symbolic function and, as such, was transmitted across this region as an idea, concept or social practice.

CHAPTER 5

Palace Ware in the Unincorporated Territories

The transmission of Neo-Assyrian culture throughout the greater Mediterranean is a well-known albeit largely unanalysed phenomenon. Geometric polychrome stone paved floors, associated with Neo-Assyrian palace and administrative complexes in Turkey and Syria, for example, are reported in 8th and 7th century BCE levels as far away as Portugal and Spain (Bláquez Martínez and Valiente Malla 1982). Phoenician trade is the hypothesised mechanism for the transmission of Assyrian material culture and technology (*cf.* Aubet 2001). Despite the widespread dissemination of Assyrian architecture and material culture throughout the Mediterranean, Palace Ware appears to be a localised phenomenon occurring only in proper Assyrian provinces and adjacent areas.

Although Palace Ware appears to be a Neo-Assyrian phenomenon, Palace Ware or Palace Ware style vessels are recovered from non-Assyrian or at least not properly Assyrian contexts such as the site of Tel Jemmeh (Petrie 1928). Jemmeh is adjacent to the Ashdod province, annexed by Sargon II (711 BCE) in order to prevent its allegiance with Egypt, however Jemmeh itself remained outside the official imperial administrative structure (Radner 2006). We selected Tel Jemmeh for inclusion in this study because of the importance of the anthropological questions surrounding 'Assyrian presence' at this site and the availability of material for scientific analysis.

Palace Ware vessels were identified by both Petrie (1928) and van Beek (1973) at Tel Jemmeh. Unfortunately, none of the 'eggshell' ware from Petrie's excavation has been found in the Petrie Palestinian Collection at UCL Institute of Archaeology and so we are unable to include it in this study. Van Beek used the field classification 'Palace Ware' to refer to all Assyrian-style ceramics at Jemmeh, incorporating both the thicker tableware and 'eggshell' thin Palace Ware under this term. We used our Palace Ware typology generated by analysis of Palace Ware vessels from the Central Polity to identify basic Palace Ware shapes and styles in this mixed assemblage and separate out potential Palace Ware vessels for morphometric analysis.

The potential Palace Ware population from Tel Jemmeh, like all archaeological ceramic assemblages, is composed of both complete and fragmentary vessels. This means that not every measurement or observation is possible for each vessel. The number of samples in a given typological or morphometric analysis reflects the total number of vessels in the population for which the observation/measurement is available and may vary from the total number of vessels in that population.

 | DOI 10.1163/9789004304123_006

Tel Jemmeh

Tel Jemmeh, also referred to in modern Hebrew as Tel Re'im or by its Biblical name Yurza, has no known Assyrian toponym. In the 1970s and 1980s, there was considerable debate about whether Jemmeh was the Akkadian 'Arṣa' from Middle Assyrian texts, and Wadi Besor, adjacent to Jemmeh, the "Brook of Egypt" mentioned in Neo-Assyrian royal annals (*cf.* Na'aman 1979; Aharoni 1979). Although complete agreement on this matter was never reached, most scholars believe the "Brook of Egypt" refers to Wadi el-Arish on the Mediterranean coast in the Sinai, which would place Arṣa significantly south and west of Tel Jemmeh (*cf.* Rainey 1982; Tadmor 1958).

The site of Tel Jemmeh is 4.9 hectares and located 10 km southeast of Gaza. Jemmeh was first excavated in 1927 by Sir W. M. Flindres Petrie, Edwards Professor of Egyptian Archaeology and Philology at UCL (Petrie 1928). The site was excavated on and off from 1970–1983 by Augustus van Beek, Smithsonian Institution National Museum of Natural History. Van Beek's excavation of Jemmeh is, to date, unpublished. In 2009, the Smithsonian Institution hired a contract archaeologist to complete and publish van Beek's excavation report. At the time of writing, these reports are in progress and will not be completed in time for inclusion in the present study. However, we were able to fully examine van Beek's notes and relevant material culture, for which my grateful thanks go to Melinda Zeder, Curator of Old World Archaeology, Smithsonian Institution National Museum of Natural History.

Understanding the nature of the relationship between Jemmeh and the Neo-Assyrian empire, and/or even if there was one, is complicated. Both Petrie and van Beek believed there was an Assyrian occupation of Jemmeh during the Late Assyrian period. Petrie (1928) argued that a series of structures in stratum EF were Assyrian in design and van Beek identified a large building of similar style as Assyrian based on architectural features and the presence at both locations of Palace Ware. As we discuss below and in chapter 6, the pottery at Tel Jemmeh is not Palace Ware and is only very generally Assyrian in style indicating that it was not produced or consumed by an Assyrian population in residence at Jemmeh. Likewise, the 'Assyrian' architecture at Jemmeh is only vaguely similar to Neo-Assyrian residential and administrative structures in the Neo-Assyrian Central Polity and Annexed Provinces (figure 5.1) (for discussion of Neo-Assyrian architecture and its adoption/adaptation throughout the empire see *i.a.* Castel 1992 and Manuelli 2009).

Palace Ware included in this study comes from van Beek's excavation of Jemmeh courtesy of the Smithsonian Institution National Museum of Natural History. The 22 vessels available for destructive and non-destructive analysis come from well-defined occupation contexts, primarily building collapse and fill.

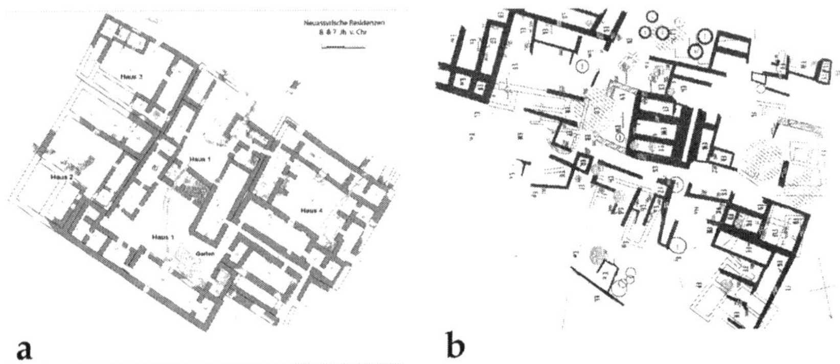

FIGURE 5.1 *Architectural comparison of the Neo-Assyrian residences at Dur-Katlimmu (a) & those described as Assyrian at Tell Jemmeh by Petrie (b). Note that the houses at Jemmeh are not oriented around courtyards; a traditional feature of Assyrian residential architecture. (reprinted with permission from Kühne 2006–2008, Abb. 3 & Petrie 1928).*

Typology

Form A

Eighteen vessels in the Jemmeh assemblage met the basic shape and style criteria for Palace Ware form A bowls: unequal biconical bodies with out-curving, horizontal, everted rims. None of the form A bowls from Jemmeh have the incurving necks found on vessels AQ, AR and AW from Aššur and form A vessels from the Annexed Provinces. Most form A bowls from Jemmeh have thinned or rounded lips, however vessels JS and JO have thickened, asymmetrical t-shaped rims and lips (figure 5.2). Sixtynine percent (9/13) of the form A population at Jemmeh have rounded or flat bases, 15% (2/13) have disk bases and another 15% have ring bases—a basal element not associated with form A Palace Ware from the Central Polity or Annexed Provinces.

Unlike Palace Ware assemblages in the Central Polity and Annexed Provinces, form A bowls are the most numerous Palace Ware shape in the Jemmeh assemblage; they are also the most elaborate in terms of decoration. Eleven vessels (61%) are decorated with registers of 2 or 3 lines around their maximum diameter or on the upper cone of the biconical body. The number of lines in the register and depth of penetration into the vessel wall are independent of other stylistic features such as base and lip type. Two vessels differ slightly from this pattern: vessel JA has a register of lines around its maximum diameter and one above its base and vessel JL has a single register of lines around its rim.

Four vessels (22%) are decorated with protruding or excised ridges around the maximum diameter or on the upper cone of the biconic body. These ridges occur singly and in pairs and are not correlated with other stylistic elements

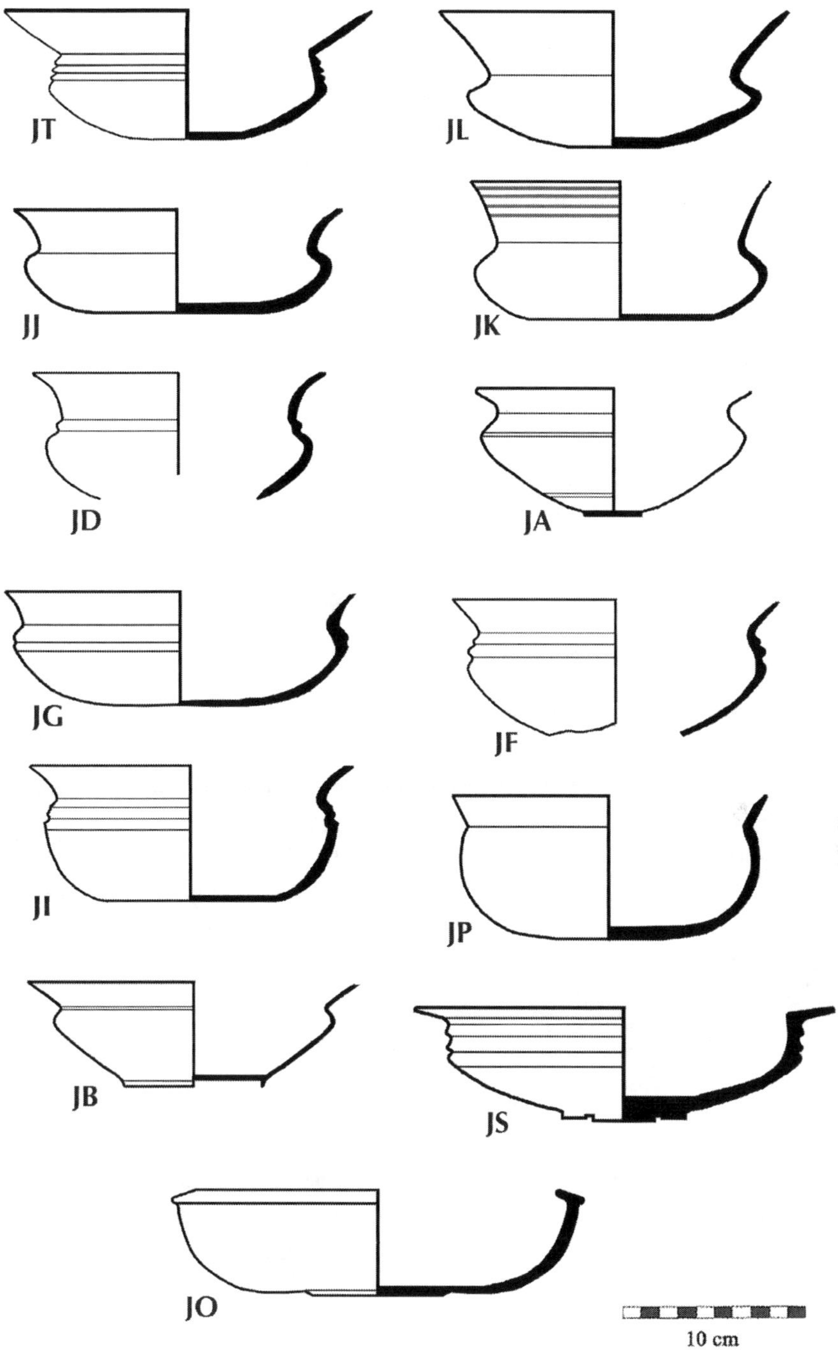

FIGURE 5.2 *Palace Ware/Assyrian style bowls from Tell Jemmeh.*

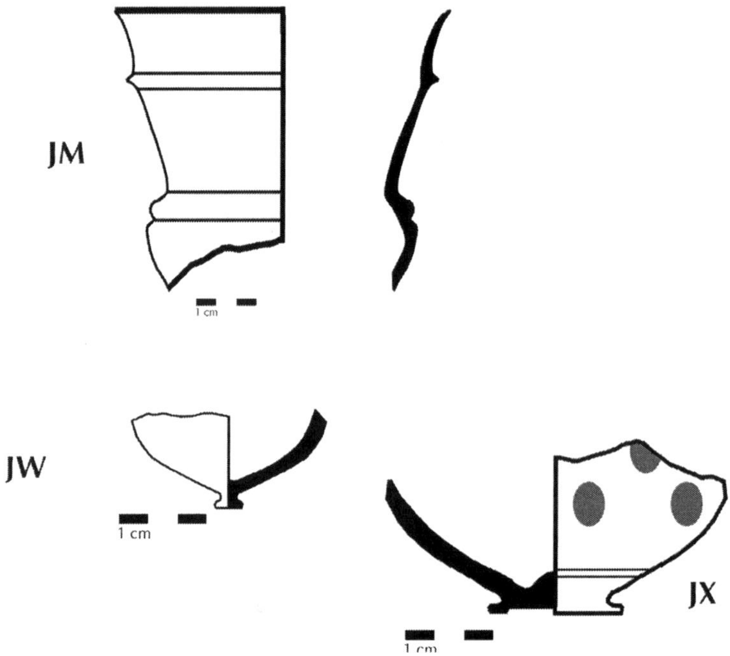

FIGURE 5.3 *Palace Ware/Assyrian style cups from Tell Jemmeh.*

such as base or lip type. Two vessels (11%) are decorated with a combination of ridges and registers of lines: vessels JF and J8 have a single ridge around their maximum diameter with two deep lines above and below the ridge. Basal elements are not available for these vessels. The remaining 3 form A vessels (17%) are undecorated, although one of these, vessel JK, has irregular bright, polished stripes where the ceramic body has been compressed, possibly indicating turning or burnishing.

Form B

Three possible form B cups were identified in the Palace Ware assemblage from Tel Jemmeh (figure 5.3). Based on the number of dimpled body sherds recovered at the site it is probable that the original form B population was larger than these three vessels. Given the similarities in shape and style between forms B and C it is not possible to positively differentiate these forms from body and rim sherds, therefore in this analysis we were only able to consider larger vessel fragments (≥ 15% complete) with diagnostic measurements and/or stylistic and decorative elements preserved.

Vessels JW and JX are basal fragments, estimated between 15–20% complete. Vessel JW has a non-functional knob base and the section of body wall preserved is undecorated. Given this limited information, vessel JW is most similar to form B3 cups from the Central Polity. Vessel JX has a ring base upon which it can stand; at least it is able to support the extant fragment. The body of JX which is preserved is decorated with a row of 6 dimples and 2 registers of 2 lines between the base and row of dimples. In terms of decorative style, vessel JX is similar to B1 and B2 cups, however, the function base suggests it is more closely related to form B1 cups. However, all of the form B1 vessels from the Central Polity have disk bases.

Vessel JM is the most complete form B cup in the assemblage (estimated at 40% extant). Although the basal element is missing, it is unequal biconical with an incurving neck, and out-curving, horizontal, everted rim with a thinned lip, similar to form B vessels from the Central Polity. Vessel JM has a single pinched ridge around its neck below the lip and a register of 3 lines around its shoulder. Not enough of the body exists to determine whether or not the vessel was dimpled. The only form B vessels from the Neo-Assyrian Central Polity with both pinched neck rings and registers of lines are form B1 cups. Based on decorative style, vessel JM is most similar to these forms.

Form C

Three possible form C jars were identified in the Palace Ware assemblage from Tel Jemmeh. Vessels JV and JN are relatively complete, estimated at 95% and 45% preserved respectively, and vessel JE is approximately 15% complete (figure 5.4). Both vessels JV and JN are unequal biconical with incurving necks, out-curving horizontal, everted rims with thinned lips, consistent with form C jars from the Central Polity. Vessel JE is unequal biconical with a vertical neck and thinned lip—a neck shape not associated with form C vessels in Assyria proper. Only vessel JV has a preserved basal element, which is non-functional and rounded.

Vessel JV has an undecorated body and a register of three lines around its lip, most closely resembling form C3 jar AH typologically. The register of incised lines around the lip of bowl AH is thick and forms a thick decorative band around the vessel's mouth 1.5 cm wide (figure 3.18). The register of lines around vessel JV is shallow and narrow, approximately 0.5 cm wide, an interesting stylistic difference. Another difference between C3 jars from the Central Polity and JV is the basal element: C3 jars typically have flat bases and JV is rounded.

Vessels JN and JE have undecorated necks and 2 rows of dimples beginning just below the shoulder, similar to form C1 vessels from the Central Polity. Due to the fragmentary nature of JE, we were not able to quantify the number of dimples per row, but vessel JN has 4 dimples per row, consistent with form C jars in the Central Polity. Form C1 vessels in the Central Polity typically have neck decoration, however vessel AJ has an undecorated neck indicating that the decorative style of JN and JE is not without precedent in Assyria proper.

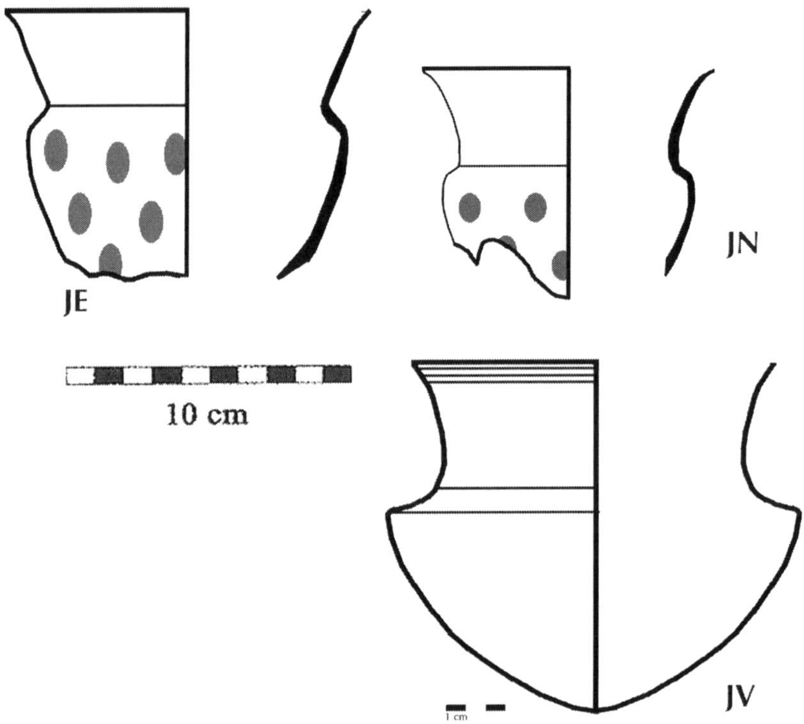

FIGURE 5.4 *Palace Ware/Assyrian style jars from Tell Jemmeh.*

Morphometric Analysis

Morphometric confirmation of Palace Ware forms at Tel Jemmeh is complicated by the small size and fragmentary nature of the sample population, particularly forms B and C, and the predominance of form A vessels—the least common form in the Central Polity.

As discussed in chapter 3, the shapes and styles of Palace Ware vessels are not unique either to Palace Ware or the Late Assyrian period, with the possible exception of form A bowls. Palace Ware is distinguished from the greater Assyrian ceramic assemblage by its thin walls (0.15–0.3 cm), fine fabric ($f{:}c_{0.062mm} = 98{:}2$), and restricted capacity. Preliminary morphometric analysis of wall thickness and vessel capacity indicate that the majority of the Palace Ware-style vessels at Jemmeh do not meet the definitional critera for Neo-Assyrian Palace Ware. Therefore, we refer to these vessels as 'Assyrian-style' or 'Palace Ware-style' to indicate typological (stylistic) similarity to the greater Assyrian ceramic corpus but not formal (morphometric) or fabric conformity to Neo-Assyrian Palace Ware diagnostic criteria.

In the Central Polity, Palace Ware vessel walls are 0.15–0.3 cm thick (mean = 0.26 cm; median = 0.25 cm; mode = 0.20 cm). Forms B and C are slightly thinner than form A and form B cups are the thinnest vessels in the assemblage (mean = 0.24 cm; median = 0.23 cm; mode = 0.20 cm). The difference in wall thickness between forms C and A is less pronounced: form C has walls with a mean thickness of 0.28 cm and median of 0.28 cm (no mode available for this data set), while form A has walls with a mean thickness of 0.3 cm, a median of 0.35 cm, and a mode of 0.3 cm.

At Tel Jemmeh, Assyrian-style vessel walls are 0.2–0.6 cm thick (mean = 0.35 cm; median = 0.35 cm, mode = 0.30 cm), considerably thicker than Palace Ware vessel walls from the Central Polity. Palace Ware-style form A bowls are the thickest population in the Jemmeh assemblage, with walls 0.25–0.60 cm thick (mean = 0.38 cm, median = 0.40 cm, mode = 0.40 cm—values which are consistently about 0.10 cm thicker than form A Palace Ware vessels in the Central Polity).

The 6 vessel fragments which constitute the form B and C Palace Ware-style vessels at Tel Jemmeh are, however, within the form specific thickness trends observed in the Central Polity: form B-style cups at Tel Jemmeh have walls 0.20–0.35 cm thick (mean = 0.25 cm, median = 0.20 cm, mode = 0.20 cm) and form C-style jars have walls 0.20–0.3 cm thick (mean = 0.25 cm, median = 0.25 cm, no mode available for this data set).

Palace Ware is discontinuous with regard to capacity in the Central Polity: form A and B vessels hold between 200–900 cm^3 while form C vessels hold 1250 cm^3 or more. At Tel Jemmeh, there is also a discontinuity in vessel capacity: one population holds between 600–1900 cm^3 and the other population holds 2800 cm^3 or more. We could not detect any subdivisions or internal structure in the cluster of vessels with capacities 600–1900 cm^3 using MRPP. This observation is, however, consistent with capacity measurements observed in the Annexed Provinces for form C jars and may indicate that any capacity specific social function of these vessels in the Central Polity was not observed or essential to their consumption and social value in both the Annexed Provinces and Unincorporated Territories.

All of the vessels complete enough for capacity analysis in the Jemmeh assemblage were form A-style bowls, except JV which is typologically form C. However, form C vessels are defined as holding ≥ 1250 cm^3 and vessel JV holds 895 cm^3 suggesting that it more closely resembles a form B cup: similar in shape to form C jars but with capacity measurements between 200 and 900 cm^3.

Form A vessels in Assyria proper hold 200–800 cm^3. Assyrian-style bowls from Tel Jemmeh hold between 600–3,400 cm^3. Only a single vessel falls within the definitional capacity range for form A Palace Ware bowls, vessel JT

(624 cm^3) and one other vessel holds just slightly more than 800 cm^3, vessel JJ (830 cm^3). However, these vessels do not meet the definitional criteria for form A wall thickness, being 0.35 and 0.4 cm thick respectively. In fact, none of the form A-style bowls from Tel Jemmeh meet the definitional criteria for Palace Ware. We include them in this analysis because their occurrence so far away from the Assyrian heartland is intriguing and may provide insight into the social function and semiotic value of Assyrian-style vessels outside Assyrian imperial borders. However, Assyrian-style form B and C vessels at Jemmeh do meet their respective form specific definitional thickness criteria and, since capacity measurements are not available for these vessels, we rely upon detailed morphometric analysis to determine their sub-form, if any.

Form A

The 18 Assyrian-style bowls from Tel Jemmeh (figure 5.2) are unrestricted-horizontal in shape, 4.2–7.8 cm in height, 10.8–21 cm at their widest, with necks 1.3–3.5 cm long, walls 0.25–0.5 cm thick and capacities between 624–3,429 cm^3. The depth of these vessels is between 20–40% (mean = 31%; median = 32%; mode = 25 and 38%). These measurements indicate that Palace Ware-style form A vessels at Jemmeh are approximately twice as high and between 2–7 cm wider than their Palace Ware counterparts.

Morphometric differences between Palace Ware form A bowls and the form A-style pottery at Jemmeh extends beyond vessel size to aspects of shape. Neck elements on Assyrian-style bowls from Jemmeh are 1.1–2.3 cm longer than their Palace Ware counterparts, outside the acceptable 1.56 cm margin of variation for approximately 70% (13/18) of the population. The ratio of height to neck length exhibits no clear pattern at Jemmeh, however clusters are observed at 4:1 and 3:1 in the form A population from the Central Polity. Of the 13 vessels for which height and neck length measurements were available, three modes or trends of 2 vessels each (15% of the population) were observed at 7:2, 6:1 and 3:1 suggesting three possible shape variants in the population, only one of which is similar to Neo-Assyrian Palace Ware.

A Sneed and Folk diagram of maximum, rim and neck diameter and analysis of vessel curvature also illustrate the difference in shape between the Assyrian-style bowls at Jemmeh and form A Palace Ware bowls. Palace Ware form A vessels form a tight cluster indicating the uniformity of the relationship among maximum, rim and neck diameter (figure 5.5); Assyrian-style bowls at Jemmeh do not. Although Palace Ware form A-style vessels from Jemmeh plot in the same general region, the grouping is disperse indicating that these vessels are either manufactured with less uniformity, according to more general criteria for vessel shape, than Palace Ware and/or that the Assyrian-style bowl

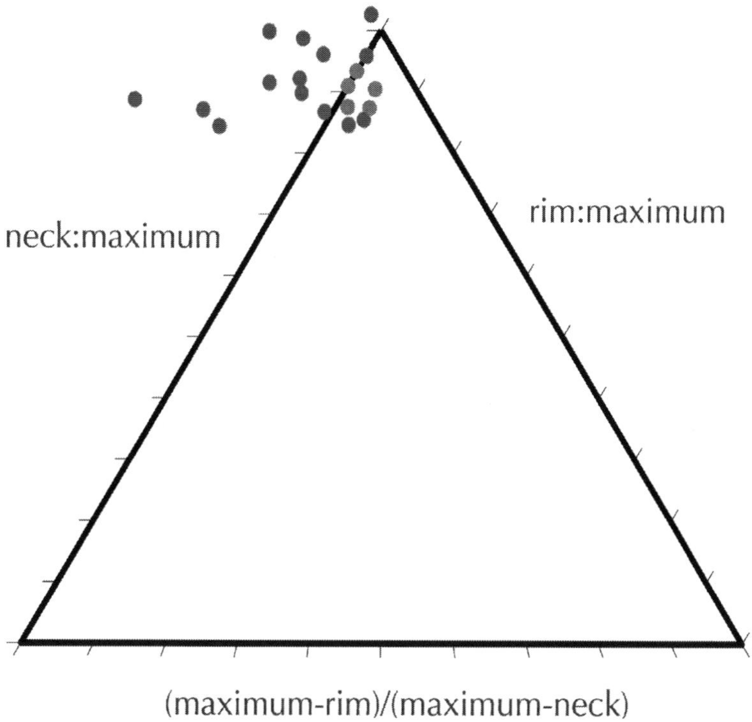

FIGURE 5.5 *Sneed & Folk ternary diagram comparing rim, neck & maximum diameters from Assyrian style bowls at Tell Jemmeh (black) and Palace Ware form A bowls from the Central Polity (grey).*

population at Jemmeh contains multiple shapes as opposed to the single shape detected in the Palace Ware assemblage. However, we did not detect internal structure or sub-groups related to maximum, rim and neck diameter in the Jemmeh population which would indicate multiple shapes.

Vessel curvature analysis of neck and shoulder angle for Palace Ware form A bowls from the Central Polity reveals 3 clusters: (a) neck = 25–28°, shoulder = 160–163°; (b) neck = 40–75°, shoulder = 112–114°; and (c) neck = 24–76°, shoulder = 135–146°. Only two of the form A-style vessels from Tel Jemmeh conform to these patterns: vessels JB and JK have neck and shoulder angles consistent with pattern c (necks = 38° and 62° and both shoulders = 135°). Another sub-population of 4 form A-style vessels almost conforms to pattern b (neck angles = 35–62° with shoulder angles = 108–110°). The shoulder angles of the latter sub-population of vessels is consistently 4° smaller than their form A pattern b counterparts which could indicate imperfect replication of the pattern b shape by multiple potters producing the same form. The remaining 60%

(9/15) of the Palace Ware-style bowls from Tel Jemmeh, form a tight grouping with neck angles between 34–67° and shoulder angles 120–126° which could indicate a form-shape variant unique to Jemmeh.

Biplots of capacity against neck length and body length reveal two potential size variants: vessels with capacities 600–2000 cm³ with neck lengths 1.3–3.5 cm and bodies 2.8–5.5 cm long; and vessels with capacities 2800–3400 cm³ with neck lengths 2.3–2.5 cm and body lengths 5–6.5 cm. MRPP analysis indicates that these groups represent statistically significant, different populations of origin ($\delta_{obs} = 0.97$; $\delta_{exp} = 1.48$; p-value = 0.0025) and that there are two formal variants related to size in the Jemmeh Palace Ware-style form A population. However, these formal variants appear to be the same shape and do not correlate with the stylistic groups previously observed in the form A-style population. For example, the 3 larger vessels, JF, JI and JO, include both vessels decorated with protruding lines and undecorated forms. Vessel JO, the undecorated form in this cluster, also differs from vessels JF and JI in terms of its lip style: JO is one of the two vessels in the population with a thickened, asymmetrical t-shaped rim and lip while vessels JF and JI have thinned lips.

These results indicate that the form A-style bowls at Tel Jemmeh are a single shape with two different sub-populations related to size. None of these vessels meet the morphometric definitional criteria for Palace Ware form A bowls nor do they exhibit the formal patterns observed in the Palace Ware form A population from the Central Polity. They do, however, exhibit stylistic and formal similarities to vessels found in the greater Neo-Assyrian ceramic assemblage, particularly tableware.

Form B

Three vessels were identified typologically as form B Palace Ware, however, preliminary morphometric analysis of vessel capacity indicates that vessel JV should also be included in this population (figure 5.3). Vessel fragments of potential form B vessels JX, JM and JW are too fragmentary for complete morphometric characterisation. Therefore, our discussion focuses on the vessel JV and it is important to note that any patterns observed are only speculative.

Vessel JV is unrestricted-vertical in shape, stands 9.7 cm high, has a 3 cm neck, and holds 896 cm³—all of which are consistent with form B vessels in the Central Polity. Vessel JV also has walls 0.3 cm thick which, while within the diagnostic limits for form B Palace Ware vessels, is at the thick end of the acceptable range. However, vessel JV has a maximum diameter of 10.4 cm, 0.7 cm wider than the widest form B cups in the Central Polity, and a neck diameter of 8 cm, 0.5 cm wider than the widest form B vessel necks, however, both are within the acceptable 1.56 cm margin of variation. A Sneed and Folk

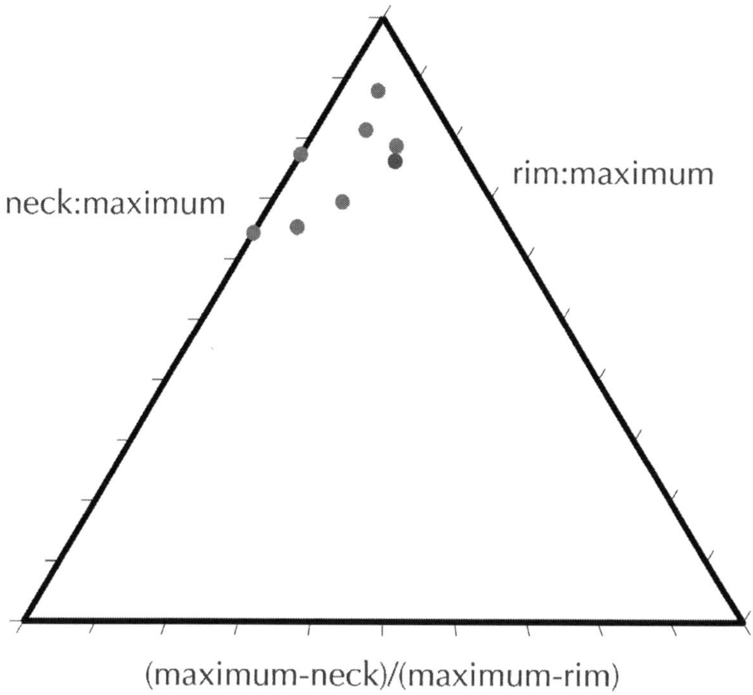

FIGURE 5.6 *Sneed & Folk ternary diagram comparing rim, neck & maximum diameters from Assyrian style cups at Tell Jemmeh (black) and Palace Ware form A bowls from the Central Polity (grey).*

diagram comparing the maximum, rim and neck diameter relationship for vessel JV and Palace Ware form B vessels illustrates that this vessel fits the observed pattern for Central Polity vessels of a x:x-1:x-2 relationship (figure 5.6). The capacity and neck length of JV are consistent with form B2 Palace Ware cups. However, vessel JV has a shorter (6.5 cm) and wider (10.4 cm) body than form B2 cups, although body length is within the acceptable margin of error.

Vessel curvature patterns for form B vessels at Jemmeh are consistent with those from the Central Polity, with one exception. Base angles are available for vessels JW, JX and JV, 26°, 32° and 17° respectively. Base angles in the Central Polity are between 25–62°, which makes JV an outlier. Neck and shoulder angles for JV are within the expected ranges for form B cups, 85° and 147° respectively. Vessel JM (neck angle = 75° and shoulder angle = 145°) also conforms to the curvature pattern for form B cups: neck angle = 69–90° and shoulder angle = 120–153°.

In summary, vessel JV meets the morphometric definitional criteria for Palace Ware form B2 vessels but, as we shall see, does not meet the fabric

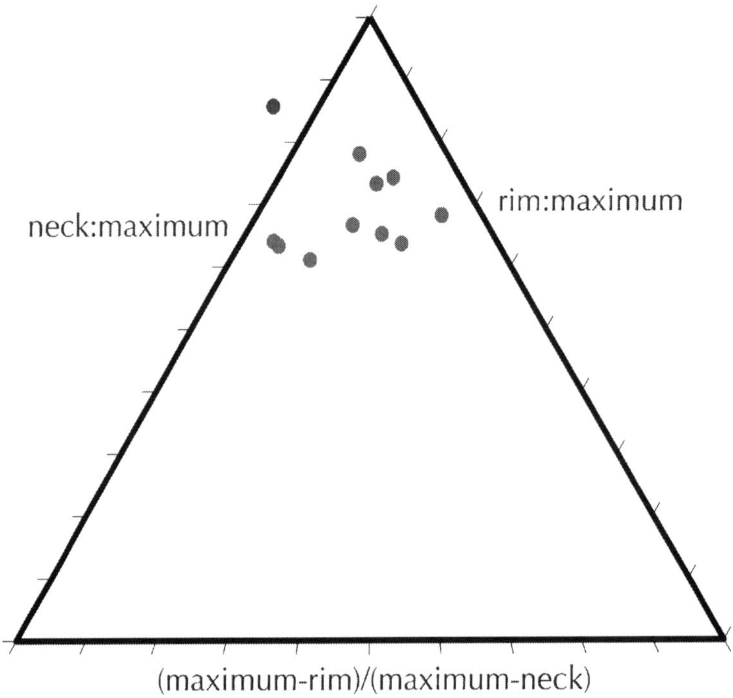

FIGURE 5.7 *Sneed & Folk ternary diagram comparing Palace Ware form B rim, neck & maximum from Assyrian style jars at Tell Jemmeh (black) and Palace Ware form A bowls from the Central Polity (grey).*

criteria. Therefore we cannot classify it as a Palace Ware form B2 and must refer to it as 'Palace Ware-style form B2'. We are unable to positively identify or exclude vessel fragments JX, JM and JW from classification as form B Palace Ware based on morphometric criteria but, like vessel JV, they cannot be classified as Palace Ware based on fabric analysis.

Form C

Vessel JN is 40% complete (basal element missing) but the extant fragment is unrestricted-vertical in form with an unequal biconical shape, incurving neck, out-curving, horizontal everted rim and thinned lip consistent with form B and C Palace Ware vessels in the Central Polity. Its maximum diameter is 9.4 cm and wall thickness 0.2 cm—consistent with Palace Ware form C jars. The neck length of vessel JN is 3.5 cm and, although this value is within the acceptable margin of variability for morphometric analysis, there is a discontinuity in form C neck lengths in the Central Polity between 3–5 cm which becomes apparent when the neck lengths of the 4 form C variants are compared (table 3.1). This means that vessel JN is an outlier with regard to neck length. Since Palace Ware form B cups also have a neck length discontinuity between 3–4.5 cm, vessel JN is an outlier in terms of its neck length for form B cups as well.

Vessel JE is 15% complete and is also missing its basal element. It is unrestricted-vertical in shape with a maximum diameter of 11 cm, neck 3 cm long and walls 0.2 cm thick. Other definitional measurements, such as capacity and body length are unavailable for this vessel.

The maximum, rim and neck diameters of vessel JN (9.4 cm, 10 cm, and 8 cm respectively) and vessel JE (11 cm, 12 cm, and 10 cm respectively) are all within definitional range for form C jars, however, a Sneed and Folk diagram comparing vessels JN and JE with form C jars from the Central Polity reveals that the relationship among these measurements is inconsistent with the patterns observed for Palace Ware jars from the Central Polity (figure 5.7).

Form C vessels in the Central Polity are very uniform in shape, particularly vessel curvature with neck angles 67–87° and shoulder angles 96–152°. Vessel JN conforms to this pattern with a neck angle of 76° and shoulder angle of 129°, while vessel JE is an outlier in terms of its neck angle (60°) but not shoulder angle (130°). This is not surprising because vessel JE has a unique neck shape; a vertical neck rather than the typical incurving neck shape of Palace Ware forms B and C.

In summary, vessels JN and JE each approximate Palace Ware form C jars but are subtly different from Palace Ware in their morphometric and stylistic attributes. Neither vessel meets the fabric critera for Palace Ware classification.

Chaîne Opératoire

Raw Materials Processing

Geological Raw Materials & Processing

Potential ceramic raw material resources in and around Tel Jemmeh come from loessial and alluvial deposits associated with the neighbouring Wadi Besor. According to Melson and van Beek (1992) Wadi Besor cuts through loess deposited during the Würmian, whose source region is the Sinai and Libya for the coarse fraction and eastern Sahara for the fine fraction. They found that alluvium from the bed of the wadi basin was suitable for potting in terms of plasticity and workability (Melson and van Beek 1992). Therefore we collected geological sediment samples for comparative raw material analysis of Assyrian-style pottery at Jemmeh from the wadi scarp adjacent to the site, approximately 400 cm below the surface in the same strata as Melson and van Beek's sample 8, which they identified as unmodified loess (1992).

The geological sediment sample is moderately sorted, light (10YR 6/4–10YR 6/6) and contains hardly any organic vegetal matter (<1%). Particle size analysis of the sediment indicates that it is trimodal; composed primarily of granules (Φ -2– -1) and coarse (Φ 1) and fine sands (Φ 4) with a small clay fraction (0.47% weight percent or 99.5% cumulative coarser). A histogram and cumulative curve of particle size distribution for the sediment resemble the sorting expected in river sediments rather than dune sediments and loess (figure 5.8). However, particle morphology is consistent with loess: particles are angular to sub-angular and prismoidal to sub-prismoidal. These results are consistent with the complexity of a wadi system, particularly one that cuts through loess and reworked loess deposits.

Mineral inclusions, identified by optical microscopy of a smear slide, include (in order of frequency): quartz, plagioclase, calcite, amphibole (hornblende), micrite, microcline, zircon, epidote and tourmaline. Opaques, probably of red and black iron and titanium rich minerals such as hematite, magnetite and rutile, are common. These observations are consistent with loess from the northwestern Negev (for petrological analyses see Engstrom 2004; Fabian and Goren 2002).

Palace Ware fabrics, as we have seen, are extremely well-sorted and fine-grained, containing no inclusions > 0.05 mm and fewer than 2% inclusions in the ceramic matrix. Petrographic analysis of Palace Ware-style ceramics from Jemmeh, discussed in detail below, are significantly coarser and less well sorted than their Palace Ware counterparts. Raw sediment from Wadi Besor has 86% cumulative coarser particles at Φ 5.5, the division between matrix material and inclusions. Palace Ware-style ceramic fabrics from Jemmeh have approximately 7% cumulative coarser particles at Φ 5.5, indicating intentional human behaviour and raw material processing (figure 5.9). Comparative analysis of particle size distribution histograms for sediment from Wadi Besor and Jemmeh Palace Ware-style ceramics also suggest raw material processing: sediments from Wadi Besor are trimodal at Φ -2, Φ 1, and Φ 4 (figure 5.8b) while Jemmeh fabrics are unimodal and exhibit a normal distribution around Φ 4 (figure 5.9).

Palace Ware-style fabrics at Jemmeh do not exhibit the sharp truncation in particle size distribution indicative of sedimentation observed in Palace Ware fabrics from the Central Polity and Annexed Provinces. Therefore, we conclude that Palace Ware-style ceramics at Jemmeh were not manufactured from raw material processed by sedimentation. According to the histogram only the coarsest fraction, granule and above (≥ Φ -1 or 2 mm), were removed from the Assyrian-style fabrics at Jemmeh. Particles this size could have been removed by hand and/or using a basket sieve: preserving the sand fraction (Φ 0–4) which is largely lost during sedimentation.

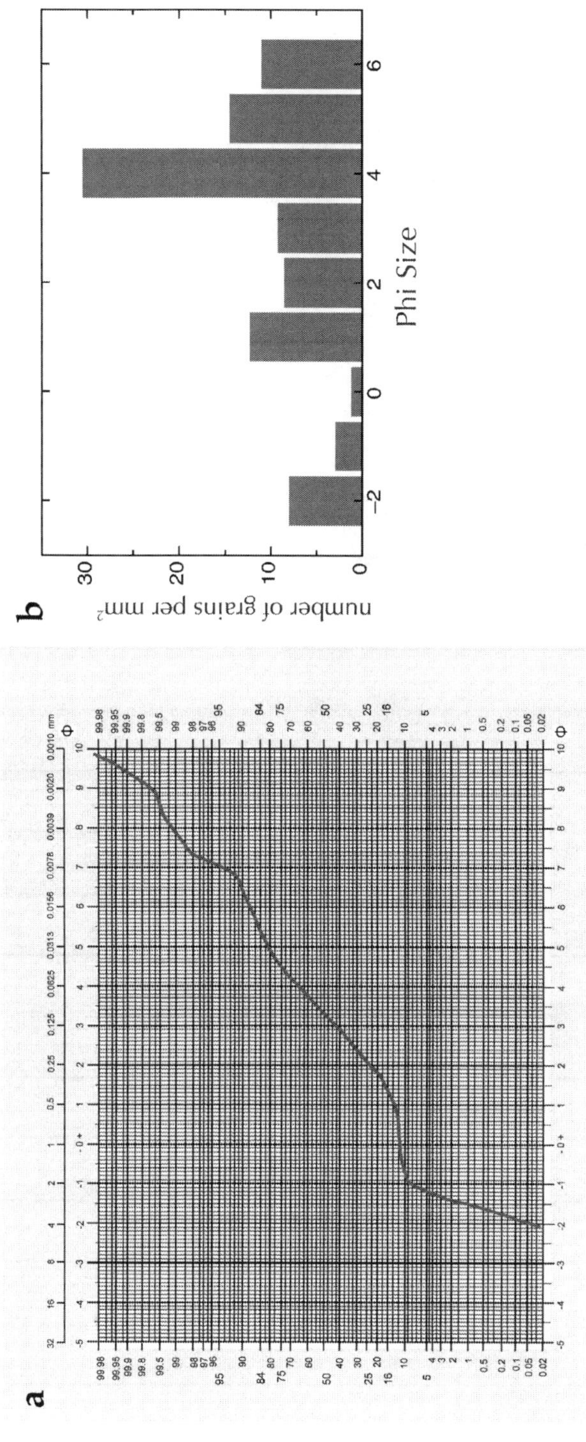

FIGURE 5.8 *Particle size analysis of sediments from the Wadi Besor. (a) cumulative coarser curve; (b) histogram.*

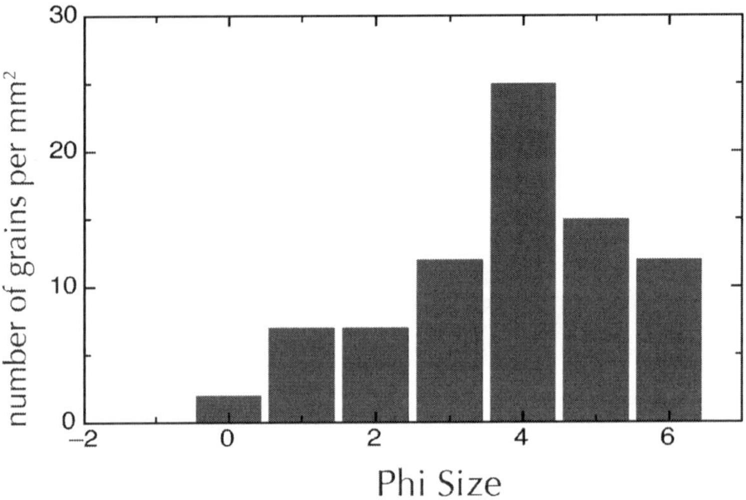

FIGURE 5.9 *Particle size histogram of inclusions in Palace Ware fabrics from Tell Jemmeh.*

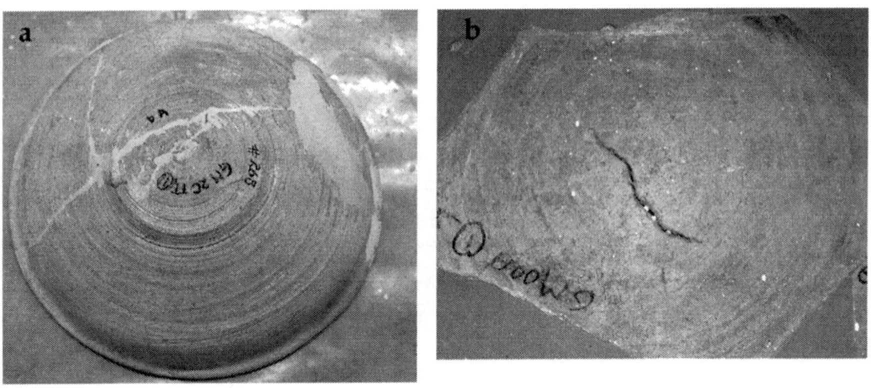

FIGURE 5.10 *Photographs of (a) rhythmic grooves & (b) s-shaped drying cracks on the vessel base of Assyrian style bowls from Tell Jemmeh. These features are typically associated with wheel thrown pottery.*

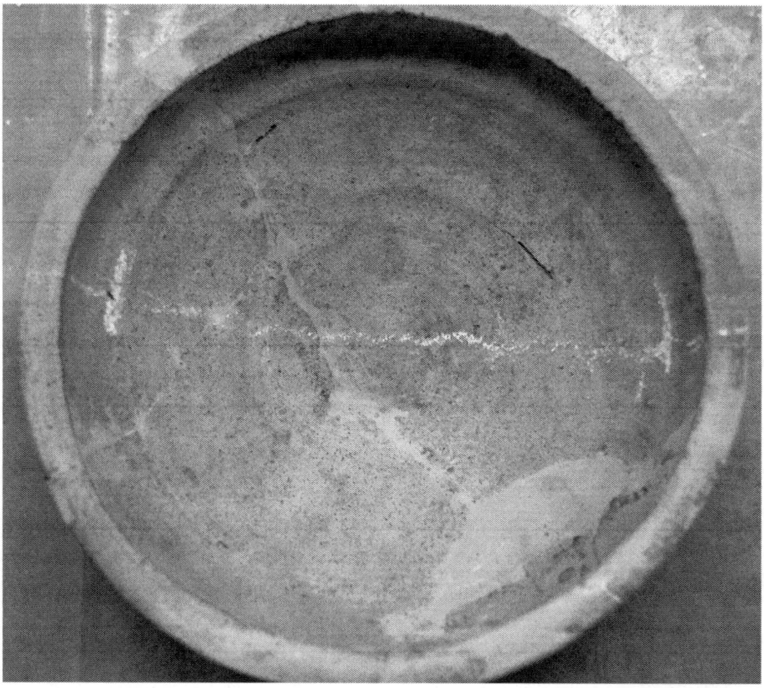

FIGURE 5.11 *Photograph of internal rilling on Assyrian style bowls from Tell Jemmeh indicative of wheel thrown pottery.*

There may be a technological rather than a cultural explanation for this change in raw material processing behaviour at Jemmeh. Sedimentation of loess from Wadi Besor could render it unsuitable for potting. Melson and van Beek observed that "much of the carbonate is concentrated in the finest... fraction" and sedimentation would produce a matrix material "higher in carbonate and thus less plastic and workable" (1992, 132). Alternatively, Palace Ware-style ceramics at Tel Jemmeh were made from a different and naturally finer raw material than the unmodified loess we collected from Wadi Besor. However, the mineralogy in the Palace Ware-style fabrics is consistent with loess from the northwest Negev, which suggests that even if these vessels were not manufactured from the unmodified loess of Wadi Besor, as suggested by Melson and van Beek, the raw materials used were local.

Formation

Formation & Shaping

Palace Ware-style vessels at Tel Jemmeh exhibit rhythmic spiral grooves and s-shaped drying cracks on the internal surface of the base indicative of wheel-thrown pottery (figure 5.10). Continuous horizontal lines associated with lifting during wheel-throwing are, for the most part, obscured by subsequent shaping stages, however, the undulating ridges and rhythmic striations produced during lifting are preserved on the internal surface of most vessels (figure 5.11) (Rye 1981; Rice 1987). Radiographs reveal subtle variations in wall thickness and the diagonal alignment of voids and inclusion normal to the vessel surface are diagnostic of wheel-thrown pottery (Middleton 1995; Berg 2008).

The external surface of Palace Ware-style vessel walls are scarred by horizontally oriented 'pull-outs' where grit has been dragged across the plastic surface of the vessel while it was rotating on the wheel (figure 5.12). This feature is common on vessels shaped by turning on a wheel whose fabric contained inclusions ≥ 0.5 mm (medium sand) (Rye 1981). Other evidence that these vessels were shaped by turning includes the pronounced continuous horizontally oriented faceting of the vessel body (figure 5.13). The external surface of most vessels also has the dull sheen indicative of turning during the leather-hard stage of drying (figure 5.14), however, on the majority of vessels it is difficult to differentiate the sheen produced during turning from what appears to be the brighter sheen of burnishing discussed in detail below.

These observations indicate that the Palace Ware-style vessels at Tel Jemmeh were manufactured using the same technology as Palace Ware in the Central Polity: formation by wheel-throwing and subsequent shaping by turning of the wheel during the leather-hard drying stage. The differences in vessel appearance, such as the pronounced faceting on Palace Ware-style vessels, are unrelated to differences in fabric coarseness and could have been removed during a subsequent smoothing stage in the Central Polity. The presence of these facets on Palace Ware-style forms at Tel Jemmeh suggests a different aesthetic or consumer for these vessels.

An alternative explanation is that the potter who produced the Palace Ware-style forms at Jemmeh was less familiar or comfortable with the technology of wheel turning and was unable to produce a smooth exterior surface. However, even if the potter was uncomfortable with wheel turning, he would have and could have removed the facets using a damp cloth if the consumer expected a smooth vessel.

Decoration

Surface Treatment

The appearance of a slip or pseudo-slip, common to Palace Ware from the Central Polity, is largely absent in the Assyrian-style assemblage at Jemmeh. Generally, Palace Ware-style vessels at Jemmeh exhibit no sign of surface

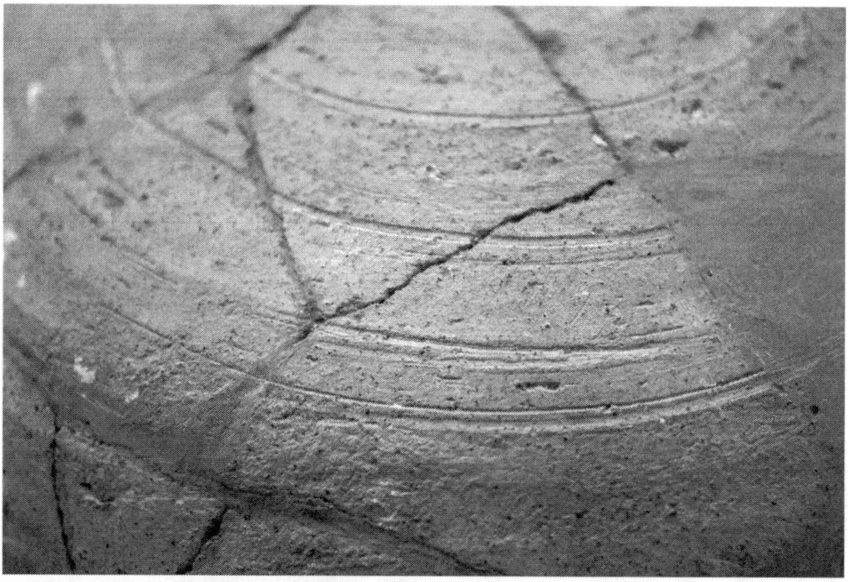

FIGURE 5.12 *Photograph of Assyrian style bowl GM 1BTT2 from Tell Jemmeh illustrating scarring on the external surface of the vessel as a result of 'pull outs' during wheel throwing.*

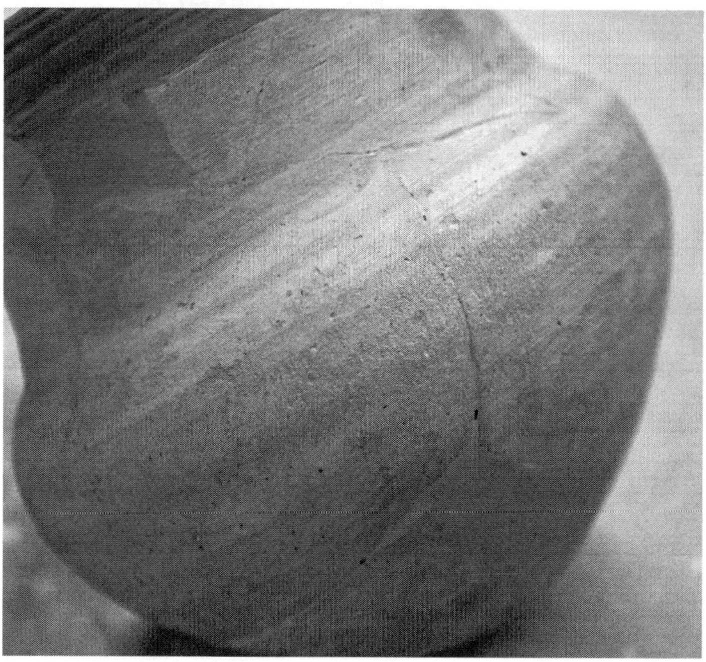

FIGURE 5.13 *Photograph of Assyrian style jar GM 1BNBR from Tell Jemmeh illustrating faceting on the vessel body.*

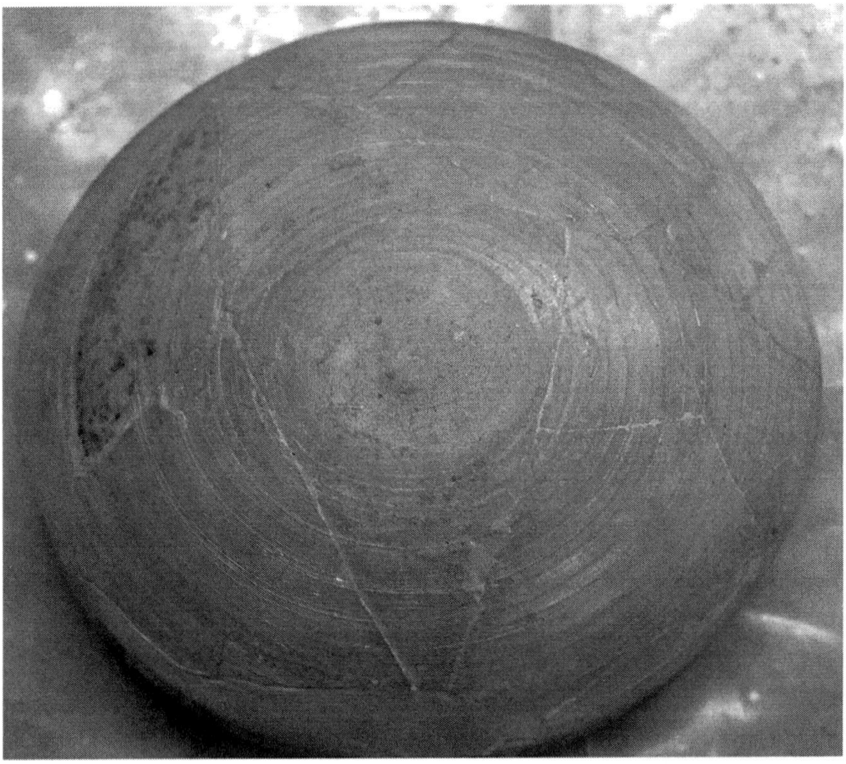

FIGURE 5.14 *Photograph of the dull sheen on the exterior surface of Assyrian style vessels from Tell Jemmeh indicative of turning.*

treatment; preserving the pullout scarring and dull sheen created during formation and shaping. The post-depositional calcite crusting, common on Central Polity Palace Ware, is also absent in the Palace Ware-style assemblage at Jemmeh. The absence of this calcium carbonate crust may indicate that a less calcareous raw materials was used at Tel Jemmeh than in the Central Polity.

Several Palace Ware-style vessels from Jemmeh (21% 5/24) exhibit circumferential regions of compressed matrix material indicative of burnishing, as opposed to the irregular patches of compressed clay associated with turning (figure 5.15). These irregular lines of compression produce a dull red sheen, which is easily distinguished from the 'flat' vessel body, and the uneven spacing of the burnished lines allows a significant portion of the body to show. Four of the vessels (16%) are red-slipped and thoroughly burnished and it is interesting to note that these vessels are the most morphometrically and typologically similar to Palace Ware from Assyria proper (figure 5.16). While red-slipped burnished pottery is not native to Assyria, it is a common decorative

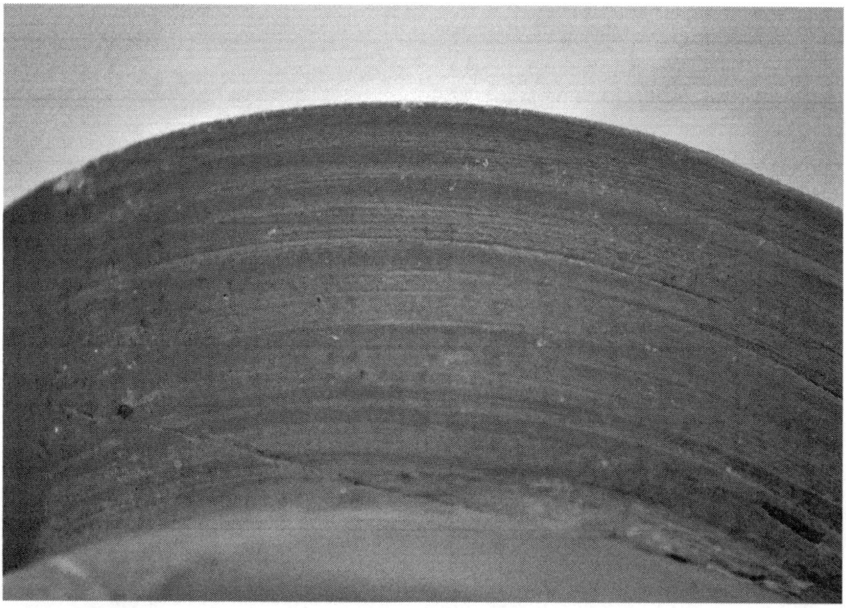

FIGURE 5.15 *Photograph of burnishing or compression marks on the exterior surface of an Assyrian style bowl (GM 3B533) from Tell Jemmeh.*

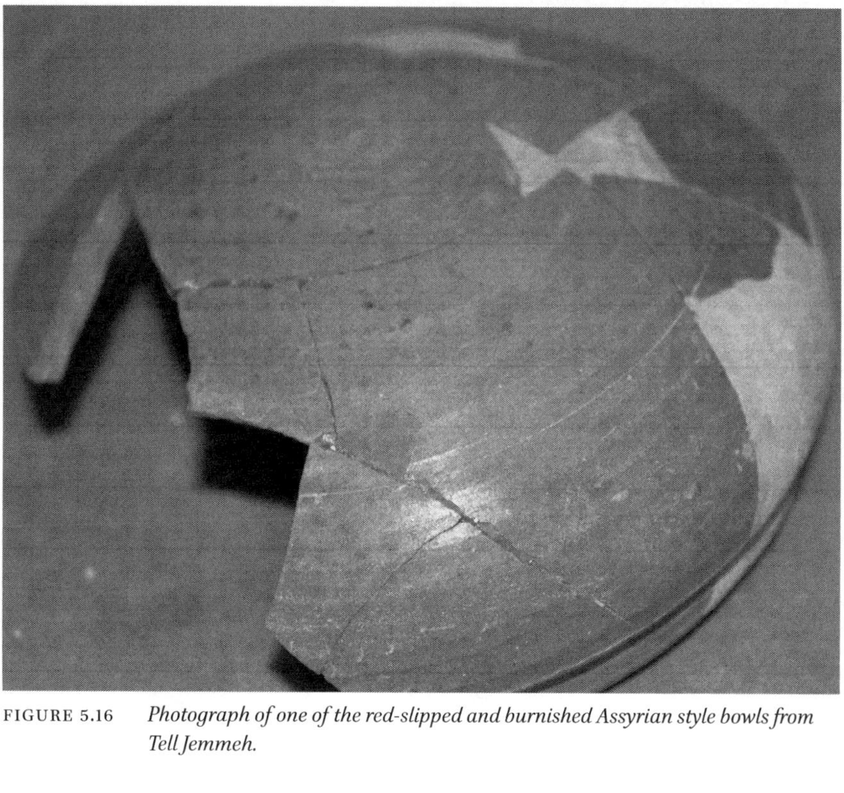

FIGURE 5.16 *Photograph of one of the red-slipped and burnished Assyrian style bowls from Tell Jemmeh.*

feature of pottery in the southern Levant, particularly southern Israel, Philistia, Judah and the Negev from the 10–9th century BCE (*e.g.* Zevit 2001; Aznar 2005). In the southern Levant, these red-slipped wheel-burnished wares are thought to imitate Phoenician pottery (*e.g.* Singer-Avitz 2010) and/or metallic vessels, particularly gold (*e.g.* King 2006; King and Stager 2001). Samaria Ware, dated to 8–7th century BCE in the southern Levant and Negev, is a fine-grained, thin-walled (0.2–0.4 cm thick) ware which is always red-slipped and burnished (King 2006). Samaria Ware vessels occur in standard 8–7th century, southern Levant shapes, styles and forms and are generally considered a prestige or luxury ware (*cf.* Aznar 2005; Docter 2012).

Burnishing and red-slipping are not decorative technologies associated with Neo-Assyrian ceramic production in general or Palace Ware specifically. The existence of burnished and red-slipped burnished Palace Ware-style vessels at Jemmeh is significant; indicating that the manufacturers and consumers of these vessels were blending local and 'foreign' or Assyrian ceramic styles and, perhaps, the semiotic function and social value of the vessels as well. This unique blending of local and Assyrian ceramic style and how it relates to the semiotics and value of the ware will be discussed in greater detail in chapter 6. However, taken together with the differences in form and production chaîne opératoire, it suggests that the manufacture and consumption of Palace Ware-style pottery at Jemmeh was done by and for a local, non-Assyrian population.

Dimples on the Palace Ware-style vessels at Jemmeh are oval and oriented with their long axis perpendicular to the base, similar to those found on Central Polity Palace Ware forms. Dendritic cracks on the reverse side of the dimple, indicative of pressure applied to the vessel wall during the leather-hard stage of drying, are absent in the Jemmeh assemblage, as are the ridged impressions similar to finger prints on their obverse face. While the absence of these features may indicate that dimpling was applied during a different, wetter stage in the drying process at Jemmeh than in Assyria Proper, we believe it more likely results from the difference in the two pastes. The coarser paste of Jemmeh Palace Ware-style vessels promotes more even drying of the vessel wall because the tension created by the drying matrix material is broken and released at and around the inclusions, equalising the surface tension and internal pressures created during drying due to shrinkage (Rice 1987). Likewise, the coarse texture of the vessel surface could obscure delicate 'fingerprint' impressions making them indistinguishable from the scarred and ridged vessel surface.

The registers of incised lines around the circumference of Palace Ware-style vessels from Jemmeh appear to be less carefully executed than their Central Polity counterparts: the lines are irregular in depth and spacing and are often

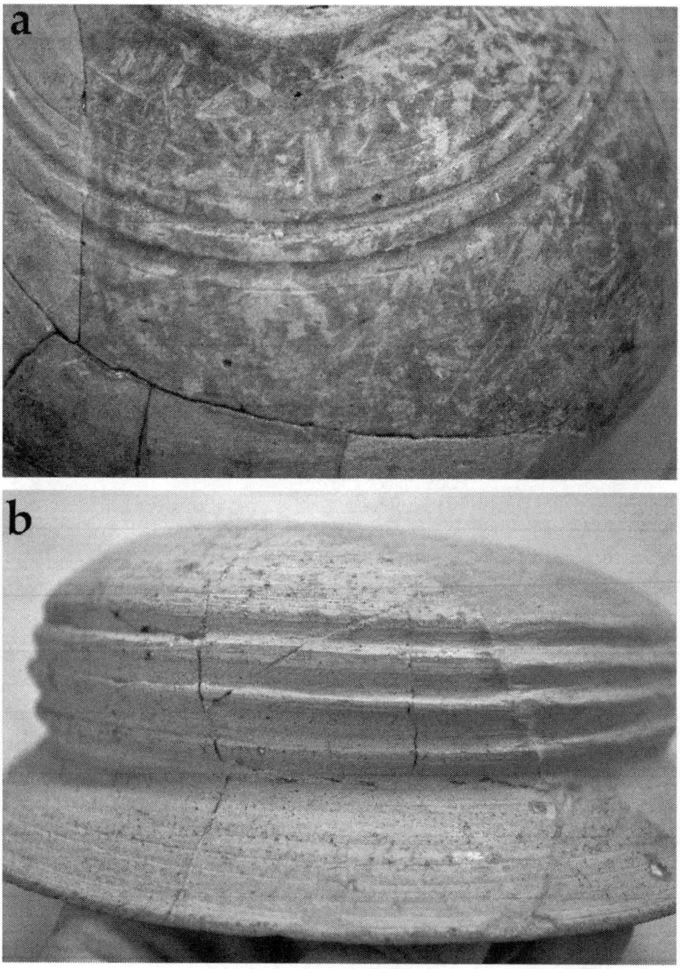

FIGURE 5.17 *Photograph of (a) fine & (b) coarse incised decoration on Assyrian style vessels from Tell Jemmeh. Note the sloppy execution compared to the precision of the incisions on vessels from the Central Provinces (figure 3.35).*

canted rather than parallel to the base (figure 5.17). It is possible that the variable depth of the incisions results from the coarseness of the fabric; when an inclusion gets caught by the tool, for example, and is dragged through the matrix material it creates an incision deeper or shallower than the others. The variable incision depth could also result from the uneven application of force during the process of incising the vessel or multiple incising events using a single pronged tool. Likewise, the rough, torn margins of the incisions could also result from the coarse nature of the fabric or indicate that the incisions were made before the vessel was leather hard (Rye 1989). The valley of the incision is round, indicating that the tool or tools used to produce them had a rounded tip. The cant to the register suggests that the vessel was rotated by hand rather than on a wheel during the application of the incisions, another potential difference in chaîne opératoire between the Jemmeh Palace Ware-style vessels and Palace Ware proper.

The protrusions and raised 'rings' around the necks and shoulders of Palace Ware-style vessels are consistent with moulding or shaping out of the ceramic body itself (figure 5.18). However, the coarseness of the fabric and, in some cases, subsequent surface treatment could potentially obscure evidence of deformation and smoothing associated with appliqué (Rye 1981). We were unable to remove a sample from the relevant portion of these vessels to confirm the observation that the rings were moulded.

Firing

Unlike Palace Ware from Assyria proper, the Palace Ware-style vessels at Jemmeh provide several indicators of firing temperature. Many vessels exhibit spalling scars on their internal and external surface where larger limestone or micrite inclusions have fractured or 'popped off' (figure 5.19). There is considerable discussion as to the exact temperature at which the reaction which results in spalling begins (*cf.* Hoard *et al.* 1995; Feathers 1993; Dunnell and Feathers 1991; Rice 1987), a reflection of the complexity of interactions between atmosphere, soak time and temperature. However, it is generally accepted that between 700–900°C the calcium carbonate ($CaCO_3$) in limestone and micrite decomposes into lime or quicklime (CaO) and carbon dioxide gas ($CO_2\uparrow$). Quicklime is hygroscopic and will readily incorporate atmospheric moisture ($H_2O\uparrow$) into its crystal lattice forming calcium hydroxide ($Ca(OH)_2$) or hydrated lime. In ceramic fabrics containing limestone and micrite inclusions, the absorption of water and subsequent formation of calcium hydroxide typically occurs after firing, while the vessel is cooling. The expansion of the crystal lattice to incorporate water molecules creates tension in the ceramic body. If the 'lime' inclusion is large enough it can spall or fracture away from the vessel body, often with explosive force leaving behind a crater-like scar. At temperatures over 900°C, the hydration of quicklime upon cooling does not occur because the calcium oxide reacts with the ceramic body to crystallise calcium ferrosilicates and calcium silicates (see discussion in chapter 3). Therefore, spalling scars on Palace Ware-style vessels at Jemmeh indicates that they were fired above 700°C but not significantly above 900°C. The presence of altered hornblende in Palace Ware-style fabrics at Jemmeh narrows the firing temperature range

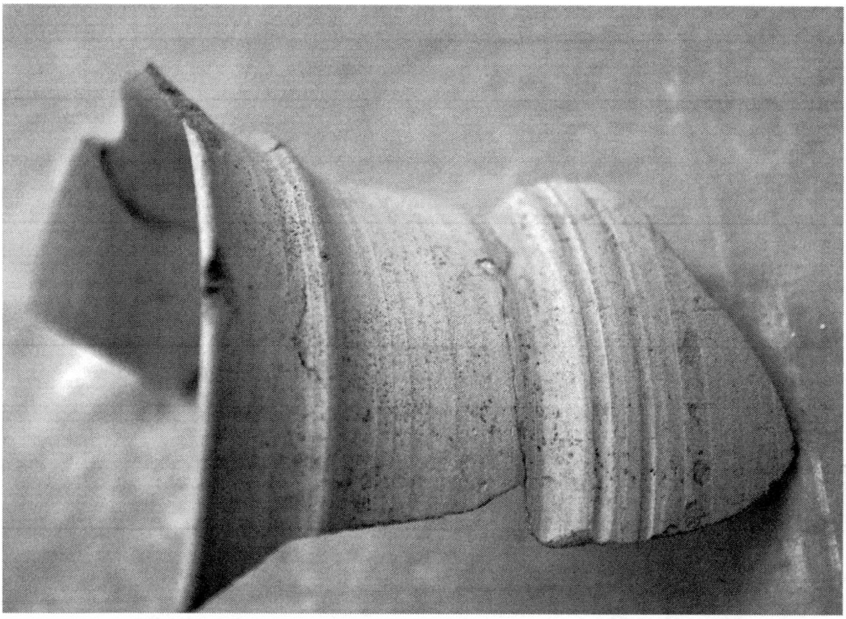

FIGURE 5.18 *Photograph of moulded neck ring on Assyrian style vessels from Tell Jemmeh.*

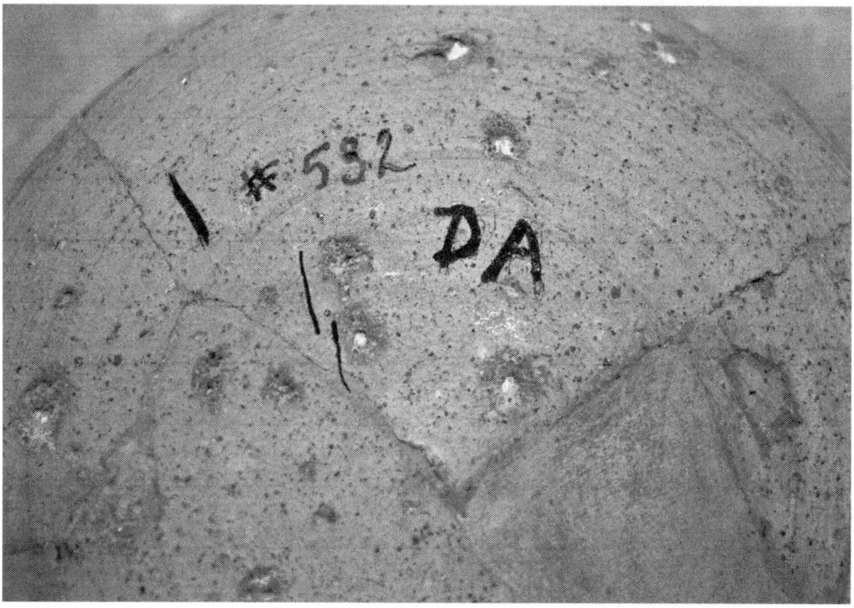

FIGURE 5.19 *Photograph of spalling scars on Assyrian style pottery from Tell Jemmeh.*

to between 800–900°C; green hornblende alters to brown oxyhornblende at temperatures of 800°C and above (Deer, Howie and Zussman 1997).
The bulk chemical composition of the Palace Ware-style ceramic matrix at Jemmeh, determined using SEM-EDS, presented in table 5.1, indicates that it is a calcareous fabric ~13 wt% CaO. Although, significantly lower in Ca content that fabrics from Central Polity and Annexed Provinces, fabric colour can be used as an indicator of firing temperature for the Palace Ware-style vessels at Tel Jemmeh. Even after we remove the red slipped burnished vessels from consideration, Palace Ware-style vessels occur in a broad range of colours—from strong brown (7.5YR 5/6) to very pale brown (10YR 7/4) to pale yellow (2.5Y 7/3) to light grey (5Y 7/2) (figure 5.20). This range of Palace Ware-style fabric colours and their frequent mottled appearance suggests either temperature fluctuations or variation in the heating chamber due to kiln inefficiency or inexpert loading of the fire box or that the ceramics were heated to between 900–1000°C, the transition temperature for calcium-iron colour dominance, and the soak time was insufficient for the complete dominance of one reaction over another. Based on the presence of spalling scars, oxyhornblende and fabric colour, we conclude that Palace Ware-style vessels at Jemmeh were fired at around 900°C.

Interestingly, contemporaneous local pottery manufactured from Negev loess is pale green or white, at least on the surface, closer to the colour range of Palace Ware than Palace Ware-style vessels from Jemmeh (figure 5.21). The light coloured surface of these local vessels results from the migration of salts in the ceramic body to the surface of the vessel during drying where they react with the iron content of the ceramic body and crystallise iron (iii) chloride ($FeCl_3$) (Matson 1971). Iron (iii) chloride is volatile above 800°C and leaves an iron depleted surface as it vaporises, producing a light coloured rind or surface on the ceramic body (Matson 1971). This suggests that the consumers of Palace Ware-style vessels at Tel Jemmeh had a different aesthetic than those in the Central Polity and Annexed Provinces and/or that the social value of Palace Ware at Jemmeh was unrelated to its colour.

Chemical and Mineralogical Characterisation

Mineralogical Profile

Assyrian-style ceramic fabrics at Jemmeh are significantly coarser (~7% inclusions; inclusions ≤1 mm) than Palace Ware fabrics and only moderately to well sorted. The inclusions themselves are angular to sub-angular and prismoidal to sub-prismoidal—consistent with loessial sediments from Wadi Besor

TABLE 5.1 *Bulk chemical composition (SEM-EDS) of Assyrian style fabrics from Tell Jemmeh*

chemical compound	weight %
Na_2O	1.64
MgO	2.98
al_2O_3	13.78
SiO_2	51.71
k_2O	4.66
CaO	13.47
TiO_2	1.01
FeO	10.76
total	100

and northwestern Negev. Despite being coarser, these Palace Ware-style fabrics are relatively homogeneous in terms of their mineralogy, including the fabrics from the possible form B Palace Ware vessels JX, JM, and JW and form C vessels JN and JE. Therefore, all potential Palace Ware ceramics at Tel Jemmeh fail to meet the definitional fabric criteria for Palace Ware and cannot, therefore, be classified as Palace Ware.

Analysis of 12 thin-sections of Assyrian-style ceramic fabrics from Tel Jemmeh reveal that they are fairly homogeneous fabric group and can be described as follows (figure 5.22):

> The matrix is reddish-brown to dark orange in PPL; optically active in XPL. Devoid of foraminifers. Very few (2–5%) vughs, vesicles and channel voids (up to 2 mm) with clear boundaries. The silt is primarily quartz but contains identifiable heavy and accessory minerals including: hornblende, plagioclase, microcline, zircon, epidote and tourmaline. Opaques (2–3%) of hematite, magnetite and rutile between a few microns and approximately 70 µm. Inclusions ($f{:}c_{0.062mm}$ = 93–90:7–10) of coarse to medium, moderately sorted, sub-angular, sub-prismoidal quartz sand, very rarely with mineral inclusions (zircon). Sub-rounded micrite (up to 0.64 mm) and limestone (up to 0.40 mm) are common. Rare accessory minerals in the fine sand fraction include hornblende (≤ 250 µm) altered to oxyhornblende, plagioclase (≤ 200 µm), microcline (≤ 180 µm) and zircon (≤ 110 µm). Very rare fragments of unfossilised land-snail shell, up to 2 mm long.

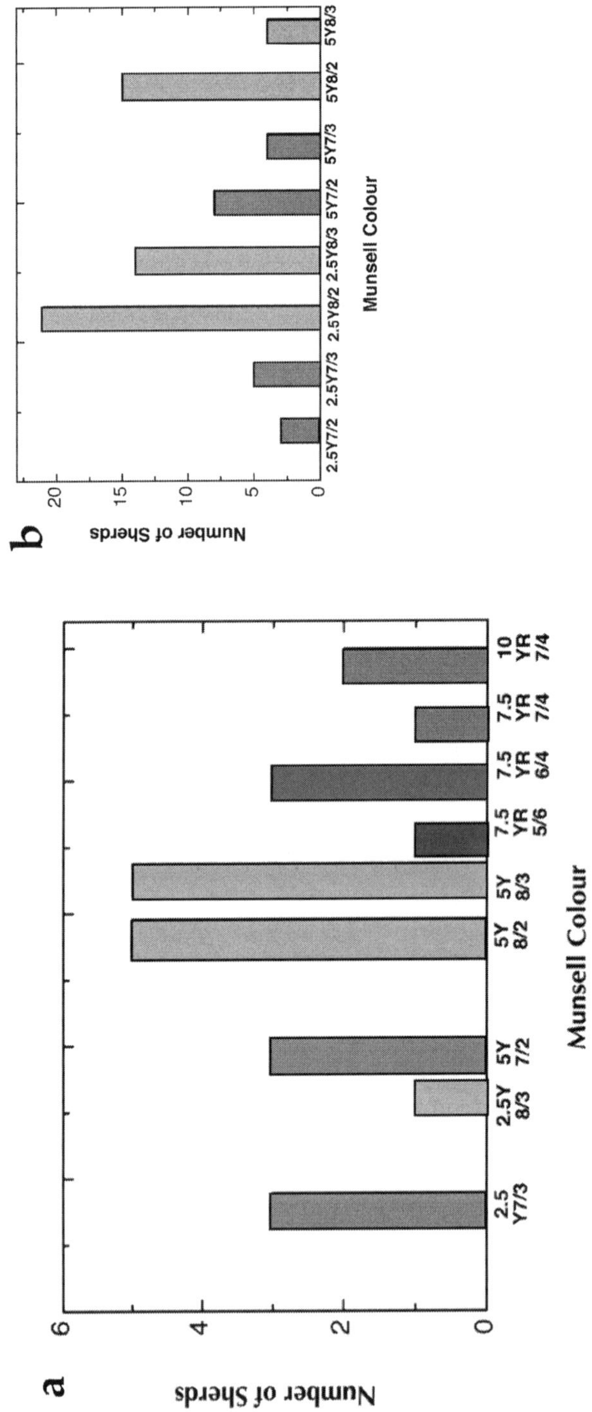

FIGURE 5.20 *Bar charts comparing colour of Assyrian style vessels from Tell Jemmeh (a) & Palace Ware vessels from the Central Polity (b).*

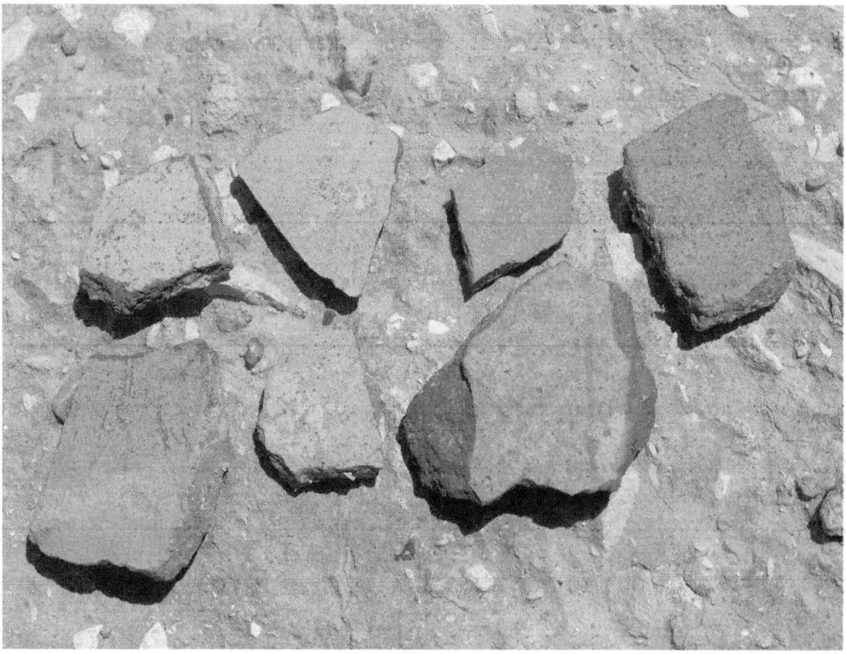

FIGURE 5.21 *Photograph of local, non-Palace Ware ceramics from Tell Jemmeh. Note the greenish-grey colour.*

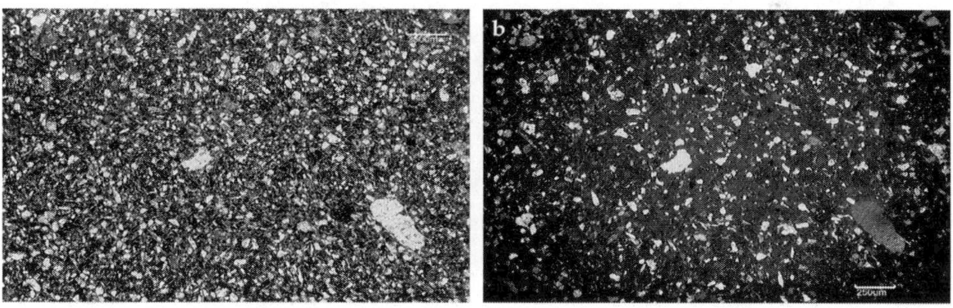

FIGURE 5.22 *Micrographs of Assyrian style fabric from Tell Jemmeh in (a)* PPL *and (b)* XPL. *(field of view = 1.7 mm)*

The mineral inclusions in the Jemmeh fabrics suggest a different material source than the ones exploited in either the Central Polity or at Dūr-Katlimmu. Microcline and tourmaline, for example, are typically found in acidic/felsic granites and pegmatites. Mineralogy in the Palace Ware fabrics from Nimrud, Nineveh and Dūr-Katlimmu is basic/mafic, suggesting that the parent rock for the ceramic raw materials used in these regions crystallised from fundamentally different magmas/melts than those at Jemmeh.

Chemical Profile

The geochemical profiles for Palace Ware from Nimrud and Nineveh and the Jemmeh Palace Ware-style fabrics using INAA is illustrated in figure 5.23. Visually the geochemical profiles from Jemmeh and the Central Polity suggest an acidic origin for the Jemmeh ceramics and a more basic origin for Central Polity Palace Ware, which is consistent with local regional geology in these areas. In fact, the two regional groups often cluster separately in biplots of element ratios, such Th:Hf against Eu:Ta (figure 5.24). Principal component analysis confirms that Assyrian-style ceramics at Tel Jemmeh are manufactured from a geochemically distinct raw material source (figures 5.25 & 5.26).

Based on the combined petrographic and geochemical analyses, we conclude that the Palace Ware-style vessels from Tel Jemmeh are (a) a different geological fabric group than either Central Polity or Dūr-Katlimmu Palace Ware and (b) they are consistent with local sediments in the Negev and were, therefore, locally manufactured and not imported.

Palace Ware Consumption

Assyrian-style pottery at Tel Jemmeh come from both primary and secondary contexts: floors and fill associated with both Petrie's 'Assyrian' residences and van Beek's 'arched' building. Palace Ware-style vessels and fragments were also recovered from pits and a well adjacent to these buildings (Petrie 1928). Interpreting contextual consumption patterns for Assyrian-style pottery at Jemmeh is complicated by the ambiguous function of the buildings from which it was recovered and the fact that comparable information from lower tel and residential contexts from the Central Polity is not available. However, *if* Petrie's 'Assyrian' residences are in fact residences and van Beek's 'arched' building functioned as a public/administrative building, then Assyrian-style pottery was consumed in both public and private contexts at Jemmeh.

The formal consumption pattern for Assyrian-style pottery at Jemmeh is significantly different than those in either the Central Polity or Annexed Provinces (table 5.2). Form A-style bowls make up 75% of the Assyrian-style population, followed by form B-style cups (17%) and form C-style jars (8%). The dramatic change in consumption of Palace Ware forms at Tel Jemmeh implies a different social function and/or semiotic meaning for these vessels in the Unincorporated Territories than in the Central Polity and Annexed Provinces.

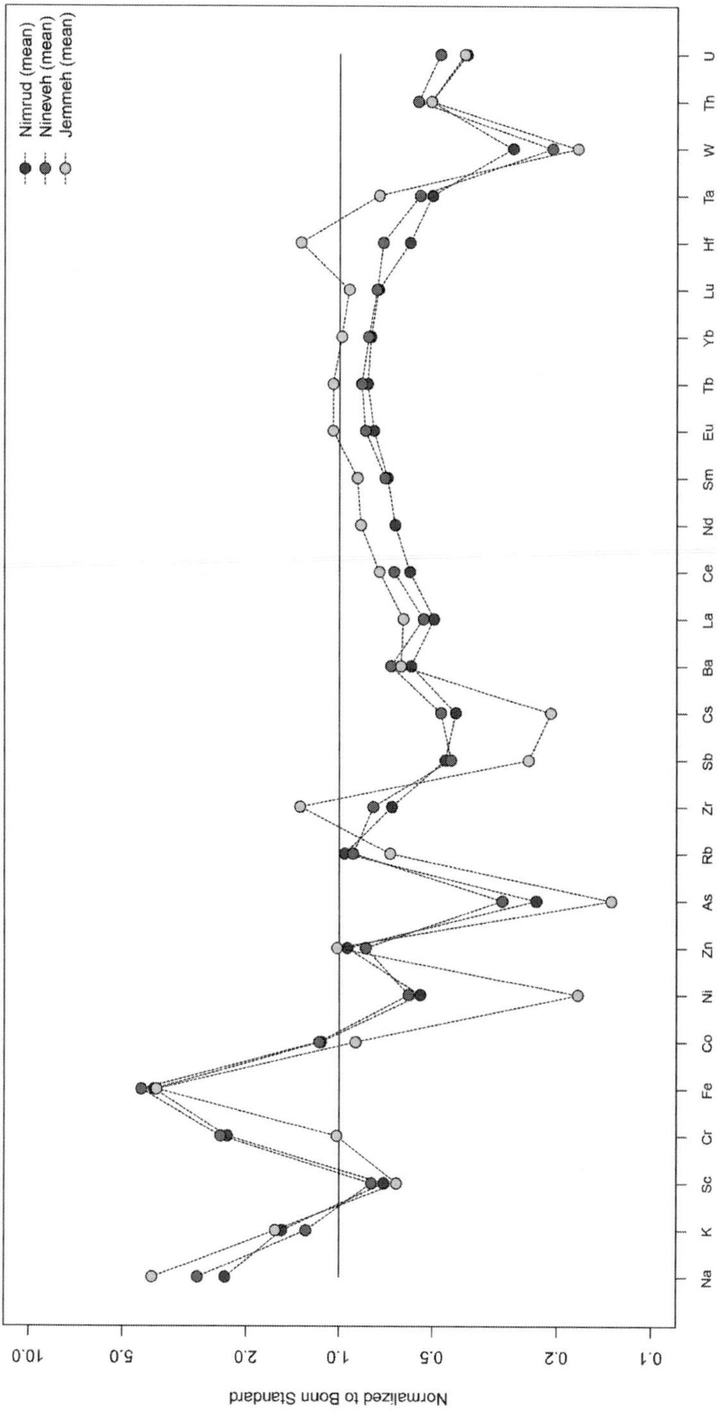

FIGURE 5.23 *Combined* INAA *bulk chemical profile for Palace Ware from Nimrud, Nineveh & Tell Jemmeh. (graph courtesy of J. Sterba)*

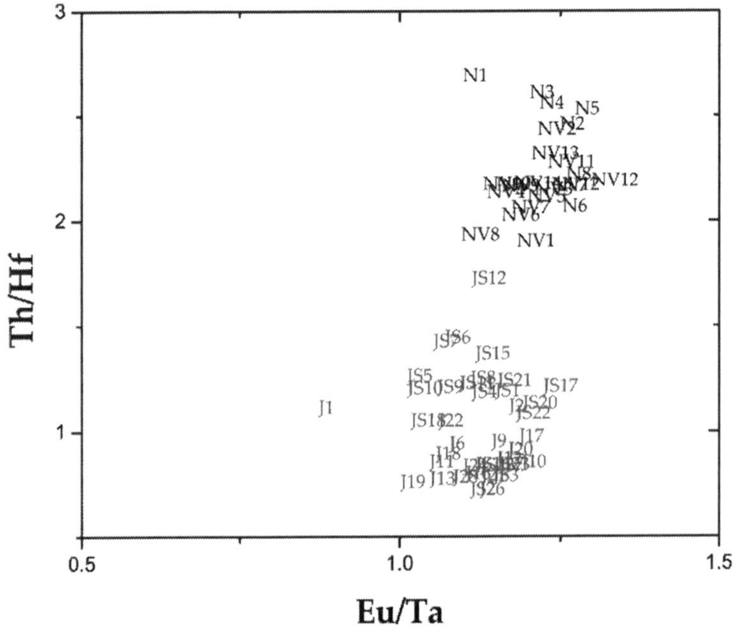

FIGURE 5.24 *Biplot of elemental ratios Eu:Ta vs. Th: Hf illustrating the chemical compositional similarity among Palace Ware from Nimrud (N), Nineveh (NV) & Assyrian style ceramics from Tell Jemmeh (J & JS).*

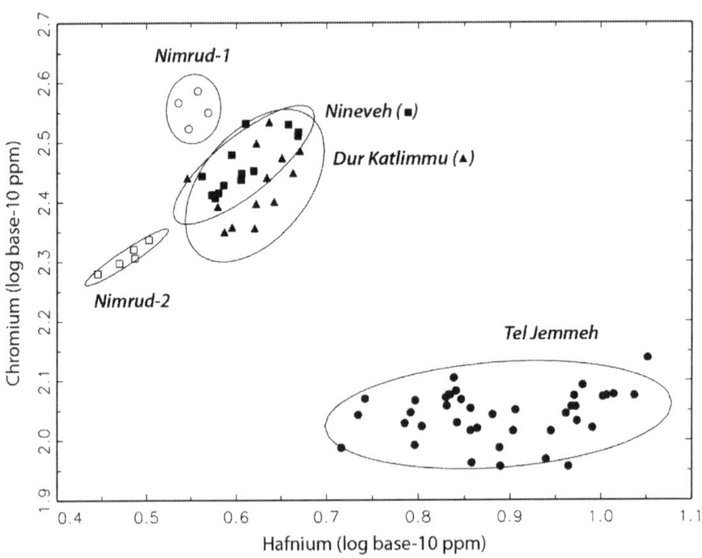

FIGURE 5.25 *Principal component analysis revealing five chemical compositional groups: Nineveh, Nimrud-1, Nimrud-2, Dur-Katlimmu & Tell Jemmeh. (figure courtesy of J. Speakman)*

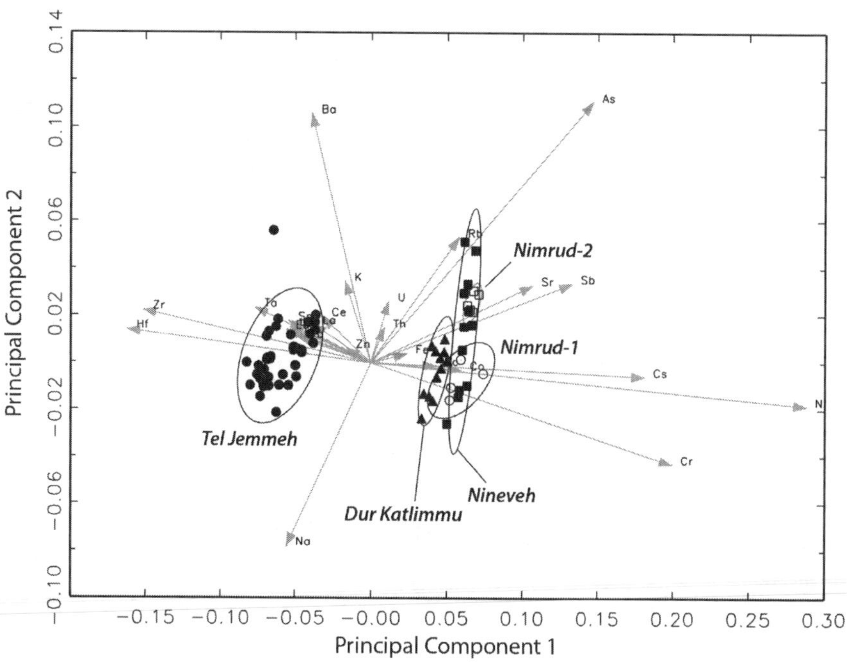

FIGURE 5.26 *PCA diagram illustrating the overall variability and relationship among the five chemical compositional groups for Palace Ware & Assyrian Style vessels in this study. (figure courtesy of J. Speakman)*

TABLE 5.2 *Assyrian style ceramic consumption patterns at Tell Jemmeh*

	Primary Context		Secondary Context	
	Public (temple, palace, etc.)	**Private (residence, etc.)**	**Public (midden, fill, etc.)**	**Private (burial, etc.)**
Tel Jemmeh				
Form A	2	2	14	
Form B	1		2	
Form C			3	

Palace Ware Transport Mechanism

Based on the geochemical and petrographic analyses, Palace Ware-style pottery in the Unincorporated Territories, like Palace Ware in the Annexed Provinces, is manufactured locally rather than imported from the Central Polity. Neither, according to our analysis, is the Palace-Ware style pottery at Jemmeh imported from the Annexed Provinces by a deported or displaced population. Tel Jemmeh was an 'improperly' Assyrian site and not incorporated into the imperial provincial administrative system. Therefore, it is unlikely that Central Polity or Central Polity trained potters would have been associated with or contracted to manufacture pottery for Tel Jemmeh or any other unincorporated site. In fact, both formal analysis of Palace Ware-style pottery at Jemmeh and the chaîne opératoire used to manufacture it suggest local potters unfamiliar with Assyrian pottery traditions.

Palace Ware in the Central Polity is homogeneous in shape, style and fabric across all three sites in the our study. Palace Ware-style pottery in the Unincorporated Territories, while similar in overall shape to Palace Ware and/or Assyrian pottery forms, is both heterogeneous intrasite and inconsistent with the formal attributes of Central Polity Palace Ware. Vessel curvature in the Unincorporated Territories, for example, varies from the expected curvature of Palace Ware vessels in the Central Polity by ≥ 40°, suggesting manufacture by potters unfamiliar with the Assyrian ceramic repertoire of forms and styles. In addition, Palace Ware-style pottery at Jemmeh blends local styles and formal attributes, such as red-slipping and burnishing, with 'Assyrian' ones which suggests both local producers and consumers of these vessels in the Unincorporated Territories.

Tel Jemmeh, like many of the buffer zones in the Unincorporated Territories, was located adjacent to Neo-Assyrian provinces, such as Ashdod and Samaria. It is possible, even probable, that the concept or symbol of Palace Ware travelled to sites in the Unincorporated Territories as a result of intraregional interaction. The 'norm' or sign for Palace Ware-style vessels in the Unincorporated Territories is less concrete than its corresponding ur-form in either the Central Polity or Annexed Provinces. Form A-style vessels occur in a range of shapes, sizes and colours and wall thickness is highly variable. Unlike Central Polity Palace Ware bowls, form A-style vessels in the Unincorporated Territories are decorated, often elaborately so, using typical Assyrian, but not Palace Ware, motifs, such as stepped bases and t-shaped lips. However, the execution of these 'Assyrian' attributes is imperfect. For example, Palace Ware form A necks are incurving, while those in the Unincorporated Territories are straight and the t-shaped lips on Assyrian Common Ware bowls flare into an out-curving tail, while those in the Unincorporated Provinces do not. As we discuss in more detail in chapter 6, these patterns, or lack thereof, indicate that when the concept of Palace Ware was translated into a local ur-form in the Unincorporated Territories, the socially significant characteristics of these vessels for the local population were those features 'foreign' to the Southern Levant and/or identifiably 'Assyrian'. In addition, the blending of local and 'foreign' attributes on form A-style plates in the Unincorporated Territories suggests a relationship between the social value and semiotic meaning of 'red slipped, burnished ware', possibly Samaria Ware, and the local form A-style ur-form.

Palace Ware-style form B and C vessels in the Unincorporated Territories are decorated and dimpled, thin-walled, unequal biconical cups and bowls with necks. The ur-form of these vessels in the Unincorporated Territories does not preserve the fine-grained fabric, and restricted colour of Central Polity Palace Ware. In addition, form B and C-style vessels have unorthodox neck styles and lengths. Unequal biconical bottles and storage jars are known throughout the Near and Middle East, and in the Southern Levant these vessels are typically neck-less storage vessels (Hendrix *et al.* 1997). It is probable, therefore, that the local ur-form for these familiar biconical storage jars was translated into the Palace Ware form B and C-style ur-form at Jemmeh, explaining the emphasis or social significance of those attributes which were 'other' such as thin walls, vessel necks and dimples. Translation from a neck-less storage jar to Palace Ware cups and bowls may also explain the unorthodox neck styles: the presence of a neck was itself a signifier of the 'Assyrian' ur-form.

We conclude, therefore, that Palace Ware-style vessels in the Unincorporated Territories were manufactured locally, by local potters to meet the social and semiotic needs of a local population. Familiarity with Assyrian-style vessels was a consequence of intraregional interaction between buffer zones and Neo-Assyrian provinces and not the result of either direct Assyrian occupation or a deported population from either the Central Polity or Annexed Provinces.

CHAPTER 6

Conspicuous Consumption: Social Function and Semiotic Meaning of Palace Ware

Palace Ware was transported across the Neo-Assyrian imperial landscape as a concept or social practice and adapted and modified to meet the social and symbolic needs of its consumers outside the imperial Central Polity. Although changes in the size, style and colour of Palace Ware in the Annexed Provinces and the blending of local and Assyrian attributes in the Unincorporated Territories indicate context driven social function and semiotic meaning, these new values, meanings and practices have their roots in the social function and symbolic meaning of Palace Ware in the Central Polity and imperial administration where the concept and social practice originated. Therefore, by understanding the function and meaning of Palace Ware in the Neo-Assyrian Central Polity for the imperial administration and examining how these concepts and social practices were modified in the Annexed Provinces and Unincorporated Territories we can begin to understand *why* Palace Ware migrated across the imperial landscape and, perhaps, the relationship to and perception of the Neo-Assyrian empire, administration and/or the concept of 'Assyrian' by its consumers outside the Central Polity.

Neo-Assyrian Central Polity

Attributes consistently and uniformly reproduced on vessels, for which there is no associated functional or manufactural behaviour or explanation, often possess social or cultural significance or value. We identified five potential indicators of social value and/or semiotic meaning in the Palace Ware assemblage from the Central Polity: thin walls; fine-grained fabric; vessel colour; vessel capacity; and dimples. These five attributes are unique within the Neo-Assyrian ceramic repertoire to Palace Ware, distinguishing it from Assyrian Common Ware or table ware and storage vessels of similar shape.

Iconographic evidence and the performance characteristics of Palace Ware vessels, such as permeability, suggest that their practical function involved the consumption of beverages (see discussion in chapter 3). A range of drinking vessel forms exists in the Assyrian ceramic repertoire, from rhytons to cups and bowls. What made Palace Ware unique within this assemblage and a symbol or

 | DOI 10.1163/9789004304123_007

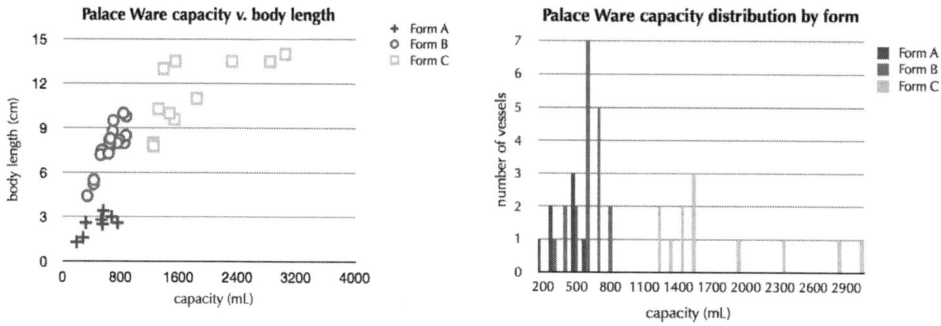

FIGURE 6.1 *Palace Ware capacity clusters from the Central Polity by form.*

icon throughout the empire was the social/symbolic practice with which it was associated and in which it was used.

Social Function of Palace Ware

Drinking vessels have few technological or formal requirements. They must hold liquid and are generally portable but occur archaeologically in a variety of shapes and sizes. Palace Ware forms A and B are relatively small (modal height of 3 and 12 cm respectively) and light (modal weight of 110 and 100 g respectively) suggesting that they were designed for individual rather than communal consumption. Form C vessels are larger (modal height 20 cm) but not significantly heavier (modal weight 200 g) suggesting that they functioned either as serving containers for the smaller form A and B vessels or were used for communal drinking. Although Palace Ware was not glazed or treated with resin, the vessel walls are partially vitrified as a result of firing, either by design or incident, which rendered the vessel body impermeable. The most significant attribute of Palace Ware vessels potentially related to their social function as drinking vessels, however, is capacity.

Palace Ware from the Assyrian Central Polity has a discontinuous capacity profile with four distinct differentiated modes (figure 6.1). The distribution around the modes is quite tight and approximates a Gaussian curve or normal distribution with a standard deviation of 100 mL for the mode at 500 mL and 500 mL for the modes at 1.5 L and 3 L respectively. The distribution around the mode at 700 mL has a standard deviation of 100 mL on one tail and 200 mL on the other. The extended tail associated with the 700 mL mode, form B vessels, results from the diminutive size of the B1 cups. When we correct for the two sizes of form B vessel, the standard deviation associated with 700 mL is

100 mL and the form B1 mode at 400 mL, convoluted by the tails of the modes at 500 mL and 700 mL, has a normal distribution with a 50 mL standard deviation. There is no practical or technological reason for these discontinuous capacity clusters, therefore we believe that they are intentional, meaningful, and socially relevant.

Several observations about the social function of Palace Ware arise from these data. First, forms A and B are different shapes although they have a similar range of capacity measurements: 200–800 mL for form A and 300–900 mL for form B. There is no practical or technological reason why two different shapes are required for the single practical function of beverage consumption. Therefore, we conclude that there is a cultural explanation and, perhaps, a different socio-cultural function for the two forms.

Another socially significant anomaly is the discontinuous capacity between form B and C vessels. Form B and C vessels are the same shape, differing in size alone. Typically, vessels of the same shape serve the same function and have a continuous capacity profile when multiple sizes are present in the population (Sinopoli 1991). In the Palace Ware population, not only is there a discontinuity in capacity measurements between these two forms but the ratio of form B to form C vessels is highly uniform, 1:3 and 1:5 respectively. The relationship between forms B and C, described by their similar shape, proportional size and discontinuity between 900 mL and 1.2 L is, therefore, significant and potentially indicative of a difference in their social function.

In addition, form B and C vessels are similar in shape to standard Middle and Neo-Assyrian bottles and storage jars, specifically Anastasio's types BT-06, BT-057b, BT-11b and SJ-03b (2010). These vessels typically hold between 1.5–3.9 L for bottles and 14.7–24.9 L for storage jars. Form B vessels, therefore, hold 1.5–2.5 times less than a standard Assyrian bottle while form C vessels approximate the volume of Assyrian bottles but are 2.5–3 times smaller than typical Assyrian storage jars. The similarity in shape and size between Palace Ware form C vessels and Assyrian bottles suggests a similar practical function; however, the specialised fabric and elaborate decorative motifs of Palace Ware form C vessels indicate a different, perhaps, more specialised social function.

Correlation of archaeological ceramics with particular vessel types or metrological units known from Assyrian texts is complicated by issues of standardisation, geography and time (see discussion by Chambon 2011). The following discussion, therefore, should be considered provisional or a working hypothesis. The basic unit of measurement in Mesopotamia for the liquid capacity of a vessel is the '*qû*' (Gaspa 2007, 165). Larger vessel capacities are measured in '*sūtu*' and '*emāru*' which are related to the '*qû*' according to a decimal ration: 100 *qû* = 10 *sūtu* = 1 *emāru* (Kinnier Wilson 1972, 114). The relationship between the Neo-Assyrian '*qû*' and modern capacity measurements based on litres is estimated at 1 *qû* = 0.8 L, according to metrological studies of the Nimrud Wine Lists (Gaspa 2007) and the Tall al-Rimāh capacity measurement obtained from an inscribed jar (Postgate 1978; Powell 1987–90). Liquid volumes less than a *qû* were measured using *kāsu* or 'cup measures', 1/10 *qû* or 80 mL, during the Neo-Assyrian period (Kinnier Wilson 1972). The five Palace Ware capacity clusters, 400, 500 and 700 mL and 1.5 and 3 L, converted to the Assyrian volumetric units *qû* and *kāsu*, approximate 5, 6 and 9 *kāsu* and 2 and 3 *qû* respectively.

Most of the vessel classes and liquid volumes described in the cuneiform texts are bulk measurements recorded in sūtu (10 *qû*) and emāru (100 *qû*) restricting their usefulness for evaluating Palace Ware function. Smaller measures of 1, 2, 3 and 5 *qû* are frequently distributed for libation offerings and monthly rations to members of the royal household. A ceramic wine container, known as a *šazamû*, is associated with libations of *lā'u* and *mēzu* wine and its estimated capacity is 3 *qû* (NWL 18 ln.7; Gaspa 2007) and it is possible that Palace Ware form C vessels were used to make these libation offerings. If this were the case, however, it would not be necessary for them to relate to form B cups in perfect capacity ratios.

The measure 'two *qû*' occurs frequently in the Nimrud Wine Lists (NWL) as the monthly allotment of wine rationed to members of the royal household and government officials. For example NWL 8 (ln. 33–37) states: 2 *qû* the chief cupbearer, ½ *qû* the son of the cupbearer, 2 *qû* the physicians, 2 *qû* the diviners, 2 *qû* the exorcists, 2 *qû* the confectioners, 2 *qû* [...].... (translation Fales 1994). Perhaps Palace Ware form C vessels were used by the imperial administration for the storage/serving of monthly wine rations. Notice also the mention of ½ *qû* or 5 *kāsu* which is approximately the capacity of Palace Ware form B1 cups.

Perhaps the most interesting references in the NWL are those describing a volume of wine 'for cups' GÚ.ZI.MES: 5 *qû*, for cups in the morning; 3 *qû*, for cups in the evening (NWL 8 ln.11–12, translation Fales 1994). The unit *kāsu* is often described as a cup measure (Kinnier Wilson 1972) and the volume of a *kāsu*, 80 mL, would indeed fill a very small cup. Perhaps the cups mentioned in these texts are Palace Ware form B vessels.

In support of these possible metrological indicators of social function, the biconical shape of Palace Ware forms B and C also suggest that these vessels were associated with the consumption of grape wine. Unlike barley and date wine, which often contain floating vegetal matter that required filtration, grape wine in antiquity contained a dense sediment which precipitated at the bottom of its storage or serving container (Moorey 1980; Formenti and Duthel 1996). This dense precipitate was likely trapped in the pointed bases of form B and C vessels and could explain why strainers and filters were not part of the

Palace Ware repertoire. If Palace Ware form B and C vessels functioned socially in the consumption of grape wine it would explain both their specific and relatively small capacity measurements.

Most of the iconographic evidence for Palace Ware forms illustrates the king or high administrative official holding or drinking from a form A bowl (*e.g.* figure 6.2). The social function of Palace Ware form A bowls, therefore, appears to be more directly related to a political or administrative social practice than that of forms B and C. The closest parallel in the cuneiform literature to these vessels is the *agannu*, typically translated as the generic 'bowl'. *Agannu* bowls were made of ceramic and metal (*i.a.* BaM 24, 11 r9'; RIMA 2, A.0.101.1, ii 122) and were used to hold a variety of fluids including beer and wine (BBR 66 7). Although *agannu* generally hold relatively large capacities (*e.g.* 1 *sūtu*), in the Governor's Palace Archive two *agannu* vessels are listed as 'drinking vessels' (155, iii 5 2). Elsewhere, *agannu* vessels are described as small enough to fit in "the palm of your hand" (BBR 61 ln. 13, translation Gaspa 2007), which suggests that *agannāte ša mašqīti* were smaller, more portable vessels; describing not only the size but the posture associated with drinking from form A vessels (*e.g.* "Garden Party" relief).

It was common practice in Mesopotamia, from at least the Old Babylonian to the Achaemenid period, for guests, officials and dignitaries at formal royal banquets and ceremonies to receive drinking bowls as honour-gifts (Sancisi-Weerdenburg 1989). The material composition of the drinking bowl varied in accordance with the social or political status of its owner and reflected the relationship of the owner to or within the royal court (*ibid.*). If Palace Ware form A bowls functioned as honour-gifts, this practice would explain the simultaneous metal-glass-crystal-ceramic skeuomorphism of this form in the archaeological record.

Royal banqueting was often a reaffirmation of loyalty between the king and participants (Radner 1999–2001) and these honour-gift drinking bowls were the material expression of this fealty. Neo-Assyrian kings required their provincial governors and vassal rulers to attend court at least once a year to pay tribute and homage to Assyria. It is possible that during this pilgrimage the *adê* contract (loyalty oath) was renewed and form A bowls, in the appropriate material, were given as honour-gifts. The *adê* contract was sealed by the ritual consumption of a *kāsu* of beer or wine from a drinking bowl (SAA 11, 6 154) which may explain the capacity cluster of Palace Ware form A bowls (and their metal counterparts) around the relatively small volume of 5–6 *kāsu*.

The social function of Palace Ware form A vessels, therefore, was likely political: honour-gifts for the ritual consumption of beer or wine as part of the adê loyalty oath. Palace Ware form B and C vessels, on the other hand,

a

b

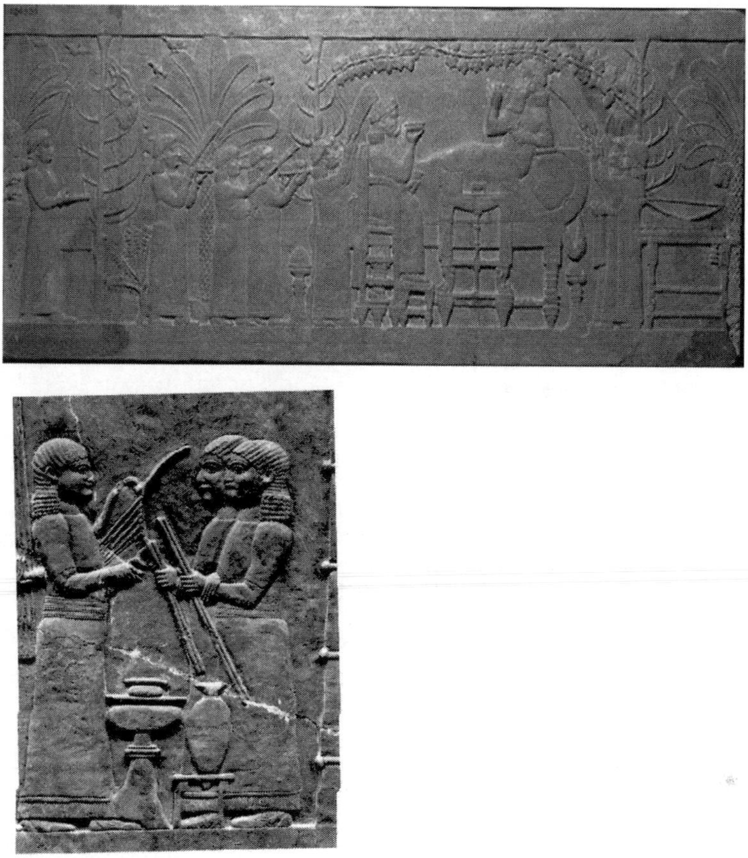

FIGURE 6.2 *Neo-Assyrian palace reliefs depicting possible Palace Ware consumption. (a) Assurbanipal banqueting relief or 'Garden Party' from the North palace, room S, at Nineveh; (b) another relief from the North palace, room S. (both images © Trustees of the British Museum)*

were probably used for the consumption of grape wine and, while this social practice may itself have been associated with Neo-Assyrian imperial administration, it is unlikely that these vessels functioned in a more overt political capacity.

Semiotic Meaning and Social Value

Social value is a conceptual construct crafted by, created for, and agreed upon by its cultural audience. As such, social value may be unrelated to concepts of economic or intrinsic value. Semiotic meaning, like social value, is context driven; a sign or icon chosen or constructed and communally agreed upon to symbolise or represent a complex of ideas, beliefs, relationships and meanings. In the case of Palace Ware, both its social value and semiotic meaning are related to its practical function. For form A bowls, that function is as honour gifts presented to dignitaries and imperial administrators at royal banquets, possibly as part of renewing the *adê* oath. In the Neo-Assyrian culture of conspicuous consumption it seems unlikely that ceramic vessels, Palace Ware, would have been greatly valued either socially or symbolically. Indeed, it has been suggested that Palace Ware vessels are merely cheap imitations of the more valued and valuable metal forms (Mallowan 1966). And yet, the inclusion of Palace Ware vessels as grave goods at Aššur and Nimrud suggests otherwise. Typically, Assyrian vessel classes or types are not restricted by material. *Kirru* vessels, for example, are attested in ceramic (SAA 7, 174 ln.4), silver (ND 2490), gold (Menzel 1981) and copper (SAA 7, 88 r. ln. 3–4). The practical and social function of these and other Assyrian vessels appears to transcend material type, being associated with the form or shape itself.

Understanding the relationship among skeuomorphs is complicated, particularly when metal is involved. Metal artefacts are subject to ancient and modern recycling and looting. The number of extant metal artefacts in the archaeological record is only an echo of the number of metal objects in use at any given point in time. Therefore, we are unable to evaluate the relative frequencies of form A bowls manufactured from metal, glass (Young *et al.* 1981), stone (Damerji 1999), and ceramic (Palace Ware fabric). Likewise, the relatively small number of metal, glass and stone bowls recovered archaeologically precludes comprehensive relative dating by material type.

Palace Ware form A bowls do not have Old or Middle Assyrian precursors or Common Ware equivalents. Oates (1959 and Curtis (1988) believe the form originates in the Middle Assyrian period as a generic Assyrian carinated bowl which, Anastasio (2010) argues, gained a 'flaring lip' during the Late Assyrian period and was subsequently exaggerated into the pronounced out-curving neck/rim of Palace Ware form A bowls. However, the earliest Palace Ware form A bowls date to the late 9th century BCE (Ohtsu 1991) and the earliest carinated Common Ware bowl with a flared rim (Anastasio type BW–05) dates to the mid-8th century (Lines 1954; Oates 1959). Given that the earliest Palace Ware form A bowls pre-date the common ware forms by 50–100 years, it is unlikely that the latter served as template for the former.

The shared practical and social function of metal, glass and stone form A bowls suggests that they are likely to have originated at the same time or slightly before ceramic Palace Ware vessels. Metal to ceramic skeuomorphism is well documented archaeologically in the Greco-Roman, Chinese and Islamic assemblages, while cases of ceramic to metal skeuomorphism are extremely rare (see discussion in Vickers *et al.* 1986). Therefore, even though the earliest metal bowls excavated in the Central Polity date to the late 9th century BCE (Stronach 1996), Neo-Assyrian Palace Ware was probably manufactured to replicate metal vessels and not vice versa (see Howes Smith 1986 and Gjerstad 1946 for discussion about the dating of metal drinking bowls in the Near East).

Rather than conduct a comprehensive survey of form A bowls in Assyria, which would itself be a subject worthy of study, we focus on those vessels excavated from Nimrud and the Neo-Assyrian tombs at Aššur. Golden form A bowls were recovered at Nimrud from the so-called Queens' tombs (tombs 2 and 3), arched subterranean chambers beneath room MM (Damerji 2008), and a silver bowl was excavated in 1990 from tomb 4 (Hussein 2008). In addition, an inscribed stone form A bowl, probably made of rock quartz crystal, was also recovered from the Queens' tombs (Damerji 1999). The overall typological similarity between these vessels and Palace Ware is striking. The silver bowl, for example, according to the drawings, has a maximum diameter, neck length and body length consistent with the formal attributes of Palace Ware form A bowls, 13 cm, 2.6 cm and 6 cm respectively, and its estimated capacity is 392.38 cm^3 or ~ 5 kāsu, also consistent with its Palace Ware counterparts.

A bronze bowl was excavated at Nimrud as part of a burial beneath the floor of room DD in the Northwest Palace, which Mallowan dated to the late 8th century BCE (Mallowan 1966). This vessel is also typologically consistent with Palace Ware form A bowls (figure 3.10) and is decorated with several registers of incised lines around the rim just below the lip, and a repoussé rosette omphalos on the interior base.

Three bronze bowls were excavated at Aššur from tomb 30, which dates to the end of the 9th century BCE: one of the bowls is decorated with a repoussé rosette omphalos, registers of engraved lines, and a 'spiked' or studded body; one is ribbed and inscribed with the name '*Aššur-taklāk*'; and the third has a plain body and an inscribed rim discussed in detail below (Haller 1954). Two additional bronze form A bowls were excavated from tomb 38 at Aššur, dating to the early 8th century BCE: one bowl is undecorated, and the other possesses a repoussé rosette omphalos and registers of incised lines (Haller 1954).

The decorative motifs on the metal vessels vary widely, from undecorated vessel bodies to intricate vertical ribbing, horizontal fluting at the shoulder, and 'studding'. Three bowls possess repoussé omphalos in a typical Assyrian floral motif and five vessels, four metal, one stone, are inscribed. The golden and stone bowls recovered from the Queens' tombs are each engraved with the name of a queen following the formula 'PN, queen of X, king of Assyria': "Belonging to Queen Yabâ, wife of Tiglath-pileser [III], king of Assyria"; "Belonging to Banîti, queen of Shalmaneser [V], king of Assyria"; "Belonging to Atalia, queen of Sargon, king of Assyria" (George 1990). The use of a formulaic titulary rather than simply a personal name suggests that these vessels had a formal or official, rather than personal, social and symbolic meaning.

One of the three form A bronze bowls from tomb 30 at Aššur is likewise inscribed with a title or administrative office: ^{amēl}*masennu ana* ^{māt}*arpada* or 'the masennu to Arpad' (Haller 1954; Millard 1994). A *masennu*, as we have seen, was a civilian magnate and a high official in the Neo-Assyrian court with a range of ritual and economic functions (Mattila 2000). It follows that the *masennu* of the important and strategic province Arpad was a powerful and highly trusted man in the Neo-Assyrian imperial administration and royal court.

A second bowl in tomb 30 is inscribed *'Aššur-taklāk'* (Haller 1954). *'Aššur-taklāk'* is a common Assyrian personal name, however it is also the eponym for the years 904 and 805 BCE (Millard 1994). The use of eponyms as a calendric device and chronicling system, and the 'office of eponym' itself, predate the Assyrian empire however, during the Late Assyrian period, the 'office of eponym' was rotated among high ranking officials in the imperial administration (*ibid.*). For example, Aššur-bani, governor of Kalḫu, and Mutakkil-Aššur, governor of Guzana, held the office of eponym in 713 and 706 BCE respectively (*ibid.*). The Aššur-taklāk who served as eponym for 805 BCE, consistent with Haller's dating of tomb 30, was probably also a high ranking Neo-Assyrian official. The collocation of these two bowls, in a single grave is highly suggestive and may describe the two most important social and political roles of its occupant: *massenu* to Arpad and eponym for 805 BCE. There is, however, no evidence to suggest that this particular bowl belonged to that Aššur-taklāk.

Additional evidence for the practice of inscribing titles or administrative offices on form A bowls comes from a bronze Neo-Assyrian bowl of unknown provenance, formerly housed in the Tehran museum and now lost: EN-URU ša URUZa-rat or the 'city ruler of Zarāt(u)' (Radner 1999–2001) The use of official titles and/or offices, rather than personal names, supports the social function of these vessels as honour gifts and a political or official, rather than personal, social value and semiotic meaning. Although to date no Palace Ware bowls with inscriptions have been excavated, the majority of the metal and stone skeuomorphs are inscribed with the official office or political rank of the owner and none of the extant vessels are inscribed with simply a personal name.

By inscribing the rank and/or administrative office of an individual on the honour-gift, drinking bowl, the vessels were elevated to symbols or icons of office and/or imperial power which, similar to imperial stamp seals, both identified the consumer to an audience as part of the Neo-Assyrian administration and reaffirmed to the consumer himself that his position was due to loyal participation in a larger system. The material composition of the bowl added another layer of meaning which, in the Neo-Assyrian culture of conspicuous consumption, served to differentiate among the imperial elite and powerful according to social and political rank: gold, glass and stone for the highest ranking members of the royal family; silver for lesser members of the royal family; bronze for the highest state officials, including provincial governors and their cabinet; and ceramic for lesser state officials. However, given that the material composition of the bowls was variable, it was the shape of these vessels that was iconic and carried their social and symbolic meaning. Perhaps this is why form A bowls alone in the Palace Ware population have no known Common Ware counterpart; the shape was universally recognised in the Central Polity as associated with and a symbol of imperial power and fealty to the Neo-Assyrian empire and its king.

The social value and semiotic function of these honour-gift drinking bowls as material expression of Assyrian fealty extended beyond the banquet itself. Treatment of the bowls was understood as a reflection of its consumer's feelings or intentions toward both the king specifically and Assyria more generally. An Old Babylonian parallel describes the established semiotic importance of the honour-gift in Mesopotamia. Ḫuzirî, king of Hazzikkannum, writes to Zimrilim, the king of Mari:

> Why is he still in favor with His Majesty? One time that man stayed with His Majesty where he drank from the cup and raised it (in salute). His Majesty counted him among his own men........ But he went back on his word and he defecated into the cup from which he had drunk; he is hostile to His Majesty! (Michalowski 1994, 35).

The social function of metal and Palace Ware form A bowls as honour-gifts given during a ritual reaffirmation of loyalty at a royal banquet explains the careful fabrication, unique shape and specific capacity of these vessels. It would also explain the inclusion of Palace Ware form A bowls as grave goods in Neo-Assyrian burials. The semiotic significance, meaning and value of this form, therefore, is Assyrian loyalty and probably has a secondary symbolic meaning related to power and prestige within the Assyrian political and administrative system.

The social function of Palace Ware form B cups and form C jars was the consumption of grape wine. In the Neo-Assyrian empire, the social practice of drinking grape wine was itself an act of conspicuous consumption symbolic of the wealth, power and royal favour enjoyed by the consumer. It is not surprising, therefore, that the vehicle of this consumption should also be a sign or icon endowed with semiotic meaning and value. Palace Ware cups and jars possessed several layers of meaning and participated in and contributed to the Neo-Assyrian imperial practice of conspicuous consumption both in a functional and symbolic capacity.

The first layer of meaning is the least subtle and relates to the social function of Palace Ware: the consumption of grape wine. Possession of Palace Ware cups and jars indicated access to grape wine, which was itself a reflection of the power and position of the consumer. A 'cupboard' of form B cups was excavated by Mallowan (1966) in the Northwest Palace at Nimrud. Room 12 is located in the public or administrative section of the Palace next to a 'presentation' or 'meeting' room (*ibid.*). The possession and display of such a large quantity of Palace Ware cups may have been an act of conspicuous consumption designed to impress upon its audience the power and wealth of the empire and its king. Perhaps wine was consumed at departmental meetings as a display of imperial abundance or perhaps individuals whose wine ration was small were expected to consume their wine ritually and return their cup—possession of personal Palace Ware cups and jars being reserved for high ranking individuals. Whatever the case, Palace Ware cups and jars were symbolic of the position and power of their consumers reflected by their access to grape wine.

The next layer of meaning is related to the conspicuous consumption of Palace Ware cups and jars themselves. Palace Ware forms B and C are easily distinguishable from Common Ware vessels of similar shape by their specialised fabric and small, specific sizes. The small capacities of forms B and C are not surprising; grape wine was an expensive and controlled commodity in the Neo-Assyrian empire and, according to the NWL, was rationed in relatively small volumes. However, Palace Ware cups and jars are consistently larger than necessary to consume the rations of grape wine described. For example, the ration of 2 *qû* from NWL 8 was approximately 1.6 L. Two *qû* was a fairly substantial volume of wine by Neo-Assyrian standards and probably distributed, stored and/or served in a form C jar. Form C jar occur in two sizes: approximately 1.5 and 3 L. Even allowing for some difference between an actual, practical qû and our best metrological estimate, the smaller of the form C jars would not comfortably hold 2 *qû* and the larger jar is conspicuously larger than necessary, perhaps indicating an intentional exaggeration. Likewise, a 'cup' measure or *kāsu* is 80 mL. The smallest Palace Ware form B cup is five times the volume necessary to comfortably hold such a small quantity of wine. If the volume of grape wine rationed to an individual was commensurate with their position and power within the Neo-Assyrian imperial administration, then the size of an individual's Palace Ware vessels would also be a reflection of their social and political importance. This may explain why more burials in the Late Assyrian cemetery at Aššur contained form C jars than form B cups, but why form B cups were still socially valuable and meaningful; limited access to and consumption of grape wine was still more prestigious than no access at all, particularly if personal possession of form B cups was restricted by rank.

If size was a socially and symbolically significant attribute of Palace Ware cups and jars, why are these vessels not grossly exaggerated? The degree to which they exceed the practical volumes they contained are relatively modest. The answer is that Palace Ware cups and jars, like grape wine itself, was a controlled commodity. Potters were contracted by institutions and/or administrative departments to manufacture Palace Ware and these institutions, not the consumers, controlled the size, shape and decoration of the finished product. It is probable that within the Central Polity social norms and expectations regulated the acceptable variation/exaggeration of Palace Ware size and the appropriate expression of conspicuous consumption.

If vessel size were a measure or means of differentiating among the powerful, so too were decoration and/or composition of Palace Ware cups and jars. Although no form C jars have been excavated in a material other than the distinctive Palace Ware ceramic fabric, form B cups were also manufactured in metal. This skeuomorphism suggests that a layer of prestige or meaning associated with material type may have existed for form B cups, similar to the ranking and conspicuous consumption of form A bowls. A metal form B cup from Fort Shalmaneser (Nimrud), dated to the 8th–7th centuries BCE (Curtis and Reade 1995; see also Oates 1959), is composed of silver with three registers of etched gold foil inlay and a fluted or ribbed body with a knob base, also covered in gold foil (figure 6.3). These decorative motifs are similar to those found on Palace Ware cups, for example moulded neck rings and registers of incised lines could be used to emulate the registers of gold foil inlay or vice versa. It is possible that the warped body created by 'dimpling' on many Palace Ware cups is meant to replicate the 'ribbed' or ridged body of the metal vessels, since the procedure required to produce ribs on a ceramic body would tear the fabric of walls as thin as Palace Ware. Although crushed, the metal cup stands 12.4 cm high, has a neck 4 cm long and a reconstructed capacity estimated between 737–869 cm^3, consistent with the typological and morphometric attributes of Palace Ware form B cups.

The most elaborately decorated Palace Ware cups and jars tend to the smaller forms. Form B1, for example, is the most ornate of the three Palace Ware cup subforms and the one most closely resembling/emulating the decorative motifs of the metal vessels. Form C jars are not as heavily decorated as form B cups in general, and the largest form C jars, form C2 and C4, are often undecorated. Perhaps this is because the social value and meaning of form C vessels was sufficiently expressed by the size of jars and/or personal possession

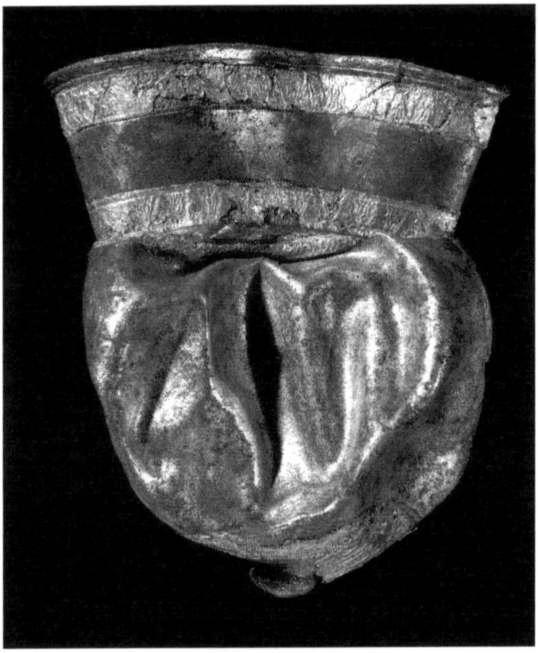

FIGURE 6.3 *Silver Palace Ware style cup from Fort Shalmaneser. (© Trustees of the British Museum)*

of Palace Ware jars at all, whereas form B cups, being smaller and perhaps more common, required allusion to more prestigious materials or vessels to function as a differentiator of rank. Additionally, form C jars were probably used for the storage, transport and presentation of grape wine, while form B cups were used in the actual social practice of grape wine consumption. As a result, form B cups were probably more visible and therefore a more obvious object of conspicuous consumption necessitating their elaborate decoration and skeuomorphism.

The social value and semiotic meaning of Palace Ware forms B and C in identifying the social and political position of the consumer was twofold. First, use and/or possession of Palace Ware cups and jars identified the consumer to an outside observer as part of the Neo-Assyrian imperial elite and someone with access to grape wine. However, the size, decorative style and/or material composition of the cups and jars related more specifically to the individual position or personal rank, power and privilege of the consumer, differentiating him from among his peers as a personal expression of conspicuous consumption.

Neo-Assyrian Annexed Provinces

Consumers of Palace Ware in the Annexed Provinces were part of the Neo-Assyrian imperial administrations serving in the provincial government. Some of these consumers were probably from the Central Polity and assigned or awarded governorship of a province by the king as a sign of trust and mark of favour. Others, though probably not the governors themselves, were local to the province and possibly members of the ruling class in the region before its annexation into the Neo-Assyrian empire. These men, in addition to their practical function of running the provincial government, had the symbolic function of personifying 'Assyria' to the province and the province to 'Assyria'. As such, they would have been fluent in the semiotics of both the Central Polity and their province and navigated the tension between establishing and maintaining a cohesive imperial identity and the ideological mandate of regional diversity.

Palace Ware, its social function, value and semiotic meaning, would have been known to the provincial governors and high officials as a result of interregional interaction between the province and Central Polity during the normal course of their duties. Form A bowls, probably in bronze like the one excavated at Dur-Katlimmu (Kreppner 2008), would certainly have been awarded to high ranking provincial officials as honour-gifts during their annual audience/royal banquet in the imperial capital and carried back to the province. Consumption of grape wine and its attendant material culture would be observed and participated in while they were staying in the Central Polity and a version of this social practice of conspicuous consumption probably existed in the provinces as well.

Despite being located adjacent to each other, the provinces in which Guzana and Dur-Katlimmu were located had very different relationships and political histories with both the Neo-Assyrian empire and Assyria in general. These different relationships and contexts altered and nuanced the social value and symbolic meaning of Assyrian material culture in these two regions, particularly material culture as rich in semiotic meaning as Palace Ware.

Social Function, Value and Semiotic Meaning of Palace Ware in the Annexed Provinces

Dur-Katlimmu

All three Palace Ware forms were consumed at Dur-Katlimmu: form C jars are the most numerous followed by form B cups and form A bowls. This pattern of consumption is most similar to that of Aššur which, as a burial context, reflects the social and symbolic importance of these vessels rather than their 'use-life' frequency. In both assemblages, the prominence of form C jars is noteworthy. In the Central Polity, Palace Ware jars were used as part of the social practice and conspicuous consumption of grape wine by the Neo-Assyrian imperial elite. Consumption of these jars, like the beverage they contained, first identified the consumer as part of the imperial administration and, second, as a powerful individual within that administration: one deserving of the distinction of a large wine ration. The jars themselves were modest in decoration and size.

At Dur-Katlimmu, Palace Ware jars have smaller capacities but are larger and more ornate than their Central Polity counterparts. Form C jars in the Central Polity occur in two basic sizes, approximately 1.5 and 3 L. The largest form C jars at Dur-Katlimmu are closest in capacity to the smaller Central Polity jars, approximately 1.5 L. The two additional smaller jar sizes at Dur-Katlimmu approximate 0.6 and 1.0 L. These volumes convert to a little less and a little more than a *qû* or 5 and 12.5 *kāsu*, respectively. It seems reasonable that the rations of grape wine for the provincial administrators would have been smaller than those listed for the officials, administrators and members of the royal household recorded in the NWL, necessitating smaller containers to distribute, transport, display and serve the wine. However, volumes of 1 *qû* and less are mentioned in the NWL with no correspondingly sized form C jars in evidence in the Central Polity.

In addition to holding a smaller volume of wine, Palace Ware jars at Dur-Katlimmu are physically larger—having significantly longer bodies and maximum diameters—and more elaborately decorated, often with traditional Assyrian motifs not typically found of Palace Ware jars, such as stepped bases. Palace Ware cups at Dur-Katlimmu are similarly larger (longer necks and bodies) and more ornate than their Central Polity counterparts but hold the same capacity of wine. This suggests that the actual standards of measurement (*qû* and *kāsu*) and social expectation about the amount a cup should hold were the same in the Central Polity and at Dur-Katlimmu but that the importance or meaning of the conspicuous consumption of these vessels was intensified at Dur-Katlimmu. Although these morphometric differences in Palace Ware jars and cups are relatively subtle and do not alter the overall form of the vessels, they indicate an emphasis on both the Assyrian-ness of these vessels and their conspicuous consumption at Dur-Katlimmu.

The social practice and semiotic significance of consuming grape wine and possessing/displaying the Palace Ware vessels used in this practice appear unchanged at Dur-Katlimmu. However, emphasis on the conspicuous consumption of these vessels and/or the beverage is heightened. The status and individual recognition associated with form C vessels was important enough to the local consumers at Dur-Katlimmu that they commissioned jars of smaller capacities to accommodate their smaller rations while at the same time making they more pronounced, more conspicuous, in height and width. What is the purpose of this emphatic and conspicuous consumption of Palace Ware at Dur-Katlimmu? Who was its cultural audience?

Cultural continuity between Dur-Katlimmu and the Central Polity existed for generations. However, under Tiglath-pilesar III administrative and imperial power in the region was reorganised and redistributed with the result that Dur-Katlimmu was annexed into a newly created province, Laqe (Radner 2002). Whether this change was motivated by real or imagined threat of insurrection, the impact of this new political reality on the administrators at Dur-Katlimmu would likely have been significant. The new provincial governor would have been chosen for his loyalty to both king and state and be aware of the reasons or fears which precipitated the creation of his province. As such, he would be particularly interested in demonstrating his loyalty to Assyria and fealty to its king. The overtly and exaggerated Assyrian decoration on the Palace Ware jars and cups at Dur-Katlimmu may be an expression of this desire to demonstrate, tangibly, oneness with Assyria; identifying these vessels and the power and prestige associated with the social practice of grape wine consumption even more symbolically and concretely with Assyria, both to its local audience and, perhaps, to Assyrian herself.

The conspicuous consumption of Palace Ware and the ritual of wine rationing were also emphasised and exaggerated at Dur-Katlimmu. The creation of additional containers (jar sizes) and, as a result, context specific layers of symbolic power and prestige within the provincial branch of the imperial government served both to identify Assyria and the Neo-Assyrian empire as the powerful and wealthy provider, to both themselves and the imperial administration in the Central Polity, and also reaffirm the Assyrian-ness of the participants in this social practice by expanding or exaggerating the ritual of wine rationing and consumption. Another possible influence on the creation of these new jar sizes and their semiotic meaning is that people in the middle or lower end of a power structure are often far more conscious and conscientious about ritual, protocol and the formality of interactions within a power structure than those in the highest positions. The creation of sub-ranks or categories of distinction and distribution deserving/requiring the acquisition of Palace Ware jars may have been used by the provincial administration to build a sense of identity and unity within themselves and also as a means of individual identification, recognition, and validation.

Consumption of form A bowls at Dur-Katlimmu supports this nuanced social and symbolic function of Palace Ware as a means of demonstrating and reaffirming cultural continuity with and loyalty to the Neo-Assyrian empire. Form A bowls are similar in capacity to their Central Polity counterparts but are more conspicuous—longer necks, wider maximum diameters and taller profiles. As with Palace Ware form B cups, conformity of form A bowls at Dur-Katlimmu to Central Polity capacity norms indicates that the social expectations associated with the function and social practice of these vessels was the same at Dur-Katlimmu as it was in the Central Polity but that the value or meaning of that consumption was heightened in the provincial setting.

Form A bowls were a symbol of Neo-Assyrian loyalty and fealty and it is unlikely that this semiotic function would change in a provincial setting, particularly for those in the highest positions of authority. The provincial governor of Dur-Katlimmu, and possibly his deputy, would have been given a bronze bowl as an honour-gifts by the king during visits to the Central Polity. Locally manufactured Palace Ware form A bowls would likely have been for the major-domo, city overseer, village inspector and possible other lower ranking officials. These ceramic Palace Ware bowls could have been used at a local, provincial banquets or rituals to reaffirm loyalty to Assyria and the province; the specific capacities of these bowls, consistent with those from the Central Polity, suggest their use in a similar ritual. Whether these vessels were symbols of personal loyalty used in ritual reaffirmation of Assyrian fealty or were simply a symbol of office representing official loyalty to and participation in the Neo-Assyrian imperial administration, their exaggerated size denotes the increased importance of their semiotic function at Dur-Katlimmu.

Guzana

Understanding the social value and semiotic meaning of Palace Ware at Guzana is complicated by the small sample size and lack of contextual information for the vessels available for inclusion in our study. Form A bowls are not represented in the Guzana population, probably an artefact of sampling. Local consumer of Palace Ware at Guzana would have included to provincial governor and members of the provincial administration, many of whom would have been presented with bronze or ceramic form A bowls as honour-gifts during banquets and loyalty rituals in the Central Polity.

As an annexed Aramean province, the provincial leadership of Guzana, particularly at the highest levels, were likely Central Polity Assyrians assigned and relocated to the provincial capital. These men would have brought with them from the Central Polity the social and symbolic meaning of Palace Ware in general and form A vessels in particular and, in the potentially hostile environment of a different cultural setting, it is probable that these meanings were maintained without alteration. Without Palace Ware form A bowls from

Guzana for analysis, it is impossible to know whether this symbol of Assyrian loyalty was exaggerated at Guzana, as it was at Dur-Katlimmu. Based on the patterns of Palace Ware cup and jar consumption at Guzana, however, we speculate it was not.

Consumption of Palace Ware at Guzana consisted primarily of form B cups, consistent with consumption patterns in Central Polity capital cities of Nimrud and Nineveh, but also a significant number of form C jars. The consumption of Palace Ware jars at Guzana may indicate an increased social value or significance of the possession, display or consumption of these vessels, as it does at Dur-Katlimmu. Alternatively, the higher proportion of jars in the Annexed Provinces in general may reflect the consolidation or centralisation of power/office space into a single structure, the governor's palace as opposed to the Central Polity practice of separate departmental 'offices'.

Technically, both the smaller (form C1) and larger (form C4) Palace Ware jar forms are represented at Guzana; although the form C4 jar is at the small end of the C4 capacity range meaning that all three jars could easily be classified within the 'small' jar category. Interestingly, the two form C1 jars have longer bodies than expected and the form C4 jar has neck and body lengths shorter than expected, despite holding the same capacities as their Central Polity counterparts. Practically speaking, all three Palace Ware jars at Guzana are the same size, shape and length. Therefore, any semiotic meaning or value attached to these vessels was associated with their shape and social function rather than their size. This is a subtle change from both the Central Polity and Dur-Katlimmu, where part of the conspicuous consumption of these vessels was their exaggerated size/length for their practical function.

Wine rations at Guzana would have been smaller than those in the Central Polity, probably similar in size to those at Dur-Katlimmu, and so even the smaller of the standard form C jars would have been conspicuously larger than necessary to hold provincial wine rations. The relative subtlety of Palace Ware jar lengths at Guzana compared with those Dur-Katlimmu suggests that the cultural audience for their conspicuous consumption was the consumers themselves and not the provincial population in general or the Central Polity administration. The status, power and social meaning of consuming Palace Ware jars at Guzana required no additional embellishment, including the creation of special jars to hold smaller rations of wine. The social practice and ritual associated with these vessels in the Central Polity was unaltered at Guzana.

All three Palace Ware jars are decorated with Assyrian motifs typical of Palace Ware jar decoration in the Central Polity, with the exception of the elaborate stepped base on jar HB. This type of basal decoration is more commonly associated with form B1 cups in the Central Polity but is quite common on both

Palace Ware cups and jars at Dur-Katlimmu. Palace Ware cups at Guzana are similar in shape and size to their Central Polity counterparts but are decidedly plainer: 100% of the form B3 population is undecorated at Guzana compared with 40% in the Central Polity. This is particularly interesting if the dimples on Palace Ware vessels were replicating the ribbing common on metal cups. The consumption of the cup shape and Palace Ware fabric appear to have been symbolic enough for their cultural audience and allusion to other more precious or prestigious materials unnecessary to their social and semiotic function at Guzana.

The similar capacity measurements of Palace Ware cups and jars at Guzana and the Central Polity indicate a high degree of cultural continuity between the two regions in terms of social practice and meaning associated with the function of these vessels; unsurprising since the consumers of Palace Ware at Guzana were likely from the Central Polity. The plainer style of the form B cups and lack of formal exaggeration of the jars, however, suggests that the social value and semiotic meaning of these vessels was simplified and restricted to the social practice of wine consumption itself rather than carrying the additional meaning of individual power/prestige differentiation associated with these forms in the Central Polity. It is almost as though the conspicuous consumption of the vessels themselves was less important at Guzana than in the Central Polity and at Dur-Katlimmu, and the semiotic meaning of these vessels was derived entirely from their social function, the conspicuous consumption of grape wine.

The consumers of Palace Ware at Guzana, members of the imperial provincial government, had nothing to prove either to the people they governed or to the Central Polity administration. The people they governed knew who they were and the power and wealth of Assyria was made tangible not only by their presence but through monumental and public architecture and the enforcement of its administrative system. Likewise, the governor of Guzana and his administrators were chosen by the king for their loyalty which was not questioned as long as they fulfilled their duties and reaffirmed their fealty annually. Displays of solidarity with the Central Polity were superfluous. The cultural audience for the conspicuous consumption of Palace Ware and grape wine was the consumers themselves. Within the ranks of the provincial leadership, the distribution of individual power and prestige was known and, if necessary, displayed by other means. Unity within the provincial administration in a potentially hostile environment, however, was essential to survival. Therefore, the social practice and conspicuous consumption of grape wine was used as a reaffirmation of their power, position and unity within the Neo-Assyrian imperial system, a means of building solidarity within the provincial administration of

Guzana, and all symbolic indicators of individual differentiation within that administration avoided to prevent insurrection.

Unincorporated Territories in the Neo-Assyrian Imperial Landscape

Identifying the consumers of Palace Ware and/or Palace Ware-style vessels in the Unincorporated Territories and the social value and semiotic meaning of these vessels outside of Assyria proper is challenging and requires a nuanced understanding of the social and political context of their consumption. Buffer zones and vassal states grateful for the protection and economic stability associated with the Neo-Assyrian empire might consume Palace Ware as a symbol of loyalty and solidarity with Assyria. On the other hand, buffer zones and vassal states who resented the interference of Assyria and/or who viewed the relationship with the Neo-Assyrian empire as a financial burden would be unlikely to consume Palace Ware or Assyrian material culture at all.

Rulers of vassal states would have been expected to have an annual audience with the king, at which time their tribute was paid and their fealty reaffirmed. Form A bowls, probably in ceramic to distinguish them from provincial governors, would have been awarded to these vassal rulers as honour-gifts and transported back to the Unincorporated Territories. While in the Central Polity, vassal rulers may have witnessed the conspicuous consumption of grape wine and Palace Ware cups and jars associated with this consumption. As persons outside the Neo-Assyrian imperial administration it is unlikely that vassal rulers would have received official wine rations themselves however, while in the Central Polity, they may have participated in the social practice of grape wine drinking.

Rulers of buffer zones may not have been considered important enough to warrant an annual audience with the king. However, we think it likely that they did. Buffer zones were often located in highly strategic regions and their loyalty was essential to preserving the integrity of imperial boundaries. From an ideological point of view, not only was the Neo-Assyrian king a 'hands on' ruler (Postgate 2007) but the cultural audience of Neo-Assyrian imperial conspicuous consumption, the monumental architecture, collecting, pageantry and public displays of wealth, was as much for those outside the empire as it was for the Assyrians themselves. The purpose of conspicuous consumption is to be observed conspicuously consuming and the larger the audience, the better. Like vassal rulers, rulers of buffer zones would probably have participated in the *adê* ritual and been awarded a form A bowl in ceramic as an honour-gift by the king. While in the Central Polity they may also have witnessed or participated in the Neo-Assyrian social practice of grape wine consumption and be familiar with Palace Ware cups and jars.

Unlike the provincial government which typically consisted of Central Polity Assyrians relocated to a provincial setting, rulers in the Unincorporated Territories were local. The social function of Palace Ware would have been known or at least familiar to rulers of vassal states and buffer zones but the semiotic value and meaning of these vessels might have been less clear. Understanding the meaning and symbolic significance of an object requires a high degree of cultural knowledge and familiarity. The more limited interregional contact between the Unincorporated Territories and Central Polity and the cultural differences between the rulers of these two areas, suggests that the social value and semiotic significance of Palace Ware in the Unincorporated Territories was related to its social function and not its symbolic meaning in Assyrian proper.

Social Function, Value and Semiotic of Palace Ware in the Unincorporated Territories

Tel Jemmeh

Tel Jemmeh was located in a buffer zone between Neo-Assyrian and Egyptian economic interests and adjacent to several vassal states and the Neo-Assyrian province Ashdod. Ashdod and the vassal states in the southern Levant had a complicated relationship with both Egypt and Assyria; switching loyalties and playing one side against the other to their own advantage for close to 100 years. Although there is no textual evidence specifically related to Jemmeh, it is reasonable to assume that the rulers of this city participated in an equally turbulent relationship with Egypt and Assyria.

Consumption of Palace Ware-style vessels at Jemmeh consists predominantly of bowls, followed by cups and jars. The relatively low proportion of Palace Ware-style cups and jars, 20% of the total population or 6 vessels, is probably a reflection of their social function in the Central Polity rather than their value or symbolic meaning. Grape wine was produced in the southern Levant and, as such, doubtlessly had a different social value in this region. If grape wine was not considered a luxury or prestige item at Jemmeh but instead was relatively common, then the social practice of consuming grape wine would likewise not be considered particularly meaningful. Material culture related to grape wine consumption, socially and symbolically significant in the Central and Annexed Provinces where grape wine was rare, would perhaps have been less consequential to the cultural audience at Jemmeh. The handful of Palace Ware-style cups and jars manufactured at Tel Jemmeh may have been novelty pieces, valued for their differentness or generic Assyrian-ness rather than their association either with grape wine or Neo-Assyrian imperial power and prestige. This change in social value and semiotic meaning is supported by the general similarity in shape and style between these vessels and Central Polity Palace Ware but the significant difference in size and fabric and the sloppy execution of stylistic attributes. The social value of these vessels was their differentness from local forms and the crudeness of their manufacture compared with actual Neo-Assyrian pottery did not detract from this value.

The presence of such a large population of form A-style bowls at Jemmeh is intriguing. In the Central Polity and Annexed Provinces, this form is associated with fealty to the king and loyalty to the Neo-Assyrian empire. Possession of these vessels identified the consumer as part of the Neo-Assyrian imperial administration and the material from which they were manufactured indicated his relative status, power and prestige within that administration. The rulers of Tel Jemmeh would likely have been aware of and participated in the social practice and ritual associated with form A honour-gift bowls. They would understand the symbolic value and meaning of these objects, if not perfectly on some level, and probably were awarded a Palace Ware form A bowls of their own. This familiarity with and ownership of a form A bowl explains how the idea, concept or shape was transported to Tel Jemmeh. However, the association of this shape with Assyrian loyalty and participation in the imperial administration combined with the, probably, troubled and changeable relationship of these rulers with that administration make them unlikely consumers of the form A-style vessels manufactured locally at Jemmeh.

It is possible that Palace Ware-style bowls were consumed by the leadership of Tel Jemmeh during a period of Assyrian alliance and discarded when the political tides shifted in favour of Egypt. A substantial amount of Assyrian-style pottery was excavated from pits and wells, presumably where it was discarded by its consumers (Petrie 1928). However, another more likely possibility is that these vessels were consumed by the upper stratum families at Tel Jemmeh, not necessarily the rulers, which could also explain their presence in private/domestic contexts.

From the perspective of the 'middle management' at Jemmeh, the rulers enjoyed international travel and brought back exotic souvenirs of their time in Assyria. Whatever these vessels meant to their owners, to their local cultural audience they represented the power and prestige associated with travel to and interaction with the world beyond Jemmeh. The locus or focus of this semiotic meaning and social value was the 'other-ness' or foreignness of these vessels. It is this aspect and those attributes of Palace Ware-style vessels identified by the local consumers as 'other' which are exaggerated and emphasised at Jemmeh, often involving a mixture of styles and motifs not typically associated with Palace Ware in the Central Polity, such as thickened t-shaped rim elements. The complete lack of conformity between these vessels, in terms of size and decoration, and Palace Ware bowls in either the Central Polity or Annexed Provinces suggests that faithful reproduction or emulation of Palace Ware was not socially meaningful to their local consumers at Tel Jemmeh. Rather the consumers at Jemmeh appear to value their idea of an Assyrian vessel.

The social value and semiotic significance of these Assyrian-style bowls was to identify the consumer as cosmopolitan, part of the elite and/or powerful at Jemmeh, familiar with the current fashion and social practices in the greater Near East. Tel Jemmeh was located along the Gaza-Petra trade route, often called the spice or incense route, and therefore its population was more familiar with and/or interested in the changing fads and fashions in the Near East in general then other small cities. Palace Ware or Assyrian-style bowls could have been one of these fads for the upper stratum families at Jemmeh.

In support of this shift in value and semiotic meaning of Palace Ware-style vessels from symbols of Assyrian loyalty and power to a more generalised sign of elite status, wealth and prestige, form A-style bowls at Jemmeh are sometimes blended with elite stylistic attributes of more local origin, such as red-slipping and burnishing. Samaria Ware, a local 'elite' ware in the southern Levant, was red-slipped and burnished and also had thin walls, similar to those characteristic of Palace Ware. The intentional blending of styles, Assyrian shape with local decorative motifs, indicates an equation of the social value of form A-style bowls and Samaria Ware and may have been a semiotic cue to the cultural audience of the conspicuous consumption of these vessels about their value and significance.

The consumers of Palace Ware-style vessels at Tel Jemmeh were likely the wealthy and privileged, interested in status and prestige and the conspicuous consumption of material culture associated with wealth and privilege. Assyrian-style vessels were valued for their foreignness and identified the consumer as cosmopolitan, part of the internationally savvy at Jemmeh. Faithful reproduction and/or emulation of Assyrian forms and styles was less important than the local idealised and exaggerated interpretation of these forms and styles. Form A-style bowls were more popular at Jemmeh both because the social practice of grape wine consumption was less valued in this community and because form A bowls were associated with the rulers of the city and/or international travel.

CHAPTER 7

Concluding Remarks

Palace Ware served an important semiotic function within the Neo-Assyrian imperial practice of conspicuous consumption. Form A bowls were given as honour-gifts by the king to members of the imperial administration and its allies in a material signifying their rank and role within the empire. Although Palace Ware bowls may have been reserved for the lower ranking members of the empire, the conspicuous consumption of the form identified the consumer as a man of importance, power and prestige, and a loyal participant in the Neo-Assyrian imperial system. As a symbol, Palace Ware bowls represented loyalty to the Assyrian king and State. Palace Ware jars and cups, forms C and B, were used in the Neo-Assyrian imperial practice of the conspicuous consumption of grape wine. The value and meaning of these vessels is derivative of the value and meaning of grape wine; a luxury good, reserved for the elect and elite. As symbols, Palace Ware jars and cups represented wealth, privilege and access, and the consumption and possession of the vessels themselves, particularly form C jars, indicated the relative status or individual power of the consumer.

Palace Ware is unique to the Neo-Assyrian empire, even if the forms themselves are not, and as such, can potentially be used as a temporal indicator of the Late Assyrian period. Given the social function and semiotic meaning of these vessels within the Neo-Assyrian imperial administration, Palace Ware can probably even be considered elite. However, the extrapolation that Palace Ware is an indicator or index artefact for Neo-Assyrian imperial occupation outside the boundaries of the provincial system is not supported by the material culture itself or the social and symbolic value of these vessels at sites in the Unincorporated Territories, such as Tel Jemmeh. At Tel Jemmeh, the social and semiotic meaning of Palace Ware-style vessels is quite independent of the symbolic and political meaning of Palace Ware in Assyria proper. In fact, faithful reproduction of Palace Ware, its form, fabric, size and style, is unimportant to the local consumers at Tel Jemmeh. The status and prestige derived from the conspicuous consumption of Palace Ware-style vessels is related to the exaggerated and idealised other-ness or foreign-ness of these vessels which identifies the consumer as metropolitan and elite.

The consumption of Palace Ware in the Annexed Provinces, on the other hand, may indeed be an indicator of Neo-Assyrian imperial presence and occupation. In the Annexed Provinces, Palace Ware was consumed by members of the imperial provincial administration, many of whom were relocated

 | DOI 10.1163/9789004304123_008

from the Central Polity. The social practice, value and symbolic meaning of these vessels was known to these consumers but often modified to meet their context specific needs. At Dur-Katlimmu, where demonstration of loyalty to and cultural continuity with Assyria were critically important to its provincial government, conspicuous consumption of Palace Ware was exaggerated: forms made bigger and more conspicuous, decoration more elaborate, and the social practice of wine consumption elaborated upon to include and extended range of vessel sizes. At Guzana, where the provincial government was in a potentially hostile environment and unity within the administration essential, indicators of individual rank, such as decoration, were downplayed.

Despite its association with the Late Assyrian period in general and the Neo-Assyrian imperial administration specifically, it is important to remember that Palace Ware was always a local phenomenon. These vessels were manufactured locally, possibly by Central Polity or Central Polity trained potters in the Annexed Provinces, for local consumers. Although it is likely that Palace Ware form A bowls from the Central Polity were transported across the imperial landscape as vessels, due to their social function as honour-gifts, Palace Ware in general was not a traded commodity. Palace Ware vessels were carefully crafted symbols and their consumption was controlled, at least within Neo-Assyrian imperial borders. Correlation of the consumption of these vessels and the annexation of territories into the Neo-Assyrian empire is explained by their social function within the imperial administration at both the State and provincial level. Adoption and adaption of these forms outside Assyria proper was voluntary and highly contextual, probably as a result of the translation of these forms into a culturally meaningful sign for the local consumers.

Detailed analysis of Palace Ware form and fabric enables us to understand the value and semiotic meaning of these vessels for their local consumers and, by extension, the relationship of these consumers with the Neo-Assyrian imperial administration and Central Polity. It is our hope that future research will expand upon our work and use the analytical and interpretive model presented here to further our understanding of relationships within and without the Neo-Assyrian provincial system.

Appendix A: Palace Ware Petrographic Thin-section Descriptions

Nimrud

N 1–1 (Body Sherd)

The matrix is olive and opaque in PPL; optically inactive in XPL. Devoid of foraminifers. Rare (0.5%) planar voids (up to 0.5mm) with frequent secondary calcite formation in the interstitial space. Opaques (2%) of hematite, rutile, magnetite, sphene and spinel, between a few microns and almost 15μm. The inclusions ($f{:}c_{0.062mm}$ = 99:1) contain very well-sorted, sub-rounded to well-rounded, fine sand particles of quartz and plagioclase, amphibole and apatite (rare) and mica (very rare), up to 0.05mm. Heavy minerals (monazite-xenotime, baryte-celestite, epidote) (very rare), up to 0.03mm, could be identified.

N 1–2 (Body Sherd)

The matrix is olive and opaque in PPL; optically inactive in XPL. Devoid of foraminifers. Rare (0.5%) planar voids (up to 0.3mm). Opaques (2%) of hematite, rutile, magnetite, sphene and spinel, between a few microns and almost 20μm. The inclusions ($f{:}c_{0.062mm}$ = 99:1) contain very well-sorted, sub-rounded to well-rounded, fine sand particles of quartz and plagioclase, amphibole and apatite (rare), up to 0.05mm. Heavy minerals (zircon, monazite-xenotime, baryte-celestite) (very rare), up to 0.02mm, could be identified.

N 1–3 (Neck Sherd)

The matrix is pale yellow-brown and opaque in PPL; optically inactive in XPL. Devoid of foraminifers. Rare (1%) planar voids (up to 0.3mm). Opaques (2%) of hematite, rutile, magnetite, sphene and spinel, between a few microns and almost 20μm. The inclusions ($f{:}c_{0.062mm}$ = 99:1) contain very well-sorted, sub-rounded to well-rounded, fine sand particles of quartz and plagioclase, amphibole and apatite (rare), up to 0.05mm. Heavy minerals (zircon, monazite-xenotime, baryte-celestite) (very rare), up to 0.03mm, could be identified.

N 1–4 (Rim Sherd)

The matrix is pale yellow-brown and opaque in PPL; optically inactive in XPL. Devoid of foraminifers. Rare (0.5%) planar voids (up to 0.3mm). Opaques (2%) of hematite, rutile, magnetite, sphene and spinel, between a few microns and almost 20μm. The

 | DOI 10.1163/9789004304123_009

inclusions ($f{:}c_{0.062mm}$ = 98:2) contain very well-sorted, sub-rounded to well-rounded, fine sand particles of quartz and plagioclase, amphibole and apatite (rare), up to 0.05mm. Heavy minerals (zircon and epidote) (very rare), up to 0.03mm, could be identified.

N1–5 (Body Sherd)

The matrix is olive and opaque in PPL; optically inactive in XPL. Devoid of foraminifers. Rare (1%) planar voids (up to 0.5mm) with frequent secondary calcite formation in the interstitial space. Opaques (2%) of hematite, rutile, magnetite, sphene and spinel, between a few microns and almost 20μm. The inclusions ($f{:}c_{0.062mm}$ = 99:1) contain very well-sorted, sub-rounded to well-rounded, fine sand particles of quartz and plagioclase, amphibole and apatite (rare), up to 0.05mm. Heavy minerals (zircon, monazite-xenotime, baryte-celestite, epidote) (very rare), up to 0.03mm, could be identified.

N1–6 (Body Sherd)

The matrix is pale yellow-brown and opaque in PPL; optically inactive in XPL. Devoid of foraminifers. Rare (0.5%) planar voids (up to 0.5mm) with common secondary calcite formation in the interstitial space. Opaques (2%) of hematite, rutile, magnetite, sphene and spinel, between a few microns and almost 25μm. The inclusions ($f{:}c_{0.062mm}$ = 99:1) contain very well-sorted, sub-rounded to well-rounded, fine sand particles of quartz and plagioclase, amphibole and apatite (rare), up to 0.04mm. Heavy minerals (monazite-xenotime, baryte-celestite, epidote) (very rare), up to 0.03mm, could be identified.

N1–7 (Body Sherd)

The matrix is olive and opaque in PPL; optically inactive in XPL. Devoid of foraminifers. Rare (0.5 %) planar voids (up to 0.4mm) with frequent secondary calcite formation in the interstitial space. Opaques (2%) of hematite, rutile, magnetite, sphene and spinel, between a few microns and almost 15μm. The inclusions ($f{:}c_{0.062mm}$ = 99:1) contain very well-sorted, sub-rounded to well-rounded, fine sand particles of quartz and plagioclase, amphibole and apatite (rare), up to 0.03mm. Heavy minerals (zircon, monazite-xenotime, baryte-celestite, epidote) (very rare), up to 0.03mm, could be identified.

N1–8 (Neck Sherd)

The matrix is pale yellow-brown and opaque in PPL; optically inactive in XPL. Devoid of foraminifers. Rare (0.5%) planar voids (up to 0.3mm) with frequent secondary calcite formation in the interstitial space. Opaques (2%) of hematite, rutile, magnetite, sphene and spinel, between a few microns and almost 20μm. The inclusions ($f{:}c_{0.062mm}$ = 98:2) contain very well-sorted, sub-rounded to well-rounded, fine sand particles of quartz and plagioclase, amphibole and apatite (rare), up to 0.03mm. Heavy minerals (monazite-xenotime, baryte-celestite, epidote) (very rare), up to 0.025mm, could be identified.

N 1–9 (Body Sherd)

The matrix is pale yellow-brown and opaque in PPL; optically inactive in XPL. Devoid of foraminifers. Rare (1%) planar voids (up to 0.5mm) with frequent secondary calcite formation in the interstitial space. Opaques (2%) of hematite, rutile, magnetite, sphene and spinel, between a few microns and almost 20µm. The inclusions ($f{:}c_{0.062mm}$ = 99:1) contain very well-sorted, sub-rounded to well-rounded, fine sand particles of quartz and plagioclase, amphibole and apatite (rare) and mica (very rare), up to 0.04mm. Heavy minerals (monazite-xenotime, baryte-celestite, epidote) (very rare), up to 0.03mm, could be identified.

N 1–10 (Body Sherd)

The matrix is pale yellow-brown and opaque in PPL; optically inactive in XPL. Devoid of foraminifers. Rare (1%) planar voids (up to 0.4mm) with frequent secondary calcite formation in the interstitial space. Opaques (2%) of hematite, rutile, magnetite, sphene and spinel, between a few microns and almost 15µm. The inclusions ($f{:}c_{0.062mm}$ = 99:1) contain very well-sorted, sub-rounded to well-rounded, fine sand particles of quartz and plagioclase, amphibole and apatite (rare), up to 0.05mm. Heavy minerals (epidote) (very rare), up to 0.03mm, could be identified.

N 1–11 (Body Sherd)

The matrix is olive and opaque in PPL; optically inactive in XPL. Devoid of foraminifers. Rare (0.5 %) planar voids (up to 0.3mm). Opaques (2%) of hematite, rutile, magnetite, sphene and spinel, between a few microns and almost 15µm. The inclusions ($f{:}c_{0.062mm}$ = 99:1) contain very well-sorted, sub-rounded to well-rounded, fine sand particles of quartz and plagioclase, amphibole and apatite (rare), up to 0.03mm. Heavy minerals (monazite-xenotime, baryte-celestite, epidote) (very rare), up to 0.03mm, could be identified.

N 1–12 (Body Sherd)

The matrix is pale yellow-brown and opaque in PPL; optically inactive in XPL. Devoid of foraminifers. Rare (0.5%) planar voids (up to 0.3mm). Opaques (2%) of hematite, rutile, magnetite, sphene and spinel, between a few microns and almost 20µm. The inclusions ($f{:}c_{0.062mm}$ = 98:2) contain very well-sorted, sub-rounded to well-rounded, fine sand particles of quartz and plagioclase, amphibole and apatite (rare) and mica (very rare), up to 0.05mm. Heavy minerals (zircon and epidote) (very rare), up to 0.03mm, could be identified.

Nineveh

NV 1–1 (Body Sherd)

The matrix is pale yellow-brown and opaque in PPL; optically inactive in XPL. Devoid of foraminifers. Rare (0.5%) planar voids (up to 0.3mm) with common (~10%) secondary calcite formation in the interstitial space. Opaques (2%) of hematite, rutile, magnetite, sphene and spinel, between a few microns and almost 20µm. The inclusions ($f{:}c_{0.062mm}$ = 97:3) contain very well-sorted, sub-rounded to well-rounded, fine sand particles of quartz and plagioclase (rare) and amphibole (very rare), up to 0.05mm. Heavy minerals (baryte-celestite, monazite-xenotime) (very rare), up to 0.03mm, could be identified.

NV 1–2 (Body Sherd)

The matrix is olive and opaque in PPL; optically inactive in XPL. Devoid of foraminifers. Rare (1%) planar voids (up to 0.3mm) with common (~15%) secondary calcite formation in the interstitial space. Opaques (2%) of hematite, rutile, magnetite, sphene and spinel, between a few microns and almost 25µm. The inclusions ($f{:}c_{0.062mm}$ = 98:2) contain very well-sorted, sub-rounded to well-rounded, fine sand particles of quartz and plagioclase (rare) and amphibole and mica (very rare), up to 0.05mm. Heavy minerals (baryte-celestite, monazite-xenotime, zircon, epidote) (very rare), up to 0.03mm, could be identified.

NV 1–3 (Rim Sherd)

The matrix is pale yellow-brown and opaque in PPL; optically inactive in XPL. Devoid of foraminifers. Rare (0.5%) planar voids (up to 0.3mm). Opaques (2%) of hematite, rutile, magnetite, sphene and spinel, between a few microns and almost 15µm. The inclusions ($f{:}c_{0.062mm}$ = 99:1) contain very well-sorted, sub-rounded to well-rounded, fine sand particles of quartz and plagioclase (rare), up to 0.03mm. Heavy minerals (epidote) (very rare), up to 0.03mm, could be identified.

NV 1–4 (Shoulder Sherd)

The matrix is yellow-brown and opaque in PPL; optically inactive in XPL. Devoid of foraminifers. Rare (0.5%) planar voids (up to 0.3mm) Opaques (2%) of hematite, rutile, magnetite, sphene and spinel, between a few microns and almost 20µm. The inclusions ($f{:}c_{0.062mm}$ = 98:2) contain very well-sorted, sub-rounded to well-rounded, fine sand particles of quartz and plagioclase (rare) and amphibole (very rare), up to 0.05mm. Heavy minerals (baryte-celestite, monazite-xenotime, apatite) (very rare), up to 0.03mm, could be identified.

NV 1–5 (*Body Sherd*)

The matrix is olive and opaque in PPL; optically inactive in XPL. Devoid of foraminifers. Rare (1%) planar voids (up to 0.3mm) with common (~10%) secondary calcite formation in the interstitial space. Opaques (2%) of hematite, rutile, magnetite, sphene and spinel, between a few microns and almost 20μm. The inclusions ($f{:}c_{0.062mm}$ = 98:2) contain very well-sorted, sub-rounded to well-rounded, fine sand particles of quartz and plagioclase (rare) and amphibole and mica (very rare), up to 0.05mm. Heavy minerals (monazite-xenotime, epidote, zircon) (very rare), up to 0.03mm, could be identified.

NV 1–6 (*Body Sherd*)

The matrix is pale yellow-brown and opaque in PPL; optically inactive in XPL. Devoid of foraminifers. Rare (0.5%) planar voids (up to 0.3mm). Opaques (2%) of hematite, rutile, magnetite, sphene and spinel, between a few microns and almost 15μm. The inclusions ($f{:}c_{0.062mm}$ = 98:2) contain very well-sorted, sub-rounded to well-rounded, fine sand particles of quartz and plagioclase (rare), up to 0.04mm.

NV 1–7 (*Body Sherd*)

The matrix is olive to pale yellow-brown and opaque in PPL; optically inactive in XPL. Devoid of foraminifers. Rare (1%) planar voids (up to 0.3mm) with common (~15%) secondary calcite formation in the interstitial space.Opaques (2%) of hematite, rutile, magnetite, sphene and spinel, between a few microns and almost 20μm. The inclusions ($f{:}c_{0.062mm}$ = 98:2) contain very well-sorted, sub-rounded to well-rounded, fine sand particles of quartz and plagioclase (rare) and mica (very rare), up to 0.05mm. Heavy minerals (baryte-celestite, monazite-xenotime) (very rare), up to 0.03mm, could be identified.

NV 1–8 (*Body Sherd*)

The matrix is pale yellow-brown and opaque in PPL; optically inactive in XPL. Devoid of foraminifers. Rare (0.5%) planar voids (up to 0.3mm). Opaques (2%) of hematite, rutile, magnetite, sphene and spinel, between a few microns and almost 15μm. The inclusions ($f{:}c_{0.062mm}$ = 99:1) contain very well-sorted, sub-rounded to well-rounded, fine sand particles of quartz and plagioclase (rare) and amphibole (very rare), up to 0.03mm.

NV 1–9 (Body Sherd)

The matrix is olive and opaque in PPL; optically inactive in XPL. Devoid of foraminifers. Rare (0.5%) planar voids (up to 0.3mm) with common (~12%) secondary calcite formation in the interstitial space. Opaques (2%) of hematite, rutile, magnetite, sphene and spinel, between a few microns and almost 20μm. The inclusions ($f{:}c_{0.062mm}$ = 97:3) contain very well-sorted, sub-rounded to well-rounded, fine sand particles of quartz and plagioclase (rare) and amphibole (very rare), up to 0.05mm. Heavy minerals (monazite-xenotime, zircon) (very rare), up to 0.03mm, could be identified.

NV 1–10 (Shoulder Sherd)

The matrix is olive and opaque in PPL; optically inactive in XPL. Devoid of foraminifers. Rare (0.5%) planar voids (up to 0.3mm). Opaques (2%) of hematite, rutile, magnetite, sphene and spinel, between a few microns and almost 15μm. The inclusions ($f{:}c_{0.062mm}$ = 98:2) contain very well-sorted, sub-rounded to well-rounded, fine sand particles of quartz and plagioclase (rare), up to 0.03mm. Heavy minerals (baryte-celestite, monazite-xenotime) (very rare), up to 0.03mm, could be identified.

NV 1–11 (Base Sherd)

The matrix is pale yellow-brown and opaque in PPL; optically inactive in XPL. Devoid of foraminifers. Rare (0.5%) planar voids (up to 0.3mm) with common (~10%) secondary calcite formation in the interstitial space. Opaques (2%) of hematite, rutile, magnetite, sphene and spinel, between a few microns and almost 20μm. The inclusions ($f{:}c_{0.062mm}$ = 98:2) contain very well-sorted, sub-rounded to well-rounded, fine sand particles of quartz and plagioclase (rare) and mica (very rare), up to 0.05mm. Heavy minerals (zircon, epidote) (very rare), up to 0.03mm, could be identified.

NV 1–12 (Base Sherd)

The matrix is pale yellow-brown and opaque in PPL; optically inactive in XPL. Devoid of foraminifers. Rare (1%) planar voids (up to 0.3mm) with common (~15%) secondary calcite formation in the interstitial space. Opaques (2%) of hematite, rutile, magnetite, sphene and spinel, between a few microns and almost 20μm. The inclusions ($f{:}c_{0.062mm}$ = 98:2) contain very well-sorted, sub-rounded to well-rounded, fine sand particles of quartz and plagioclase (rare) and amphibole and mica (very rare), up to 0.04mm. Heavy minerals (baryte-celestite) (very rare), up to 0.03mm, could be identified.

Dur-Katlimmu

SH 1–1 (*Body Sherd*)

The matrix is pale yellow brown and opaque in PPL; optically inactive in XPL. Devoid of foraminifers. Rare (1%) planar voids (up to 0.7mm) with frequent secondary calcite formation in the interstitial space. Opaques (3%) of magnetite, ilmenite and spinel between a few microns to almost 20μm. The inclusions ($f{:}c_{0.062mm}$ = 96:4) contain very well-sorted, sub-rounded to well-rounded, fine sand particles of relict calcite, calcic plagioclase, quartz, pyroxene and olivine-like minerals, up to 0.06mm.

SH 1–2 (*Rim Sherd*)

The matrix is olive and opaque in PPL; optically inactive in XPL. Devoid of foraminifers. Rare (0.5%) planar voids (up to 0.5mm). Opaques (2%) of magnetite, ilmenite and spinel between a few microns to almost 15μm. The inclusions ($f{:}c_{0.062mm}$ = 97:3) contain very well-sorted, sub-rounded to well-rounded, fine sand particles of relict calcite, calcic plagioclase, and quartz, up to 0.04mm.

SH 1–3 (*Base Sherd*)

The matrix is pale yellow brown and opaque in PPL; optically inactive in XPL. Devoid of foraminifers. Rare (1%) planar voids (up to 0.7mm) with frequent secondary calcite formation in the interstitial space. Opaques (3%) of magnetite, ilmenite and spinel between a few microns to almost 20μm. The inclusions ($f{:}c_{0.062mm}$ = 96:4) contain very well-sorted, sub-rounded to well-rounded, fine sand particles of relict calcite, calcic plagioclase, quartz, pyroxene and olivine-like minerals, up to 0.06mm.

SH 1–4 (*Base Sherd*)

The matrix is pale yellow brown and opaque in PPL; optically inactive in XPL. Devoid of foraminifers. Rare (1%) planar voids (up to 0.5mm) with frequent secondary calcite formation in the interstitial space. Opaques (2%) of magnetite, ilmenite and spinel between a few microns to almost 20μm. The inclusions ($f{:}c_{0.062mm}$ = 97:3) contain very well-sorted, sub-rounded to well-rounded, fine sand particles of relict calcite, calcic plagioclase, quartz, and pyroxene (rare), up to 0.05mm.

SH 1–5 (*Rim Sherd*)

The matrix is olive and opaque in PPL; optically inactive in XPL. Devoid of foraminifers. Rare (0.5%) planar voids (up to 0.3mm) with frequent secondary calcite formation in the interstitial space. Opaques (3%) of magnetite, ilmenite and spinel between a few microns to almost 15μm. The inclusions ($f{:}c_{0.062mm}$ = 97:3) contain very well-sorted, sub-rounded to well-rounded, fine sand particles of relict calcite, calcic plagioclase, and quartz, up to 0.05mm.

SH 1–6 (*Shoulder Sherd*)

The matrix is pale yellow brown and opaque in PPL; optically inactive in XPL. Devoid of foraminifers. Rare (0.5%) planar voids (up to 0.5mm) with frequent secondary calcite formation in the interstitial space. Opaques (3%) of magnetite, ilmenite and spinel between a few microns to almost 20µm. The inclusions ($f{:}c_{0.062mm}$ = 96:4) contain very well-sorted, sub-rounded to well-rounded, fine sand particles of relict calcite, calcic plagioclase, quartz, pyroxene and olivine-like minerals, up to 0.06mm.

SH 1–7 (*Body Sherd*)

The matrix is pale yellow brown and opaque in PPL; optically inactive in XPL. Devoid of foraminifers. Rare (1%) planar voids (up to 0.5mm) with frequent secondary calcite formation in the interstitial space. Opaques (3%) of magnetite, ilmenite and spinel between a few microns to almost 20µm. The inclusions ($f{:}c_{0.062mm}$ = 96:4) contain very well-sorted, sub-rounded to well-rounded, fine sand particles of relict calcite, calcic plagioclase, quartz, pyroxene and olivine-like minerals, up to 0.05mm.

SH 1–8 (*Body Sherd*)

The matrix is olive and opaque in PPL; optically inactive in XPL. Devoid of foraminifers. Rare (0.5 %) planar voids (up to 0.3mm). Opaques (3%) of magnetite, ilmenite and spinel between a few microns to almost 15µm. The inclusions ($f{:}c_{0.062mm}$ = 98:2) contain very well-sorted, sub-rounded to well-rounded, fine sand particles of relict calcite, calcic plagioclase, and quartz, up to 0.04mm.

SH 1–9 (*Neck Sherd*)

The matrix is pale yellow brown and opaque in PPL; optically inactive in XPL. Devoid of foraminifers. Rare (1%) planar voids (up to 0.5mm) with frequent secondary calcite formation in the interstitial space. Opaques (3%) of magnetite, ilmenite and spinel between a few microns to almost 20µm. The inclusions ($f{:}c_{0.062mm}$ = 96:4) contain very well-sorted, sub-rounded to well-rounded, fine sand particles of relict calcite, calcic plagioclase, quartz and pyroxene, and olivine-like minerals (rare), up to 0.06mm.

SH 1–10 (*Body Sherd*)

The matrix is pale yellow brown and opaque in PPL; optically inactive in XPL. Devoid of foraminifers. Rare (1%) planar voids (up to 0.7mm) with frequent secondary calcite formation in the interstitial space. Opaques (3%) of magnetite, ilmenite and spinel between a few microns to almost 20µm. The inclusions ($f{:}c_{0.062mm}$ = 96:4) contain very well-sorted, sub-rounded to well-rounded, fine sand particles of relict calcite, calcic plagioclase, quartz and pyroxene, up to 0.05mm.

SH 1–11 (Body Sherd)

The matrix is pale yellow brown and opaque in PPL; optically inactive in XPL. Devoid of foraminifers. Rare (0.5%) planar voids (up to 0.4mm). Opaques (2%) of magnetite, ilmenite and spinel between a few microns to almost 15μm. The inclusions ($f{:}c_{0.062mm}$ = 97:3) contain very well-sorted, sub-rounded to well-rounded, fine sand particles of relict calcite, calcic plagioclase, and quartz, and olivine-like minerals (rare), up to 0.05mm.

SH 1–12 (Body Sherd)

The matrix is pale yellow brown and opaque in PPL; optically inactive in XPL. Devoid of foraminifers. Rare (1%) planar voids (up to 0.7mm) with frequent secondary calcite formation in the interstitial space. Opaques (3%) of magnetite, ilmenite and spinel between a few microns to almost 20μm. The inclusions ($f{:}c_{0.062mm}$ = 97:3) contain very well-sorted, sub-rounded to well-rounded, fine sand particles of relict calcite, calcic plagioclase, quartz, pyroxene and olivine-like minerals, up to 0.06mm.

Tell Jemmeh

JS 1–1 (Body Sherd)

The matrix is reddish-brown in PPL; optically active in XPL. Devoid of foraminifers. Very few (4%) vughs, vesicles and channel voids (up to 2mm) with clear boundaries. The silt is primarily quartz but contains identifiable heavy and accessory minerals including: hornblende, plagioclase, microcline, zircon, and epidote. Opaques (3%) of hematite, magnetite and rutile between a few microns and approximately 70μm. Inclusions ($f{:}c_{0.062mm}$ = 95:5) of coarse to medium, moderately sorted, sub-angular, sub-prismoidal quartz sand, very rarely with mineral inclusions (zircon). Sub-rounded micrite (up to 0.6mm) and limestone (up to 0.4mm) are common. Rare accessory minerals in the fine sand fraction include hornblende (≤ 250μm) altered to oxyhornblende, plagioclase (≤ 200μm), microcline (≤ 180μm) and zircon (≤ 110μm).

JS 1–2 (Rim Sherd)

The matrix is reddish-brown in PPL; optically active in XPL. Devoid of foraminifers. Very few (2%) vughs, vesicles and channel voids (up to 1mm) with clear boundaries. The silt is primarily quartz but contains identifiable heavy and accessory minerals including: hornblende, plagioclase, microcline, zircon, epidote and tourmaline. Opaques (2%) of hematite, magnetite and rutile between a few microns and approximately 50μm. Inclusions ($f{:}c_{0.062mm}$ = 93:7) of coarse to medium, moderately sorted, sub-angular, sub-prismoidal quartz sand. Sub-rounded micrite (up to 0.4mm) and limestone (up to 0.4mm). Rare accessory minerals in the fine sand fraction include hornblende (≤ 200μm) altered to oxyhornblende, plagioclase (≤ 200μm), microcline (≤ 150μm) and zircon (≤ 100μm).

JS 1–3 (Body Sherd)

The matrix is dark orange in PPL; optically active in XPL. Devoid of foraminifers. Very few (5%) vughs, vesicles and channel voids (up to 2mm) with clear boundaries. The silt is primarily quartz but contains identifiable heavy and accessory minerals including: hornblende, plagioclase, microcline, and epidote. Opaques (3%) of hematite, magnetite and rutile between a few microns and approximately 70 μm. Inclusions ($f{:}c_{0.062mm}$ = 90:10) of coarse to medium, moderately sorted, sub-angular, sub-prismoidal quartz sand, very rarely with mineral inclusions (zircon). Sub-rounded micrite (up to 0.7mm) is common. Rare accessory minerals in the fine sand fraction include hornblende (≤ 250 μm) altered to oxyhornblende, plagioclase (≤ 200 μm), microcline (≤ 180 μm) and zircon (≤ 110 μm). Very rare fragments of unfossilised land-snail shell, up to 2 mm long.

JS 1–4 (Base Sherd)

The matrix is reddish-brown in PPL; optically active in XPL. Devoid of foraminifers. Very few (5%) vughs, vesicles and channel voids (up to 2mm) with clear boundaries. The silt is primarily quartz but contains identifiable heavy and accessory minerals including: hornblende, plagioclase, microcline, epidote and tourmaline. Opaques (2%) of hematite, magnetite and rutile between a few microns and approximately 70μm. Inclusions ($f{:}c_{0.062mm}$ = 90:10) of coarse to medium, moderately sorted, sub-angular, sub-prismoidal quartz sand. Sub-rounded micrite (up to 0.6mm) and limestone (up to 0.4mm) are common. Rare accessory minerals in the fine sand fraction include hornblende (≤ 250μm) altered to oxyhornblende, plagioclase (≤ 230μm), microcline (≤ 200μm) and zircon (≤ 110μm). Very rare fragments of unfossilised land-snail shell, up to 2mm long.

JS 1–5 (Rim Sherd)

The matrix is dark orange in PPL; optically active in XPL. Devoid of foraminifers. Very few (2%) vughs, vesicles and channel voids (up to 1.3mm) with clear boundaries. The silt is primarily quartz but contains identifiable heavy and accessory minerals including: hornblende, plagioclase, microcline, and epidote. Opaques (3%) of hematite, magnetite and rutile between a few microns and approximately 70μm. Inclusions ($f{:}c_{0.062mm}$ = 93:7) of coarse to medium, moderately sorted, sub-angular, sub-prismoidal quartz sand, very rarely with mineral inclusions (zircon). Sub-rounded micrite (up to 0.64mm) and limestone (up to 0.4mm) are common. Rare accessory minerals in the fine sand fraction include hornblende (≤ 250μm) altered to oxyhornblende, plagioclase (≤ 200μm), and microcline (≤ 180μm).

JS 1–6 (Base Sherd)

The matrix is dark orange in PPL; optically active in XPL. Devoid of foraminifers. Very few (4%) vughs, vesicles and channel voids (up to 2.5mm) with clear boundaries. The silt is primarily quartz but contains identifiable heavy and accessory minerals including: hornblende, plagioclase, epidote and tourmaline. Opaques (2%) of hematite, magnetite and rutile between a few microns and approximately 50μm. Inclusions ($f{:}c_{0.062mm}$ = 94:6) of coarse to medium, moderately sorted, sub-angular, sub-prismoidal quartz sand. Sub-rounded micrite (up to 0.6mm) and limestone (up to 0.3mm) are common. Rare accessory minerals in the fine sand fraction include hornblende (≤ 250μm) altered to oxyhornblende, plagioclase (≤ 200μm), microcline (≤ 150μm) and zircon (≤ 90μm).

JS 1–7 (Base Sherd)

The matrix is reddish-brown in PPL; optically active in XPL. Devoid of foraminifers. Very few (5%) vughs, vesicles and channel voids (up to 2mm) with clear boundaries. The silt is primarily quartz but contains identifiable heavy and accessory minerals including: hornblende, plagioclase, microcline, and epidote. Opaques (3%) of hematite, magnetite and rutile between a few microns and approximately 50μm. Inclusions ($f{:}c_{0.062mm}$ = 90:10) of coarseto medium, moderately sorted, sub-angular, sub-prismoidal quartz sand. Sub-rounded micrite (up to 0.6mm) and limestone (up to 0.4mm) are common. Rare accessory minerals in the fine sand fraction include hornblende (≤ 250μm) altered to oxyhornblende, plagioclase (≤ 200μm), microcline (≤ 180μm) and zircon (≤ 110μm).

JS 1–8 (Rim/Neck Sherd)

The matrix is reddish-brown in PPL; optically active in XPL. Devoid of foraminifers. Very few (3%) vughs, vesicles and channel voids (up to 1.5mm) with clear boundaries. The silt is primarily quartz but contains identifiable heavy and accessory minerals including: hornblende, plagioclase, zircon, and tourmaline. Opaques (3%) of hematite, magnetite and rutile between a few microns and approximately 50μm. Inclusions ($f{:}c_{0.062mm}$ = 93:7) of coarse to medium, moderately sorted, sub-angular, sub-prismoidal quartz sand. Sub-rounded micrite (up to 0.5mm) and limestone (up to 0.2mm) are common. Rare accessory minerals in the fine sand fraction include plagioclase (≤ 200μm) and microcline (≤ 200μm). Very rare fragments of unfossilised land-snail shell, up to 1.5mm long.

JS 1–9 (Body Sherd)

The matrix is reddish-brown in PPL; optically active in XPL. Devoid of foraminifers. Very few (4%) vughs, vesicles and channel voids (up to 2mm) with clear boundaries.

The silt is primarily quartz but contains identifiable heavy and accessory minerals including: hornblende, plagioclase, microcline, epidote and tourmaline. Opaques (3%) of hematite, magnetite and rutile between a few microns and approximately 70µm. Inclusions ($f{:}c_{0.062mm}$ = 95:5) of coarse to medium, moderately sorted, sub-angular, sub-prismoidal quartz sand. Sub-rounded micrite (up to 0.4mm) and limestone (up to 0.4mm) are common. Rare accessory minerals in the fine sand fraction include hornblende (≤ 200 µm) altered to oxyhornblende, plagioclase (≤ 150 µm), and microcline (≤ 150 µm).

JS 1–10 (Body Sherd)

The matrix is reddish-brown in PPL; optically active in XPL. Devoid of foraminifers. Very few (3%) vughs, vesicles and channel voids (up to 2mm) with clear boundaries. The silt is primarily quartz but contains identifiable heavy and accessory minerals including: hornblende, plagioclase, microcline, epidote and zircon. Opaques (2%) of hematite, magnetite and rutile between a few microns and approximately 70µm. Inclusions ($f{:}c_{0.062mm}$ = 96:4) of coarse to medium, moderately sorted, sub-angular, sub-prismoidal quartz sand, very rarely with mineral inclusions (zircon). Sub-rounded micrite (up to 0.3mm) and limestone (up to 0.3mm) are common. Rare accessory minerals in the fine sand fraction include hornblende (≤ 150µm) altered to oxyhornblende, plagioclase (≤ 100µm), and zircon (≤ 150µm). Very rare fragments of unfossilised land-snail shell, up to 1mm long.

JS 1–11 (Body Sherd)

The matrix is reddish-brown in PPL; optically active in XPL. Devoid of foraminifers. Very few (5%) vughs, vesicles and channel voids (up to 2mm) with clear boundaries. The silt is primarily quartz but contains identifiable heavy and accessory minerals including: hornblende, plagioclase, microcline, epidote and tourmaline. Opaques (3%) of hematite, magnetite and rutile between a few microns and approximately 70µm. Inclusions ($f{:}c_{0.062mm}$ = 93:7) of coarse to medium, moderately sorted, sub-angular, sub-prismoidal quartz sand. Sub-rounded micrite (up to 0.6mm) and limestone (up to 0.5mm) are common. Rare accessory minerals in the fine sand fraction include hornblende (≤ 250µm) altered to oxyhornblende, plagioclase (≤ 200µm), microcline (≤ 200µm) and zircon (≤ 100 µm).

JS 1–12 (Body Sherd)

The matrix is dark orange in PPL; optically active in XPL. Devoid of foraminifers. Very few (3%) vughs, vesicles and channel voids (up to 2mm) with clear boundaries. The silt is primarily quartz but contains identifiable heavy and accessory minerals including: hornblende, plagioclase, microcline, zircon, and epidote. Opaques (3%) of hematite, magnetite and rutile between a few microns and approximately 50μm. Inclusions (f:$c_{0.062mm}$ = 93:7) of coarse to medium, moderately sorted, sub-angular, sub-prismoidal quartz sand, very rarely with mineral inclusions (zircon). Sub-rounded micrite (up to 0.5mm) and limestone (up to 0.4mm) are common. Rare accessory minerals in the fine sand fraction include hornblende (≤ 150μm) altered to oxyhornblende, plagioclase (≤ 200μm), microcline (≤ 150μm) and zircon (≤ 100μm).

Appendix B: INAA Bulk Chemical Data

	sample	Na	K	Sc	Cr	Fe	Co	Ni	Zn	As	Rb	Sr	Zr	Sb
Nimrud	N 1.1	3057	18900	14.7	190.0	43520	24.3	201	85	11.4	68	781	120	0.972
	N 1.2	3074	18600	15.4	202.0	45080	24.7	187	81	10.4	66	684	108	0.860
	N 1.3	3499	18200	15.6	198.0	45940	26.5	198	89	10.5	67	710	113	0.876
	N 1.4	3196	19400	16.4	217.0	48060	27.5	204	91	10.9	72	724	133	0.948
	N 1.5	3528	21400	15.9	209.0	46480	26.0	192	87	10.3	64	811	120	0.862
	N 1.6	5647	18600	15.2	333.0	43860	25.8	200	81	7.2	68	710	136	0.745
	N 1.7	6736	19300	17.7	386.0	50690	32.2	262	88	6.3	64	1770	138	0.714
	N 1.8	7513	23000	17.1	355.0	48980	28.9	235	85	6.0	71	453	161	0.827
	N 1.9	8018	22300	13.5	369.0	40020	21.3	176	80	4.5	79	588	119	0.686
Nineveh	NV 1.1	5793	18700	15.9	339.0	46800	27.1	230	86	9.8	82	517	165	0.905
	NV 1.2	3588	21200	18.6	258.0	53760	26.9	235	70	16.3	86	530	170	0.808
	NV 1.3	4940	19200	18.0	302.0	52540	29.0	245	83	8.7	73	655	156	0.821
	NV 1.4	4106	20000	15.9	268.0	47270	24.4	218	65	9.9	70	593	107	0.803
	NV 1.5	7905	18100	17.6	340.0	51960	27.5	226	75	4.8	62	410	151	0.638
	NV 1.6	4503	19500	19.0	329.0	55960	30.7	236	82	14.7	69	775	188	0.861
	NV 1.7	5317	15400	14.5	290.0	40950	24.4	222	63	9.5	65	721	118	0.601
	NV 1.8	7153	14700	17.2	324.0	50550	22.6	221	55	20.9	54	603	170	0.766
	NV 1.9	5302	20900	17.1	274.0	51060	26.8	221	78	7.7	78	537	137	0.875
	NV 1.10	8376	9590	16.4	260.0	47930	26.4	224	74	8.8	40	516	140	0.819
	NV 1.11	4924	18700	14.6	230.0	42600	23.2	189	76	7.4	68	743	118	0.775
	NV 1.12a	6311	11200	17.4	255.0	49840	25.2	200	67	16.1	46	748	115	0.730
	NV 1.12b	6544	11800	18.8	281.0	53800	26.5	211	70	16.0	50	797	185	0.791
	NV 1.13	6464	20000	19.4	278.0	56580	31.6	267	97	5.1	85	386	116	0.854
	NV 1.14	9229	11700	18.1	283.0	53550	28.5	224	75	10.0	41	417	160	0.911
Dur-Kat	SH 1.1	7999	27300	18.0	251.0	55170	27.2	162	126	8.7	77	360	136	0.775
	SH 1.2	5823	24200	19.0	294.0	55190	28.6	224	82	7.9	87	484	153	0.859
	SH 1.3	9503	11200	16.9	277.0	48770	25.2	203	67	3.2	27	434	134	0.650
	SH 1.4	4250	19200	16.7	227.0	50120	26.3	179	92	8.4	73	433	128	0.680
	SH 1.5	9607	23900	19.1	548.0	54680	32.5	245	100	4.1	71	341	143	0.564
	SH 1.6	7251	21800	15.2	297.0	46740	24.7	169	105	7.0	59	496	155	0.660
	SH 1.7	6159	18600	12.9	275.0	39470	21.4	140	76	8.6	56	473	121	0.537
	SH 1.8	8536	23100	15.2	314.0	45990	24.5	146	88	10.1	64	612	166	0.709
	SH 1.9	12200	12600	17.0	280.0	50990	25.8	160	75	7.5	39	492	146	0.595

 | DOI 10.1163/9789004304123_010

Cs	Ba	La	Ce	Nd	Sm	Eu	Tb	Yb	Lu	Hf	Ta	W	Th	U
4.04	430	23.7	43.2	19.5	4.71	0.917	0.619	2.08	0.304	2.79	0.846	1.8	7.48	2.32
3.85	400	24.0	47.3	21.5	4.54	1.050	0.626	2.14	0.309	3.07	0.846	1.1	7.52	2.13
3.94	399	23.7	47.3	22.9	4.51	1.030	0.618	2.15	0.325	2.95	0.867	–	7.68	2.28
4.25	427	25.7	50.8	25.5	4.91	1.090	0.649	2.29	0.367	3.18	0.909	1.4	8.12	2.41
3.61	410	24.8	49.1	23.8	4.67	1.080	0.649	2.34	0.346	3.06	0.855	–	7.72	2.24
3.53	397	25.7	48.2	24.3	5.17	1.080	0.662	2.24	0.318	3.53	0.876	–	7.27	2.89
3.71	321	27.6	52.3	20.8	5.47	1.160	0.705	2.47	0.329	3.61	0.939	–	7.80	2.72
3.60	353	26.7	51.8	22.1	5.34	1.180	0.811	2.46	0.378	3.71	0.951	–	8.21	2.18
3.98	503	22.9	43.9	18.3	4.45	0.934	0.601	2.20	0.330	3.44	0.822	1.0	7.43	2.10
4.36	440	27.6	55.3	–	5.02	1.160	0.736	2.53	0.350	4.55	0.994	0.7	8.62	2.29
4.68	444	29.2	58.6	–	5.70	1.190	0.773	2.48	0.374	3.74	0.991	1.4	9.09	6.53
3.79	842	27.1	52.4	–	4.88	1.130	0.691	2.27	0.350	3.94	0.945	1.1	8.42	2.30
3.88	390	25.7	52.0	–	4.97	1.060	0.597	2.13	0.328	3.86	0.947	0.8	8.21	2.70
4.60	346	26.7	55.6	–	4.61	1.140	0.621	2.27	0.320	4.08	0.961	0.7	8.58	2.01
3.82	830	29.3	59.2	–	5.62	1.270	0.832	2.52	0.431	4.67	1.110	2.3	9.42	2.54
3.50	596	22.9	47.6	–	4.24	0.993	0.668	2.14	0.293	3.51	0.857	1.5	7.21	2.26
4.15	596	28.4	57.3	–	5.31	1.110	0.667	2.47	0.346	4.66	1.030	0.5	8.97	3.00
4.34	363	25.9	54.0	–	4.68	1.120	0.696	2.29	0.335	4.03	0.976	1.1	8.69	2.15
4.64	304	28.6	50.3	–	5.59	1.070	0.690	2.28	0.348	3.81	0.958	1.0	8.26	3.81
3.76	309	23.3	46.7	–	4.27	0.980	0.601	2.04	0.295	3.21	0.806	0.9	7.29	1.97
4.28	402	27.2	54.7	–	4.76	1.180	0.727	2.34	0.311	3.77	0.963	0.5	8.16	3.38
4.59	412	27.6	59.1	–	4.88	1.260	0.770	2.49	0.343	4.03	0.982	0.9	8.82	3.55
5.09	419	27.6	52.7	–	4.68	1.110	0.632	2.31	0.349	3.65	0.931	0.8	8.44	2.07
4.78	340	28.2	56.3	–	5.02	1.160	0.652	1.97	0.291	4.16	0.997	–	9.03	2.68
5.00	313	31.5	62.1	–	5.72	1.270	0.681	2.35	0.365	4.38	1.140	1.1	9.19	3.00
4.52	331	28.8	59.3	–	4.96	1.220	0.752	2.69	0.371	4.22	0.971	–	9.26	2.35
4.51	299	26.3	51.0	–	4.39	1.060	0.653	2.27	0.309	3.97	0.941	–	8.22	2.02
4.30	275	27.8	57.3	–	4.91	1.230	0.727	2.41	0.342	3.94	1.060	1.2	8.81	2.15
3.68	248	27.6	53.3	–	4.94	1.160	0.668	2.74	0.331	4.53	0.934	–	7.84	2.06
3.30	262	24.8	55.1	–	4.55	1.180	0.739	2.36	0.298	4.48	1.030	1.1	8.12	2.05
3.11	251	23.9	44.8	–	4.43	1.030	0.651	2.13	0.316	3.52	0.881	0.9	6.72	1.87
4.03	346	27.7	52.4	–	4.66	1.190	0.682	2.31	0.312	4.19	0.944	1.7	7.48	2.18
4.30	282	32.6	58.4	–	5.88	1.320	0.778	2.45	0.374	4.61	1.090	–	8.75	3.32

(cont.)

	sample	Na	K	Sc	Cr	Fe	Co	Ni	Zn	As	Rb	Sr	Zr	Sb
	SH 1.10	7270	23400	17.7	305.0	53430	27.3	159	105	9.8	70	548	177	0.628
	SH 1.11	7314	15900	17.5	275.0	50630	26.5	182	83	11.8	47	402	143	0.961
	SH 1.12	7432	19000	13.5	494.0	41110	21.9	130	83	7.0	54	532	143	0.588
	SH 2.4	8094	25400	15.3	341.0	46390	24.1	154	85	9.5	53	617	118	0.631
	SH 2.5	7267	11600	15.8	317.0	47440	25.8	174	70	1.5	22	517	170	0.238
	SH 3.1	8996	20300	11.3	390.0	34220	18.3	119	65	10.1	45	546	141	0.562
	SH 3.4	7230	22800	16.6	226.0	50720	26.4	161	101	9.3	66	479	147	0.703
	SH 3.6	7676	29900	16.3	246.0	49370	25.6	172	114	9.9	54	591	109	0.633
	SH 3.7	5211	22100	17.2	249.0	52480	27.8	168	109	8.3	71	655	151	0.712
	SH 4.1	7013	16800	14.2	223.0	43450	23.5	170	77	5.8	61	424	147	0.708
Jemmeh	JS 1.1	8476	28000	14.3	118.0	46270	19.6	57	96	4.7	51	341	223	0.418
	JS 1.2	7876	14300	13.3	108.0	41770	20.7	47	67	4.3	44	324	310	0.319
	JS 1.3	10210	20200	13.8	111.0	43110	20.2	48	92	5.0	47	343	294	0.385
	JS 1.4	7322	20400	14.6	121.0	46770	21.2	65	103	4.1	56	379	227	0.476
	JS 1.5	8026	23000	13.2	107.0	42700	18.8	65	94	6.0	48	357	220	0.442
	JS 1.6	6775	20000	15.3	117.0	50130	21.5	71	100	5.1	59	403	239	0.520
	JS 1.7	6694	20800	12.5	97.2	40640	18.1	60	82	6.8	47	373	191	0.451
	JS 1.8	7935	24800	15.4	127.0	48790	19.6	61	100	5.5	58	354	214	0.586
	JS 1.9	8213	20600	13.4	106.0	43270	19.1	65	93	7.4	49	383	214	0.743
	JS 1.10	9032	20600	14.2	117.0	46560	19.5	63	81	2.2	49	316	252	0.415
	JS 1.11	9018	24000	13.9	111.0	43800	18.0	59	91	6.0	51	342	210	0.405
	JS 1.12	7798	33600	17.9	117.0	58630	23.9	66	128	5.5	59	346	205	0.573
	JS 1.13	10040	21300	14.9	257.0	39800	16.9	199	74	6.5	63	447	90	0.591
	JS 1.14	16920	8330	22.9	242.0	57090	32.8	210	103	8.5	25	424	99	0.805
	JS 1.15	8393	25600	13.6	110.0	44020	21.3	60	92	5.5	47	398	180	0.441
	JS 1.16	9706	20400	14.5	119.0	44610	20.2	53	92	6.2	53	297	336	0.390
	JS 1.17	8435	23900	15.2	119.0	48930	21.2	59	103	4.1	55	349	214	0.453
	JS 1.18	8238	24300	14.8	112.0	47670	20.8	62	105	4.9	54	333	276	0.529
	JS 1.20	8078	24300	14.3	114.0	45790	20.5	56	96	3.5	51	351	238	0.402
	JS 1.21	7425	20900	14.7	119.0	47380	21.3	65	101	3.6	54	340	235	0.443
	JS 1.22	9237	27500	14.7	113.0	47130	20.8	52	103	3.5	55	224	239	0.427
	JS 1.23	9082	17800	15.8	138.0	49630	22.0	54	89	3.5	55	369	357	0.389
	J01	6893	22300	14.8	107.0	46840	21.6	55	96	6.4	46	400	246	0.411
	J02	7810	20500	12.1	98.1	39560	19.1	51	88	4.3	45	421	211	0.401
	J06	7727	24200	12.5	97.1	40840	20.3	54	83	3.8	40	329	272	0.390

Cs	Ba	La	Ce	Nd	Sm	Eu	Tb	Yb	Lu	Hf	Ta	W	Th	U
4.01	322	29.5	63.3	–	4.87	1.370	0.774	2.67	0.368	4.68	1.080	1.0	8.61	2.31
3.47	315	29.4	53.9	–	4.99	1.160	0.647	2.65	0.331	4.30	0.928	–	8.41	2.44
3.10	295	23.0	49.3	–	3.95	1.070	0.639	2.14	0.281	4.30	0.907	0.9	7.10	1.86
2.82	292	29.4	57.0	–	4.85	1.170	0.703	2.29	0.348	4.33	0.939	–	7.70	2.19
3.77	301	26.8	56.6	–	4.87	1.240	0.802	2.44	0.335	4.98	1.040	–	8.46	1.88
2.50	247	21.4	38.7	–	3.94	0.907	0.573	1.76	0.269	3.85	0.787	–	5.91	1.81
4.41	339	29.6	59.5	–	5.15	1.280	0.740	2.92	0.357	4.17	1.050	1.3	8.54	2.43
3.13	269	27.4	53.6	–	4.87	1.140	0.781	2.15	0.325	3.80	1.010	–	8.22	2.32
4.19	347	26.3	59.0	–	4.34	1.240	0.689	2.36	0.322	4.18	1.030	–	8.33	2.15
3.85	325	28.6	50.1	–	5.41	1.090	0.722	2.17	0.352	3.86	1.000	1.1	7.90	2.28
1.95	458	34.1	63.8	–	6.27	1.520	0.780	2.75	0.406	6.76	1.340	0.9	8.00	2.31
1.56	335	29.0	55.9	–	5.64	1.370	0.778	2.81	0.454	9.41	1.250	0.8	6.74	2.91
1.76	500	31.0	58.2	–	5.66	1.440	0.816	2.90	0.385	9.15	1.270	0.8	7.14	2.05
2.12	460	32.4	68.2	–	6.07	1.550	0.961	3.04	0.416	6.93	1.420	0.6	8.17	2.17
1.60	354	32.8	61.0	–	6.34	1.370	0.909	2.51	0.389	6.10	1.370	0.9	7.65	2.48
2.22	557	27.5	73.0	–	5.21	1.600	1.010	3.28	0.346	6.26	1.520	0.8	9.00	2.07
1.96	350	32.7	57.2	–	6.34	1.320	0.830	2.37	0.418	5.20	1.270	0.8	7.38	2.24
2.32	395	35.1	69.2	–	6.62	1.600	0.871	3.11	0.485	6.89	1.460	0.9	8.58	2.43
1.78	472	33.1	60.0	–	6.58	1.380	0.883	2.69	0.416	6.37	1.320	0.8	7.66	2.33
1.81	404	32.1	64.1	29.3	6.01	1.420	0.885	2.85	0.413	7.02	1.420	0.4	8.40	2.33
1.75	399	34.6	62.1	–	6.74	1.430	0.875	2.63	0.438	6.19	1.330	0.5	7.56	2.44
2.37	346	39.8	83.4	36.3	7.18	1.770	1.060	3.31	0.425	5.52	1.610	1.2	9.48	2.24
3.89	157	18.4	31.6	–	4.10	0.790	0.508	1.58	0.283	2.30	0.601	0.8	5.55	3.81
2.63	136	18.4	36.0	–	3.71	0.994	0.626	2.55	0.282	2.55	0.592	–	5.69	1.76
2.12	711	34.4	62.1	–	6.25	1.460	0.882	2.66	0.394	5.42	1.330	0.6	7.38	2.20
1.93	507	31.2	63.3	–	6.10	1.480	0.829	3.05	0.423	10.10	1.340	0.7	8.45	3.78
2.06	357	38.6	67.4	–	7.10	1.640	0.892	2.74	0.477	6.80	1.350	1.1	8.20	2.39
2.15	376	32.0	68.6	–	6.21	1.500	0.896	3.13	0.443	8.05	1.500	1.0	8.40	2.20
1.89	384	37.1	63.6	23.9	6.74	1.530	0.837	2.87	0.489	6.77	1.300	0.7	7.63	2.27
2.04	363	33.7	68.7	–	6.08	1.560	0.920	3.00	0.394	6.83	1.370	1.5	8.42	2.13
2.23	374	34.4	62.3	–	6.42	1.510	0.833	2.54	0.461	7.18	1.300	0.9	7.75	2.44
1.78	504	31.4	72.3	–	5.67	1.610	0.936	3.31	0.418	11.30	1.450	–	9.34	2.45
1.69	339	33.3	60.2	28.9	6.92	1.520	0.914	2.87	0.404	6.95	1.770	–	7.68	2.56
1.65	311	28.8	55.7	27.6	5.88	1.390	0.819	2.64	0.378	6.25	1.200	–	6.95	2.10
1.29	367	26.7	52.6	31.5	5.95	1.300	0.789	2.63	0.345	7.73	1.220	–	7.23	2.13

(cont.)

sample	Na	K	Sc	Cr	Fe	Co	Ni	Zn	As	Rb	Sr	Zr	Sb
J 09	7329	24200	13.7	104.0	44100	20.3	52	124	3.9	41	324	249	0.395
J 10	8367	18900	13.3	114.0	42680	19.7	49	78	4.0	46	459	324	0.392
J 11	8414	21900	14.6	124.0	47170	23.1	51	88	3.0	50	328	325	0.363
J 12	6756	18800	11.9	104.0	37680	16.5	42	74	4.6	36	393	283	0.319
J 13	8772	16400	12.3	104.0	38460	17.2	47	83	9.7	45	441	313	0.317
J 16	6876	22300	11.5	90.3	36870	15.4	38	108	4.4	41	282	312	0.463
J 17	5712	22000	11.7	91.6	38390	19.1	43	89	4.5	36	277	263	0.351
J 18	7012	17300	11.2	90.4	35320	17.5	44	88	4.1	36	313	268	0.353
J 19	8391	14100	11.7	105.0	36880	16.5	45	70	3.3	44	381	340	0.395
J 20	6053	21100	12.0	105.0	38560	16.0	44	88	8.3	38	425	257	0.384
J 21	8058	13000	13.5	119.0	42850	19.8	45	76	3.3	46	356	367	0.432
J 22	7663	22900	14.4	110.0	46960	22.6	55	103	3.5	40	326	265	0.411
J 23	9486	13900	13.3	114.0	43050	19.4	45	69	4.4	45	361	327	0.359

Cs	Ba	La	Ce	Nd	Sm	Eu	Tb	Yb	Lu	Hf	Ta	W	Th	U
1.35	511	28.9	54.2	29.6	6.12	1.430	0.851	2.73	0.360	7.19	1.260	–	6.79	2.30
1.59	337	32.3	60.1	27.9	6.46	1.460	0.870	2.90	0.422	9.38	1.250	–	7.93	2.04
1.67	536	31.7	60.3	34.2	6.49	1.540	0.911	3.12	0.436	9.55	1.490	–	8.09	2.35
1.39	400	27.7	52.2	26.5	5.69	1.310	0.810	2.78	0.441	8.00	1.150	–	6.90	1.97
1.47	454	27.0	50.6	24.9	5.85	1.300	0.815	2.69	0.421	8.81	1.250	–	6.74	2.44
1.27	345	29.5	54.9	30.3	6.04	1.320	0.822	2.90	0.414	9.20	1.210	1.0	7.29	2.15
1.36	391	29.0	54.3	27.8	6.08	1.380	0.840	2.63	0.374	7.20	1.180	–	6.97	1.69
1.37	315	26.8	50.0	23.2	5.58	1.220	0.770	2.46	0.396	7.75	1.170	–	6.87	1.95
1.43	401	28.1	51.6	24.0	5.84	1.270	0.854	2.85	0.634	9.78	1.280	–	7.34	2.36
1.19	2120	27.3	49.2	20.8	5.57	1.310	0.742	2.62	0.365	7.31	1.130	–	6.61	2.11
1.62	403	31.4	60.4	31.7	6.51	1.480	0.901	3.04	0.449	10.30	1.330	–	8.09	3.43
1.36	815	29.3	59.7	26.2	6.37	1.420	0.852	2.79	0.442	7.60	1.350	–	7.92	2.47
1.56	347	32.4	61.4	30.2	6.70	1.490	0.907	3.09	0.448	9.28	1.300	–	7.73	2.90

Bibliography

Adams, W. Y. and Adams, E. W. 1991. *Archaeological typology and practical reality: a dialectical approach to artifact classification and sorting.* Cambridge: Cambridge University Press.

Aharoni, Y. 1979. *The Land of the Bible: A Historical Geography.* Philadelphia: Westminster Press.

Akkermans, P. M. M. G. and Duistermaat, K. 2001. A Middle Assyrian Kiln at Tell Sabi Abyad. In: W. Orthmann, J. W. Meyer, M. Novák and A. Pruss (eds.) *Beiträge zur Vorderasiatischen Archäologie—Winfried Orthmann gewidmet.* Frankfurt: Johann Wolfgang Goethe-Universität, Archäologisches Institut, 12–19.

Al-Amiri, S. 1983. Types of Vegetation of al. Zubair Desert, Southern Iraq. *GeoJournal* 7, 83–86.

Al-Ansari, N. and Romawi, O. 1997. The influence of the Mosul dam on the bed sediments and morphology of the River Tigris. Human Impact on Erosion and Sedimentation. In *Proceedings of Rabat Symposium S6, April 1997.* IAHS Publication Number 245.

Al-Asil, N. 1955. The Archaeological Exhibition of 1955. *Sumer: A Journal of Archaeology and History in Iraq* 11, 3–4.

Al-Bassam, K. S. and Hak, J. 2006. Metallic and Industrial Rocks and Minerals. In: S. Z. Jassim and J. C. Goff (eds.) *Geology of Iraq.* Prague: Nolin, 288–302.

Al-Juboury, A., Ismail, S. A. and Ghazal, M. M. 1999. Chromite Enrichment in the Recent Fluvatile Sediments, North Iraq. *Qatar University Science Journal* 18, 159–167.

Alcock, S. E. and Morrison, K. D. 2001. Imperial Ideologies. In: S. E. Alcock, T. N. D'altroy, K. D. Morrison and C. M. Sinopoli (eds.) *Empires.* Cambridge: Cambridge University Press, 279–282.

Ali Jawad, A. 1984. Some Trace-Element Analyses of Pliocene Molasse and Recent Euphrates and Tigris Fluvial Sediments. *Chemical Geology* 45, 213–224.

Allaby, A. and Allaby, M. 2003. *Oxford Dictionary of Earth Sciences.* Oxford: Oxford University Press.

Anastasio, S. 2010. *Atlas of the Assyrian Pottery of the Iron Age.* Turnhout, Belgium: Brepols.

Andre, W. 1909. *Der Anu-Adad-tempel in Assur.* Leipzig: J. C. Hienrichs.

Anthony, J. W., Bideaux, R. A., Bladh, K. W. and Nichols, M. C. 2004–2011. *Handbook of Mineralogy.* Retrieved from World Wide Web: http://www.handbookofmineralogy.org/.

Aqrawi, A. A. M., Domas, J. and Jassim, S. Z. 2006. Quaternary Deposits. In: S. Z. Jassim and J. C. Goff (eds.) *Geology of Iraq.* Prague: Dolin, 185–198.

Arnold, D. 1985. *Ceramic theory and cultural process.* Cambridge: Cambridge University Press.

Aubet, M. E. 2001. *The Phoenicians and the West*. Cambridge: Cambridge University Press.

Aznar, C. A. 2005. *Exchange Networks in the southern Levant during the Iron Age II: A Study of Pottery Origin and Distribution*. Unpublished Ph.D. thesis, Harvard University.

Barnett, R. D. 1957. *A catalogue of the Nimrud ivories: with other examples of ancient Near Eastern ivories in the British Museum*. London: The Trustees of the British Museum.

Beier, T. and Mommsen, H. 1994. Modified Mahalanobis filters for grouping pottery by chemical composition. *Archaeometry* 36, 287–306.

Bennett, C.-M. 1982. Neo-Assyrian Influence in Transjordan. *Studies in the History and Archaeology of Jordan* 1, 181–187.

Bentz, M. 2009. Masse, Form und Funktion Die attische-schwarzfigurigen Halsamphoren. In: A. Tsingarida (ed.) *Shapes and Uses of Greek Vases (7th-4th centuries BC): Proceedings of the Symposium held at the Université libre de Bruxelles 27–29 April 2006*. Bruxelles: CreA-Patrimoine, 79–87.

Berg, I. 2008. Looking through pots: recent advances in ceramics X-radiography. *Journal of Archaeological Science* 35, 1177–1188.

Berry, K. J., Kvamme, K. L. and Mielke, P. W., JR. 1980. A Permutation Technique for the Spatial Analysis of the Distribution of Artefacts into Classes. *American Antiquity* 45, 55–59.

———. 1983. Improvements in the Permutation Test for the Spatial Analysis of the Distribution of Artifacts into Classes. *American Antiquity* 48, 547–553.

Berry, R. W., Brophy, G. P. and Nagash, A. 1970. Mineralogy of the Suspended Sediment in the Tigris, Euphrates, and Shatt-al-Arab Rivers of Iraq, and the Recent History of the Mesopotamian Plain. *Journal of Sedimentary Research* 40, 131–139.

Bikai, P. 30 July 2010. Personal Communication RE: Neo-Assyrian ceramic workshop at Nineveh.

Bishop, R. L. and Blackman, M. J. 15 December 2010. Personal Communication RE: Geochemistry of the Habur.

Bishop, R. L., Rands, R. L. and Holley, G. R. 1982. Ceramic Compositional Analysis in Archaeological Perspective. *Advances in Archaeological Method and Theory* 5, 275–330.

Blackman, M. J., Stein, G. J. and Vandiver, P. B. 1993. The Standardization Hypothesis and Ceramic Mass Production: Technological, Compositional, and Metric Indexes of Craft Specialization at Tell Leilan, Syria. *American Antiquity* 58, 60–80.

Bláquez Martínez, J. M. and Valiente Malla, J. 1982. El poblado de La Muela y la fase orientalizante en Cástulo (Jaén). In: H. G. Niemeyer (ed.) *Phönizer im Westen: Die Beiträge des Internationalen Symposiums über "Die phönizische Expansion im westlichen Mittlemeerraum" in Köln vom 24. bis 27. April 1979*. Mainz: Philipp von Zabern, 407–428.

Botta, P.-É. and Flandin, E. 1849. *Monument de Ninive: Architecture et Sculpture*. Paris: Imprimerie Nationale.

Brinkman, J. A. 1997. Unfolding the Drama of the Assyrian Empire. In: S. Parpola and R. M. Whiting (eds.) *Assyria 1995: Proceedings of the 10th Anniversary Symposium on the Neo-Assyrian Text Corpus Project, Helsinki, September 7–11, 1995*. Helsinki: The Neo-Assyrian Text Corpus Project, 1–16.

Brown, A. G. 2001. *Alluvial Geoarchaeology: floodplain archaeology and environmental change*. Cambridge: Cambridge University Press.

Brunke, H. 2011. Feasts for the Living, the Dead, and the Gods. In: K. Radner and E. Robson (eds.) *The Oxford Handbook of Cuneiform Culture*. Oxford: Oxford University Press, 167–183.

Buday, T. and Jassim, S. Z. 1987. *The Regional Geology of Iraq: Techtonism, Magmatism and Metamorphism. Volume 2*. Baghdad: State Establishment of Geological Survey and Mineral Investigation.

Bunnens, G. 1997. Til Barsib under Assyrian Domination: A Brief Account of the Melbourne University Excavations at Tell Ahmar. In: S. Parpola and R. M. Whiting (eds.) *Assyria 1995: Proceedings of the 10th Anniversary Symposium on the Neo-Assyrian Text Corpus Project, Helsinki, September 7–11, 1995*. Helsinki: The Neo-Assyrian Text Corpus Project, 17–28.

Butler, C. and Seiler, C. 1984. *Hegel: The Letters*. Bloomington, IN: Indiana University Press.

Caesar, M. 1999. *Umberto Eco: Philosophy, Semiotics and the Work of Fiction*. Cambridge: Polity Press.

Campbell Thompson, R. 1923. Some Notes on Modern Babylonia. *Journal of the Royal Asiatic Society* 55, 233–242.

———. 1931. *The prisms of Esarhaddon and Ashurbanipal found at Nineveh: 1927–8*. London: Bernard Quazritch Ltd..

Campbell Thompson, R. and Hutchinson, R. W. 1929. *A century of exploration at Nineveh*. London: Luzac and Co.

Castel, C. 1992. *Habitat urbain néo-assyrien et néo-babylonien: de l'espace bâti à l'espace vécu*. Paris:

Caubet, A. 1992. Reoccupation of the Syrian Coast after the Destruction of the 'Crisis Years'. In: W. A. Ward and Joukowsky (eds.) *Crisis Years: The 12th Century BC From Beyond the Danube to the Tigris*. Dubuque, Iowa: Kendall/ Hunt Publishing Company, 123–131.

Chambon, G. and Kreppner, F. J. 2008. Hohlmaßsysteme und deren Standardisierung in Assyrien und Volumina von Gefäßkeramik aus Dūr-Katlimmu. In: H. Kühne (ed.) *Dūr-Katlimmu 2008*. Wiesbaden: Harrassowitz, 11–32.

Chapoulie, R., Delery, C., Daniel, F. and Vendrell-Saz, M. 2005. Cuerda Seca Ceramics from Al-Andalus, Islamic Spain and Portugal (10th-12th Centuries AD): Investigation with SEM-EDX and Cathodoluminescence. *Archaeometry* 47, 519–534.

Charters, S., Evershed, R. P., Goad, L. J., Leyden, A., Blinkhorn, P. W. and Denham, V. 1993. Quantification and Distribution of Lipid in Archaeological Ceramics: Implications for Sampling Potsherds for Organic Residue Analysis and the Classification of Vessel Use. *Archaeometry* 35, 211–223.

Cholidis. 2010. *Tell Halaf-Projekt. Tell Halaf-Projekt, Vorderasiatisches Museum.* Retrieved 17 March 2010 from World Wide Web: www.tell-halaf-projekt.de.

Collins, S. 15 February 2010. Personal Communication RE: Late Assyrian material culture at Sidon.

Collon, D., 1987. *First Impressions: Cylinder Seas in the Ancient Near East.* Chicago: University of Chicago Press

———. 1996. Review of S. Herbordt, Neuassyrische Glyptik des 8.–7. Jh. V. Chr. (State Archives of Assyria Studies I). *Orientalia* 65, 185–187.

Cooper, N. and Bowman, J. 1985–6. Studying the effect of heat on clay using x-ray diffraction analysis: the role of firing duration in the assessment of ancient firing. *Bulletin of the Experimental Firing Group* 4, 37–48.

Courtois, L. C. and Doray, A. M. 1983. Technologie et céramiques Levantines au temps de la domination Assyrienne. *Comptes Rendus du 108e Congrès National des Sociétés Savantes, Grenoble: Ministere de L'éducation Nationale Comité des travaux historiques et scientifiques.* Paris: CTHS, 125–136.

Courty, M. A. and Roux, V. 1995. Identification of wheel throwing on the basis of ceramic surface features and microfabrics. *Journal of Archaeological Science* 22, 17–50.

Crosby, A. W. 2004. *Ecological Imperialism: The Biological Expansion of Europe, 900–1900.* Cambridge: Cambridge University Press.

Curtis, J. 1988. Assyria as a Bronzeworking Centre in the Late Assyrian Period. In: J. Curtis (ed.) *Bronze-Working Centres of Western Asia.* London: Kegan Paul International in association with the British Museum, 83–96.

———. 1989. *Excavations at Qasrij Cliff and Khirbet Qasrij.* London: British Museum Publications.

———. 1997. Nimrud. In: E. M. Myers (ed.) *The Oxford Encyclopedia of Archaeology in the Near East.* Oxford: Oxford University Press.

Curtis, J. and Reade, J. E. (eds.) 1995. *Art and empire: treasures from Assyria in the British Museum.* New York: Metropolitan Museum of Art.

Damerji, M. S. B. 1999. *Gräber assyrischer Königinnen aus Nimrud.* Mainz: Zabern.

Darvill, T. and Timby, J. 1982. Textural analysis: A review of potentials and limitations. In: I. Freestone, C. Johns and T. Potter (eds.) *Current Research in Ceramics: Thin-Section Studies.* London: British Museum, 73–88.

Daszkiewicz, M., Bobryk, E. and Schneider, G. 2006. Neuassyrische Kochtopfkeramik vom Roten Haus: Chemisch-Mineralogische Zusammensetzung und Funktionseigenschaften. In: F. J. Kreppner (ed.) *Die Keramik des "Roten Hauses" von Tall Šēḫ Ḥamad/Dur-Katlimmu: eine Betrachtung der Keramik Nordmesopotamiens aus der zweiten Hälfte des 7. und aus dem 6. Jahrhundert v. Chr.* Wiesbaden: Harrassowitz Verlag, 421–437.

Davidson, T. E. and McKerrell, H. 1976. Pottery Analysis and Halaf Period Trade in the Khabur Headwaters Region. *IRAQ* 38, 45–56.

———. 1980. The Neutron Activation Analysis of Halaf and 'Ubaid Pottery from Tell Arpachiyah and Tepe Gawra. *IRAQ* 42, 155–167.

Deer, W. A., Howie, R. A. and Zussman, J. 1997–2011. *Rock Forming Minerals*. Bath: The Geological Society Publishing House.

Deller, K. 1999. The Assyrian Eunuchs and Their Predecessors. In: K. Watanabe (ed.) *Priests and Officials in the Ancient Near East: Papers of the Second Colloquium on the Ancient Near East—The City and its Life held at the Middle Eastern Culture Centre in Japan (Mitaka, Tokyo)*. Heidelberg: Universitätsverlag C. Winter, 303–312.

Delougaz, P., 1952. *Pottery from the Diyala region*. University of Chicago Press, Chicago.

Descantes, C. H., Intoh, M., Neff, H. and Glascock, M. D. 2004. Chemical characterization of Yapes clays and ceramics by instrumental neutron activation analysis. *Journal of Radioanalytical and Nuclear Chemistry* 262, 83–91.

Descantes, C. H., Speakman, R. J. and Glascock, M. 2008. Compositional Studies of Caribbean Ceramics: An Introduction to Instrumental Neutron Activation Analysis. *Journal of Caribbean Archaeology* 2, 1–14.

Dietrich, M. 2003. *The Neo-Babylonian Correspondence of Sargon and Sennacherib*. Helsinki: Helsinki University Press.

Docter, R. F. 2012. *Samaria ware*. Retrieved from World Wide Web: http://referenceworks.brillonline.com/entries/brill-s-new-pauly/samaria-ware-e1100070.

Dornemann, R. 1997. Tell Ḥalaf. In: E. M. Meyers (ed.) *The Oxford Encyclopedia of Archaeology in the Near East*. Oxford: Oxford University Press, 460–462.

Dunnell, R. C. and Feathers, J. K. 1991. Late Woodland manifestations of the Malden Plain, southeast Missouri. In: M. S. Nassaney and C. R. Cobb (eds.) *Stability, Transformation, and Variation: The Late Woodland in the Southeast*. New York: Plenum, 21–45.

Eco, U. 1979. *Theory of Semiotics*. Bloomington, IN: Indiana University Press.

El-Daywachi, S. I. 1954. Mosul Citadel in Various Periods (Arabic). *Sumer: A Journal of Archaeology and History in Iraq* 10, 94–116.

Elat, M. 1977. The Economic Relations of the Neo-Assyrian Empire with Egypt. *Journal of the American Oriental Society* 98, 20–34.

Engstrom, C. 2004. The Neo-Assyrians at Tell el-Hesi: A Petrographic Study of Imitation Assyrian Palace Ware. *Bulletin of the American Schools of Oriental Research* 333, 69–81.

Ericson, J. and Stickel, E. G. 1973. A proposed classification system for ceramics. *World Archaeology* 4, 357–367.

Evans, G. 1950. Ancient Mesopotamian Assemblies. *Journal of the American Oriental Society* 78, 1–11.

Fabian, P. and Goren, Y. 2002. A new type of Late Roman storage jar from the Negev. In: J. H. Humphrey (ed.) *The Roman and Byzantine Near East Volume 3*. Portsmith, RI: Journal of Roman Archaeology, 145–153.

Fales, F. M. 1994. A fresh look at the Nimrud Wine Lists. In: L. Milano (ed.) *Drinking in Ancient Societies*. Padova: Sargon, 361–380.

Fales, F. M. and Postgate, J. N. 1995. *Imperial Administrative Records, Part II: Provincial and Military Administration*. Helsinki: Helsinki University Press.

Feathers, J. K. 1991. Estimating Original Firing Temperature in Low Fired Prehistoric Ceramics. In: P. B. Vandiver, J. Druzik and G. Wheeler (eds.) *Materials Issues in Art and Archaeology II: Symposium held April 17–21, 1990, San Francisco, California, U.S.A.* Pittsburg (PA): Materials Research Society.

Finkbeiner, U. and Pongratz-Leisten, B. 1992. Beispiele Altorientalischer Städte. Residenzen des assyrischen Reiches. Assur. *Tübinger Atlas des Vorderen Orients der Universität Tübingen*, IV, 21.

Ford, J. A. 1954. Comment on A. C. Spaulding, "Statistical Techniques for the Discovery of Artifact Types". *American Antiquity* 19, 390–391.

Formenti, F. and Duthel, J. M. 1996. The Analysis of Wine and Other Organics Inside Amphoras of the Roman Period. In: P. E. McGovern, S. J. Fleming and S. H. Katz (eds.) *The Origins and Ancient History of Wine*. London: Routledge, 79–88.

Foster, G. M. 1965. The Sociology of Pottery: Questions and Hypotheses Arising from Contemporary Mexican Work. In: F. R. Matson (ed.) *Ceramic and Man*. Chicago: Aldine Publishing Company, 43–61.

Foster, K. P. 1998. *Gardens of Eden: Exotic Flora and Fauna in the Ancient Near East. Transformations of Middle Eastern Natural Environments: Legacies and Lessons*. New Haven: Yale University Press.

Freestone, I. C. 1982. Applications and Potential of Electron Probe Micro-Analysis in Technological and Provenance Investigations of Ancient Ceramics. *Archaeometry* 24, 99–116.XX

———. 1995. Ceramic Petrography in Science in Archaeology: a Review (ed. P. E. McGovern). *American Journal of Archaeology* 99, 111–115.

Freestone, I. C. and Hughes, M. J. 1989. Appendix III: Examination of Ceramics from Qasrij Cliff and Khirbet Qasrij. In: J. Curtis (ed.) *Excavations at Qasrij Cliff and Khirbet Qasrij*. London: British Museum Publications Ltd., 61–75.

Fuchs, A. and Parpola, S. 2001. *The Correspondence of Sargon II, Part III: Letters from Babylonia and the Eastern Provinces*. Helsinki: Helsinki University Press.

Gaspa, S. 2007. Vessels in Neo-Assyrian Documents: Capacity Measures and Listing Conventions. *State Archives of Assyria Bulletin* 16, 145–184.

Gatti, M. A. 1986–7. *La Ceramica Neo Assira (X–VII Sec.): Tupologie e Diffusione.* Unpublished Ph.D. thesis, Università Degli Studi di Padova.

George, A. R. 1990. Royal Tombs at Nimrud. *Minerva* 1, 29–31.

Gilboa, A. 1996. Assyrian Pottery at Dor and the Status of the Town During the Assyrian Occupation Period (Hebrew). *Eretz Israel* 25, 122–35.

Gitin, S. 1997. The Neo-Assyrian Empire and its Western Periphery. In: S. Parpola and R. M. Whiting (eds.) *Assyria 1995: Proceedings of the 10th Anniversary Symposium on the Neo-Assyrian Text Corpus Project, Helsinki, September 7–11, 1995*. Helsinki: The Neo-Assyrian Text Corpus Project, 77–104.

———. 2010. Personal Communication RE: Palace ware from the Negev.

Gjerstad, E., 1946. Decorated Metal Bowls from Cyprus. *Opuscula Archaeologica* 4, 1–19.

Goethe, J. W. 1970. *The Theory of Colours*. Boston: The MIT Press.

Goldstein, J., Newbury, D. E., Joy, D. C., Lyman, C. E., Echlin, P., Lifshin, E., Sawyer, L. C. and Michael, J. R. 2003. *Scanning Electron Microscopy and X-ray Microanalysis*. London: Kluwer Academic/Plenum Publishers.

Goren, Y., Finkelstein, I. and Na'aman, N. 2004. *Inscribed in Clay: Provenance Study of the Amarna Tablets and Other Near Eastern Texts*. Tel Aviv: Tel Aviv University.

Goren, Y., Mommsen, H., Finkelstein, I. and Na'aman, N. 2009. A Provenance Study of the Gilgamesh Fragment from Megiddo. *Archaeometry* 51, 763–773.

Goren, Y., Mommsen, H. and Klinger, J. 2010. Non-destructive provenance study of cuneiform tablets using portable x-ray fluorescence (pXRF). Journal of Archaeological Science 38, 684–696.

Grayson, A. K., 1993. Assyrian Officials and Power in the Ninth and Eighth Centuries. *State Archives of Assyria Bulletin* 7, 19–52.

———. 1999. The Struggle for Power in Assyria: Challenge to Absolute Monarchy in the Ninth and Eighth Centuries BC. In: K. Watanabe (ed.) *Priests and Officials in the Ancient Near East: Papers of the Second Colloquium on the Ancient Near East—The City and its Life held at the Middle Eastern Culture Centre in Japan (Mitaka, Tokyo)*. Heidelberg: Universitätsverlag C. Winter, 253–270.

Greenwood, K. 2010. The Hearing Gods of the Assyrian Royal Inscriptions. *Journal of Ancient Near Eastern Religions* 10, 211–218.

Haines, R. C. 1971. *Excavations in the Plain of Antioch II: The Structural Remains of the Later Phases: Chatal Hoyuk, Tell al-Judaidah, and Tell Ta'yinat*. Chicago: University of Chicago Press.

Haller, A. 1954. *Die Gräber und Grüfte von Assur*. Berlin: Gerb. Mann.

Hally, D. J. 1986. The Identification of Vessel Function: A Case Study from Northwest Georgia. *American Antiquity* 51, 267–295.

Hausleiter, A. 1999. Neo-Assyrian Pottery from Kalḫu/Nimrud: with special reference to the Polish excavations in the "central Building". In: A. Hausleiter and A. Reiche (eds.) *Iron Age Pottery in Northern Mesopotamia, Northern Syria and South-Eastern Anatolia.* Münster: Ugarit-Verlag, 17–60.

———. 2008. Nimrud in the context of Neo-Assyrian Pottery Studies. In: J. Curtis, H. McCall, D. Collon and L. Al-Gailani Werr (eds.) *New Light on Nimrud: Proceedings of the Nimrud Conference 11–13th March 2008.* London: British Institute for the Study of Iraq in association with The British Museum, 215–224.

———. 2010. *Neuassyrische Keramik im Kerngebiet Assyriens—Chronologie und Formen.* Wiesbaden: Harrassowitz.

Hawkins, J. D. 1995. The Political Geography of North Syria and South-East Anatolia in the Neo-Assyrian Period. In: M. Liverani (ed.) *Neo-Assyrian Geography.* Rome: Università di Roma, 87–101.

Hendrickson, E. F. and McDonald, M. M. A. 1983. Ceramic Form and Function: An Ethnographic Search and an Archaeological Application. *American Anthropologist* 85, 630–643.

Hendrickson, R. C. 1989. The Buff and the Grey: Ceramic Assemblages and Cultural Process in the Third Millennium BC Central Zagros, Iran. In: P. E. Mc Govern and M. D. Notis (eds.) *Cross-Craft and Cross-Cultural Interactions.* Westerville, OH: The American Ceramic Society, Inc, 81–146.

Hendrix, R. E., Drey, P. R. and Storfjell, J. B. 1997. *Ancient Pottery of Transjordan: An Introduction Utilizing Published Whole Forms.* Berrien Springs, MI: Institute of Archaeology/Horn Archaeological Museum Andrews Museum.

Herbordt, S. 1992. *Neuassyrische Glyptik des 8.–7. Jh. v. Chr.: unter besonderer Berücksichtigung der Siegelungen auf Tafeln und Tonverschlüssen.* Helsinki: Neo-Assyrian Text Corpus Project.

Hoard, R. J., O'Brien, M. J., Khorasgany, M. G. and Gopalaratnam, V. S. 1995. A materials-science approach to understanding limestone-tempered pottery from the Midwestern United States. *Journal of Archaeological Science* 22, 823–832.

Holloway, S. W. 2002. *Aššur Is King! Aššur Is King!: Religion in the Exercise of Power in the Neo-Assyrian Empire.* Leiden: Brill.

Howes Smith, P. H. G., 1986. A Study of 9th–&th Century Metal Bowls from Western Asia, *Iranica Antiqua* 21, 1–88.

Hughes, M. J., Freestone, I. C. and Humphrey, M. S. 1997. Neutron Activation and Petrographic Analysis of Pottery. In: J. Curtis and A. Green (eds.) Excavations at Khirbet Khatuniyeh. London: British Museum Press, 95–101.

Humbert, J.-B. 15 January 2010. Personal Communication RE: Neo-Assyrian excavations in Gaza and Amman.

Hunt, A. M. W. 2012. On the Origin of Ceramics: moving toward a common understanding of 'provenance'. *Archaeological Reviews from Cambridge* 27, 84–96.

Hunt, J. H. 2010. *Mesopotamian Šuilla Prayers to Ea, Marduk, and Nabû: Exegetical Studies.* Lewiston: The Edwin Mellen Press.

Hussein, M. M. 2008. Recent Excavations at Nimrud. In: J. Curtis, H. McCall, D. Collon and L. Al-Gailani Werr (eds.) *New Light on Nimrud: Proceeeds of the Nimrud Conference 11th–13th March 2002*. London: British Institute for the Study of Iraq in association with The British Museum, 83–98.

Jacobs, L. 1992. Causes for the pale colour of second millennium BC pottery from several sites in Mesopotamia. In: S. Méry (ed.) *Sciences de la terre at céramiques archéologiques: expérimentations, applications*. Cergy: Documents et Travaux de l'Institut Géologique Albert-de-Lapparent, Centre Polytechnique Saint-Louis, 121–136.

Jacobsen, T. 1943. Primative Democracy in Ancient Mesopotamia. *Journal of Near Eastern Studies* 2, 159–172.

Jacobsen, T. and Lloyd, S. 1935. *Sennacherib's Aqueduct at Jerwan*. Chicago: University of Chicago Press.

Jassim, S. Z. 2006. Late Precambrian Development of the Arabian Plate. In: S. Z. Jassim and J. C. Goff (eds.) *Geology of Iraq*. Prague: Dolin, 27–31.

Jassim, S. Z. and Buday, T. 2006a. Tectonic Framework. In: S. Z. Jassim and J. C. Goff (eds.) *Geology of Iraq*. Prague: Dolin, 45–56.

———. 2006b. Units of the Unstable Shelf and the Zagros Suture. In: S. Z. Jassim and J. C. Goff (eds.) *Geology of Iraq*. Prague: Dolin, 71–83.

Jassim, S. Z., Suk, M. and Waldhausrová, J. 2006. Magmatism and Metamorphism in the Zagros Suture. In: S. Z. Jassim and J. C. Goff (eds.) *Geology of Iraq*. Prague: Nolin, 212–231.

Karkanas, P. 2010. Identifying Minerals Using Microchemical Analysis. In: S. Weiner (ed.) *Microarchaeology: Beyond the Visible Archaeological Record*. Cambridge: Cambridge University Press, 317–319.

Kerr, P. F. 1977. *Optical Mineralogy*. London: McGraw-Hill.

Kessler, K. 1997. "Royal Roads" and other Questions of the Neo-Assyrian Communication System. In: S. Parpola and R. M. Whiting (eds.) *Assyria 1995: Proceedings of the 10th Anniversary Symposium on the Neo-Assyrian Text Corpus Project, Helsinki, September 7–11, 1995*. Helsinki: The Neo-Assyrian Text Corpus Project, 129–136.

Kilikoglou, V., Hein, A. and Maniatis, Y. (eds.) 2002. *Modern Trends in Scientific Studies on Ancient Ceramics: Papers presented at the 5th European Meeting on Ancient Ceramics, Athens 1999*. Oxford: Archaeopress.

King, P. J. 2006. The Eighth, the Greatest of Centuries? In: H. Attridge and J. V. D. Kam (eds.) *Presidential Voices: The Society of Biblical Literature in the 20th Century*. Society of Biblical Literature, 233–246.

King, P. J. and Stager, L. E. 2001. *Life in Biblical Israel*. Westminster John Knox Press.

Kinnier Wilson, J. V. 1972. *The Nimrud Wine Lists: A study of men and administration at the Assyrian capital in the Eighth Century, BC*. London: British School of Archaeology in Iraq.

Klauber, E., 1910. *Assyrisches Beamtentum nach Briefen aus der Sargonidenzeit.* Leipziger Semitistische Studien V/3. Leipzig: J. C. Hinrich.

Klengel-Brandt, E., 1994. *Einige Siegelabdrücke wohl nachassyrischer Zeit aus Assur.* Münster: Ugarit-Verlag.

Krásny, J., Alsam, S. and Jassim, S. Z. 2006. Hydrogeology. In: S. Z. Jassim and J. C. Goff (eds.) *Geology of Iraq*. Prague: Dolin, 251–287.

Kraus, F. R. 1982. 'Kārum', ein Organ städtischer Selbstverwaltung der altbabylonischen Zeit. In: A. Finet (ed.) *Les pouvoirs locaux en Mésopotamie et dans les régions adjacentes*. Brussels: Institut des hautes études de Belgique, 24–42.

Kreppner, F. J. 2006. *Die Keramik des "Roten Hauses" von Tall Šēḫ Ḥamad/Dur-Katlimmu: eine Betrachtung der Keramik Nordmesopotamiens aus der zweiten Hälfte des 7. und aus dem 6. Jahrhundert v. Chr.* Wiesbaden: Harrassowitz.

———. 2008. The Collapse of the Assyrian Empire and the Continuity of Ceramic Culture: The Case of the Red House at Tall Sheikh Hamad. *ANES* 45, 147–165.

Kühne, H. 1995. The Assyrians on the Middle Euphrates and the Ḫābūr. In: M. Liverani (ed.) *Neo-Assyrian Geography*. Rome: Università di Roma, 69–85.

———. 1996. Tell Sheikh Hamad/Dur-Katlimmu. In: S. Muhesen (ed.). Institut Français d'Etudes Arabes de Damas.

———. 2008. Šaiḫ Ḥamad, Tall. B. Archäologisch. *Reallexikon der Assyrologie und Vorderasiatischen Archäologie* 11, 543–551.

———. 2010. The Rural Hinterland of Dūr-Katlimmu. In: H. Kühne (ed.) *Dūr-Katlimmu 2008 and beyond.* Wiesbaden: Otto Harrassowitz GmbH & Co, 115–128.

Kühne, H. and Luther, A. 1998. Tall Seh Hamad / Dur-Katlimmu / Magdalu? *Nouvelles Assyriologiques Brèves et Utilitaires*, 106–109.

Kuhrt, A. 1995. *The Ancient Near East: c. 3000–330 BC*. London: Routledge.

Labat, R. 1976. *Manuel d'épigraphie akkadienne: signes, syllabaire, idéogrammes*. Paris: Imperimerie Nationale.

Lambert, W. G. 1983. The God Aššur. *Iraq* 45, 82–86.

Lamprichs, R. 1997. Aššur. In: E. M. Meyers (ed.) *The Oxford Encyclopedia of Archaeology in the Near East.* Oxford: Oxford University Press, 225–228.

Lanfranchi, G. 1997. Consensus to Empire: Some Aspects of Sargon II's Foreign Policy. In: H. Waetzoldt and H. Hauptmann (eds.) *Assyrien im Wandel der Zeiten: XXXIXe Rencontre Assyriologique Internationale 6.–10. Juli 1992*. Heidelberg: Heidelberger Orientverlag, 81–87.

Lanfranchi, G. and Parpola, S. 1990. *The Correspondence of Sargon II, Part II: Letters from the Northern and Northeastern Provinces*. Helsinki: Helsinki University Press.

———. 2000. The ideological and political impact of the Assyrian imperial expansion on the Greek World in the 8th and 7th centuries BC. In: Aro, S. (Ed.) *The Heirs of Assyria*. Helsinki: The Neo-Assyrian Text Corpus Project, 7–34.

Layard, A. H. 1849. *Nineveh and its remains: with an account of a visit to the Chaldaean Christians of Kurdistan, and the Yezidis, or devil-worshipers, and an enquiry into the manners and arts of the ancient Assyrians*. London: John Murray.

———. 1852. *A popular account of discoveries at Nineveh*. London: John Murray.

Lie, A. G. 1929. *The Inscriptions of Sargon II, king of Assyria: The Annals*. Paris: P. Geuthner.

Lines, J. 1954. Late Assyrian Pottery from Nimrud. *Iraq* 16, 164–167.

Liverani, M. 1979. The Ideology of the Assyrian Empire. In: M. Trolle Larsen (ed.) *Power and Propaganda: A Symposium on Ancient Empires*. Copenhagen: Akademisk Forlag, 297–318.

Liverani, M., 2003. *Oltre la Bibbia*. Rome: Laterza.

Livingstone, A. 1997. New Dimensions in the Study of Assyrian Religion. In: S. Parpola and R. M. Whiting (eds.) *Assyria 1995: Proceedings of the 10th Anniversary Symposium on the Neo-Assyrian Text Corpus Project, Helsinki, September 7–11, 1995*. Helsinki: The Neo-Assyrian Text Corpus Project, 165–178.

Lumsden, S. 15 September 2009. Personal Communication RE: Neo-Assyrian ceramic workshop at Nineveh.

Luukko, M. and Van Buylaere, G. 2002. *The Political Correspondence of Esarhaddon*. Helsinki: Helsinki University Press.

Mallowan, M. E. L. 1950. The excavations at Nimrud (Kalḫu), 1949–1950. *Iraq* 12, 147–183.

———. 1966. *Nimrud and its remains*. London: Collins.

Maniatis, Y. 2009. The Emergence of Ceramic Technology and its Evolution as Revealed with the use of Scientific Techniques. In: A. J. Shortland, I. C. Freestone and Th. Rehren (eds.) *From Mine to Microscope: Advances in the Study of Ancient Technology*. Oxford: Oxbow Books, 1–18.

Maniatis, Y. and Tite, M. S. 1981. Technological examination of Neolithic–Bronze Age pottery from Central and Southeast Europe and from the Near East. *Journal of Archaeological Science* 8, 59–76.

Manuelli, F., 2009. Assyria and the Provinces: survival of local features and imposition of new patterns in the peripheral regions of the empire. *Mesopotamia* 44, 113–128.

Marcus, M. I. 1996. *Emblems of Identity and Prestige: The Seals and Sealings from Hasanlu, Iran—Commentary and Catalog*. Philadelphia: University Museum University of Pennsylvania.

Martínez-Carrillo, A., Lucena, M. J., Fuertes, J. M. and Ruiz, A. 2012. Morphometric Analysis Applied to the Archaeological Pottery of the Valley of Guadalquivir. In: A. Elewa (ed.) *Morphometrics for Nonmorphometricians*. Berlin: Springer-Verlag, 307–324.

Matson, F. R. 1971. A study of temperatures used in firing ancient Mesopotamian pottery. In: R. H. Brill (ed.) *Science and Archaeology*. Cambridge (MA): MIT Press, 65–79.

———. 1989. Ceramics: The Hub of Ancient Craft Interplay. In: P. E. Mc Govern and M. D. Notis (eds.) *Cross-Craft and Cross-Cultural Interactions*. Westerville, OH: The American Ceramic Society, Inc., 13–28.

Mattila, R. 2000. *The King's Magnates: A Study of the Highest Officials of the Neo-Assyrian Empire*. Helsinki: The Neo-Assyrian Text Corpus Project.

Melson, W. G. and Beek, G. W. V. 1992. Geology and the Loessial Soils, Tell Jemmeh, Israel. *Geoarchaeology* 7, 121–147.

Menzel, B., 1981. *Assyrische Tempel*. Studia Pohl, Series Maior 10. Rome: Biblical Institute Press.

Meskell, L., 1998. An archaeology of social relations in an Egyptian village. *Journal of Archaeological Method and Theory* 5, 209–243.

Michalowski, P. 1990. Presence at Creation. In: I. T. Abusch, J. Huehnergard and P. Steinkeller (eds.) *Lingering Over Words: Studies in Ancient Near Eastern Literature in Honor of William L. Moran*. Atlanta: Scholars Press, 381–396.

———. 1994. The Drinking Gods: alcohol in early Mesopotamian ritual and mythology. In: Milano, L. (ed.) *Drinking in Ancient Societies: History and Culture of Drinks in the Ancient Near East*. Padua: Sargon, 27–44.

Middleton, A. 1997. Ceramics. In: A. Middleton and J. Lang (eds.) *Radiography of cultural materials*. Cornwall: Butterworth—Heinemann, 76–95.

Middleton, A. and Lang, J. 1997. Radiography: Theory and Practice. In: A. Middleton & J. Lang (eds.) *Radiography of cultural materials*. Cornwall: Butterworth—Heinemann, 1–32.

Mielke, P. W., JR. and Berry, K. J. 2001. *Permutation methods: A distance function approach*. New York: Springer.

Mielke, P. W., JR., Berry, K. J. and Johnson, E. S. 1976. Multi-responsive Permutation Procedures for a priori Classifications. *Communications in Statistics—Theory and Methods* A5, 1409–1424.

Millard, A. R. 1994. *The Eponyms of the Assyrian Empire, 910–612 BC*. Helsinki: Neo-Assyrian Text Corpus Project.

Minarikova, D. 1979. The results of the Quaternary sediments investigations in the northern part of the Mesopotamian Plain. Unpublished report. Baghdad: GEOSURV.

Mirti, P. and Davit, P. 2004. New Developments in the Study of Ancient Pottery by Colour Measurement. *Journal of Archaeological Science* 31, 741–751.

Molera, J., Pradell, T. and Vendrell-Saz, M. 1998. The colours of Ca-rich ceramic pastes: origin and characterization. *Applied Clay Science* 13, 187–202.

Mommsen, H. 2004. Short Note: Provenancing of Pottery—The Need for an Integrated Approach? *Archaeometry* 46, 267–271.

Montana, G., Mommsen, H., Iliopoulos, I., Schwedt, A. and Denaro, M. 2003. The Petrography and Chemistry of Thin-Walled Ware from an Hellensistic-Roman Site at Segesta (Sicily). *Archaeometry* 45, 375–389.

Moorey, P. R. S. 1980. Metal Wine Sets in the Ancient Near East. *Iranica Antiqua* 15, 181–197.

———. 1994. *Ancient Mesopotamian materials and industries: the archaeological evidence.* Winona Lake: Eisenbrauns.

Muscarella, O. W. 1986. The Location of Ulhu and Uiše in Sargon II's Eighth Campaign, 714 BC. *Journal of Field Archaeology* 13, 465–475.

Na'aman, N. 1979. Sennacherib's Campaign to Judah and the Date of the lmlk Stamps. *Vetus Testamentum* 29, 61–86.

———. 1995. Province System and Settlement Pattern in Southern Syria and Palestine in the Neo-Assyrian Period. In: M. Liverani (ed.) *Neo-Assyrian Geography*. Rome: Università di Roma, 103–115.

———. 2009. Was Dor the Capital of an Assyrian Province? *Tel Aviv* 36, 95–109.

Nadali, D., 2009–2010. Neo-Assyrian State Seals: an allegory of power. *State Archives of Assyria Bulletin* 13, 215–244.

Nakai, I., 2005. Synchrotron Radiation X-Ray Fluorescence Analysis of Archaeological Ceramics and Glass. In: Uda, M., Demortier, G., Nakai, I. (eds.) *X-rays for Archaeology*. Dordrecht: Springer, 183–198.

Neff, H. and Glascock, M. 2002. *Report on Instrumental Neutron Activation of Olmec Pottery*. Columbia, MO: University of Missouri.

Nicholson, P. T. and Patterson, H. L. 1989. Ceramic Technology in Upper Egypt: A Study of Pottery Firing. *World Archaeology* 21, 71–86.

Nissen, H.-J. 1988. *The Early History of the Ancient Near East 9000–2000*. Chicago: University of Chicago Press.

Oates, D. and Oates, J. 1976. *The rise of civilisation*. Oxford: Elsevier/Phaidon.

Oates, J. 1959. Late Assyrian pottery from Fort Shalmaneser (8th-7th century). *Iraq* 21, 130–146.

Oates, J. and Oates, D. 2001. *Nimrud: An Assyrian Imperial City Revealed*. London: British School of Archaeology in Iraq.

Oded, B. 1970. Observations on Methods of Assyrian Rule in Transjordania after the Palestinian Campaign of Tiglath-Pileser III. *Journal of Near Eastern Studies* 29, 177–186.

———. 1979. *Mass Deportations and Deportees in the Neo-Assyrian Empire*. Weisbaden: Reichert.

———. 1995. Observations on the Israelite/Judean Exiles in Mesopotamia During the Eighth-Sixth Centuries BC. In: K. Van Lerberghe and A. Schoors (eds.) *Immigration and Emigration within the Ancient Near East: Festschrift E. Lipiński*. Leuven: Uitgeverij Peeters en Departement Oriëntalistiek, 205–212.

Ohtus, T. 1991. Late Assyrian "Palace Ware"—concerning dimpled goblet. In: H. I. H. P. T. Mikasa (ed.) *Essays on Ancient Anatolian and Syrian Studies in the 2nd and 1st Millennium BC*. Wiesbaden: Otto Harrassowitz, 131–154.

Önal, M. 2006. Determination of chemical formula of a smectite. *Communications of the Faculty of Science, University of Ankora (series B)* 52, 1–6.

Oppenheim, A. L., 1964. *Ancient Mesopotamia: portrait of a dead civilization*. Chicago: University of Chicago Press.

———. 1969. The banquet of Ashurnasipal II. In: J. Pritchard (ed.) *Ancient Near Eastern texts relating to the Old Testament*. Princeton: Princeton University Press, 558–561.

Oppenheim, A. L., Brill, R. H., Barag, D. and Von Saldern, A. 1970. *Glass and glassmaking in ancient Mesopotamia; an edition of the cuneiform texts which contain instructions for glassmakers with a catalogue of surviving objects*. Corning, N. Y.: Corning Museum of Glass.

Orton, C., Tyres, P. and Vince, A. 1993. *Pottery in Archaeology*. Cambridge: Cambridge University Press.

Otzen, B. 1979. Israel under the Assyrians. In: M. Trolle Larsen (ed.) *Power and Propaganda: A Symposium on Ancient Empires*. Copenhagen: Akademisk Forlag, 251–262.

Parker, B. 2001. *The Mechanics of Empire: The Northern Frontier of Assyria as a Case Study in Imperial Dynamics*. Helsinki: Vammalan Kirjapaino Oy.

Parpola, S. 1987a. *The Correspondence of Sargon II, Part I: Letters from Assyria and the West*. Helsinki: Helsinki University Press.

———. 1987b. Neo-Assyrian Treaties from the Royal Archives of Nineveh. *Journal of Cuneiform Studies* 39, 161–189.

———. 1999. Sons of God—The Ideology of Assyrian Kingship. Retrieved on 3 August 2007 from World Wide Web: http://www.gatewaystobabylon.com/introduction/sonsofgod.htm.

———. 2000. Monotheism in Ancient Assyria. In: B. Porter (ed.) *One God or Many?: Concepts of Divinity in the Ancient World (Transactions of the Casco Bay Assyriological Institute 1)*. Casco Bay: Casco Bay Assyrological Institute, 165–209.

———. 2003. Assyria's Expansion in the 8th and 7th Centuries and Its Long-Term Repercussions in the West. In: W. G. Dever and S. Gitin (eds.) *Symbiosis, Symbolism, and the Power of the Past*. Winona Lake, Indiana: Eisenbrauns, 99–106.

———. 2004. National and Ethnic Identity in the Neo-Assyrian Empire and Assyrian Identity in Post Assyrian Times. *Journal of Assyrian Academic Studies* 18, 5–22.

Parpola, S. and Watanabe, K. 1988. *Neo-Assyrian Treaties and Loyalty Oaths*. Helsinki: Helsinki University Press.

Pedersén, O. 1985. *Archives and Libraries in the City of Assur: A Survey of Material from the German Excavations (Pt. 1)*. Uppsala/Stockholm: Almqvist & Wiksell Internat.

———. 1986. *Archives and Libraries in the City of Assur: A Survey of Material from the German Excavations (Pt. 2)*. Uppsala/Stockholm: Almqvist & Wiksell Internat.

Perlman, I. and Asaro, F. 1969. Pottery Analysis by Neutron Activation. *Archaeometry* 11, 21–38.

Petrie, W. M. F. 1928. *Gerar*. London: British School of Archaeology in Egypt.

Pezzotti, G., Matsutani, A., Munisso, M. C. and Zhu, W. L. 2009. Advanced Nano-Scale Metrology for the Characterisation of Ceramic Materials in the Scanning Electron Microscope. *Materials Science Forum* 606: Advances in Ceramic Materials, 93–101.

Pfälzner, P. 1995. *Mittanische und Mittelassyrische Keramik: eine chronologische, funktionale und produktionsökonomische Analyse*. Berlin: D. Riemer.

Philip, G. 1968. Mineralogy of the Recent sediments of Tigris and Euphrates rivers and some of the older detrital deposits. *Journal of Sedimentary Research* 38, 35–44.

Pollard, A. M., Batt, C. M., Stern, B. and Young, S. M. M. 2007. *Analytical Chemistry in Archaeology*. Cambridge: Cambridge University Press.

Ponchia, S., 2012. Administrators and Administrated in Neo-Assyrian Times. In: Wilhelm, G. (Ed.) *Organization, Representation, and Symbols of Power in the Ancient Near East*. Winona Lake, IN: Eisenbrauns, 213–224.

Porter, B. 1997. The Relative Status of Nabû and Marduk in the Late Assyrian Period. In: S. Parpola and R. M. Whiting (eds.) *Assyria 1995: Proceedings of the 10th Anniversary Symposium on the Neo-Assyrian Text Corpus Project, Helsinki, September 7–11, 1995*. Helsinki: The Neo-Assyrian Text Corpus Project, 253–260.

Postgate, J. N. 1973. *The Governor's Palace Archive*. London: British School of Archaeology in Iraq.

———. 1978. An Inscribed Jar from Tell al Rimah. *Iraq* 40, 71–75.

———. 1979. The Economic Structure of the Assyrian Empire. In: M. Trolle Larsen (ed.) *Power and Propaganda: A Symposium on Ancient Empires*. Copenhagen: Akademisk Forlag, 193–222.

———. 1990. Excavations at Abu Salabikh 1988–9. *Iraq* 52, 95–114.

———. 1992. The Land of Assur and the Yoke of Assur. *World Archaeology* 23, 247–263.

———. 1995. Assyria: the Home Provinces. In: M. Liverani (ed.) *Neo-Assyrian Geography*. Rome: Università di Roma, 1–17.

———. 2007. The invisible hierarchy: Assyrian military and civilian administration in the 8th and 7th centuries BC. In: Postgate, J. N. (ed.) *The Land of Assur and the Yoke of Assur: Studies on Assyria 1971–2005*. Oxford: Oxbow Books, 331–360.

Potts, D. 1997. *Mesopotamian civilisation: The Material Foundations*. London: Athlone Press.

Powell, M. A. 1987–1990. Masse und Gewichte. *Reallexikon der Assyrologie und Vorderasiatischen Archäologie* 7, 457b–517a.

———. 1996. *Wine and Vine in Ancient Mesopotamia: the Cuneiform Evidence*. McGovern, P. E.

Pratt, M. L. 2008. *Imperial Eyes: Travel Writing and Transculturation*. New York: Routledge.

Pucci, M. 2010. The Discovery of the City-Canal Dūr-Katlimmu. In: H. Kühne (ed.) *Dūr-Katlimmu 2008 and Beyond*. Wiesbaden: Harrassowitz Verlag, 163–174.

Radner, K. 1999–2001. Eine Bronzeschale mit neuassyrischer Inschrift. *State Archives of Assyria Bulletin* 13, 17–25.

———, mit Beiträgen von Wolfgang Röllig zu den aramäischen Beischriften, 2002. *Die neuassyrischen Texte aus Tall Šēh Ḥamad*. Berlin: Dietrich Reimer Verlag.

———. 2006. Provinz: Assyrien. In: M. P. Streck (ed.) *Reallexikonder Assyriologie unde Vorderasiatischen Archäologie*. Berlin: Walter de Gruyter, 42–68.

———. 2008. The delegation of power: Neo-Assyrian bureau seals. In: P. Briant, W. F. M. Henkelman and M. W. Stolper (eds.) *L'archive des fortifications de Persépolis : état des questions et perspectives de recherches*. Paris: De Boccard, 481–516.

———. 2010a. Central Assyria, the lands between Assur, Nineveh, and Arbela. Retrieved 12 October 2010 from World Wide Web: http:www.ucl.ac.uk/sargon/essentials/countries/centralassyria/: University College London.

———. 2010b. The stele of Sargon II of Assyria at Kition: A focus for an emerging Cypriot identity? In: R. Rollinger, B. Gufler, M. Lang and I. Madreiter (eds.) *Interkulturalität in der Alten Welt: Vorderasien, Hellas, Ägypten und die viefältigen Ebenen des Kontakts*. Wiesbaden: Harrassowitz Verlag, 429–450.

———. 2011. The Assyrian Empire and its Vassals at the Close of the 8th century BC: The Siege of Jerusalem in Context. Anglo-Israel Archaeological Society. Clore Centre, The British Museum.

———, Mit Beiträgen von W. Röllig zu den Aramäischen Beischriften. 2002. *Die neuassyrischen Texte aus Tall Šēh Ḥamad*. Berlin: Dietrich Reimer Verlag.

Rainey, A. 1982. Toponymic Problems (cont.), Syria, The Brook of Egypt, Shur = The Wall of Egypt, Egyptian TJ = Semitic Samech. *Tel Aviv* 9, 130–136.

Rapp JR., G. and Hill. 1998. *Geoarchaeology: The Earth-Science Approach to Archaeological Interpretation*. New Haven: Yale University Press.

Rawson, P. S. 1954. Palace Ware from Nimrud: Technical Observations. *Iraq* 16, 168–172.

Rehder, J. E. 2000. *Mastery and Uses of Fire in Antiquity: A Sourcebook on Ancient Pyrotechnology*. Montreal: McGill-Queen's University Press.

Reynolds, F. S. 2003. *The Babylonian Correspondence of Esarhaddon and Letters to Assurbanipal and Sin-šarru-iškun from Northern and Central Babylonia*. Helsinki: Helsinki University Press.

Rice, P. M. 1976. Rethinking the Ware Concept. *American Antiquity* 41, 538–543.

———. 1982. Pottery Production, Pottery Classification, and the Role of Physicochemical Analyses. In: Olin, J. S., Franklin, A. D. (eds.) *Archaeological Ceramics: Papers presented at a seminar on Ceramics as Archaeological Material held at the Smithsonian Institution, Washington, D.C. and the National Bureau of Standards, Gaithersburg, Maryland, 29 September–1 October 1980, one of the Smithsonian Institution/National Bureau of Standards seminars on the Application of the Materials and Measurement Sciences to Archaeology and Museum Conservation*. Washington, D.C.: Smithsonian Institution Press, 47–56.

———. 1987. *Pottery Analysis*. Chicago: University of Chicago Press.

Rice, P. M. and Saffer, M. E. 1982. Cluster analysis of mixed-level data: Pottery provenience as an example. *Journal of Archaeological Science* 9, 395–409.

Rijad, D. 2002. *Aus den irakischen Ausgrabungen in Assur 2001. Spätneuassyrische Wohnbebauung, parthische Grabbauten und der Ostpalas. Mitteilungen der Deutschen Orient Gesellschaft*. Berlin: Deutsche Orient-Gesellschaft.

Rye, O. 1981. *Pottery Technology: Principles and Reconstruction*. Washington, D.C.: Taraxacum.

Sancisi-Weerdenburg, H. 1989. Gifts in the Persian Empire. In: P. Briant and C. Herrenschmidt (eds.) *Le tribut dans l'Empire perse: Actes de la table ronde de Paris, 12–13 décembre 1986*. Paris: Peeters, 129–146.

Sayce, A. H. 1900. *Babylonians and Assyrians: Life and Customs*. New York: Charles Schribner's Sons.

———. 1908. *The Archaeology of the Cuneiform Inscriptions*. London: Society for Promoting Christian Knowledge Subjects.

Schachner, G., Huntley, D. and Duff, A. 2011. Changes in regional organization and mobility in the Zuni region of the American Southwest during the Pueblo III and IV periods: insights from INAA studies. *Journal of Archaeological Science* 38, 2261–2273.

Schneider, G. 2006. Mineralogisch-Chemische Untersuchungen der Mittel- und Neuassyrischen Keramik von Tall Šēḫ Ḥamad. In: F. J. Kreppner (ed.) *Die Keramik des "Roten Hauses" von Tall Šēḫ Ḥamad/Dur-Katlimmu: eine Betrachtung der Keramik Nordmesopotamiens aus der zweiten Hälfte des 7. und aus dem 6. Jahrhundert v. Chr.* Wiesbaden: Harrassowitz Verlag, 391–420.

———. 2010. Personal Communication RE: XRD of ceramics.

Schreiber, K., 2005. Imperial Agendas and Local Agency: Wari Colonial Strategies, in: Stein, G. J. (Ed.). *The Archaeology of Colonial Encounters*. Santa Fe: School of American Research Press, 237–262.

Scott, M. L. and MacGinnis, J. 1990. Notes on Nineveh. *Iraq* 52, 63–73.

Senior, L. M. and Birnie, D. P. 1995. Accurately Estimating Vessel Volume from Profile Illustrations. *American Antiquity* 60, 319–334.

Shackley, M. S. 2010. Is there reliability and validity in portable x-ray fluorescence spectrometry (pXRF). *The SAA Archaeological Record* November, 17–20.

Shoval, S. 2003. Using FT-IR Spectroscopy for Study of Calcareous Ancient Ceramics. *Optical Materials* 24, 117–122.

Singer-Avitz, L. 2010. A Group of Phoenician Vessels from Tel Beersheba. *Tel Aviv: Journal of the Institute of Archaeology of Tel Aviv University* 37, 188–199.

Sinopoli, C. M. 1991. *Approaches to Archaeological Ceramics*. New York: Plenum Press.

———. 2001. Imperial Integration and Imperial Subjects. In: S. E. Alcock, T. N. D'altroy, K. D. Morrison and C. M. Sinopoli (eds.) *Empires*. Cambridge: Cambridge University Press, 195–200.

Smettan, U. 2008. Bodenpotentiale in Nordost-Syrien, Region Tall Šēḫ Ḥamad. In: H. Kühne (ed.) *Umwelt und Subsistenz der Assyrischen Stadt Dūr-Katlimmu am Unteren Ḫābūr*. Wiesbaden: Harrassowitz Verlag, 7–28.

Smith, G. 1873. Nineveh and its Records: Inscribed Stone, giving an account of the deluge—the site of Nineveh from a sketch. *The London Illustrated News*.

Spaulding, A. C. 1953. Statistical Techniques for the Discovery of Artifact Types. *American Antiquity* 18, 305–313.

———. 1954. Reply to Ford. *American Antiquity* 19, 391–393.

Speakman, R. J. 2010. Personal Communication RE: Neutron activation analysis

Stein, G., 1998. World Systems Theory and Alternative Modes of Interaction in the Archaeology of Culture Contact, in: Cusick, J. G. (Ed.). *Studies in Culture Contact: Interaction, Culture Change and Archaeology*. Carbondale, IL: Center for Archaeological Investigations, Southern Illinois University, 220–255.

———. 2002. From Passive Periphery to Active Agents: Emerging Perspectives in the Archaeology of Interregional Interaction. *American Anthropologist* 104, 903–916.

———. 2005. Introduction: The Comparative Archaeology of Colonial Encounters, in: Stein, G. (Ed.). *The archaeology of colonial encounters: comparative perspectives*. Santa Fe: School of American Research Press, 3–31.

Sterba, J. H. 20 August 2009. Personal Communication RE: Strengths and Weaknesses of INAA analysis.

Sterba, J. H., Mommsen, H., Steinhauser, G. and Bichler, M. 2009. The influence of different tempers on the composition of pottery. *Journal of Archaeological Science* 36, 1582–1589.

Strawn, B., Melville, S., Greenwood, K. and Noegel, S. 2006. Neo-Assyrian and Syro-Palestinian Texts III. In: M. Chavalas (ed.) *The Ancient Near East: Historical Sources in Translation*. Oxford: Blackwell Publishing, 331–380.

Stronach, D. 1990. The Garden as a Political Statement: Some Case Studies from the Near East in the First Millennium BC. *Bulletin of the Asia Institute* 4, 171–180.

———. 1996. The Imagery of the Wine Bowl: Wine in Assyrian in the Early First Millennium BC. In: P. E. McGovern, S. J. Fleming and S. H. Katz (eds.) *The Origins and Ancient History of Wine*. London: Routledge, 175–196.

Stronach, D. and Lumsden, S. 1992. UC Bekeley's Excavations at Nineveh. *The Biblical Archaeologist* 55, 227–233.

Tadmor, H. 1958a. The Campaigns of Sargon II of Assur: A Chronological-Historical Study. *Journal of Cuneiform Studies* 12, 22–40.

———. 1958b. The Campaigns of Sargon II of Assur: A Chronological-Historical Study (Conclusion). *Journal of Cuneiform Studies* 12, 77–100.

———. 1999. *The Inscriptions of Tiglath-Pileser III: King of Assyria: Critical Edition with Introduction, Translations and Commentary*. Jerusalem: Israel Academy of Sciences and Humanities.

Taylor, J. 2011. Tablets as Artefacts, Scribes as Artisans. In: K. Radner and E. Robson (eds.) *The Oxford Handbook of Cuneiform Culture*. Oxford: Oxford University Press, 5–31.

Thomas, N., 1994. *Colonialism's culture : anthropology, travel, and government.* Princeton: Princeton University Press.

Thomason, A. K. 2005. *Luxury and Legitimation: Royal Collecting in Ancient Mesopotamia*. Aldershot, Hampshire: Ashgate Publishing Limited.

———. 2010. Banquets, Bronzes, and Baubles: material comforts in Neo-Assyrian palaces. In: Cohen, A., Kangas, S. (Eds.) *Assyrian Reliefs at Dartmouth College: A Cultural Biography*, Lebanon, NH: Hood Museum of Art at Dartmouth University and University Press of New England, 198–214.

Tite, M. S. 1999. Pottery Production, Distribution, and Consumption—The Contribution of the Physical Sciences. *Journal of Archaeological Method and Theory* 6, 181–233.

Tite, M. S., Freestone, I. C., Meeks, N. D. and Bimson, M. 1982. The Use of Scanning Electron Microscopy in the Technological Examination of Ancient Ceramics. In: J. S. Olin and A. D. Franklin (eds.) *Archaeological Ceramics: Papers presented at a seminar on Ceramics as Archaeological Material held at the Smithsonian Institution, Washington, D.C. and the National Bureau of Standards, Gaithersburg, Maryland, 29 September–1 October 1980, one of the Smithsonian Institution/National Bureau of Standards seminars on the Application of the Materials and Measurement Sciences to Archaeology and Museum Conservation*. Washington, D.C.: Smithsonian Institution Press, 109–120.

Tite, M. S., Kilikoglou, V. and Vekinis, G. 2001. Strength, Toughness and Thermal Shock Resistance of Ancient Ceramics, and Their Influence on Technological Choice. *Archaeometry* 43, 301–324.

Tite, M. S. and Mantatis, Y. 1975. Examination of Ancient Pottery Using the Scanning Electron Microscope. *Nature* 257, 122–123.

Turner, G. 1970. Tell Nebi Yūnus: The Ekal Māšarti of Nineveh. *Iraq* 32, 68–85.

Van As, A. and Jacobs, B. 1986. Technological Research of Palaeo- and Meso-Babylonian Pottery—a report on the 1986 season at Tell at Der (Iraq) and some preliminary results. *Newsletter of the Department of Pottery Technology Leiden University* 4.

Van Beek, G. W. 1973. Assyrian Vaulted Buildings at Tell Jemmeh (Hebrew). *Qadmoniot* 6, 23–26.

———. 1997. Tell Jemmeh. In: E. M. Meyers (ed.) *The Oxford Encyclopedia of Archaeology in the Near East*. Oxford: Oxford University Press, 213–215.

Van Der Mieroop, M. 1999. The Government of an Ancient Mesopotamian City: what we know and why we know so little. In: K. Watanabe (ed.) *Priests and Officials in the Ancient Near East: Papers of the Second Colloquium on the Ancient Near East—The City and its Life held at the Middle Eastern Culture Centre in Japan (Mitaka, Tokyo)*. Heidelberg: Universitätsverlag C. Winter, 139–162.

Van Dommelen, P., 1998. *On Colonial Grounds: a comparative study of colonialism and rural settlement in first millenium BC west central Sardinia.* Leiden: Faculty of Archaeology, University of Leiden.

Van Sickle, J. 1997. Using mean similarity in dendrograms to evaluate classifications. *Journal of Agricultural, Biological, and Environmental Statistics* 2, 370–388.

Veldhuis, N. 1996. Cuneiform Tablet as an Educational Tool. *Dutch Studies on Near Eastern Languages and Cultures* 2, 11–26.

Vickers, M., Impey, O. and Allan, J. 1986. *From Silver to Ceramic: the potter's debt to metalwork in the Graeco-Roman, Oriental and Isalamic Worlds.* Oxford: Ashmolean Museum.

Von Oppenheim, M. 1931. *Der Tell Halaf: Eine neue Kultur im ältesten Mesopotamien.* Leipzig: F. A. Brockhaus.

Waetzoldt, H. 1970–1971. Zwei unveröffentiche Ur III-Texte über die Herstellung von Tongerfäßen. *Die Welt des Orients* 7, 7–41.

Wallerstein, I., 1974. *The Modern World-System: Capitalist Agriculture and the Origin of the European World-Economy in the Sixteenth Century.* New York: Academic Press.

———. 1980. *The Modern World-System: Mercaltilism and the Consolodation of the European World-Economy, 1600–1750.* New York: Academic Press.

———. 1989. *The Modern World-System: The Second Era of Great Expansion of the Capitalist World-Economy, 1730's–1840's.* New York: Academic Press.

Watanabe, K. 1993. Neuassyrische Siegellegenden. *Orient* 29, 109–138.

———. 1999. Seals of Neo-Assyrian Officials. In: K. Watanabe (ed.) *Priests and Officials in the Ancient Near East: Papers of the Second Colloquium on the Ancient Near East—The City and its Life held at the Middle Eastern Culture Centre in Japan (Mitaka, Tokyo).* Heidelberg: Universitätsverlag C. Winter, 313–366.

Waters, M. R. 1992. *Principles of Geoarchaeology: A North American Perspective.* Tucson: The University of Arizona Press.

Weigand, P., Harbottle, G. and Sayre, E. 1977. Turquoise Sources and Source Analysis: Mesoamerica and the Southwestern U.S.A. In: T. Earle and J. Ericson (eds.) *Exchange Systems in Prehistory.* New York: Academic Press, 15–34.

Weisberg, D. 1967. *Guild Structure and Political Allegiance in Early Achaemenid Mesopotamia.* New York: AMS Press.

Whitbread, I. K. 1995. *Greek transport amphorae: a petrological and archaeological study.* London: British School at Athens.

Winter, I. J. 1977. Perspective on the "Local Style" of Hasanlu IVB: A Study in Receptivity. In: L. D. Levine and T. C. Young JR. (eds.) *Mountains and Lowlands: Essays in the Archaeology of Greater Mesopotamia.* Malibu: Undena, 371–386.

———. 1993. "Seat of Kingship"/"A Wonder to Behold": The Palace as Construct in the Ancient near East. *Ars Orientalis* 23, 27–55.

Winter, I., 2000. Le Palais imaginaire: scale and meaning in the iconography of Neo-Assyrian cylinder seals. In: Uehlinger, C. (Ed.) *Images as Media*. Fribourg: Academic Press, 51–87.

Wolf, S. 2002. Estimation of the Production Parameters of Very Large Medieval Bricks from St. Urban, Switzerland. *Archaeometry* 44, 37–65.

Wood, I. 30 July 2011. Personal Communication RE: Manufacture of Neo-Assyrian Palace Ware.

Woolley, C. L. 1956. *Ur Excavations IV: The Early Periods*. London and Philadelphia: British Museum and Museum of the University of Pennsylvania.

Young, R. C., Devries, K., Kohler, E. L., McClellan, J. F., Mellink, M. J. and Sams, G. K. 1981. *Three Great Early Tumuli*. Philadelphia: University of Pennsylvania, University Museum.

Zettler, R. 1992. *The Ur III Temple of Inanna at Nippur: the Operation and Organization of Urban Religious Institutions in Mesopotamia in the Late Third Millennium BC*. Berlin: Reimer.

Zevit, Z. 2001. *The Religions of Ancient Israel: A Synthesis of Parallactic Approaches*. New York: Continuum.

Index